KU-007-468

Business research ✓

THE LEARNING CENTRE
HAMMERSMITH AND WEST
LONDON COLLEGE
GLIDDON ROAD
LONDON W14 9BL

WITHDRAWN

HAMMERSMITH WEST LONDON COLLEGE

346953

second edition

Business research

A practical guide for undergraduate
and postgraduate students

Jill Collis and Roger Hussey

© Jill Collis & Roger Hussey 1997, 2003

All rights reserved. No reproduction, copy or transmission of this
publication may be made without written permission.

No paragraph of this publication may be reproduced, copied or transmitted
save with written permission or in accordance with the provision of the
Copyright, Designs and Patents Act 1988, or under the terms of any licence
permitting limited copying issued by the Copyright Licensing Agency,
90 Tottenham Court Road, London W1P 4LP.

Any person who does any unauthorised act in relation to this publication
may be liable to criminal prosecution and civil claims for damages.

The authors have asserted their rights to be identified as the authors of
this work in accordance with the Copyright, Designs and Patents Act 1988

First edition 1997
Reprinted 9 times
Second edition 2003
Published by
PALGRAVE MACMILLAN
Houndmills, Basingstoke, Hampshire RG21 6XS and
175 Fifth Avenue, New York, N.Y. 10010
Companies and representatives throughout the world

PALGRAVE MACMILLAN is the global academic imprint of the Palgrave
Macmillan division of St. Martin's Press, LLC and of Palgrave Macmillan Ltd.
Macmillan® is a registered trademark in the United States, United Kingdom
and other countries. Palgrave is a registered trademark in the European
Union and other countries.

ISBN–10: 0–333–98325–4 paperback
ISBN–13: 978–0–333–98325–6 paperback

This book is printed on paper suitable for recycling and made from fully
managed and sustained forest sources.

A catalogue record for this book is available from the British Library.

A catalog record for this book is available from the Library of Congress

10   9   8   7   6   5   4
12 11 10 09 08 07 06 05

Printed in China

HAMMERSMITH AND WEST
LONDON COLLEGE
LEARNING CENTRE

3 1 JUL 2006

346953   £25–49
W/STONES
650.072 COL
Business

346953

Contents

10   **Trouble shooting** *322*

Introduction *322*

Getting started *323*

Managing the research *324*

Identifying a research topic *325*

Making a preliminary plan of action *326*

Applying a theoretical framework *327*

The research proposal *328*

Deciding the methodology *329*

Searching and reviewing the literature *330*

Collecting data *331*

Organising the data in a phenomenological study *332*

Analysing data *333*

Structuring the research report *334*

Writing the research report *335*

Dealing with writer's block *336*

Achieving the standards *337*

Preface to the second edition

This second edition of *Business Research* has the same aim as the first edition: to give practical guidance to business students who are required as part of their course to carry out a research project. The immense popularity of the first edition demonstrates that there is a great need for such a text. This present book retains the successful format of the first, but the presentation has been improved to give greater clarity and certain sections have been extended. In particular, we have concentrated on those parts where students have expressed a desire for greater practical advice.

Many first-time researchers find the concepts and jargon of research off-putting. Each chapter is clearly structured around a particular topic and the different aspects are simply described and explained. New terms are introduced gradually and the glossary provides clear explanations.

Undergraduate and postgraduate students on taught courses are often required to complete a research project within tight time limits. They have to balance these pressing practical aspects with the conceptual demands of research. M.Phil. and doctoral students usually find that they must spend a considerable amount of time studying the conceptual aspects of research. For all students the main problem is how to find the most efficient way of collecting, analysing and presenting data whilst maintaining academic rigour.

Students studying by themselves are likely to know where they are experiencing problems with their research and can go directly to the relevant chapters. At any time, students can refer to the 'Trouble shooting' section at the end of the book for advice. Instructors using *Business Research* as a course text will find the chapters logically follow the research process from the introductory stages of research to writing up the project. The wealth of references given throughout the text can be used as discussion topics or further reading.

There are few short cuts that one can take with research, but this book will speed the process and help students to use their time effectively and successfully.

Jill Collis
Kingston University, UK

Roger Hussey
University of Windsor, Canada

Acknowledgements

We would like to thank our colleagues in the UK and abroad and the many cohorts of students who have kindly commented on the first edition of this book. We are also grateful to our publishers for their continued support and encouragement.

1 Understanding research

Introduction

Whether you are at the stage of merely contemplating carrying out business research, or have already started a business research project, you will find this chapter useful for clarifying your thoughts. The objectives of this chapter are:

▶ to examine the definition and purpose of research
▶ to identify the qualities of a good researcher
▶ to describe the main types of research
▶ to give an indication of the different stages in conducting research
▶ to identify the characteristics of a good research project.

1.1 Definition and purpose of research

Although research is central to both business and academic activities, there is no consensus in the literature on how it should be *defined*. One reason for this is that research means different things to different people. However, from the many different definitions offered, there appears to be agreement that:

▶ research is a process of enquiry and investigation
▶ it is systematic and methodical
▶ research increases knowledge.

Your investigations must be thorough and rigorous at all stages of the research process. If your research is to be conducted in an efficient manner and make the best use of the opportunities and resources available, it must be organised. If it is to provide a coherent and logical route to a reliable outcome, it must be conducted systematically using appropriate *methods* to collect and analyse the *data*. Finally, your research must address a specific problem or issue, sometimes referred to as the *research problem*, in order to set a definable objective for the research activity.

Research offers both undergraduates and postgraduates an opportunity to identify and select a research problem and investigate it independently. A research project allows you to apply theory to, and/ or analyse, a real problem, or to explore and analyse more general issues. It also enables you to apply research procedures in order to illuminate the problem and contribute to our greater understanding of the problem or to generate solutions. Thus, the *purpose* of research can be summarised as follows:

- to review and synthesise existing knowledge
- to investigate some existing situation or problem
- to provide solutions to a problem
- to explore and analyse more general issues
- to construct or create a new procedure or system
- to explain a new phenomenon
- to generate new knowledge
- a combination of any of the above.

Our summary illustrates that research is purposeful since it is conducted with a view to achieving an outcome. The outcome may be presented in the form of a *consultancy research report*, an undergraduate or taught Master's *dissertation*, a M.Phil. or Ph.D. *thesis* and/or an *article* for an academic journal. In this book we focus on the needs of students carrying out some form of business research for a qualification. Therefore, we concentrate on undergraduate and postgraduate dissertations and theses.

1.2   Qualities of a good researcher

Research requires a number of *qualities* and *skills*, some of which you may already have; others you will need to develop during the course of your research. This book will help. Figure 1.1 summarises the main qualities and skills you need. Perhaps the most important of these is the ability to persevere, especially when you are faced with a setback. As the diagram shows, perseverance contributes to the development of all the other skills and qualities which will help you achieve a successful outcome.

1.2.1   Communication skills

A key skill you will require as a researcher is the ability to *communicate* your understanding of the research area. For example, you will have to submit a dissertation or thesis which will demonstrate your written communication skills. In addition, some students, and all M.Phil. and Ph.D. students, must undertake a *viva*, which is a defence of your thesis by oral examination. We will look more closely at these topics in Chapter 9.

Figure 1.1 Research qualities and skills

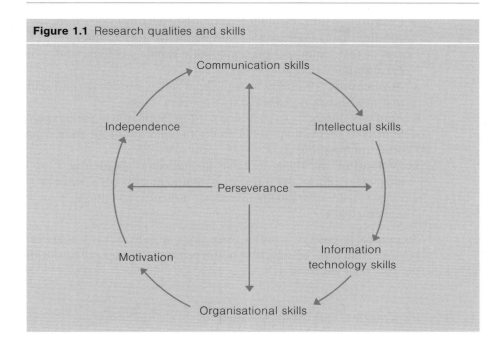

Written and verbal communication skills will also be needed when:

- applying for funding
- discussing your project with your supervisor
- negotiating access to sources of data
- conducting interviews
- designing a questionnaire
- leading a focus group
- writing and presenting conference papers
- writing your report
- writing academic journal articles.

1.2.2   Intellectual skills

As well as communication skills, you will also need to develop the following *intellectual skills*. We have taken the definitions from Bloom (1956), who sees learning as the mastering of a hierarchy of skills. Of course, there are other models of critical thinking skills (for example, see Haywood, 1989).

- **Knowledge** (or memory): the ability to recall facts, nomenclature, classifications, practical techniques, laws and theories; simple calculation and computation

- **Comprehension**: the ability to translate data from one form to another (for example, verbal into mathematical); to interpret or deduce the significance of data; to solve simple problems relying on these abilities
- **Application**: the ability to apply knowledge, experience and skill to a new situation presented in a novel manner
- **Analysis**: the ability to break down information into its various parts
- **Synthesis** (or creativity): the ability to build up information from other information
- **Evaluation**: the ability to make qualitative or quantitative judgements; to set out a reasoned argument through a series of steps, usually of gradually increasing difficulty; to criticise constructively.

You probably possess many of these skills already and will therefore have a sound base on which to build; you will develop others during the course of your research.

1.2.3   Information technology skills

In addition to being an intellectual activity, any research study involves a certain amount of routine work, parts of which will be fairly tedious. Wherever appropriate in this book, we explain how you can use *information technology* (IT) to help you with such tasks.

To attempt to conduct any research without access to a computer and basic IT skills makes the task harder. At the very least, you should have *word-processing* skills. A word-processing program such as *Word* can assist you to create, edit and print text. Typical features allow you:

- to design the **page layout**, including margin widths, page length, line spacing and justification of text
- to **highlight** text using different sized fonts, italics, bold and underline
- to **move** a section of text to another part of the document
- to **insert** and **delete** text so that changes can easily be made
- to **search** for and **replace** text, for example replace the word 'chapter' with the word 'section' throughout a file
- to **spell check** and **grammar check** text, so that mistakes can be identified and easily corrected
- to **count** the number of words in a selected piece of text or file
- to **merge print** files, for example insert an individual's name and address from one file into another file containing a standard letter and a questionnaire, at the time of printing.

A key element of success in research, which we cannot stress too strongly, is to write up as you go along. You should word-process your *research proposal* (see Chapter 5), your notes, any quotations and references you have selected from the literature, the results of any surveys, observations, and so on. Later on you can manipulate, refine, add to and otherwise amend this draft material for your final report (see Chapter 9). It is important to check any regulations regarding line spacing, margins, font size, etc., as well as the word count of your completed project at an early stage.

If you have decided to adopt a *quantitative* approach to your research (see Chapter 3), you will find that you also need to use *spreadsheets* and *statistical packages* to help you analyse and interpret your data (see Chapter 7). A spreadsheet program such as *Excel* performs calculations on numerical data which is entered into a worksheet. A worksheet is a large matrix of rectangles called cells. A cell can contain numbers, words or a formula. Facilities available on most spreadsheet programs include:

- ► **mathematical functions** such as addition, subtraction, multiplication and division
- ► **statistical functions** such as percentage, mean, standard deviation and regression
- ► **financial functions** such as net present value
- ► **graphics** such as line graphs, bar charts and pie charts.

Statistical packages are used for describing, summarising and analysing any quantitative data you have collected. We look at methods for analysing quantitative data in Chapter 7. Examples of statistical packages include *Minitab and SPSS (Statistical Package for the Social Sciences)*. Like any other piece of software, the user is removed from actual programming and is only required to learn a simple set of instructions to start analysing the data.

You are probably familiar with the concept of a *database* and may already have experience of using one. A database is a comprehensive and coordinated, consistent and controlled collection of structured data items. The data held may be quantitative, qualitative or both, and is organised in a useful form. For example, quantitative data you might want to keep in a database include financial information about companies in your sample, numbers of employees; in fact any numerical data relating to your research which you may want to add to, amend or retrieve at a later date. Examples of qualitative data you may want to keep in a database include the names and addresses of interviewees or questionnaire respondents on a database, or quotations and references you have collected from the literature.

A *database management system* such as *Access* enables you to create, access, expand and update a computerised database. The main advantages of a computerised database over a manual filing system are:

- the **speed** with which specific records can be accessed
- the **variety of ways** in which records can be accessed
- the **different criteria** which can be used to select records.

You will need to know how to use the computerised library catalogue and the on-line and CD-ROM databases of abstracts and indexes in the library when carrying out your *literature search* (see Chapter 4). Examples include FAME, LEXIS/NEXIS and ABI INFORM. This type of computerised database only allows you to display and/or print the information it contains; in other words, you cannot amend the files it contains in any way.

You will also need to know how to use the Internet. Anyone familiar with the *Windows* or *Apple Mac* interface can instantly use the Internet. However, searching the Internet can be very time consuming. The amount of information available is vast and touches every area of human endeavour and interest. Therefore, you need to use a search engine, such as *Google*, *Lycos* or *Yahoo*. You may not be able to find what you want, or even what you expect, but you will probably be able to communicate with others who are interested in your research area.

A key aspect of using information technology is the importance of regularly saving your work on disk. Many software programs have in-built features which do this automatically at specified intervals. We recommend that you take advantage of such features and save your work onto a floppy disk at ten-minute intervals. This will ensure that in the event of a electrical or other fault you should be able to retrieve the majority of your work. You will find it helpful to create directories on your disk which will allow you to categorise your saved files. At the end of each session, you should make a back-up copy of the master disk in case it gets lost or corrupted in some way.

1.2.4   Organisational skills

The most important *organisational skill* you will need to develop is *time management*. You will find that some of the tasks you set yourself are very time consuming but may not be immediately productive; examples include applying for funding, finding a supervisor, *negotiating access* to sources of data (see Chapter 2), investigating *sources of information* (see Chapter 4) or writing a *research proposal* (see Chapter 5). However, such tasks cannot be disregarded and you must allot time to them in addition to those activities which contribute more directly to the production of your dissertation or thesis.

As part of your *research proposal*, which we discuss in Chapter 5, you will have to construct a *timetable* for your research. We suggest that you do this as soon as possible and use it as a guide for managing your time. You may also find it useful to list all the activities you have to undertake and estimate the time you think it will take to complete them. If you wish, this can be developed into a *critical path analysis*. Critical path analysis is a simplified model of a project which can be used to plan when tasks should be carried out. The project is represented as a network diagram using two symbols: nodes, which represent the activities, and arrows, which show the sequence of the activities. Critical activities are those which cannot be delayed without holding up the project and the path they lie on is called the critical path (Morris, 1993).

If you are an undergraduate on an industrial placement, you will probably have to juggle the demands of your employer whilst working on your dissertation; research associates and teaching assistants may have to cope with preparing and giving lectures for the first time, whilst studying for a higher degree. Whatever your circumstances, you must also find time for family relationships and some social life.

Thus, the ability to manage your time effectively is vital to a successful outcome. Many of the research activities you will be involved in require a fairly large span of time devoted to them at one time. You will quickly find that tackling tasks in short bursts is very unproductive. To write a satisfactory first draft of your proposal, you will probably find it best to shut the door, unplug the telephone and sit down with your books and papers for five or six hours without interruption. After this initial stint you may be able to make progress by working in shorter periods of time as you correct, improve and edit each section.

In addition to managing your time, you will also have to develop your own systems for managing the administration of your research. These will include record keeping, filing, correspondence and building up a personal library of books, articles, cuttings, etc. If you decide to conduct a large postal questionnaire survey, for example, you need to be confident that you can manage the administration involved.

1.2.5   Motivation

Being well *motivated* is essential to the successful completion of a research project. You will find it helpful to analyse your own reasons for becoming a researcher. Figure 1.2 shows a number of examples of reasons given by students.

Whatever your reason for doing research, you need to ask yourself whether it is powerful enough to see you through to completion. It is also possible that your motivation will fluctuate during the course of your study and this could affect the quality of your research. For example, 'I love the subject' or 'I love studying' might gradually change to 'I just want it to be over!' There is no 'right' motivator, but it is important to be aware of the factors that affect you and how they influence your research.

Figure 1.2 Students' reasons for doing research

I love the subject

I love studying

I want to be an intellectual

I have a personal question I want to answer

I want to be creative and useful

I want to be a member of the research community

I haven't been able to get a job

Employers want people with this qualification

All my friends are doing it

It's part of my course

My family/superiors want me to do it

There are a number of ways in which you can maintain and increase your interest in your research. One is to choose a subject in which you are passionately interested. You will also find discussing your research with your supervisors and other students helps to sustain you interest. Finally, we would recommend that at a very early stage you attend presentations, seminars and conferences where you can listen to other researchers. This is imperative for M.Phil. and Ph.D. students who should also aim to present seminar and conference papers themselves and write articles about their research for publication in academic journals.

1.2.6   Independence

Many students on taught courses feel dependent on their lecturers, notes and the 'system' which forces them to learn. However, in research students are required to be empowered, self-motivated and highly *independent*. Sometimes they find conducting research a lonely process, since it requires considerable self-discipline. If you are an M.Phil. or Ph.D. student you will find that there is no structure, lecture notes or reading list to fall back on; nor are there any assignments or exams, which do at least provide feedback.

Although your supervisor will provide guidance, you may find an increased need for support from colleagues and peers. Suggestions for helping you to adjust to your role as an independent researcher include:

▶ conducting collaborative research – working or publishing with others

▶ finding a mentor who will be interested in your work and agree to be a role model and friend for support, guidance, introductions, etc.

▶ building up a network of contacts with those engaged in similar research areas through local organisations, conferences or the Internet

▶ attending any training sessions that may be available, such as methodology lectures or workshops on using statistical packages.

1.2.7   Personal strengths and weaknesses

Before taking on a new project of any kind, it is often useful to appraise your personal *strengths* and *weaknesses* in order to check your chances of success. Easterby-Smith, Thorpe and Lowe (1991) offer a helpful checklist which is shown in Table 1.1. It is based on Burgoyne and Stuart's (1976) work on the attributes of effective managers, because managing a research project is both a management challenge as well as an intellectual challenge.

Ideally, you should possess all these core qualities to a moderate extent. However, 'knowledge can be acquired by reading and talking, or by attending courses; skills can be acquired through practising them, in either a simulated or a real environment; and personal qualities can

Table 1.1 Qualities of competent researchers

Knowledge	Skills	Personal qualities
Awareness of different assumptions about the world	Ability to plan, organise and manage own time	Awareness of own strengths, weaknesses and values
Awareness of methods of data collection	Ability to search libraries and other sources	Clarity of thought
Awareness of different methodologies	Ability to gain support and cooperation from others	Sensitivity to events and feelings
Knowledge of immediate subject of study	Ability to structure and argue a case in writing	Emotional resilience
Knowledge of related subjects/disciplines	Ability to defend and argue views orally	Flexibility
Knowledge of key networks and contacts in chosen field	Ability to learn from experience	Creativity

Source: Adapted from Easterby-Smith, Thorpe and Lowe (1991) p. 17.

be acquired, with much difficulty, through life or educational experience' (Easterby-Smith, Thorpe and Lowe, 1991, p. 17).

1.3   Types of research

The many different *types* of research can be classified according to:

- the **purpose** of the research – the reason why are you conducting it
- the **process** of the research – the way in which you will collect and analyse your data
- the **logic** of the research – whether you are moving from the general to the specific or vice versa
- the **outcome** of the research – whether you are trying to solve a particular problem or make a general contribution to knowledge.

For example, the aim of your research project might be to describe a particular business activity (purpose) by collecting data (process) which will be used to solve a problem (outcome). Table 1.2 shows the classification of the main types of research according to the above criteria.

1.3.1   Exploratory, descriptive, analytical and predictive research

If we are classifying research according to its purpose, we can describe as being either exploratory, descriptive, analytical or predictive. These four different types of research are examined below in order of their increasing sophistication.

   Exploratory research is conducted into a research problem or issue when there are very few or no earlier studies to which we can refer for information about the issue or problem. The aim of this type of study is to look for patterns, ideas or *hypotheses*, rather than testing or confirming a hypothesis. A hypothesis is an idea or proposition which can be tested for association or causality by deducing logical consequences which can be tested against *empirical evidence*. Empirical evidence is data based on observation or experience. In exploratory

Table 1.2 Classification of main types of research	
Type of research	*Basis of classification*
Exploratory, descriptive, analytical or predictive research	Purpose of the research
Quantitative or qualitative research	Process of the research
Deductive or inductive research	Logic of the research
Applied or basic research	Outcome of the research

research the focus is on gaining insights and familiarity with the subject area for more rigorous investigation at a later stage.

Typical techniques used in exploratory research include case studies, observation and historical analysis which can provide both quantitative and qualitative data. Such techniques are very flexible since there are few constraints on the nature of activities employed or on the type of data collected. The research will assess which existing theories and concepts can be applied to the problem or whether new ones should be developed. The approach to the research is usually very open and concentrates on gathering a wide range of data and impressions. As such, exploratory research rarely provides conclusive answers to problems or issues, but gives guidance on what future research, if any, should be conducted.

Descriptive research is research which describes phenomena as they exist. It is used to identify and obtain information on the characteristics of a particular problem or issue. For example, descriptive research may answer such questions as:

- ▶ What is the absentee rate in particular offices?
- ▶ What are the feelings of workers faced with redundancy?
- ▶ What are the qualifications of different groups of employees?

The data collected is often quantitative and statistical techniques are usually used to summarise the information. Descriptive research goes further in examining a problem than exploratory research, since it is undertaken to ascertain and describe the characteristics of the pertinent issues.

Analytical or **explanatory research** is a continuation of descriptive research. The researcher goes beyond merely describing the characteristics, to analysing and explaining why or how it is happening. Thus, analytical research aims to understand phenomena by discovering and measuring causal relations among them. For example, information may be collected on the size of companies and the levels of labour turnover. Analytical research attempts to answer such questions as:

- ▶ How can we reduce the number of complaints made by customers?
- ▶ How can we improve the delivery times of our products?
- ▶ How can we expand the range of our services?

An important element of explanatory research is identifying and, possibly, controlling the *variables* in the research activities, since this permits the critical variables or the causal links between the characteristics to be better explained. A variable is an attribute of an entity that can change and take different values which can be observed and/or measured. We will be looking more closely at variables in Chapter 6.

Predictive research goes even further than explanatory research. The latter establishes an explanation for what is happening in a particular situation, whereas the former forecasts the likelihood of a similar situation occurring elsewhere. Predictive research aims to generalise from the analysis by predicting certain phenomena on the basis of hypothesised, general relationships. For example, predictive research attempts to answer such questions as:

- In which city would it be most profitable to open a new retail outlet?
- Will the introduction of an employee bonus scheme lead to higher levels of productivity?
- What type of packaging will improve the sales of our products?
- How would an increase in interest rates affect our profit margins?

Thus, the solution to a problem in a particular study will be applicable to similar problems elsewhere, if the predictive research can provide a valid, robust solution based on a clear understanding of the relevant causes. Predictive research provides 'how', 'why' and 'where' answers to current events and also to similar events in the future. It is also helpful in situations where 'what if' questions are being asked.

Table 1.3 shows the above classifications by level of sophistication and gives examples. One drawback of increasing the level of sophistication in research isthat the level of complexity and detail also increases. This, in turn, increases the likelihood of failure or non-completion of the research.

Table 1.3 Research types by increasing level of sophistication

Type of research	Example
Exploratory research	An interview survey among clerical staff in a particular office, department, company, group of companies, industry, region, etc., to find out what might motivate them to increase productivity (i.e. to see if a research problem can be formulated)
Descriptive research	A description of how the selected clerical staff are rewarded and what measures are used to record their productivity levels
Analytical research	An analysis of any relationships between the rewards given to the clerical staff and their productivity levels
Predictive research	A forecast of which variable should be changed in order to bring about a change in the productivity levels of clerical staff

1.3.2   Quantitative and qualitative research

Research can also be differentiated by looking at the approach adopted by the researcher. Some people prefer a *quantitative approach* which is objective in nature and concentrates on measuring phenomena. Therefore, a quantitative approach involves collecting and analysing numerical data and applying statistical tests. Others prefer a *qualitative approach*, which is more subjective in nature and involves examining and reflecting on perceptions in order to gain an understanding of social and human activities.

One of your early decisions will be to decide which is the best approach for your research. Some students avoid taking a quantitative approach because they are not confident with statistics and think a qualitative approach will be easier. Many students find that it is harder to start and decide an overall design for a quantitative study, but it is easier to conduct the analysis and write up because it is highly structured. Qualitative research is normally easier to start, but students often find it more difficult to analyse the data and write up their final report.

For example, if you were conducting a study into stress caused by working night shifts, and you were taking a quantitative approach, you might want to collect objective, numerical data such as absenteeism rates, productivity levels, etc. However, if you were taking a qualitative approach, you might want to collect subjective data about how stress is experienced by night workers in terms of their perceptions, health, social problems, and so on.

There are many arguments in the literature regarding the merits of qualitative versus quantitative approaches, which we will examine in Chapter 3. At this stage you simply need to be aware that your choice will be influenced by the nature of your research project as well as your own philosophical preferences. Moreover, you may find that the access you have been able to negotiate (see Chapter 2), the type of data available and the research problem persuade you to put your philosophical preferences to one side.

1.3.3   Applied and basic research

A standard classification of research divides projects into either *applied* or *basic research*. Basic research is also referred to as *fundamental* or *pure* research. Applied research is research which has been designed to apply its findings to solving a specific, existing problem. For example, the reorganisation of an office layout, the improvement of safety in the workplace or the reduction of wastage of raw materials in a factory process.

When the research problem is of a less specific nature, and the research is being conducted primarily to improve our understanding

!

The following quiz will help you check your understanding. Beware, more than one answer may apply!

1 An advertising agency wants to know what factors made the last campaign they ran for a major brewery such a success. This is an example of:

   a exploratory research ☐
   b descriptive research ☐
   c analytical research ☐
   d predictive research ☐

2 Classify the following questions as exploratory, descriptive, analytical or predictive research:

   a Why have the sales of our products in Scotland been so high? ☐
   b What are our sales in Scotland compared to our sales in France? ☐
   c How can we improve our sales in France? ☐
   d Is it possible to identify those factors that affect our sales in Scotland? ☐
   e What has been the level of our sales in Germany over the last five years? ☐
   f Why are our sales lower in France than in either Scotland or Germany? ☐
   g Will a change in the packaging improve our sales in France? ☐

3 Pilot projects are a common type of:

   a exploratory research ☐
   b descriptive research ☐
   c analytical research ☐
   d predictive research ☐

3 Research that tests relationships between different variables is:

   a exploratory research ☐
   b descriptive research ☐
   c analytical research ☐
   d predictive research ☐

5 A factory manager notes from his records that productivity levels are higher when the weather is cooler and concludes that employees work harder in cold weather. This is an example of:

   a an inductive process ☐
   b a deductive process ☐

The answers are given at the end of the chapter.

of general issues, without emphasis on its immediate application, it is classified as basic research. For example, you might be interested in whether personal characteristics influence people's career choices. Basic research is regarded as the most academic form of research, since the principal aim is to make a contribution to knowledge, usually for the general good, rather than to solve a specific problem for one organisation.

1.3.4 Deductive and inductive research

Deductive research is a study in which a conceptual and theoretical structure is developed and then tested by empirical observation; thus particular instances are deduced from general inferences. For this reason, the deductive method is referred to as moving from the general to the particular. For example, you may have read about theories of motivation and wish to test them in your own workplace.

Inductive research is a study in which theory is developed from the observation of empirical reality; thus general inferences are induced from particular instances, which is the reverse of the deductive method. Since it involves moving from individual observation to statements of general patterns or laws, it is referred to as moving from the specific to the general. For example, you may have observed from factory records in your company that production levels go down after two hours of the shift and you conclude that production levels vary with length of time worked.

All the different types of research we have discussed can be helpful in allowing you to understand your research and the best way to conduct it, but do not feel too constrained. It is important to recognise that one particular project may be described in a number of ways as it will have purpose, process, logic and outcome. For example, you may conduct an applied, analytical study using a quantitative approach. In a long-term project you may wish to use qualitative and quantitative approaches, deductive and inductive methods, and you will move from exploratory and descriptive research to analytical and predictive research.

Knowledge of the key classifications we have examined will allow you to describe what you are doing and to ascertain which particular phase of research you are in.

1.4   The research process

Whatever type of research or approach is adopted, there are several fundamental stages in the *research process* which are common to all scientifically based investigations. These are shown in Figure 1.3.

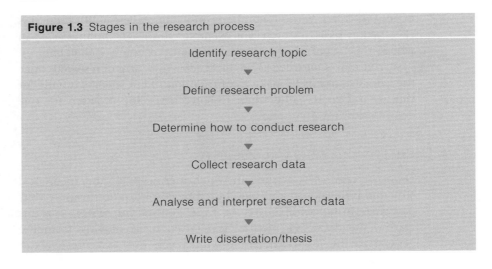

Figure 1.3 Stages in the research process

Identify research topic

▼

Define research problem

▼

Determine how to conduct research

▼

Collect research data

▼

Analyse and interpret research data

▼

Write dissertation/thesis

This simplified diagram is a traditional and highly structured view of the research process. In later chapters we will examine other approaches. This model also presents research as a neat, orderly process, with one stage leading logically on to the next. However, in practice, research is rarely like that! For example, failure at one stage means returning to an earlier stage and many stages overlap. Thus, if you were unable to collect the research data, it may be necessary to revise your definition of the research problem or amend the way you conduct the research. This is often a good reason for conducting some exploratory research before commencing a full project.

We will now look briefly at each of the stages in the research process to give you an overview; greater detail is given in later chapters.

1.4.1   Identifying a research topic

You may find a *research topic* suggests itself as a result of your course work, job, interests or general experience. For example, you may be interested in the employment problems of minority groups in society, the difficulties of funding small businesses, what makes managers successful, or the commercial sponsorship of sport. The possibilities are endless, but having identified a research topic which is of general interest to you, you can move on to the next stage.

1.4.2   Defining the research problem

All students experience some difficulty in narrowing down their general interest in a research topic in order to focus on a particular research problem which is small enough to be investigated. This is often referred to as *defining* the research problem and leads on to setting the *research questions*. The classic way in academic research to identify a research problem is to consider the *literature* and identify any gaps, since these indicate original areas to research (see Chapter 4).

If you have conducted an undergraduate dissertation already, that subject area may lead you to your M.Phil. or Ph.D. research questions. Alternatively, management consultancy or commissioned research may suggest research questions

1.4.3 Determining how to conduct the study

Your general approach to the research is known as your *research paradigm*. The term *paradigm* refers to the progress of scientific practice based on people's philosophies and assumptions about the world and the nature of knowledge; in this context, about how research should be conducted. Your approach to the entire process of the research study is known as your research *methodology*. Although, in part, this is determined by the research problem, the assumptions you use in your research and the way you define your research problems will influence the way you conduct the study. We examine these important aspects of research in Chapter 3.

1.4.4 Collecting the research data

There are a variety of ways in which you can *collect* your research data and we look at the main *data collection methods* in Chapter 6. If you have a *quantitative* methodology you will be attempting to measure variables or count occurrences of a phenomenon. On the other hand, if you have a *qualitative* methodology, you will emphasise meanings and experiences related to the phenomena.

1.4.5 Analysing and interpreting the research data

The *analysis* and *interpretation* of your research data forms the major part of your research project. The tools of analysis you will use will depend on whether you have collected quantitative or qualitative data. An introduction to the various methods and techniques is given in Chapters 7 and 8.

1.4.6 Writing the report

It is at the *writing up* stage that many students experience problems, usually because they have left it until the very last minute! It is important to start writing up your research in draft as soon as you start the early stages of the project, and continue to do so until it is completed.

Table 1.4 Typical structure of a dissertation or thesis

Chapter/section	Description
Introduction	A precise explanation of what research is about, why it is important and interesting; the research questions or hypotheses should also be stated
Literature review	A critical analysis of what other researchers have said on the subject and where your project fits in
Methodology	An explanation of why you collected certain data, what data you collected, from where you collected it, when you collected it, how you collected it and how you analysed it
Results	A presentation of your research results
Analysis and discussion	An analysis of your results showing the contribution to knowledge and pointing out any weaknesses/limitations
Conclusions	A description of the main lessons to be learnt from your study and what future research should be conducted
References	A detailed, alphabetical or numerical list of the sources from which information has been obtained and which have been cited in the text
Appendices	Detailed data referred to but not shown elsewhere

To a large extent, the stages outlined above will be captured in the *structure* of your dissertation or thesis. It is valuable at the outset to consider a possible structure, since it will give you an idea of what you are aiming for. The title should be descriptive but not lengthy. Remember that any planned structure will have the disadvantage of making the research process look much more orderly than it really is. Although all research reports differ in structure according to the problem being investigated and the methodology employed, there are some common features. Table 1.4 shows a typical structure.

1.5   Characteristics of a good research project

Many of the characteristics of a *good* research project can be developed by adopting a systematic and methodical approach. You may come across the term *methodological rigour* applied to research. It refers to the clarity, appropriateness and intellectual soundness of the overall methodology and the conduct of the study. Methodological rigour

Table 1.5 Characteristics of good and poor research projects

Good project	Poor project
Good literature review	Poor/uncritical literature review
Sound primary research	Poor/little primary research
Logical structure	Haphazard structure
Analytical	Descriptive
Theory integrated	Theory tacked on
Underpinned by conceptual framework	Little/no conceptual framework
Integration between methodology, literature, analysis, conclusions, etc.	Little/no integration between elements

implies the application of systematic and methodical methods in conducting the study and a careful, detailed, exacting approach.

As we have already suggested, this does not mean that research is a neat and orderly process. Above all, it is a process of discovery and it is not possible to contain all the new developments which will take place. However, a soundly based research project should be capable of being flexible and allowing for new developments. In subsequent chapters we will explain how this can be achieved, but at this stage it is useful to have an overview. Therefore, in Table 1.5 we compare good and poor research projects.

Conclusions

In this chapter we have examined the purpose and nature of research, and the ways in which it can be classified. We have also looked at some of the more important qualities and skills you will need as a researcher. A research project offers an opportunity to identify and select a problem or issue and to investigate it independently with the guidance of your supervisor. It gives you the opportunity to apply theory/analysis to a real business problem or issue and apply research procedures in a manner that will illuminate it and contribute towards greater understanding of that problem or issue, or even generate solutions.

Answers to the classifying research quiz

1. (c) analytical research

2. (a) analytical research

      (b) descriptive research
      (c) predictive research
      (d) exploratory research
      (e) descriptive research
      (f) analytical research
      (g) predictive research

3. (a) exploratory research
      and
   (b) descriptive research
      and
   (c) analytical research

4. (c) analytical research

5. (a) an inductive process

2 Dealing with practical issues

Introduction

Although you may be thinking hard about your research already, before you can start it you will need to look at any regulations or procedures with which you must comply. Even if you are writing an internal consultancy report, you will be working within terms of reference; if your research is being conducted with a view to achieving an academic qualification, you will find there are a number of rules and regulations you will need to adhere to. As regulations vary from one institution to another, we can only provide a general guide, but this chapter should alert you to the main points.

As well as ensuring that you are aware of the regulations, there are many practicalities involved in research activities. In this chapter we offer general advice on:

- ▶ course requirements
- ▶ choosing an academic institution and a supervisor
- ▶ sources of funds
- ▶ negotiating access to companies
- ▶ ethics
- ▶ managing the research.

2.1 Course requirements

In this section we can only offer some benchmarks as the actual entry requirements and standards you must achieve in your research will be defined by your own institution, the type of research you are undertaking and whether it is going to be submitted in part or whole assessment for a particular qualification. When you have completed your research, you will present it in the form of a written report, usually known as a *dissertation* or *thesis* depending on the type of qualification. However, there are no hard and fast rules and this is largely a matter of convention. Table 2.1 ranks the main degrees, starting with the undergraduate degrees and ending with the highest award of the postgraduate degrees, a doctorate.

Table 2.1 The main degrees and associated research reports

Level and type of degree	Research report
Undergraduate or first degrees	
Bachelor of Arts (B.A.)	Dissertation
Bachelor of Science (B.Sc.)	Dissertation
Postgraduate or second degrees	
Taught:	
Master of Arts (M.A.)	Dissertation
Master of Science (M.Sc.)	Dissertation
Master of Business Administration (M.B.A.)	Dissertation
By research:	
Master of Philosophy (M.Phil.)	Thesis
Doctoral degree	
Doctor of Philosophy (Ph.D.)	Thesis
Doctor of Business Administration (D.B.A.)	Thesis

The table concentrates on research reports which lead directly to an award, such as a M.Phil., or an important part of an award, such as an undergraduate degree. However, you may be conducting a group assignment which involves research or you may be carrying out some form of consultancy project. In such cases the regulations may be quite loose or even non-existent and therefore it is important to establish *terms of reference* for the project.

In such cases, the terms of reference will establish the scope and purpose of your investigation. They will set out the nature of the enquiries you will report and whether your final report will be of an exploratory nature, or set out firm recommendations or somewhere in between. As the researcher, you will negotiate the terms of reference with the person requesting the research and therefore the responsibility for satisfying the terms of reference will rest with you. Whether you are studying for an award, conducting a consultancy project or carrying out a research project with a group of other students, you will find that many of the processes are the same. These processes are fully described in this book.

For all levels of researchers, including experienced researchers, conducting any type of research project is a process of enquiry and therefore a learning experience. In business research, as in other subject areas, a student project at undergraduate or postgraduate level affords a medium through which you can acquire the following skills and knowledge:

- skills for **independent research**, such as problem identification, problem definition, and the ability to plan and execute a research project appropriate to the problem under investigation; also, the ability to collect and analyse data, form conclusions and make practical recommendations
- skills for **effective communication**, such as verbal and presentational skills as well as written and organisational skills
- knowledge of research **methodologies, methods** and **analytical techniques**
- detailed knowledge of a particular **topic**, including the literature published in that area, its underlying concepts, theories and assumptions
- **personal skills**, such as resourcefulness, flexibility, creativity and clarity of thought, also the self-confidence that is gained as a result of managing an independent research project
- the ability to **critically analyse** a situation and to draw conclusions.

We looked at some of these skills and concepts in Chapter 1, and will be examining many of them in more detail in this and subsequent chapters.

2.1.1   Bachelor's degrees

In the UK, and other parts of the world, it is common for under-graduates on a *Bachelor's degree* (*B.A.* or *B.Sc.*) to undertake a research project towards the end of their course which will result in a report usually known as a *dissertation*. This is not restricted to business or management degrees, but increasingly in disciplines such as law, engineering and science, students must demonstrate an appreciation of business and this is often achieved by means of a research project. You may find that you must have reached a prescribed standard in your course in order to proceed to this stage.

If you are on a part-time degree or full-time degree course with a year's industrial placement, your research project will normally be based on your experience and knowledge of business acquired at work. If you are a student on a full-time course with no placement year, you will normally be expected to complete a library-based research project. However, there is often scope for some original research as well. Certain named awards may specify the general topic area for the project.

Typically, the aims of an undergraduate research project are:

- to enable students to acquire analytical and problem-solving skills based on evaluation and synthesis within a work environment or a simulation of a practical situation

- ▶ to provide for active learning where the student identifies and defines the problem to be explored and the work to be completed, thus learning from the experience, rather than passive learning methods
- ▶ to develop skills for independent research
- ▶ to develop the ability to operationalise a business problem or issue (in other words, describe it in such a way that it can be measured)
- ▶ apply academic knowledge in the investigation of a business problem or issue.

In general, you will be expected to demonstrate that you have an understanding of research methods appropriate to the chosen field and to have investigated and evaluated an approved topic. Such research projects often fall into the category of *applied research* (see Section 1.3.3) and are mainly *descriptive* in nature (see Section 1.3.1). This does not mean that you are not expected to adopt a critical and analytical approach. Indeed, students who can demonstrate these intellectual skills at the undergraduate level are likely to achieve high marks.

2.1.2   Master's degrees

There are 'no laws that specify which degrees can be awarded, by which institutions, to whom and on what basis, as is the case in Continental countries' (Philips and Pugh, 1994, p. 18). Therefore, it is difficult to give more than a general guide to what constitutes a Master's degree, and you will need to refer to your chosen institution for specific details.

The dissertation is an important part of a taught *Master of Arts (M.A.)*, *Master of Science (M.Sc.)* or *Master of Business Administration (M.B.A.)* degree. The requirements are similar to those for an undergraduate dissertation, but the standard of work demanded is higher with greater emphasis on the student demonstrating a critical and analytical approach.

To undertake a taught Master's degree, other than an M.B.A., you would normally be required to have a first degree in a relevant discipline. Sometimes, professional qualifications or experience may be substituted and this is often the case with M.B.A. students.

A *Master of Philosophy (M.Phil.)* degree is a programme of supervised research. The student must demonstrate an understanding of research methods appropriate to the chosen field and have critically investigated and evaluated an approved topic. As this is a degree by research, there is considerable emphasis on the *rigour* with which the student conducts the research. As you will remember from Chapter 1, this means that it must be systematic and methodical.

Entry requirements for a M.Phil. are normally a good honours degree, that is one where you have achieved a specified high standard. In the UK this is often an upper second or first class honours degree.

Experience and relevant professional qualifications may be taken into consideration if your qualifications do not comply exactly with the entry criteria.

2.1.3   Doctoral degrees

As with the M.Phil., it is only possible to offer a general description of a *Doctor of Philosophy (Ph.D.)* award. Usually it is a programme of supervised research, although a taught doctorate which includes an independent research component is offered by some institutions. The student must have critically investigated and evaluated an approved topic, but must also have made an independent and original contribution to knowledge. This contribution need not be revolutionary, but the research must result in an increase in our understanding.

For a Ph.D. award some institutions would expect you to have a relevant Master's degree which encompassed a research training programme, such as a methodology course. If you are unable to register directly for a Ph.D., you may find it is possible to register for a M.Phil. and transfer to a Ph.D. part way through, before completing the M.Phil. Of course, this is only possible if your research project can be extended to meet the criteria of a Ph.D.

2.1.4   Standards

Table 2.2 shows that the length of your research report will vary according to the level and type of the research project. It will also depend on the requirements of your own institution, so the following must be taken as a general guide only.

We have described the length of the various research reports in terms of the number of words they contain. You will be able to calculate this quite easily by using the word-count facility on your word-processing package. If you find the word count measure hard to visualise, you may prefer to estimate the length of your report in terms of number of pages. One A4 page contains approximately 500 words, but since research

Table 2.2 Approximate length of research reports

Level	Research report	Typical length
Bachelor's degree	Dissertation	10 000–15 000 words
Taught Master's degree	Dissertation	20 000 words
Master's degree by research	Thesis	40 000 words
Doctoral degree	Thesis	80 000 words

reports are traditionally presented in double spacing, you should halve this. Therefore 10 000 words constitute about 40 pages. Tables, graphs, diagrams and other illustrations will extend your report, as will the inclusion of appendices. The latter are not normally included in the word count.

More important than the difference in length is the difference in substance between reports at different levels. Although all academic

Table 2.3 Criteria to be satisfied by research reports

Level	Research report	Criteria
Bachelor's degrees and some Master's degrees which require the completion of a project	Dissertation	A well-structured and convincing account of a study, the resolution of a problem or the outcome of an experiment Evidence of awareness of the literature
Taught Master's degree	Dissertation	An ordered, critical and reasoned exposition of knowledge gained through the student's efforts A comprehensive review of the literature
Master's degree by research	Thesis	Evidence of an original investigation or the testing of ideas Competence in independent work or experimentation An understanding of appropriate techniques Ability to make critical use of published work and source materials Appreciation of the relationship of the special theme to the wider field of knowledge Worthy, in part, of publication
Doctoral degree	Thesis	As for Master's degree by research, plus: Originality as shown by the topic researched or the methodology employed Distinct contribution to knowledge

Source: Adapted from Howard and Sharp (1994) p. 177.

research should focus on one specific *research problem* (see Chapter 1), and in many cases its resolution, a dissertation is normally limited in terms of the extent of original inquiry; a M.Phil. thesis requires carrying out some original research, normally within the scope of existing theories; whilst a Ph.D. thesis is expected to make some contribution to knowledge.

Howard and Sharp (1994) advise that it is important not to lose sight of the fact that the prime aim of writing up is to convince your examiners that you have satisfied the appropriate criteria laid down by your institution. Table 2.3 shows the main criteria to be satisfied by level of research.

2.2 Choosing an academic institution

Academic institutions differ in their interests in subjects and teach them in a variety of different ways. Research benefits greatly from the help of an experienced and interested *supervisor,* a member of the academic staff who will oversee and guide your research. We look at supervision in some detail in Section 2.2.1. You will find that even if you have a good personal relationship with your supervisor, strong supervision is insufficient on its own and you need to consider other aspects when choosing an academic institution. Figure 2.1 draws from research by Johnston (1995) and our own experience to provide a

Figure 2.1 Checklist for postgraduate research students selecting an academic institution

▶ Are you provided with an information booklet at the outset which gives information on research and the regulations and procedures which apply?

▶ Are you offered an interview with the director of research studies, or a potential supervisor, to explore the match between your research interests and the research activities and supervisors' abilities of the institution?

▶ Is there some form of research design or methodology programme or, at the very least, a series of seminars on research methods to provide you with knowledge as well as an opportunity to meet other researchers?

▶ If the institution is fairly large, is there a regular newsletter to help you keep in touch?

▶ Is there a culture of conference attendance by supervisors and researchers that will give you the opportunity to present papers and discuss your research with others?

▶ Are the library and computer resources adequate?

▶ Will you have access to common rooms where you can meet fellow researchers?

checklist for choosing an academic institution. Although some features may be of interest to undergraduate researchers, it is mainly aimed at postgraduate research students.

It is unlikely that all the institutions you approach will be able to offer all these features. However, the checklist provides an easy way of verifying that your final choice will provide access to the maximum number of resources and facilities for your needs, thus enhancing your chances of successfully completing your studies.

2.2.1   Choosing a supervisor

In both undergraduate and postgraduate degrees, having a supervisor is a formal requirement. For a postgraduate qualification, more than one supervisor is required. Therefore, you may need to find specialist supervisors who will be interested in your research, supportive and, most important, whom you will be able to get on with. At the very least you should be able to bounce ideas off your supervisor. Philips and Pugh (1994, p. 16) offer the following advice to Ph.D. (and M.Phil.) students. If you are an undergraduate or on a taught Master's course, some of their advice will also apply to you.

- ▶ Get as much information as you can before choosing your academic institution. Visit the college or university beforehand; talk to potential supervisors and view the facilities/resources. Discuss with potential supervisors what research experience they have, their publications record and their preferred style of supervision
- ▶ Once you have selected an institution and a supervisor, carry out a small pilot project with definite deadlines to get you into the system. On completion, discuss not only the results with your supervisor, but how you conducted it and what you can learn from the process
- ▶ Work at personal relationships with your supervisor(s) and fellow students
- ▶ Talk to fellow researchers in your subject area about how their approach to research works in practice
- ▶ Set limited goals and achieve them.

The longer the period of research, the greater the importance of the supervisor. According to Philips (1984), the supervisor/researcher relationship should be resilient enough to cope with the stages in the student's research process which are shown in Figure 2.2.

The emotional effects of conducting research should not be underestimated. Research involving independent inquiry and considerable intellectual activity can entail considerable stress. This is especially true

Figure 2.2 Stages in the research process

Early enthusiasm

▼

Increasing interest in the work

▼

Transfer of dependence from
supervisor to information
resulting from effort

▼

Generating own ideas
based on that information

▼

Frustration at being unable
to develop these ideas

▼

Boredom with original problem

▼

Determination to finish
with original problem

Source: Adapted from Philips (1984) p. 16.

of postgraduate degrees, where a major piece of research may be conducted over a period of several years. Your initial enthusiasm and interest may turn into frustration, boredom and writer's block, and you may begin seriously to question your ability to continue. However, with the help of your supervisor, you can minimise the likelihood of serious stress through careful planning and time management, and eventually reach the final phase when your main concern is to get the research finished.

The ideal relationship is one where the researcher is initially tutored by the *supervisor* and eventually becomes a respected colleague. Thus, they start as master and pupil, and end up as equals. Therefore, it is important that you and your supervisor are well matched. This is not so difficult if the staff at the institution are known to you, perhaps because it is where you studied for your first degree. You may have been stimulated by a particular subject and a particular lecturer, and wish to approach that person to supervise your present research. On the other hand, you may be registering for your degree at an institution which is new to you, and where you do not know the staff. In this case, you may have only a few days in which to talk to various people.

It is important to be aware of the dominant value system in your college or university when attempting to assess the suitability of a potential supervisor. Most lecturers are involved in four main activities:

▶ teaching
▶ research
▶ administration
▶ publishing papers, articles and, sometimes, books.

The best supervisor is one who has knowledge and interest in the area you have chosen to research, and one who has experience of carrying out research and successfully supervising students. An understanding of the theoretical concepts of research methodologies may not be enough. An academic with a good record of publications, but without these other attributes, does not necessarily make a good supervisor; he or she may be too preoccupied with his or her own research activities.

If possible, you should talk to other researchers who are being supervised, or have experience of being supervised by the academic you have in mind, before making your decision. However, you should bear in mind that the decision is a two-way process in which you and your *research proposal* (see Chapter 5) will also be assessed. A supervisor may decline to supervise a student who is researching an area which holds no interest for him or her, or if in his or her opinion the student's research proposal is seriously flawed. Moreover, a potential supervisor will want to feel that you are sufficiently motivated to complete your research successfully.

It is usually the responsibility of the head of the department or director of research to exercise as much care as possible in matching students to supervisors. He or she will take into account such factors as the research topic, the number of students already being supervised by that member of staff, the student's academic ability and personality, etc. Sometimes the student is accepted on condition that he or she undertakes to do a project in one of the ongoing areas of research in the department. Students who only have a general idea about their research topic may develop their ideas after discussions with their supervisors. However, a final decision should be made as soon as possible.

Once you have agreed who your supervisor(s) will be, it is important to realise that this is a two-way relationship in which you play an active part. Howard and Sharp (1994) recommend that the student should:

▶ attempt at the outset to find out the supervisor's views of the supervisor/student relationship; for example, on impromptu versus formal meetings, punctuality, etc.
▶ agree with the supervisor the routine aspects of the relationship and take responsibility for their implementation; for example, agree the maximum interval between meetings and ensure it is not breached
▶ produce written lists of queries prior to meetings with the supervisor in order to define the agenda and structure the meeting

▶ keep written notes of meetings with the supervisors (even if the supervisor also does so) and submit copies to him/her

▶ agree with the supervisor the nature and timing of written material, such as progress reports and drafts chapters, to be submitted to him/her.

Research into the supervision of postgraduate students by Phillips (1984) shows that supervisory style is important. She found that the more supervisors left their students to get on with their work, intervening only when specifically asked for help, the shorter the length of time before the students became independent researchers. She argues that too much contact and cosseting delays the necessary weaning process.

2.2.2   Other models of supervision

It would be a mistake to think exclusively in terms of one supervisor for each researcher, although this is likely to be the model for undergraduate research. In postgraduate research it is normal to have two supervisors, although three are not unusual. Some colleges and universities delegate the administrative, pastoral and academic roles of supervision to separate individuals within the institution. This enables them to reduce the risk of failure by closely monitoring progress.

An alternative approach is that of *de facto* supervision. This model encourages the researcher to develop a number of different surrogate supervisors, possibly in other establishments, who have particular skills which the main supervisor lacks. This is particularly useful where company-based projects are concerned and a combination of academic and consultancy skills are required.

In the physical sciences, group and team projects are a widely used approach. Research students are often clustered round a major research issue and each student is part of the team. This allows specific areas of work within the same problem area to be the responsibility of individual researchers. Such approaches are research-skills based. On the other hand, research in the social sciences, which include management and business topics, is more likely to involve solitary, knowledge-based activities and includes a relationship with one or more supervisors which covers many more activities.

2.2.3   Other sources of support

The isolation which can be felt by students whilst conducting their research projects can be lessened by developing *support sets*. A set comprises approximately five students and a tutor and meets for a full day every one or two months. Each person is given an hour or so of the time available during which the group focuses on their particular project or problem. This provides an opportunity to use the group as a sounding board, in addition to exchanging experiences and ideas. It also enables group members to support and encourage one another.

Set members need to be working in loosely related areas, in order to increase the chances of cross-fertilisation of ideas without undue competition. The main requirement is that there are sufficient numbers of students attached to a department or faculty to produce viable group sizes. They may be supplemented by managers from companies who are not registered for a degree, but who wish to conduct their own in-company research.

Support sets can be a feature of more traditional research activities in the social sciences and need not be exclusively founded on process. They should be seen as being additional to normal supervision arrangements and are particularly valuable in the early stages of a research project.

Other potential sources of support can be found from sharing experiences with colleagues and mentors, and by networking. You should also attend any taught sessions offered, such as methodology courses, doctoral colloquiums and conferences.

2.3 Funding

Research is not a cost-free activity. Even if you were to conduct all your research in your college or university library, you would incur minor expenses, such as photocopying and printing. As soon as you start visiting other libraries and institutions, you will begin to incur more substantial expenses, such as travelling and subsistence costs. If you decide to conduct a postal questionnaire, for example, you will incur considerable printing and postage costs, and this assumes that your time is completely free!

Unfortunately *funding* for research is very difficult to obtain. You may find that you need to apply to more than one potential source of funds before you are successful. Therefore, you should allow plenty of time for this stage in your research. Assuming that your research has not been commissioned, and you are looking for funds, you should consider the following sources.

2.3.1 Your employer

If you are a part-time student or conducting a project as part of an industrial placement, your *employer* is likely to provide an opportunity for you to conduct your research into some aspect of management within your own workplace. Therefore, you will probably find that your employer is willing to reimburse any expenses you may incur in connection with your research.

2.3.2   Commercial funding

If you are working on a project which you consider to be of *commercial interest*, but which is not sponsored, you may be able to find an interested organisation which is willing to meet your costs. However, any such institution, whether it is your employer or an outside agency, is likely to want considerable influence over the project. This may give you problems with your academic requirements. If funding is critical, you may end up writing one report for the sponsoring organisation and another for your supervisor which meets the requirements of your academic institution, and you should not underestimate the pressure the extra work will give you.

2.3.3   Professional bodies

Many *professional bodies* of accountants, lawyers, bankers, marketing, personnel and purchasing managers, etc., hold research funds. Competition for such funds is keen and only those applications which are relevant to the interests of the professional body concerned are likely to be successful. You may find that preference is given to applicants who are members, but it is worth applying as sums can be relatively generous.

2.3.4   Individual benefactors

You may be lucky enough to find an *individual benefactor* who wants the research done. This may be because the individual is particularly interested in the topic or because he or she is conducting a larger project and is willing to meet the costs of your research if it feeds into the larger study. If you obtain funding from such a source, you must check the ownership of the data you generate and your independence.

2.3.5   Government bodies

Although there are substantial *government funds* available, obtaining them is a very competitive process and this makes it difficult for an inexperienced researcher. However, you should make early enquiries to see whether your college or university holds any government research funds or can direct you to such funds.

2.3.6   Charities and associations

Substantial funding is available from some *charities* and *associations*, although strict criteria often have to be met. More modest amounts to cover limited expenses such as travelling, postage and printing are less difficult to obtain.

2.3.7 Existing research projects

Many universities attract research funds and you may be able to help on an *existing research project*. In return for your help with the research your expenses will be reimbursed and you may be paid a salary. You may also be able to use the part of the project you are working on as the basis for your thesis or dissertation. However, there are some drawbacks to this sort of arrangement. You will have to demonstrate that the research is your own individual piece of work and you may find that the demands of the entire project supplant any of your own needs. You may be required to do some teaching. However, if you are able to agree a suitable arrangement, you stand to benefit not only from the financial rewards but from the advantage of working with more experienced researchers. Furthermore, in all probability you will have a ready access to data.

2.4 Negotiating access

If you are a part-time student or doing a placement project as part of a degree, your employer may give you *access* to sources where you can collect research data. Other students need to find their own sources and negotiate access to them. For example, if you have decided to collect your research data by designing a questionnaire and posting it to potential respondents, you will need to determine what types of people to send it to and obtain their names and addresses.

You may want to conduct a study which requires access to one or more organisations. The first step is to make use of any contacts you may already have. For example, your parents, relatives and friends may provide an introduction to an organisation which might be interested in your research. Remember that they will only be able to supply an introduction; it will be up to you to negotiate the *terms of access*.

If the above fails, then you may have to *cold canvass* firms; that is, approach the organisation without an introduction. This will require more confidence. Send a letter enclosing an outline of your *research proposal*, suitably modified for the organisation. The letter must be addressed to an appropriate named person whose name you should be able to obtain from company literature. Alternatively, telephone the firm and ask the switchboard operator for the name of the finance, marketing, personnel director or manager, or whoever is most likely to be interested in your research. If you do not receive a reply after ten days, you should follow your letter up with a telephone call to the manager or director concerned.

Whether you are using a contact or cold canvassing, you must present your project in the form of a brief research proposal, usually not more than two pages of A4. This should set out clearly the benefits to the organisation and what you want. Remember that the organisation will not want an academic document with citations, but a clear, concise, non-technical explanation of what the project is about in report form. If you can demonstrate that your research may provide answers to problems which their managers may be experiencing, you are more likely to be successful. Remember, the company will believe that it is doing you a favour, not vice versa, so be very sensitive in the requests you make.

Although you may be successful in finding an interested organisation, you may find that certain restrictions are placed on your research. These include constraints in terms of how long you can spend in the organisation, the documents you can see, the methods you can use, the personnel you can interview and the questions you can ask.

If the firm is interested, your contact is likely to respond by suggesting an informal discussion. This will enable management to assess you and your project in greater depth than can be gleaned from your proposal. It is important to be aware of and sympathetic to the norms and procedures of the firm you are approaching. Some organisations may be willing to make verbal agreements on the telephone or at an informal meeting; others may require all the issues to be agreed in writing with formal terms of reference. However, even if the agreement has been verbal, we recommend that you write a letter confirming what has been agreed. You should ensure that all correspondence is copied to all relevant members of staff in the organisation.

We discuss the main terms and conditions you may wish to consider in any agreement next.

2.4.1   Anonymity

In principle you should offer all the participants in your research the opportunity to remain *anonymous*. This means assuring participants that they will not be identified with any of the opinions they express. If you are conducting a large-scale survey by questionnaire, this should cause no problem, although you may collect some personal details, such as age and job title. In some interview surveys, for example, it may be vital to ensure anonymity, since this will encourage greater freedom of expression.

In other situations it may be very important that the name or position of the participant is stated. This may be because their status or responsibilities are such that their opinions can only be appreciated with this knowledge. In these circumstances it is imperative that the participant gives his or her consent. Other examples where permission must be sought include naming the author of a particular internal document. Sometimes it is possible to resolve problems of anonymity by agreeing on confidentiality, which we discuss next.

2.4.2   Confidentiality

Closely related to anonymity, the issue of *confidentiality* focuses on the data collected. You should discuss the issues of anonymity and confidentiality with your supervisors and the organisation(s) where you intend to collect your data as soon as possible to clarify these issues. In many cases this is relatively straightforward. You will need to reassure the organisation that all the data and information collected will be treated in the strictest confidence; although you will collate the data provided and use it in your research, you will ensure that no sensitive information is disclosed.

You will need to confirm that the data you collect will be used in such a way that it is not traceable to any particular individual. For example, your research report need not name the company or companies where you have negotiated access to data; it is sufficient to refer to the organisation as an engineering company, a food retailer, etc. Similarly, with individuals, they can simply be identified by reference to their position, since if the name of the company is not known, they cannot be identified, even if it is the managing director you are referring to. When writing to potential participants, or at the top of a questionnaire, you might include a sentence referring to this, such as: 'Your name, address and telephone number will remain confidential to the researcher(s), unless you have given permission otherwise. Any information you give will not be associated with your name in any way.'

Sometimes these measures are not enough and the company or individual is not sufficiently protected. In such circumstances, if the company or individuals are agreeable, it should be possible for your research report to be granted confidentiality terms. This would mean that no one but your supervisor(s) and examiners will have access to it; it will not be put in the public domain, either by placing it in the library or by publishing extracts from it. Obviously this would prevent you from presenting any seminar or conference papers on your research, or publishing any academic articles.

2.4.3   Publication permission

Obtaining *permission to publish* is not usually an issue at the undergraduate level since it is unlikely that there will be any intention to publish the results externally. For M.Phil. and Ph.D. students, it is essential that research results are published if you are pursuing an academic career. You will need to explain that the research report will be used for your degree. If you wish to publish from the research at a later date, it is normal practice to seek prior permission from the organisation. It is important to clarify who owns the data you have collected. At the end of your research you should provide the organisation with a copy of your report, but beware of offering them a special or interim report, since this can be very time consuming and expensive. However, if you have agreed to supply a report in exchange for access, you may have to write a special versions as your academic report is unlikely to be sufficiently user-friendly.

2.5.4   Agreeing a timetable

You will need to agree a *timetable* with the organisation for your research investigations and completion of the research report. You may find that you need to negotiate access with more than one person in the organisation and you should therefore plan to allow plenty of time for this stage in your research. It is likely that the individuals concerned will be helping you with your research in addition to doing their normal jobs. Therefore the time they are able to allocate to your research interests will be limited and must be arranged at their convenience.

2.4.5   Personal safety

It is important to consider your *personal safety* when conducting research. You will be exposing yourself to new situations and meeting people of whom you have no previous knowledge. Fortunately, few problems arise, but it is important that you are aware of potential dangers and take the necessary steps to minimise them.

If you are negotiating access with a well-known organisation, your safety is reasonably well assured, but with small, unknown organisations or individual interviews 'on site', caution is required. You should ensure that you have the full name, title and postal address of anyone you intend to visit. Attempt to establish their credibility beforehand by seeing if they are known to any of your colleagues and checking with your original source for the contact. If you have any doubts, ask your supervisor or a colleague to accompany you.

2.5   Ethics

It is easy to think of *ethics* being important in the natural sciences, such as medicine, but even in the social sciences it is 'difficult to conduct much research at all without running in to ethical arguments' (Coolican, 1992 p. 249). Therefore, you will need to consider a number of different ethical issues and find out what rules there may be for conducting research at an early stage in your studies. The American Psychological Association has established its own ethical principles for conducting research which are reproduced by Rudestam and Newton (1992). However, in business research there is no written code and it is up to you, in conjunction with your supervisor, to determine what is ethical. Before we offer our advice on the subject, it is worthwhile examining some of the problems which can arise.

- ► **The subject firm:** You may have spent some time negotiating access to an organisation in order to conduct your research. Naturally, you will be grateful to them for their help and will spend some time developing a good relationship, but what would you do if during the course of your research you found out that the company was doing something illegal? For example, imagine that you are conducting research in a small factory which employs a hundred people in an economically depressed area. During your research you observe that proper safety guards are not fitted to the machines, but you know that fitting them would bankrupt the company and put people out of work. What action should you take?
- ► **Confidentiality/anonymity:** It is normal to offer confidentiality or anonymity to participants in a research project. This encourages them to give more open and honest responses. However, it may present you with the problem that you receive information that you might consider should be passed on to someone else. For example, perhaps you are conducting research into the reasons for high wastage levels of materials in a production process. During interviews you discover that part of the wastage is due to one employee stealing goods. What should you do?
- ► **Informed consent:** In any research project it is ethical to inform potential participants of the purpose of the research and to obtain their agreement to their participation. This can present problems in gaining access and obtaining valid responses. For example, if you were to inform the participants in a laboratory experiment of the purpose of the research, it might alter their behavioural responses and thus distort your findings. Perhaps you are collecting your research data through participant observation (see Chapter 6). In business research this would involve becoming a full member of a work group and participating in all their activities as if you, too, were an ordinary employee. However, you would not be an ordinary employee since your purpose in joining them is to study some aspect of the way they work. Would you tell them that you are a researcher and risk distorting your findings, or would you deceive them?
- ► **Dignity:** In research it would not be ethical to embarrass or ridicule participants, but unfortunately this can easily be done. The relationship between the researcher and the phenomenon being studied is often complex. It is important to remember that you may be considered by the participants in your research as someone in

authority. For this reason, they may feel obliged to participate in your study or answer your questions, and do not feel that they have any choice in the matter.

▶ **Publications:** The career of an academic is developed through publications and the success of a research student is achieved through the acceptance of their thesis or dissertation. History shows that there are some who are willing to falsify their research findings in order to achieve publication success. This is undoubtedly highly unethical, but it is also unethical to exaggerate or omit results in order to present your research in a more favourable light. A more complex situation arises when your publication casts a bad light on an individual, group or organisation. This can arise if you are conducting a comparative study, when you must discuss your results with great sensitivity.

As you can imagine, there are no easy answers to most ethical dilemmas. Some commentators believe that firm ethical principles should be established for business research; others believe that such codes would be too simplistic and rigid. It has been argued that it is sometimes necessary to be vague about the purpose of the research and even covert in collecting data in order to achieve findings of value. It will be your responsibility to resolve these issues before you embark on your research study. Your own ethical position will help you determine how to design your research project. You may find the checklist shown in Figure 2.3 a useful starting point.

You may find that these questions expose a number of dilemmas and we will explore these in subsequent chapters when we look at the design of a research project and the methods for collecting data.

Related to ethics are matters which can be referred to as common *courtesy*. It is important that you conduct yourself in a manner which is beyond reproach. This entails consideration of the ethical issues we have discussed and also manners. It is essential that you thank

Figure 2.3 Checklist for ethical research

1. Will the research process harm participants or those about whom information is gathered (indirect participants)?

2. Are the findings of this research likely to cause harm to others not involved in the research?

3. Are you violating accepted research practice in conducting the research and data analysis, and drawing conclusions?

4. Are you violating community standards of conduct?

Source: Kervin (1992) p. 38.

individuals and organisations for their assistance with you research, both verbally at the time and afterwards by letter. If you have promised to provide copies of transcripts of interviews, for example, or your final report, make certain that you do so promptly. If any of your work is published, even if you do not need to obtain consent, as a matter of courtesy you should send a copy of the article to the participants.

2.6 Managing the research

Your research will cause you many intellectual and methodological problems which we will discuss in subsequent chapters. In this chapter we are focusing on the main practical issues, which once dealt with will free you to concentrate on the research itself. The solution to many of the practical problems you will face is to set up systems and procedures to manage the research. In this section we consider various aspects of the research which require managing from setting a timetable to keeping records.

2.6.1 Setting a timetable

Research is a time-consuming activity and if you do not set yourself a *timetable* you run the risk of failure due to not completing the project on time. To plan your time you need to know how long your institution allows for the submission of your dissertation or thesis. You also need to know how to allocate your time across the different activities you will undertake.

A Bachelor's or taught Master's dissertation is normally completed within one academic year. Table 2.4 shows the approximate length of the registration period for research degrees, but you should check with your own institution's regulations, as times can vary.

Table 2.4 Approximate length of research degrees

	Minimum	Maximum
M.Phil. thesis		
Full-time	18 months	36 months
Part-time	30 months	48 months
Ph.D. thesis (transfer)		
Full-time	33 months	60 months
Part-time	45 months	72 months
Ph.D. thesis (direct)		
Full-time	24 months	60 months
Part-time	36 months	72 months

Table 2.5 Approximate time allowances for main stages of research

Stage in research process	Time required (%)
Identifying research topic	15
Identifying research problem	10
Determining how to conduct research	10
Collecting research data	20
Analysing and interpreting research data	20
Writing dissertation or thesis	25
Total	100

There is no doubt that time is a major enemy of the research student. The secret of completing on time is to have a plan and your should draw up your own timetable as soon as possible. You may find Table 2.5 a useful guide when apportioning the amount of time you have available. As the table shows, this will vary according the to research qualification you are working for. Of course, the figures are only indicative and you may have to adjust your personal research timetable to reflect the *research design* you have adopted (see Chapter 5). You should also allow some time for solving any problems you may encounter.

However a major weakness of the analysis is that it implies that research takes place in orderly, discrete and sequential stages. Throughout this book you will find reminders that this is definitely not the case! Although we will be encouraging you to be methodical in your approach, you will find that all research contains stages which overlap. For example, you may need to go on collecting information about current research in your chosen field right up to the final draft, in order to be sure that you present an up-to-date picture.

Also, we must emphasise that although the writing-up stage is shown as a distinct activity at the end of the research process, you must get into the good habit of writing up your notes straight away. This means that you will start to write up your research, albeit in draft form, as soon as you start your project. When you have decided on the structure for your dissertation or thesis you can amend and refine your notes, and place them in the appropriate chapters. It is important not to underestimate how long the writing up stage takes, even when you have good notes and references on which to base your research report.

!   Experiential learning | **Managing your research**

Draw up a timetable for your own research, based on Table 2.5. If applicable, include key dates for submitting your proposal and any progress reports.

You may find it useful to look at some of the reasons for long completion times or, in the worst scenario, failure to complete. For a start, if you are inexperienced, you will find that everything takes longer than you expect. Therefore, it is important to plan your time carefully, with advice from your supervisor. If you are an undergraduate student you will only have a matter of months in which to complete your dissertation. You may have to balance your research activities against the demands of an industrial placement and/or your final year subjects. If you are a postgraduate student without funding, you may have to juggle the demands of paid work with your research; indeed, you may be lecturing to students yourself. If you are a mature student, you may have both paid work and family life to fit in.

Many students go on to study for a postgraduate degree straight after their finals. Because they know that they have several years in which to complete their research, they often overlook the importance of planning. The result is a slow start and this is a very common reason for late completion. A second common reason is perfectionism. Some students find it difficult to bring things to a conclusion. They are never satisfied with their results and are always thinking of ways in which to improve them, even before they have written them up. Thus, the writing-up stage is always postponed. Such students find it hard to see whether improvement really is necessary and whether it is desirable to spend so much time on that stage of the research to the detriment of later stages.

A third reason for late completion is that the student becomes distracted from the main research problem. Sometimes the facilities offered by information technology, such as on-line information systems, CD-ROMs, word-processing programs, databases, spreadsheets, graphical and statistical packages, can become so absorbing that it is hard to contain the literature search, the data is overanalysed or too much time spent on presentation of the results. Consequently, meeting the deadline is jeopardised. Sometimes the reason for the delay is exactly the opposite, and there has been insufficient collation and analysis of the data. In this case the student does not realise the inadequacy until he or she begins to write up and has to break off to complete this earlier stage, often resulting in a delay of months rather than weeks.

An experienced supervisor will be aware of these and other problems. The best way to overcome them is to draw up a realistic timetable with your supervisor which shows the dates on which the various stages in the research process should be completed. It is important to do this at the earliest possible stage. Many students find it extremely helpful to know that they are expected to reach certain stages at certain times, as this removes some of the pressure of managing their time and organising their research.

2.6.2 Organising materials

It will not take you too long to realise that a large part of research is concerned with *organising materials*, which may range from articles copied from journals, questionnaires returned, newspaper cuttings, transcripts of interviews or odd notes you have made. Everyone devises their own system, but we find it useful to sort the materials into their different types and order them according to this classification.

Copies of articles and conference papers can be kept in a file alphabetically under the name of the author. For a Ph.D. you may have several hundred articles; for an undergraduate project only a dozen or so. No matter how many you collect, it is important that they are stored systematically so that you can easily find them.

Primary materials such as questionnaires, transcripts of interviews, etc., should be numbered and dated and then filed in numerical order. You may find it useful to draw up an index for each set of files. In Chapter 8 we discuss the analysis of qualitative data and you will see that, to a large extent, the success of this rests on the efficient storing and referencing of primary materials. We give some examples in that chapter on how this can be achieved.

During your research you will probably collect a certain amount of miscellaneous materials, such as odd notes, quotations or cuttings, which may be important when you are writing your dissertation or thesis. Once you have decided on a draft structure (see Chapter 1), which you should do as early as possible, you can set up a file with dividers to separate each anticipated chapter and place these miscellaneous materials in the most appropriate chapter. As your research progresses you can expand and modify the report structure (see Chapter 9).

2.6.3 Networking

In this context *networking* simply means setting up and maintaining links with individuals in business and academic life during the course of your research. We have already discussed the importance of negotiating access and the courtesies required. Remember that all the contacts you make may be useful at some future date. Research is not a simple linear process of moving from one stage to the next, but often involves retracing your steps. The contacts you have made and maintained will assist you to do this.

There is nothing worse when you are writing up your research to find that you have not collected an essential statistic from a company or one of your interviews is incomplete. If you wrote to the individuals who have helped you along the way, thanking them for their assistance, it is easier to go back to them for the missing data. Similarly, if you have sent them any reports or articles resulting from your research, you are more likely to be successful if you approach them at a later date with a request to conduct further research.

It is also important to establish and maintain links with academic colleagues in your own and other institutions. These may be people interested in the same or a similar area of research who you meet in the common room, on courses or at academic conferences, etc., with whom you can exchange articles and talk over ideas and problems. You may also be able to exchange early drafts of your dissertation or thesis for mutual comment and criticism.

2.6.4   Keeping records

Keeping *records* is a very important component in the management of your research. In Chapter 4 we discuss an important aspect of your research known as the literature review and how to reference articles and books properly. It is essential that you keep a record of every article and book you read which might be useful in your own research. By this we mean a full reference (see Chapter 4). The references for articles and books can be kept either on a computer or on index cards; the latter are convenient to take with you to the library and can be completed there and then.

You will need to set up a filing system for your correspondence so that you can find the letter you wish to refer to. It is also important to maintain a record of contacts' names, addresses, telephone numbers, etc. A computerised record system is particularly useful if you are planning to send out a number of standard letters as the names and addresses can be merged with the standard letter at the time of printing (mail merge).

Finally, one further file you may wish to keep is one in which you can store instructions for using the library catalogue system, computerised databases and various software packages. This is also a good place to put leaflets on library opening times, safety requirements in laboratories and maps of various locations you may have to visit.

Conclusions

In this chapter we have examined some of the practical issues you will encounter when you become a researcher. Many of the practicalities you will have to deal with, such as course requirements and regulations, vary from one institution to another, and it is important that you find out what they are at an early stage. You may have to find funding for your research and you will certainly need to find a supervisor who is able and willing to advise you and guide your research. Some students will need to find more than one supervisor.

By the time you have read Chapter 1 and dealt with the practical issues raised in this chapter, you should be ready to move on to some of the more conceptual issues we discuss in Chapter 3.

3 Dealing with conceptual issues

Introduction

Now you have begun to understand the nature of research and we have dealt with some of the practical issues, it is time to look at the main conceptual issues which underpin research. The objectives of this chapter are:

▶ to examine the two main research paradigms
▶ to identify the key methodologies associated with each paradigm
▶ to examine the possibility of using triangulation.

Do not be put off if you are not yet familiar with these terms. In this chapter we introduce the concepts one at a time, so that you can gradually build up your knowledge. You will soon find yourself using them when talking to your supervisor and other researchers, as they provide a valuable framework for expressing your thoughts about your research. In addition, your new knowledge will help you make the most of any preliminary reading you may be doing.

If you are conducting research as part of an undergraduate degree or a taught Master's degree, you will probably face two major constraints compared with students taking a research degree. These relate to the relatively short period in which you must conduct your research and the relatively small size of your final research report. Therefore, you may not find it possible or necessary to explore the concepts and ideas in this chapter in such depth as M.Phil. or Ph.D. students. These students need greater understanding and should use the references at the end of the book as a guide to further reading.

3.1 Research paradigms

The term *paradigm* refers to the progress of scientific practice based on people's philosophies and assumptions about the world and the nature of knowledge; in this context, about how research should be conducted. Paradigms are 'universally recognised scientific achievements that for a time provide model problems and solutions to a community of practitioners' (Kuhn, 1962, p. viii). They offer a framework comprising an accepted set of theories, methods and ways of defining data.

Unfortunately, the term *paradigm* is used quite loosely in academic research and can mean different things to different people. To help clarify the uncertainties, Morgan (1979) suggests that the term can be used at three different levels:

▸ at the *philosophical* level, where it is used to reflect basic beliefs about the world
▸ at the *social* level, where it is used to provide guidelines about how the researcher should conduct his or her endeavours
▸ at the *technical* level, where it is used to specify the methods and techniques which ideally should be adopted when conducting research.

Thus, your basic beliefs about the world will be reflected in the way you design your research, how you collect and analyse your data, and even the way in which you write your thesis. Therefore, it is important to recognise and understand your personal paradigm as this will determine the entire course of your research project.

There are two main research *paradigms* or *philosophies*. Although there is considerable blurring, the two paradigms can be labelled *positivist* and *phenomenological* and these are the terms we shall used in this book. During the course of your studies you may come across authors who use other terms, the most common of which are *quantitative* and *qualitative*. Some authors prefer to use the term *interpretivist* rather than phenomenological because it suggests a broader philosophical perspective and prevents confusion with a methodology known as phenomenology. Table 3.1 summarises some of the more common terms.

The terms shown under each paradigm in the table are not necessarily interchangeable and in many cases have arisen as a result of the author wishing to denote a different approach. At the undergraduate level these nuances may not be important, but in postgraduate research considerable study may be required to argue the appropriateness of a particular paradigm.

Table 3.1 Alternative terms for the main research paradigms

Positivistic paradigm	Phenomenological paradigm
Quantitative	Qualitative
Objectivist	Subjectivist
Scientific	Humanistic
Experimentalist	Interpretivist
Traditionalist	

Although we have identified two main paradigms, it is best to regard them as the two extremes of a continuum. As you move along the continuum, the features and assumptions of one paradigm are gradually relaxed and replaced by those of the other paradigm. We will be looking at this more closely in the next section.

3.1.1   Assumptions of the main paradigms

Creswell (1994) draws on a number of other authors to show the different *assumptions* of the two main paradigms. These are shown in Table 3.2. You will see that he refers to the positivistic paradigm as *quantitative* and the phenomenological paradigm as *qualitative.*

With the *ontological assumption*, you must decide whether you consider the world is objective and external to the researcher, or socially constructed and only understood by examining the perceptions of the human actors.

Epistemology is concerned with the study of knowledge and what we accept as being valid knowledge. This involves an examination of the relationship between the researcher and that which is being researched. Positivists believe that only phenomena which are observable and measurable can be validly regarded as knowledge. They try to maintain an independent and objective stance. On the other hand, phenomenologists attempt to minimise the distance between the researcher and that which is being researched. They may be involved in different forms of participative enquiry (see Section 3.5.7). This polarity between the two approaches has been captured by Smith (1983, p. 10) who argues, 'In quantitative research facts act to constrain our beliefs; while in interpretive research beliefs determine what should count as facts.'

The *axiological assumption* is concerned with values. Positivists believe that science and the process of research is value-free. Therefore, positivists consider that they are detached from what they are researching and regard the phenomena which are the focus of their research as objects. Positivists are interested in the interrelationship of the objects they are studying and believe that these objects were present before they took an interest in them. Furthermore, positivists believe that the objects they are studying are unaffected by their research activities and will still be present after the study has been completed. These assumptions are commonly found in research studies in the natural sciences, but they are less convincing in the social sciences which are concerned with the activities and behaviour of people.

At the other extreme, phenomenologists consider that researchers have values, even if they have not been made explicit. These values help to determine what are recognised as facts and the interpretations

Table 3.2 Assumptions of the two main paradigms

Assumption	Question	Quantitative	Qualitative
Ontological	What is the nature of reality?	Reality is objective and singular, apart from the researcher	Reality is subjective and multiple as seen by participants in a study
Epistemological	What is the relationship of the researcher to that researched?	Researcher is independent from that being researched	Researcher interacts with that being researched
Axiological	What is the role of values?	Value-free and unbiased	Value-laden and biased
Rhetorical	What is the language of research?	Formal Based on set definitions Impersonal voice Use of accepted quantitative words	Informal Evolving decisions Personal voice Use of accepted qualitative words
Methodological	What is the process of research?	Deductive process Cause and effect Static design – categories isolated before study Context-free Generalisations leading to prediction, explanation and understanding Accurate and reliable through validity and reliability	Inductive process Mutual simultaneous shaping of factors Emerging design – categories identified during research process Context-bound Patterns, theories developed for understanding Accurate and reliable through verification

Source: Adapted from Creswell (1994) p. 5.

which are drawn from them. Although there are a range of positions under the phenomenological paradigm, phenomenologists believe that the researcher is involved with that which is being researched.

You will appreciate that the above three assumptions are inter-related. Logically, if you accept one assumption that is within the positivistic paradigm, the other two complement it.

The *rhetorical assumption* is concerned with the language of research. This is particularly important when you write your *research proposal* (see Chapter 5) and your final *dissertation* or *thesis* (see Chapter 9). These documents should be complementary to your paradigm, but they must also be written in a style which is acceptable to your supervisors and examiners.

In a positivistic study it is usual to write in a formal style using the passive voice. For example, instead of writing, 'As part of my research, I observed a group of employees ...' you would write, 'As part of the research, observations were made of a group of employees ...' This is because you should be trying to convey the impression that your research is objective, that rigorous procedures have been adopted and any personal opinions and values you possess have not been allowed to distort the findings. In your proposal you will write in the future tense, but in your final report you will use the past tense. For example, 'Interviews were held with ...' rather than, 'I held interviews with ...'

In a phenomenological study the position is less clear. In many disciplines the preferred style of writing is one which fully reflects the immediacy of the research and demonstrates the researcher's involvement. Therefore, you should write in the first person; in the future tense in the project proposal and more often than not in the present tense in the final report. However, you should review the *literature* relating to your discipline (see Chapter 4) and discuss with your supervisor whether this style is acceptable. We will be looking more closely at the writing-up stage in Chapter 9.

The *methodological assumption* is concerned with the process of the research. Having determined which paradigm to adopt, you will find that your choice of *methodology* is largely determined. The term *methodology* refers to the overall approach to the research process. We will be looking more closely at this in Section 3.2.

If you are a positivist, you are likely to be concerned with ensuring that any concepts you use can be operationalised; that is, described in such a way that they can be measured. Perhaps you are investigating a topic which includes the concept of intelligence, and you want to find a way of measuring the particular aspect of intelligence you are interested in. You will probably use large *samples* (see Section 3.2.2) and reduce the phenomena you are examining into their simplest parts. You will focus on what you regard are objective facts and formulate *hypotheses* (see Section 3.2.3). In your analysis you will be seeking associations or causality.

If you are a phenomenologist, you will be examining small *samples*, possibly over a period of time. You will use a number of different

Figure 3.1 Continuum of core ontological assumptions

Positivist	*Approach to social sciences*				Phenomenologist
Reality as a concrete structure	Reality as a concrete process	Reality as a contextual field of information	Reality as a realm of symbolic discourse	Reality as a social construction	Reality as a projection of human imagination

Source: Adapted from Morgan and Smircich (1980) p. 492.

research methods to obtain different perceptions of the phenomena and in your analysis you will be seeking to understand what is happening in a situation and looking for patterns which may be repeated in other similar situations.

Of course, the positivistic and phenomenological paradigms are two extremes and very few people would operate within their pure forms. There are a number of alternative classifications and alternative paradigms, most of which underline the fact that there are not just two paradigms but a whole range. Morgan and Smircich (1980) identify a *continuum* of these assumptions with six identifiable stages which is shown in Figure 3.1.

Starting at the left-hand side, at the extreme positivist end of the continuum, which Morgan and Smircich refer to as the *objectivist* end, there are those who assume that the social world is the same as the physical world. Their ontological assumption is that reality is an external, concrete structure which affects everyone. As the social world is external and real, the researcher can attempt to measure and analyse it using research methods such as *laboratory experiments* (see Section 3.4.2) and *surveys* (see Section 3.4.4).

At the second stage of the continuum reality is regarded as a concrete process where 'the world is in part what one makes of it' (Morgan and Smircich, 1980, p. 492). The third stage is where reality is derived from the transmission of information which leads to an ever-changing form and activity. At the fourth stage 'the social world is a pattern of symbolic relationships and meanings sustained through a process of human action and interaction.' (Morgan and Smircich, 1980, p. 494) At the fifth stage the social world is created by individuals through language, actions and routines. At the sixth, and extreme phenomenologist end of the continuum, which Morgan and Smircich refer to as the *subjectivist* end, reality is seen as a projection of human imagination. Under this assumption there may be no social world apart from that which is inside the individual's mind.

For the time being it is best to concentrate on the main assumptions we have described, but to be aware that these are pure forms.

You will certainly encounter further examples in the course of your studies. You need to remember that your choice of *paradigm* has implications for your choice of *methodology* (the overall approach to the research process) and, to a lesser extent, your research *methods* (the ways in which you collect data). When we look at research methods in Section 3.4, you will see that there is considerable development of approaches which attempt to bridge the two paradigms or serve as middle ground.

The particular paradigm you adopt for your research will be partly determined by the nature of the *research problem* (see Chapter 1) you are investigating, but it will also be shaped by your assumptions. It is important to remember that one paradigm is not 'wrong' and the other 'right', and you may find a particular paradigm is more acceptable to your supervisors, examiners and, indeed, to the editors of journals in which you may wish to publish your research. Unfortunately, it may not always be clear as to why they favour a particular paradigm, as they may merely be following a tradition in the discipline. Therefore, it is essential that you check which is the dominant paradigm in your chosen area of research and agree it with your supervisor at an early stage.

3.1.2   Positivistic paradigm

Historically the *positivistic paradigm* in the social sciences is based on the approach used in the natural sciences, such as biology, botany and physics. The approach used by the natural scientists had been highly successful and it is not surprising that when the social sciences were emerging towards the end of the nineteenth century, social scientists adopted their practices. It was argued that social scientists could adopt the role of observers of an independent and pre-existing reality; they should remain distant when conducting their research and not allow values and bias to distort their objective views.

The positivistic approach seeks the facts or causes of social phenomena, with little regard to the subjective state of the individual. Thus, logical reasoning is applied to the research so that precision, objectivity and rigour replace hunches, experience and intuition as the means of investigating research problems. Positivism is founded on the belief that the study of human behaviour should be conducted in the same way as studies conducted in the natural sciences. It is based on the assumption that social reality is independent of us and exists regardless of whether we are aware of it. Therefore, the ontological debate of 'What is reality?' can be kept distinct from the epistemological question of 'How do we obtain knowledge of that reality?' The act of investigating reality has no effect on that reality.

According to positivists, laws provide the basis of explanation, permit the anticipation of phenomena, predict their occurrence and therefore allow them to be controlled. Explanation consists of establishing causal relationships between the *variables* by establishing causal laws and linking them to a deductive or integrated *theory*. Thus, social and natural worlds are both regarded as being bound by certain fixed laws in a sequence of cause and effect. You will remember from Chapter 1 that a variable is an attribute of an entity that can change and take different values which are capable of being observed and/or measured. A theory is a set of interrelated variables, definitions and propositions that presents a systematic view of phenomena by specifying relationships among *variables* with the purpose of explaining natural phenomena.

3.1.3   Phenomenological paradigm

It was not long before some social scientists began to argue against positivism. They pointed out that the physical sciences deal with objects which are outside us, whereas the social sciences deal with action and behaviour which are generated from within the human mind. Moreover, they argued that the 'interrelationship of the investigator and what was being investigated was impossible to separate, and what existed in the social and human world was what we (investigators and laymen) thought existed' (Smith, 1983, p. 7).

Phenomenology is the science of phenomena. A *phenomenon* is 'a fact or occurrence that appears or is perceived, especially one of which the cause is in question' (Allen, 1990, p 893). The word is derived from the Greek verb to appear or show. Therefore, the *phenomenological paradigm* is concerned with understanding human behaviour from the participant's own frame of reference. A reaction to the positivistic paradigm, it is assumed that social reality is within us; therefore the act of investigating reality has an effect on that reality. Considerable regard is paid to the subjective state of the individual. This qualitative approach stresses the subjective aspects of human activity by focusing on the meaning, rather than the measurement, of social phenomena.

To varying degrees, phenomenologists believe that social reality is dependent on the mind. There is no reality independent of the mind; therefore, what is researched cannot be unaffected by the process of the research. The research methods used under this approach are 'an array of interpretative techniques which seek to describe, translate and otherwise come to terms with the meaning, not the frequency of certain more or less naturally occurring phenomena in the social world' (Van Maanen, 1983, p. 9).

The phenomenological paradigm developed as a result of criticisms of the positivistic paradigm. Figure 3.2 gives a brief review of

Figure 3.2 Main criticisms of the positivistic paradigm

1. It is impossible to treat people as being separate from their social contexts and they cannot be understood without examinng the perceptions they have of their own activities.

2. A highly structured *research design* (see Chapter 5) imposes certain constraints on the results and may ignore more relevant and interesting findings.

3. Researchers are not objective, but part of what they observe. They bring their own interests and values to the research.

4. Capturing complex phenomena in a single measure is, at best, misleading. For example, is it possible to assign a numerical value to a person's intelligence?

the main criticisms and this helps to explain the differences between the two paradigms.

You may find a bewildering array of terms under the phenomenological paradigm, which different authors refer to as paradigms or methodologies, particularly if they are labelled as a *qualitative* approach. However, on closer examination you will find that many are little more than *methods* for collecting data; in other words, they are not concerned with the overall approach to the research but with one aspect of it. Sometimes the author has used the term *methodology* to emphasise the overall approach to the research process. On other occasions the word *paradigm* has been used to distinguish a different assumption the author is using from that normally associated with a phenomenological paradigm.

Do not be confused by these different terms; in the main they are merely devices whereby the researcher, once close to the phenomena, can gain the sort of insights into people or situations he or she requires. Others are useful tools which help participants in the research think about their own worlds and consider, possibly for the first time, the way in which they construct their own reality.

Experiential learning | **Your views on the nature of reality**

In small groups or with your supervisor, discuss where you fit on the continuum of core ontological assumptions in Figure 3.1.

3.2   Paradigms and methodology

During the course of your studies you will come across the words *methodology* and *methods* and their importance to research. Some writers use them interchangeably. One reason for this is that it makes them sound more impressive. Another reason, particularly with the

Table 3.3 Features of the two main paradigms

Positivistic paradigm	Phenomenological paradigm
Tends to produce quantitative data	Tends to produce qualitative data
Uses large samples	Uses small samples
Concerned with hypothesis testing	Concerned with generating theories
Data is highly specific and precise	Data is rich and subjective
The location is artificial	The location is natural
Reliability is high	Reliability is low
Validity is low	Validity is high
Generalises from sample to population	Generalises from one setting to another

research methods used under a phenomenological paradigm, is that the method is so closely interwoven with the assumptions and the philosophies of the paradigm that it permeates the entire *research design* (see Chapter 5).

We prefer to distinguish between the two terms. *Methodology* refers to the overall approach to the research process, from the theoretical underpinning to the collection and analysis of the data. 'Like theories, methodologies cannot be true or false, only more or less useful' (Silverman, 1994, p. 2). *Methods*, on the other hand, refer only to the various means by which data can be collected and/or analysed. Thus, methodology is concerned with the following main issues:

► why you collected certain data
► what data you collected
► from where you collected it
► when you collected it
► how you collected it
► how you will analyse it.

The paradigm you adopt has great importance for the methodology you use. Table 3.3 shows the main features of the two paradigms. We have polarised the features in order to contrast them. However, as we have already suggested, it is helpful to think of them as being on a continuum. Regardless of which paradigm you are employing, it is important that you pay attention to all the features, and ensure that there are no contradictions or deficiencies in your methodology. The table introduces some new terms and concepts which we will now discuss.

3.2.1   Qualitative and quantitative data

In contrast with a number of other authors, you will see from the table that we prefer to use the terms *positivistic*, rather than *quantitative*, and *phenomenological*, rather than *qualitative*, for the paradigms because it is possible for a positivistic paradigm to produce qualitative data and vice versa. However, it is usual to associate a positivistic paradigm with measurement.

3.2.2   Sample size

A *sample* is a subset of a population and should represent the main interest of the study. A *population* is any precisely defined set of people or collection of items which is under consideration. Examples of a set of people in a business research project might be the working population of a particular country; all skilled people in a particular industry; all workers of a certain grade in a particular company, or all trainees in a particular department. A collection of items might be all green Ford Fiestas registered in a particular year in a particular region, or one day's production of medium-sliced wholemeal bread at a particular factory.

Because of the need to conduct statistical analysis, a positivistic paradigm often uses large samples; results from a representative sample can be taken to be true for the whole population. However, the aim of a phenomenological paradigm is to get depth, and it is possible to conduct such research with a sample of one. We look at samples again in Chapter 6.

3.2.3   Theories and hypotheses

The normal process under a positivistic paradigm is to study the literature to establish an appropriate *theory* and construct a *hypothesis*. A hypothesis is an idea or proposition which you test using statistical analysis. With a phenomenological approach, there may be no relevant existing theory or you may not wish to be restricted by existing theories. Therefore, you may carry out your investigation in order to construct a new theory to explain the phenomena or to describe different patterns which emerge in the data. Alternatively, you may

Table 3.4 Basic concepts in research

Concept	Meaning	Relevance
Theory	A set of explanatory concepts	Usefulness
Hypothesis	A testable proposition	Validity
Methodology	A general approach to studying research topics	Usefulness
Method	A specific research technique	Good fit with theory, hypothesis and methodology

Source: Silverman (1994) p. 1.

use the early part of the research study to develop hypotheses which are tested in subsequent stages of the research. Silverman (1994) offers a useful clarification of the basic research concepts and this is shown in Table 3.4.

You will find that some authors use the word *models* as an alternative for theories or, more often, to refer to theories with a narrow focus. A discussion on theories is beyond the scope of this book, although we discuss the importance of a theoretical framework when determining your *research design* (see Chapter 5).

3.2.4   Type of data

If you adopt a positivistic paradigm, it is essential that the *data* you use is highly specific and precise. Therefore, the data you collect will be mainly *quantitative data*. Because measurement is an essential element of the research process under this paradigm, you must apply considerable rigour to ensure the accuracy of the measurement. Under a phenomenological paradigm, the emphasis is on the quality and depth of the data. Therefore, the data you collect will be mainly *qualitative data*. The data is often referred to as being *rich*, since it captures the richness of detail and nuance of the phenomena being studied.

Bonoma (1985) argues that all researchers desire high levels of data integrity and results currency. *Data integrity* is a term used to describe those characteristics of research which affect error and bias in the research results. *Results currency* refers to the *generalisability* (see Section 3.2.8) of results. Bonoma claims that positivistic methodologies, such as laboratory experiments, are higher in data integrity than more phenomenological methodologies. However, phenomenological methodologies, such as case studies, tend to be high in results currency because they have contextual relevance across measures, methods, paradigms, settings and time. In any research project the researcher normally operates a trade-off between data integrity and results currency. In other words, data integrity can only be achieved by sacrificing results currency.

3.2.5   Location

Location refers to the setting in which the research is conducted. The best example of a positivistic paradigm is a scientist in a laboratory conducting a controlled experiment. By placing the research in a laboratory it is possible to isolate and control those variables which are being investigated. It is important to investigate some research problems in an artificial setting. For example, if you were investigating the effect of lack of sleep or alcohol on a health worker, it would not be safe to do it in a hospital.

Under a phenomenological paradigm, the research is usually conducted in the field. This term refers to a natural location as opposed to an artificial location. In business research projects, this is likely to be the workplace, and usually the researcher does not attempt to control any aspects of the phenomena.

3.2.6   Reliability

Reliability is concerned with the findings of the research and is one aspect of the credibility of the findings; the other is *validity* (see Section 3.2.7). You need to ask yourself 'will the evidence and my conclusions stand up to the closest scrutiny?' (Raimond, 1993, p. 55). If a research finding can be repeated, it is reliable. In other words, if you or anyone else were to repeat the research, you or they should be able to obtain the same results. For example, if you found that a group of workers who had attended a training course doubled their previous productivity levels, would another researcher obtain very similar results? Repeating a research study to test the reliability of the results is known as *replication* and is very important in positivistic studies where reliability is usually high.

Under a phenomenological paradigm the criterion of reliability may not be given so much status, or it may be interpreted in a different way. It is not important whether qualitative measures are reliable in the positivistic sense, but whether similar observations and interpretations can be made on different occasions and/or by different observers. Phenomenologists follow a number of procedures to ensure reliability or the authenticity of their findings and we will be discussing these in subsequent chapters.

It is often possible to design a research study where reliability is high, but validity, which we discuss in the next section, is low. For example, perhaps you are attempting to establish the criteria on which bank managers decide to grant overdrafts to customers. There are some very rational criteria, such as income levels, security of employment, past evidence of repayment and home ownership and it is possible that repeated questionnaire surveys of bank managers would demonstrate that these are the important criteria. However, observation or in-depth interviews might establish other criteria which are equally important. These could be apparently less rational criteria such as the bank manager not liking the look of the applicant or how he or she speaks.

3.2.7   Validity

Validity is the extent to which the research findings accurately represent what is really happening in the situation. 'An effect or test is valid if it demonstrates or measures what the researcher thinks or claims it does' (Coolican, 1992, p. 35). Research errors, such as faulty research procedures, poor samples and inaccurate or misleading measurement, can undermine validity. For example, you may be interested in whether employees understand their company occupational pension scheme and therefore you ask them to calculate their pension entitlements. The question is, do their answers reflect their understanding of the scheme, or whether they have read the scheme, or how good they are at remembering the details of the scheme, or even their ability to make calculations?

Because a positivistic paradigm focuses on the precision of measurement and the ability to be able to repeat the experiment reliably, there is always a danger that validity will be very low. In other words, the measure does not reflect the phenomena the researcher claims to be investigating. On the other hand, a phenomenological paradigm is aimed at capturing the essence of the phenomena and extracting data which is rich in its explanation and analysis. The researcher's aim is to gain full access to the knowledge and meaning of those involved in the phenomenon and consequently validity is high under such a paradigm.

There are a number of different ways in which the validity of research can be assessed. The most common is *face validity* which simply involves ensuring that the tests or measures used by the researcher do actually measure or represent what they are supposed to measure or represent. Another form of validity which is important in business research is *construct validity*. This relates to the problem that there are a number of phenomena which are not directly observable, such as motivation, satisfaction, ambition and anxiety. These are known as *hypothetical constructs* which are assumed to exist as factors which explain observable phenomena. For example, you may be able to observe someone shaking and sweating before an interview. However, you are not actually observing anxiety, but a manifestation of anxiety.

With hypothetical constructs, you must be able to demonstrate that your observations and research findings can be explained by the construct. It would be easy to fall into the trap of claiming that employees are highly motivated because they achieve high levels of productivity, when in fact they are working hard because they are anxious about the security of their jobs because the economy is in recession.

3.2.8   Generalisability

Generalisation is concerned with the application of research results to cases or situations beyond those examined in the study. *Generalisability* is 'the extent to which you can come to conclusions about one thing (often a population) based on information about another (often a sample).' (Vogt, 1993, p. 99). If you are following a positivistic paradigm, you will have constructed a *sample* (see Chapter 6) and you will be interested in determining how confident you are in stating that the characteristics found in the sample will be present in the *population* from which you have drawn your sample.

However, Gummesson (1991) argues that using statistics to generalise from a sample to a population is just one type of generalisation; in a phenomenological study you may be able to generalise from one setting to another. He supports the view of Normann (1970) who contends that it is possible to generalise from a very few cases, or even a single case, if your analysis has captured the interactions and characteristics of the phenomena you are studying. Thus, you will be concerned with whether the patterns, concepts and theories which have been generated in a particular environment can be applied in other environments. To do this, you must have a comprehensive understanding of the activities and behaviour you have been studying.

3.3 Types of research methodology

In the previous section we looked at the impact of your choice of *paradigm* on your *research design* and *methodology*. There are a number of different types of research methodology, some of which lend themselves more to one paradigm than another. Therefore, the type of methodology you choose should reflect the assumptions of your research paradigm. For example, an *experiment* conducted in a laboratory to measure the productivity of workers where the temperature of the room is deliberately varied would be positivistic. However, some methodologies can be used under either a positivistic or a phenomenological paradigm, depending on the assumptions of the researcher.

In this section we discuss the main methodologies used in business research. During the course of your studies you may come across others and you should bear in mind that your choice is not limited to

Figure 3.3 Methodological assumptions of the main paradigms

Positivistic	*Approach to social sciences*	**Phenomenological**
◄———————————————————————————————————————►		
Associated methodologies		*Associated methodologies*
Cross-sectional studies		Action research
Experimental studies		Case studies
Longitudinal studies		Ethnography
Surveys		Feminist perspective
		Grounded theory
		Hermeneutics
		Participative enquiry

those discussed in this chapter. In Figure 3.3 we have grouped the key methodologies together under the two main paradigms. However, you should remember that these two paradigms are near the extremities of the continuum; each methodology can be moved some way along the continuum according to the individual researcher's assumptions.

3.4 Positivistic methodologies

3.4.1 Cross-sectional studies

Cross-sectional studies are a positivistic methodology designed to obtain information on variables in different contexts, but at the same time. Normally, different organisations or groups of people are selected and a study is conducted to ascertain how factors differ. For example, if you are investigating associations between labour turnover and productivity, you need to select a sample of work groups where you know that labour turnover or productivity is different. You can then conduct statistical tests to find out whether there is any correlation between these two variables. We explain how this can be done in Chapter 7.

Cross-sectional studies are conducted when there are constraints of time or resources. The data is collected just once, over a short period of time, before it is analysed and reported. Thus, cross-sectional studies take a snapshot of an on-going situation. They are often used to investigate economic characteristics of large numbers of people or organisations, but a number of problems are associated with them. The first is how to select a large enough sample to be representative of the total population. The second is how to isolate the phenomena you are particularly interested in from all the other factors which may influence any correlation. Finally, cross-sectional studies do not explain why a correlation exists, only that it does or does not. On the other hand, cross-sectional studies are inexpensive and are conducted simultaneously, so that there is no problem of chronological change and few of the subjects studied are lost.

3.4.2 Experimental studies

Experimental studies are a positivistic methodology. Experiments are conducted either in a laboratory or in a natural setting in a systematic way. The former permit considerable control by allowing the researcher to eliminate certain variables or keep some variable constant. Experimental studies permit causal relationships to be identified. The aim is to manipulate the *independent variable* (for example, the intensity of lighting in a room) in order to observe the effect on the *dependent variable* (for example, productivity levels of office workers).

Problems include *confounding variables* which the researcher attempts to control. A confounding variable is one which obscures the effects of another, for example, the novelty of having so much attention or working in an unfamiliar place. In business research it is difficult to arrange experiments. Furthermore, laboratory settings do not reflect the actual environment. Many laboratory experiments have been criticised because they use students as subjects, the lack of reality in concentrating narrowly on certain variables, and the artificial nature of the environment compared with the real world. Barber (1976) identifies a number of problems which relate to the *investigator* (the person in overall control of the research) and the *experimenter* (the person actually carrying out the experiment). These range from poor research design and inaccurate recording to fudging the results.

Despite these drawbacks, Dobbins, Lane and Steiner (1988) argue that laboratory experiments are valuable and that even studies using students as subjects have validity. They argue that investigations into the use of *laboratory experiments* reveal that they can have substantial external validity. Dobbins, Lane and Steiner recommend that the choice of research method should be based on the purpose of the research and the investigator's orientation. In their view, laboratory experiments are useful for examining work behaviour at the individual level.

Although *field experiments* offer the advantage that they are conducted in a real situation, and thus avoid many of the drawbacks of the laboratory experiment, there may be problems establishing and conducting the research. In particular, you may not have such strong control over *confounding* and *extraneous variables*. You will remember that a confounding variable is one which obscures the effects of another. An extraneous variable is any variable other than the independent variable which might have an effect on the dependent variable. For example, if your study involves an investigation of the relationship between productivity and motivation, you may find if difficult to exclude the effect on productivity of other factors such as a heat wave, a work to rule, a takeover or domestic problems.

There are a number of approaches to designing an experimental study, and we discuss the main ones below:

▶ **Repeated-measures design:** In this type of study the experiment is repeated under different conditions. For example, perhaps you are interested in assessing employees' performance in operating complicated machinery under noisy conditions. You could ask the employees (who would be the subjects of the experiment) to operate the machinery when it was noisy and gauge their performance by measuring the time taken to perform a particular task and the number of errors. You might ask the same employees to conduct the same task under quiet conditions. If the results are not the same under both noisy and quiet conditions, and all other variables have been controlled, it would be reasonable to assume that the change in performance is due to the level of noise

One problem with this approach is that an employee's performance may be better on the second occasion because they have rehearsed the task by doing it the first time. Alternatively, they may perform less well the second time because they have become bored. These are examples of the *order effect*. There are a number of solutions to this problem, but the easiest is to ensure that there is sufficient time between the experiments to remove any ordering effects (Coolican, 1992)

▶ **Independent-samples design:** In this type of experiment two groups of employees would be selected; one to operate the machinery under noisy conditions, the other under quiet conditions. The two groups' results can then be compared. The major problem with this approach is that there may be differences between the two groups. For example, one group might contain a greater number of trainees than the other group. One solution to inequalities such as this is to allocate employees randomly to each group

▶ **Matched-pairs design:** This is a more rigorous approach which attempts to ensure that the two groups do not differ in respect of such characteristics as training, age, skill, etc. by matching pairs of employees and allocating one to each group. Of course, there may be some difficulty in identifying which characteristics should be matched and ensuring that there are enough employees to obtain a sufficient number of matched pairs

▶ **Single-subject design:** This approach is useful when only a few subjects are available, but there is the problem of how to generalise from the result with confidence. However, despite this drawback, findings from such a study can be useful in particular circumstances.

The nature of the research problem and the access you have managed to negotiate is likely to play a significant role in determining the specific design you choose. To select the most appropriate design, you need to consider a number of different factors which Kervin (1992) classifies as follows:

▶ **the number of groups:** you will either compare two or more groups of cases, or look for variations within one group

▶ **the nature of groups:** it will be important to know how the group is formed, for example by using random allocation or matched cases

▶ **the time of the experiments:** in the repeated-measures design, the experiment was conducted twice, but it could be repeated more often (in our example, with varying levels of noise). However, these options may not be possible and you could find that you are restricted in collecting evidence at one point of time only, at least with the same groups.

Once you have decided on the type of experimental design, you need to determine the size of your sample. One criterion to use is what you intend to do with the data. Coolican (1992) argues that when the experimental independent variable can be assumed to have a similar effect on most people, the optimum sample size is about 25 to 30.

Although we have referred to experimental studies as a positivistic methodology, a phenomenological approach can be adopted, even in a laboratory study. Some commentators suggest that laboratory procedures are inconsistent with the epistemology implied by the interaction theory and they are artificial (for example, Blumer, 1980). The relationship between the researcher and the participants will have a certain level of authoritarianism and the experiments do not give a faithful representation of social action in everyday life.

Couch (1987) rejects many of these criticisms and claims that laboratory experiments can be used fruitfully in a phenomenological study, but that care must be taken with the research design. He recommends that the situation should be structured so that participants only pay minimal attention to the researcher. If possible, a mini-social world of short duration, but with a high level of authenticity, should be created in the laboratory. This may require an elaborate layout and the researcher being involved in a particular role within the phenomenon being studied.

The analysis of the data will be based on video recordings and transcriptions. 'The use of the laboratory and recording devices ... [does not] require acceptance of the positivistic ontology.' (Couch, 1987, p. 166). The results of the field studies can then be compared to the results of laboratory studies so that 'grounded theories of social construct that have universal application can be constructed' (Couch, 1987, p. 175).

Experimental studies, both in the laboratory and the field, present specific challenges to the researcher. Although the methodology is more frequently used in positivistic studies, there are arguments that it is appropriate in phenomenological studies. If you choose to conduct an experimental study, you will need to concentrate on the research design and recognise the limitations of the study. These issues are discussed in Chapter 5.

3.4.3   Longitudinal studies

A *longitudinal study* is often, but not always, associated with a positivist methodology. It is a study, over time, of a variable or group of subjects.

The aim is to research the dynamics of the problem by investigating the same situation or people several times, or continuously, over the period in which the problem runs its course. This is often many years. Repeated observations are taken with a view to revealing the relative stability of the phenomena under study; some will have changed considerably, others will show little sign of change. Such studies allow the researcher to examine change processes within a social, economic and political context. Therefore, it should be possible to suggest likely explanations from an examination of the process of change and the patterns which emerge. It has been argued (Adams and Schvaneveldt, 1991) that the observation of people or events over time can offer the researcher the opportunity to exercise some control over the variables being studied.

It can be argued that a longitudinal study can be based primarily on a qualitative approach. Stebbins (1992) refers to this as *concatenated exploration*. A distinctive feature of this approach is that there is a chain of studies. Each link in the chain is an examination or re-examination of a related group or social process, or an aspect of a broader category of groups or social processes. The early studies in the chain are mainly exploratory, but as the chain of studies progresses, grounded theory is generated.

Stebbins argues that the chain of qualitative case studies improves the applicability and validity of the findings. In addition, the researcher gains in knowledge and understanding of the subject as the research develops, and can take account of social processes instead of concentrating only on individuals. Because of the smaller sample size, it is easier to negotiate access for a longitudinal study than for a cross-sectional study, and to produce significant results. However, once started, the study must be continued and there is the problem of losing subjects during the course of the study. Moreover, this methodology is very time-consuming and expensive to conduct. It is unlikely to be appropriate for research students on taught courses, since it requires the researcher to be involved for a number of years for the advantages to be enjoyed.

For undergraduates, a longitudinal study is usually not possible because the course does not allow sufficient time to collect *primary data*. However, it is possible to base your research on *secondary data*. The government and other bodies publish a considerable amount of data on various social and economic factors, such as employment, home ownership, household expenditure and income. By concentrating on a specific area, you could investigate whether there have been significant changes over a period of time and how these changes might be explained. In Chapter 7 we explain a technique known as *time series analysis*, which is useful for analysing data collected in longitudinal studies.

3.4.4   Surveys

A *survey* is a positivistic methodology whereby a *sample* of subjects is drawn from a *population* and studied to make inferences about the population. When the total population is small, it is normal to collect data about each member of the population. When the population is large, it would be too time consuming and expensive to collect data about every member, and therefore only a sample of the whole population is used. If the sample is representative, it is possible to use statistical techniques to demonstrate the likelihood that the characteristics of the sample will also be found in the population. In other words, it may be possible to generalise from the findings. These statistical techniques are discussed in Chapter 7.

The first and most critical stage of the survey is to select the sample. It is important to ensure that your sample is not *biased* and is representative of the population from which it is drawn. An example of a biased sample is where you asked for volunteers to participate in the research, because these people may possess certain characteristics which the others, who did not volunteer, do not possess. The various methods you may use to attempt to select an unbiased sample are discussed in Chapter 6.

Having decided on a sample, it is necessary to decide how to ask the survey questions. The alternatives are face-to-face or telephone *interviews* or *questionnaires*, and these too are examined in Chapter 6. As far as possible, all participants will be asked exactly the same questions in the same circumstances.

There are two major types of survey. A *descriptive survey* is concerned with identifying and counting the frequency of a specific population, either at one point in time or at various times for comparison. Such surveys are often associated with political elections, but are frequently used in business research in the form of attitude surveys. For example, you might wish to assess customers' attitudes to the products or services of a company or to find out the views of employees on specific issues.

The other major type of survey is the *analytical survey* where the intention is to determine whether there is any relationship between different variables. If you wish to carry out this type of survey, you will need to be familiar with the theoretical context so that you can identify the independent, dependent and extraneous variables. We look at variables more closely in Chapter 6.

3.5   Phenomenological methodologies

3.5.1   Action research

The assumptions on which *action research* are based place it within the phenomenological paradigm. It is an approach which assumes that the social world is constantly changing, and the researcher and the research itself are part of this change. The term was coined by Lewin (1946) who saw the process of enquiry as forming a cycle of planning, acting, observing and reflecting. The planning stage is concerned with identifying an objective, which it is intended to achieve, and how this may be done. The first phase of action is implemented and its effects observed and reflected on before modifying the overall plan, if appropriate.

Action research is a type of *applied research* (see Chapter 1) designed to find an effective way of bringing about a conscious change in a partly controlled environment; for example, a study aimed at improving communications between management and staff in a particular company. It is usual to conduct action research within a single organisation and it is therefore similar to a case study approach in many of its procedures.

The main aim of action research is to enter into a situation, attempt to bring about change and to monitor the results. The close collaboration required between the researcher and the client company poses a number of problems. Some action research may not be very far removed from a problem-solving, consultancy project. From the beginning, the researcher and the client must be agreed on the aims of the study. There will be mutual control of the research and analysis of the results. The final action plan to be implemented is usually the client's responsibility, supported by the researcher. The research report is often published jointly.

There is considerable debate among academics as to the nature of this methodology, although 'improvement and involvement seem central to all users of the term' (Robson, 1993, p. 439). Furthermore, there is collaboration between researchers and practitioners, with the latter participating in the research process. However, it is argued that these features alone do not make for good research and some projects labelled action research 'have been closer to consultancy or journalism' (Gummesson, 1991, p. 102). To avoid such criticisms, some researchers prefer the term *action science*, the main characteristics of which are described by Gummesson as follows:

- Action science always involves two goals: solve a problem for the client and contribute to science
- The researcher and the client should learn from each other and develop their competencies
- The researcher must investigate the whole, complex problem, but make it simple enough to be understood by everyone
- There must be cooperation between the researcher and the client, feedback to the parties involved and continuous adjustment to new information and new events

▶ Action science is primarily applicable to the understanding and planning of change in social systems and thus is a suitable research and consulting strategy for business organisations

▶ The corporate environment and the conditions of business must be understood before the research starts

▶ The methodology should not be judged solely by the criteria used for the positivistic paradigm, but by criteria more appropriate for this particular methodology.

3.5.2   Case studies

A *case study* is an extensive examination of a single instance of a phenomenon of interest and is an example of a phenomenological methodology. The importance of the context is essential and Eisenhardt (1989) refers to the case study as 'a research study which focuses on understanding the dynamics present within single setting' (Eisenhardt, 1989, p. 534). Bonoma (1985) notes that it must be 'constructed to be sensitive to the context in which management behaviour takes place' (Bonoma, 1985, p. 204).

A *unit of analysis* is the kind of case to which the variables or phenomena under study and the research problem refer, and about which data is collected and analysed. A case study approach implies a single unit of analysis, such as a company or a group of workers, an event, a process or even an individual. It involves gathering detailed information about the unit of analysis, often over a very long period of time, with a view to obtaining in-depth knowledge. You may have a single case of a number of cases in a research study.

Case studies are often described as *exploratory research*, used in areas where there are few theories or a deficient body of knowledge. However, this is not their only form. Scapens (1990) adds the following types:

▶ **descriptive** case studies where the objective is restricted to describing current practice

▶ **illustrative** case studies where the research attempts to illustrate new and possibly innovative practices adopted by particular companies

▶ **experimental** case studies where the research examines the difficulties in implementing new procedures and techniques in an organisation and evaluating the benefits

▶ **explanatory** case studies where existing theory is used to understand and explain what is happening.

Otley and Berry (1994) add another type. This is a case study which arises by chance; circumstances occur which give the researcher access and the opportunity to examine a phenomenon. Although such a study may be limited to just a few aspects of organisational life, the results can be extremely stimulating and original. The different types of case study are not well delineated and one type may be combined with or merge into another. The methods used to collect data in a case study include documentary analysis, interviews and observation (see Chapter 6).

Yin (1994) identifies the following characteristics of case study research:

▶ The research aims not only to explore certain phenomena, but to understand them within a particular context
▶ The research does not commence with a set of questions and notions about the limits within which the study will take place
▶ The research uses multiple methods for collecting data which may be both qualitative and quantitative.

These characteristics are open to debate and are set in a phenomenological paradigm. If you were taking a more positivistic approach, you might wish to commence with a strong theoretical foundation and specific research questions. Whichever paradigm you operate under, there are similarities in the research process. The main stages are discussed below.

▶ **Selecting your case:** It is not usually necessary to find a representative case or set of cases because you will not be attempting statistical generalisations to show that you can generalise from your sample to a larger population. However, you may be attempting theoretical generalisations where you propose that the theory applied in one set of circumstances can generalised to another. You may wish to select a critical case which encompasses the issues in which you are most interested. You may also decide that you require more than one case. Similar cases will help to show whether your theory can be generalised and dissimilar cases will help to extend or modify any theory
▶ **Preliminary investigations:** This has been referred to as drift (Bonoma, 1985) and is the process of becoming familiar with the context in which you are going to conduct your research. Some researchers believe that it is best to keep your mind free of any prior beliefs and to learn from the naturalistic evidence at this stage. Others disagree with this approach and consider that the researcher approaches the project with either explicit or implicit theories. To determine your approach, it may be helpful to reflect on your paradigm and also to consider the purpose you attribute to your research
▶ **The data stage:** You will need to determine how, where and when to collect data. It is usually best to 'combine data collection

methods such as archive searching, interviews, questionnaires and observations. The evidence may be qualitative (e.g. words), quantitative (e.g. numbers) or both' (Eisenhardt, 1989, p. 534)

▶ **The analysis stage:** At the analysis stage you have a choice between within-case analysis or cross-case analysis. If you use the former it is essential that you become totally familiar with the material. This should enable you to build up separate descriptions of events, opinions and phenomena which can be used to identify patterns. If you use cross-case analysis you may wish to identify the similarities and differences which will help you to identify common patterns

▶ **The report stage:** There can be considerable difficulties in writing up case study material, both in determining an appropriate structure and demonstrating that your analysis and conclusions can be linked to the masses of data you will have collected. Students often find a chronological structure is the easiest to adopt since this means they can relate the unfolding of events as they occur. We consider the writing up stage in detail in Chapter 9.

In a phenomenological study, it is essential that you quote extensively from the data you have collected through *interviews* and other means (see Chapter 6). *Diagrams* are often helpful for explaining the patterns you see emerging.

Although a case study approach can be a very satisfying methodology, there are some weaknesses. Access to a suitable organisation is often difficult to negotiate and the process of the research can be very time consuming. It is also difficult to decide on the *delimitations* of your study; in other words, where you are going to place the boundaries. Although you may be focusing on a particular organisation or group of individuals, they do not exist in a vacuum, but interact with the rest of society. Whatever your *unit of analysis* (see Chapter 5), it will have a history and a future which will influence your understanding of the present. You may find it difficult to understand the events in a particular period of time without knowledge of what went before and what may follow.

3.5.3   Ethnography

Ethnography is a phenomenological methodology which stems from anthropology. *Anthropology* is the study of people, especially of their societies and customs. Ethnography is an approach in which the researcher uses socially acquired and shared knowledge to understand the observed patterns of human activity. *Ethno-* means folk and *-graphy* means description. Werner and Schoepfle (1987) claim that ethnography is any full or partial description of a group. The main method of collecting data is *participant observation* (see Chapter 6) where the researcher becomes a full working member of the group being studied. The research normally takes place over a long period of time, often many months, in a clearly defined location such as a factory floor, and involves direct participation in the activities of that particular workplace.

The aim of the methodology is to be able to interpret the social world in the way that the members of that particular world do. Bogdan and Taylor (1975) and Patton (1990) offer a number of suggestions for researchers conducting ethnographic studies which can be summarised into the following stages:

▶ Build trust as early as possible
▶ Become as involved as you can with the phenomena, but maintain an analytical perspective
▶ Develop strong contacts with a few key informants
▶ Gather data from as many different sources as possible, using multiple methods
▶ Capture participants' views of their experiences in their own words, but remember the limitations of their perspectives
▶ Write up field notes as soon as possible after leaving the setting and do not talk to anyone until you have done so
▶ Be descriptive when taking your field notes and draw diagrams of physical layouts
▶ Include your own experiences, thoughts and feelings as part of your field notes
▶ As field work draws to a close, concentrate on making a synthesis of your notes.

A considerable number of disciplines have used an ethnographic approach, and business is no exception. Some of them are reviewed by Gill and Johnson (1991). However, there are a great many factions and schisms and 'ethnography is perhaps the most hotly contested site in qualitative research today' (Denzin and Lincoln, 1994, p. 203) This has led to the emergence of a number of different styles of ethnography which depend on the skills and training of the researcher and the nature of the group with which the ethnographer is working. Whatever the type of ethnography adopted, it 'provides insights about a group of people and offers us an opportunity to see and understand their world' (Boyle, 1994, p. 183).

Students conducting ethnographical studies face a number of problems. First, you have to select an organisation in which your particular research interests are present and negotiate access. Secondly, you have to develop a high degree of trust in those you work with to ensure that you collect the data. Thirdly, if you are using full participation to do your research, you must cope with being a full-time member of a work group as well as doing the research. Finally, there is the issue of whether the particular setting or group best reflects the research interests and whether it will be possible to generalise from the findings.

Despite these difficulties, students can find ethnography a very rewarding methodology. You obtain first-hand experience of the context being studied. By direct observation, you are able to better understand and interpret the phenomenon being studied, and participation in events may lead participants to reveal maters which would otherwise be left unsaid. When writing up your research it is important to capture the experiences that the group have gone through by quoting the participants' own words and describing the context in which they were uttered.

3.5.4   Feminist perspective

In its broadest sense, feminism is about change for women and parity with men in society. At a methodological level a *feminist perspective* is concerned with challenging 'the traditional research paradigm from the point of view of the politics and ideology of the women's movement.' (Coolican, 1992, p. 27). Thus, it challenges the methods by which knowledge is currently generated and the source of the views of the world it reflects.

One approach to a feminist perspective is that expressed by Hyde (1994), who lists the following three principles which captured her initial understanding of it:

► knowledge is grounded in the experiences of women
► research benefits women
► the researcher immerses herself or himself in or exhibits empathy for the world being studied.

Advocating a feminist methodology does not mean that the full range of methodologies are not open and useful to everyone. 'It would fall back onto old stereotypes to suggest that women didn't tend to use quantification or feel happy testing hypotheses statistically' (Coolican, 1992, p. 127). It is also possible to combine a feminist perspective with another methodology; for example, Treleaven's (1994) collaborative enquiry with women as staff development.

However, adopting a feminist methodology can present both theoretical and practical problems. Gregg (1994) describes difficulties when she interviewed women who held contrasting opinions to her own. Sometimes there was 'a tension between accepting what the women said ... and wanting to hold onto a particular feminist view, a vision of a feminist future as part of a commitment to social change' (Gregg, 1994, p. 53).

Even the language of research can be a barrier. 'It is quite difficult for women to be speaking subjects – harder than for men – and that is true both for women as our research subjects and for us as researchers when we write and talk about our research' (DeVault, 1990, p. 112). Despite these difficulties, feminism brings a new perspective to research and offers insights and understanding of problems which would otherwise be unavailable.

3.5.5   Grounded theory

Grounded theory is 'but one of the interpretive methods that share the common philosophy of phenomenology – that is, methods that are used to describe the world of the person or persons under study' (Stern, 1994, p. 273). The methodology was conceived by Glaser and Strauss (1967) in the medical field, but has now been developed in many disciplines. It uses 'a systematic set of procedures to develop an inductively derived grounded theory about a phenomenon. The findings of the research constitute a theoretical formulation of the reality under investigation, rather than consisting of a set of numbers, or a group of loosely related themes' (Strauss and Corbin, 1990, p. 24). Thus, the theory is generated by the observations rather than being decided before the study. This contrasts with positivist research where speculation and reflection lead to the development of hypotheses. The hypotheses are then translated into predictions, often by a process of deduction. Next, they are tested in controlled circumstances or experiments designed to generate data which will confirm (or otherwise) the hypothesis. Finally, this is used to confirm or modify the theory.

The purpose of grounded theory is to build theory that is faithful to and which illuminates the area under investigation. The intention is to arrive at prescriptions and policy recommendations with the theory which are 'likely to be intelligible to, and usable by, those in the situation being studied, and is often open to comment and correction by them' (Turner, 1981, p. 226).

The theoretical framework is developed by the researcher alternating between inductive and deductive thought. First, the researcher inductively gains information which is apparent in the data collected. Next, a deductive approach is used which allows the researcher to turn away from the data and think rationally about the missing information and form conclusions based on logic. When conclusions have been drawn, the researcher reverts to an inductive approach and tests these tentative hypotheses with existing or new data. By returning to the data, the deducted suggestions can be supported, refuted or modified. Then supported or modified suggestions can be used to form hypotheses and investigated more fully. It is this inductive/deductive approach and the constant reference to the data which helps *ground* the theory.

'Joint collection, coding and analysis of data is the underlying operation. The generation of theory, coupled with the notion of theory as process, requires that all three operations be done together as much as possible' (Glaser and Strauss, 1967, p. 43). The relationships between categories and subcategories which are discovered during the research should be as a result of information contained within the data, or from deductive reasoning which has been verified within the data. They should not arise from previous assumptions which have not been supported.

Any views held by the researcher prior to the study may restrict his or her perceptions of the phenomenon under investigation. This might lead to important links and relationships remaining undiscovered or inaccurate deductions about the data, for example. Glaser (1978) suggests that the researcher should enter the research setting with as few predetermined ideas as possible. Of course, no one can completely distance themselves from the beliefs and structures which they have grown up with or have developed. However, the researcher needs to be aware of the presence of such prejudices. Once a prejudice has been recognised, its validity can be questioned, and it no longer remains a bias.

The overall features of grounded theory have been summarised by Silverman (1993, p. 46) into the following three stages:

- ▶ an initial attempt to develop categories which illuminate the data
- ▶ an attempt to 'saturate' these categories with many appropriate cases in order to demonstrate their importance
- ▶ developing these categories into more general analytic frameworks with relevance outside the setting.

Grounded theory presents a number of problems. There is the difficulty of dealing with the considerable amount of data which is generated during the course of the research and the problem of *generalisability* of the findings (see Section 3.2.8).

3.5.6   Hermeneutics

Hermeneutics is a phenomenological methodology which was originally concerned with interpreting ancient scriptures. Dilthey (1976) and others have formalised the technique and broadened its scope. Essentially, this methodology involves paying particular attention to the historical and social context surrounding an action when interpreting a text. It is assumed that there is a relationship between the direct conscious description of experience and the underlying dynamics or structures. Whilst a text can provide an important description of the conscious experience, analysis and interpretation of the underlying conditions which led to the experience are also required. Thus, the hermeneutic process involves interpreting the meaning of a text through continual reference to its context (Ricoeur, 1977).

Although more usually associated with the interpretation of historical text, hermeneutics has been applied to research in law where the reasons behind judgments or statutes are sought. According to Lindlof (1995, p. 31), 'The method can be applied to any situation in which one wants to "recover" historical meaning.' Taylor (1990) links hermeneutics with *repertory grid technique* (see Chapter 8). Her rationale for doing this is that five criteria for text set down by Ricoeur (1981) can be rewritten for data sets as follows:

► Words and numbers convey meaning
► Numbers are chosen according to a structured rationale
► There is a relationship between this structured rationale and the intended meaning
► The work of this intended meaning is a projection of a world
► The uncovering of this meaning is through the mediation of self-understanding.

Taylor stresses the importance of the researcher as an interpreter and a reiterative process of relabelling and reanalysing the data in a hermeneutic circle. Although hermeneutics is not a widely used methodology in business research, her unusual approach illustrates the importance of being flexible in classifying methodologies and methods and the value of creativity.

3.5.7   Participative enquiry

Participative enquiry is a phenomenological methodology and is 'about research with people rather than research on people.' (Reason, 1994a, p. 1). The participants in such a research study are involved as fully as possible in the research which is conducted in their own group or organisation. The research may even be initiated by a member of the group. Participants are involved in the data gathering and analysis. They also debate and determine the progress and direction of the research, thus enabling the researcher to develop questions and answers as a shared experience with a group as co-researchers (Traylen, 1994).

Concerns about the traditional model of research, which implies an authority imbalance in the relationship between the researcher and the researched, together with ethical issues (see Chapter 2), have led some researchers to seek a methodology which involves the

participants more in the study. One reason for this is that such involvement will produce better quality data; another is more concerned with
philosophical arguments and the democratic rights of individuals to
participate in a study. As one commentator puts it, 'I believe and hope
that there is an emerging world view, more holistic, pluralist and
egalitarian, that is essentially participative' (Reason, 1994b, p. 324). De
Venney-Tiernan, Goldband, Rackham and Reilly (1994) contend that
the methodology can be employed successfully by novices and those
who would not consider themselves to be academics.

There are a number of different approaches to participative enquiry.
Reason (1994b) identifies three. With *cooperative enquiry* all those
involved in the research are coresearchers whose thinking and decision-
making contribute to generating ideas, designing and managing the
project, and drawing conclusions form the experience; they are also
cosubjects who participate in the activity being researched. In *participatory action research* the aim is to challenge the power relationship in
society. Such studies are often concerned with capturing the knowledge and experiences of oppressed groups. The final term is *action
science* which we have discussed already under action research. The
basis for all these approaches is that they see 'human beings as co-
creating their reality through participation, experience and action'
(Denzin and Lincoln, 1994, p. 206)

3.6   Mixing methodologies

You will need to make a choice about the *paradigm* you will adopt
at an early stage in your research. Once this is established, it is not
unusual in business research to take a mixture of approaches, particularly in the methods of collecting and analysing data. This allows
you to take a broader, and often complimentary, view of the research
problem or issue. What is central, is how well you pull the data
together to make sense of it. We will be looking at this in later chapters.
You may find it helpful at this point to investigate your personal
predisposition towards particular research approaches.

It can be argued that the dominant paradigm in business research is
the positivistic paradigm. If this is acceptable in your discipline, and
to your supervisor, you will not need to expend much energy in justifying the methodology you adopt for your research. However, a more
phenomenological or qualitative approach is becoming more acceptable and, arguably, is more appropriate for many business research
studies. This means that your study could be entirely phenomenological in its approach, or there might be a qualitative aspect within a
positivistic paradigm. If you decide on a phenomenological approach,
you may have to spend more time explaining and justifying your

!

Experiential learning | **Diagnosing your research paradigm**

Indicate whether you agree or disagree with the following statements. There are no right or wrong answers, and the exercise should not be taken too seriously!

	Agree	Disagree	Don't know
1 Quantitative data is more scientific than qualitative data	☐	☐	☐
2 It is important to state the hypotheses before data collection	☐	☐	☐
3 Surveys are probably the best way to investigate business issues	☐	☐	☐
4 Unless a phenomenon can be measured reliably, it cannot be investigated	☐	☐	☐
5 A good knowledge of statistics is essential for all approaches to business research	☐	☐	☐
6 Case studies should only be used as a pilot project before the main research is conducted	☐	☐	☐
7 Using participant observation to collect data is of little value in business research	☐	☐	☐
8 Laboratory experiments should be used more widely in business research	☐	☐	☐
9 It is impossible to generate theories during the course of research into business issues	☐	☐	☐
10 Researchers must remain objective and independent from the phenomena they are studying	☐	☐	☐

If you have more 'agrees' than 'disagrees', you are likely to adopt a positivist paradigm. If you have more 'disagrees' than 'agrees', you are likely to adopt a phenomenological paradigm. If you have an equal number of 'agrees' and 'disagrees', you are probably quite flexible about your research approach. If you have more 'don't knows' than other answers, we suggest you study this chapter again.

methodology. It is important to remember that the two main paradigms represent two extremes of a continuum and your study may represent a blend of assumptions and methodologies.

There is some difficulty in mixing the two main paradigms in the same study, since it is difficult to argue simultaneously that you believe that social reality is separate and external *and* that it is merely a construction of the mind! Therefore, it is easier, particularly at the undergraduate level or at the early stages of the research, to remain within one paradigm. However, it is perfectly possible, and even advantageous, to use both qualitative and quantitative methods for collecting data. For example, a questionnaire survey providing quantitative data could be accompanied by a few in-depth interviews to provide qualitative insights and illuminations.

3.6.1   Triangulation

The use of different research approaches, methods and techniques in the same study is known as *triangulation* and can overcome the potential bias and sterility of a single-method approach. For example, we might want to ask a number of people to describe a bunch of flowers by using only one of their senses. We could get a perfectly adequate description of the flowers if we asked one person to describe the colour only. But we would get a much fuller picture if we asked each person to describe a different aspect, such as the smell, the texture and shape of the petals and leaves, etc. By collecting all these separate impressions together we can get a fuller and richer picture of the way the respondents experience the flowers.

Denzin (1970, p. 297) defines triangulation as 'the combination of methodologies in the study of the same phenomenon'. He argues that the use of different methods by a number of researchers studying the same phenomenon should, if their conclusions are the same, lead to greater *validity* and *reliability* than a single methodological approach.

Easterby-Smith, Thorpe and Lowe (1991) identify four types of triangulation:

- ► **data triangulation**, where data is collected at different times or from different sources in the study of a phenomenon
- ► **investigator triangulation**, where different researchers independently collect data on the same phenomenon and compare the results
- ► **methodological triangulation**, where both quantitative and qualitative methods of data collection are used
- ► **triangulation of theories**, where a theory is taken from one discipline (for example, marketing) and used to explain a phenomenon in another discipline (for example, accounting).

Unless you are part of a research team, it is unlikely that you will be able to consider investigator triangulation as an option. However, most students, including undergraduates, should be able to use triangulation of theories, data triangulation or methodological triangulation at some stage in their research.

Jick (1979) contends that triangulation has vital strengths, encourages productive research, enhances qualitative methods and allows the complementary use of quantitative methods. However, replication is exceedingly difficult to perform where you have a mixed method approach, particularly where qualitative data is generated, and data collection and analysis is time consuming and expensive. Moreover, triangulation cannot be used to rectify a poor research design, but must be integral to a good design.

Conclusions

We have introduced a number of concepts in this chapter which may be new to you. The relationship between these concepts can be summarised as follows. Your personal research paradigm helps you to determine which methodology to adopt and, in turn, the methodology you adopt helps you to determine how you will use different methods to collect your data.

Although this chapter is difficult because it deals with abstract ideas, once you have studied it, you will find that it gives you a very valuable framework which you can then use in a practical way to plan your *research design*. Once you have chosen your research design, you will be in a position to develop your *research proposal*. We look at these two important stages of your research in the next chapter.

4 Searching the literature

Introduction

Now that you understand the principal conceptual issues which underpin research, you should have been able to decide your research paradigm and be ready to select a research topic. In this chapter we will be examining how you can generate research topics and conduct a comprehensive literature search, the outcome of which will be a literature review. The objectives of this chapter are:

▶ to help you to select a research topic
▶ to explain how to carry out a literature search
▶ to describe potential sources of secondary data
▶ to illustrate how to make citations and references
▶ to examine the purpose of the literature review.

4.1 Generating a research topic

In determining your research *paradigm*, you may have already settled on a *research topic*. This is the subject area in which you would like to conduct your research. Some students already have an interest in a particular topic when they decide to become researchers; others delay starting their project because they have difficulty in identifying potential areas for research.

If you are having a problem finding a research topic, the best advice is to start by trying to identify a general subject area which is of interest to you. Naturally, you are more likely to have a successful and enjoyable experience if you find the subject matter interesting! You could try using *brainstorming* in that general subject area to generate potential research topics. Brainstorming is a very simple technique. You need at least one other interested person with whom to generate spontaneous ideas. In the first instance, you could try jotting down a list of all the ideas that come up. Then you need to review them by deciding what you mean by each idea. For example, if you were interested in financial reporting, you might try asking yourself the following questions:

- What is financial reporting?
- Do I mean internal or external financial reporting?
- Is there a particular aspect of financial reporting I am interested in?
- Am I interested in the regulation of financial reporting?
- Am I interested in voluntary disclosure?
- Am I interested in the communication aspects?

Once you have begun to focus your ideas about financial reporting, you could turn your attention to such questions as:

- What is reported?
- When is it reported?
- To whom is it reported?
- What is the purpose of reporting?
- Are there any ethical issues?

Another way of approaching the problem might be to examine the various ways in which research can be designed or conducted. Howard and Sharp (1994) offer the suggestions we discuss below. Although these do not lead directly to subject ideas, they may offer a number of leads.

4.1.1   Analogy

Analogy involves designing a research project in one subject by importing ideas and procedures from another area where you consider there are similarities. Thus, you are using the research developments in one area to illuminate how you could conduct your own study. It is also possible to develop a research topic if you are aware of some methods of analysis that have been used in one particular study, which can be applied in your own work. This use of existing analytical techniques in a completely new and different area can result in a very interesting study which makes a contribution to our knowledge of the subject.

4.1.2   Morphological analysis

Morphological analysis is another technique which you may find useful. *Morphology* is concerned with the study of form. Essentially, morphological analysis is a 'mix and match' approach which involves drawing up a table and using it to analyse the particular subject you are interested in. First, you define the key factors or dimensions of the subject. These will become the column headings. Then you list the various attributes of the factor or the ways in which it can occur under the headings. Finally, you define all feasible combinations of the attributes to generate a number of potential research projects. Obviously, your choice is tempered by the paradigm you have adopted.

Table 4.1 Example of morphological analysis. General subject area: Research

Type of research	Methodology	Unit of analysis
Exploratory	Cross-sectional studies	An individual
Descriptive	Experimental studies	An event
Analytical	Longitudinal studies	An object
Predictive	Surveys	A body of individuals
Quantitative	Action research	A relationship
Qualitative	Case studies	An aggregate
Deductive	Collaborative research	
Inductive	Ethnography	
Applied	Grounded theory	
Basic		

In the example in Table 4.1, we have used the general subject area of research. We have defined our key dimensions as the *type of research* (see Chapter 1), the *methodology* (see Chapter 3) and the *unit of analysis* (see Chapters 3 and 5).

The result of your analysis might indicate a *descriptive* research project which uses a *survey* for its methodology and focuses on a *body of individuals* as its unit of analysis; for example professional associations of accountants or lawyers. Another analysis might suggest an *exploratory* research project which uses a *case study* approach and is conducted in one division of a particular company. A third analysis might generate a *predictive* research project which uses *experiments* with individuals; perhaps a project where you test how alcohol abuse affects individual students' examination performance.

You should restrict yourself to defining only the key dimensions of your chosen subject, as you can see that morphological analysis can generate a huge number of potential projects!

4.1.3   Mind maps

Another way of focusing your general interest in a topic is to use *diagrams*. There are a number of ways of constructing diagrams, depending on the purpose you have in mind. Whilst diagrams show how things depend on one another, maps show relationships in space or time. A *mind map* is a highly creative and personal form of diagram. The process is not particularly systematic and focuses on key aspects, rather than detail. These key aspects are jotted down haphazardly, without any particular thought as to their position and are usually joined by lines to indicate connections and relationships

Figure 4.1 shows our mind map which focuses on the general subject area of research. The map was commenced by writing the word

Figure 4.1 Example of a mind map. General subject area: Research

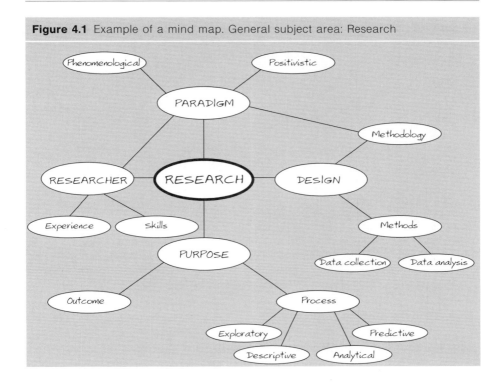

'research'. Other associated words were written nearby and lines were drawn to connect these words with the word 'research' and with the other words, gradually working outwards.

4.1.4 Relevance trees

Relevance trees are a particular type of diagram which can be used as a device for generating research topics or for focusing your interest in a research topic. The idea is to develop clusters of related ideas from a starting concept. To be most effective, the starting concept should be fairly broad. Figure 4.2 shows an example of a relevance tree from the starting concept of communication. Using the relevance tree we identified a number of potential research topics. For example, one-way presentations in the workplace or, at a more general level, the different forms of two-way communications used in social and workplace situations.

> **!**
>
> Experiential learning | **Brainstorming exercise**
>
> If you are having difficulty in finding a researchable topic, try brainstorming ideas in small groups or with your supervisor.

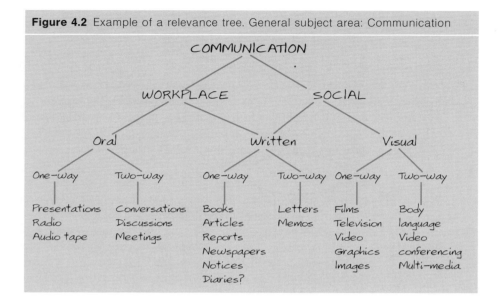

Figure 4.2 Example of a relevance tree. General subject area: Communication

4.2 Overview of the literature search

Once you have decided on your research topic you are ready to start your *literature search*. This is the process of exploring the existing literature to ascertain what has been written or otherwise published on your chosen research topic, how previous research has been conducted and how this impacts on your own *research problem* The literature search should increase your knowledge of the subject area and the application of different research methodologies, as well as help you to focus on your own *research topic*, develop and support it. It will also help you to determine whether your intended project is feasible. If not, you may have to amend it in some way or even seek a new project.

The aim of the literature search is to identify as many items of *secondary data* as possible which are relevant to your research topic. Secondary data is data which already exists. Examples of sources of secondary data include:

► books
► articles in journals, magazines and newspapers
► conference papers
► reports
► archives
► published statistics
► companies' annual reports and accounts
► organisations' internal records

> newspapers
> films, videos and broadcasts
> electronic databases
> the Internet.

In this context, the term *literature* refers to all sources of published data. By exploring what others have contributed to your area of interest, you will be able to find out what is already known, identify any gaps, see how your ideas compare with what has gone before, and develop existing ideas or create new ones. In Figure 4.3 we offer a guide to conducting a literature search.

The *literature review* is a written summary of the findings from your literature search. It is an important part of any research activity and should provide the background to and justification for your research project. It will be written up as part of your *proposal* (see Chapter 5) and will become one of the early chapters in your final research report. It is not sufficient merely to describe other research studies which have taken place; you need to appraise critically the contributions of others, and identify trends in research activity and define any areas of weaknesses. You must show that you are familiar with the literature on your chosen research topic. Cooper (1988, p. 107) provides a useful definition which covers all styles of literature review.

'First, a literature review uses as its database reports or primary or original scholarship, and does not report new primary scholarship

Figure 4.3 Guide to conducting a literature search

> It is very important to start exploring the literature as soon as possible. If, initially, your research project is still fairly unfocused, your search will be in general terms only
> Decide the scope of your research and set your parameters accordingly (for example, by period of time, geography or industry)
> Determine the key words, including alternative spellings, synonyms and differences in usage
> Only collect articles, books, papers, etc., which are relevant to your research (for example, in terms of subject matter, methodology, research instrument, theoretical discussion). Good research articles should review the literature, describe the research methodology used in the study, discuss the results and draw conclusions
> Use the references given in the literature you have collected to guide you to other articles you should collect
> When you start to recognise the references cited in other works, you are nearing the end of your first search
> In order to keep up to date with the literature, it is important that you continue your literature search throughout your study

itself. The primary reports used in the literature may be verbal, but in the vast majority of cases reports are written documents. The types of scholarship may be empirical, theoretical, critical/ analytic, or methodological in nature. Second, a literature review seeks to describe, summarise, evaluate, clarify and/or integrate the content of primary reports.'

When you are ready to write your literature review, you will need to:

- Define your terms
- Select only relevant material
- Group your material into categories
- Draw out the important features
- Make comparisons of results
- Be critical
- Demonstrate relevance to your own research
- Use the literature to set the context for your own research.

You should start your literature search as early as possible and continue throughout your research, since you will need to show that you are aware of the current state of knowledge, discuss it and comment on it. You will need to set up a filing system for storing copies of articles, notes, quotations, references, etc. You will soon find that your material can be collated into different categories and a number of large files with dividers will be useful for this purpose. You may find that you want to maintain an alphabetical index of the material you have collected, either on index cards or on computer.

4.3　Starting a literature search

The first step is to define the scope, context and parameters for your work. These might include the following limitations:

- **Time:** for example, between certain dates. It may not be worth searching more than five years back on a topic that is concerned with some kind of new technology for instance. Find an appropriate cut-off date. It can always be moved and it will avoid wasting time
- **Geography:** for example, a single city, region, country or a comparison of more than one of these
- **Single** or **multidisciplinary** approach: for example, the application of IT in accounting
- **Single discipline**, but **multiconcept** approach: for example, the role of appraisal in staff development.

This process will help you to identify and collect only that information which is relevant to your research project.

The next step is to decide what sort of information you require. Very recent topics are not likely to be covered by books; journals and newspapers will be the most relevant places to look for information relating to recent events. You may find that some information, for example about a company's corporate strategy or organisational structure, may only be available in internal documents. These may be confidential or difficult to obtain. However, by considering carefully what type of information you expect to find, you can restrict your search to those types only, thus saving yourself valuable time.

You may be able to find much of the information you need from your own institution's library. However, you may need to search further afield, since college and university libraries are primarily (undergraduate and postgraduate) course-related collections, and may not be able to provide all the detailed specialist information you need. You need to bear in mind that if you are not a member of a particular library, there may be a charge for using the facilities.

You will need to plan well ahead so that you have plenty of time to acquire information from alternative sources, make visits to other libraries and apply for interlibrary loans. At this stage the aim is to collect and read the literature which is relevant to your research project. Initially you may only be collecting references to the literature, and you should write these on index cards or, preferably, keep a computerised record on disk. You may have access to specialist bibliographic software, such as *Reference Manager for Windows*, or you can create your own using a database (see Chapter 1). If you are keeping manual records, you will need to keep your references in some kind of order, usually alphabetical by author's surname, as this is the form you will need for your own list of references (see Section 4.6). Later you will need to obtain and read abstracts and, if they prove to be relevant to your research, you will need to borrow or obtain a copy of the actual book, article, paper, etc.

Before you can begin searching the literature you must determine the *key words* which are associated with your chosen research topic. You will need these search words to guide you to the most relevant and appropriate literature. To take a simple example, perhaps your chosen research topic is the marketing of beer and cider in the UK. In this case, your key words would be 'Marketing', 'Beer', 'Cider' and 'UK'. As you develop your literature search you will need to amend your list of key words in order to widen or narrow your search as necessary. For example, to widen your search you might try 'Alcoholic beverages' and to narrow it, 'Lager', 'Mild', 'Bitter', 'Real ale', 'Stout', 'Apple juice', 'Perry', 'Scrumpy'. Some lateral thinking is sometimes necessary when

Table 4.2 Suggested order for conducting a literature search

Information source	Suggested reference
Dictionaries and encyclopaedias	
Books	Library catalogue
	British National Bibliography
Journal articles	Indexes and abstracts
Newspaper articles	Times Index
	Guardian Index
	Monthly Index to the Financial Times
Government publications	Annual catalogue (HMSO)
	Catalogue of British Official Publications
Theses	Index to Theses (UK)
	Dissertations Abstracts (USA)
Conference proceedings	Index of Conference proceedings
(published conference papers)	(British Library)
Standards	BSI Standards Catalogue
Statistics	Guide to Official Statistics (UK)
	Sources of Unofficial Statistics
Directories	Current British Directories
Company annual reports	Companies/library reference area
Market reports and surveys	Marketing Surveys Index

selecting your search words; it is often useful to include *synonyms* and consider American as well as English spellings.

Having identified your key words, you are now ready to start searching. Table 4.2 shows the order in which you might set about conducting a literature search. For every source of secondary data there is often a published guide or index which will help you locate and identify the material speedily and effectively. We look at the main sources of information in the following sections, but remember, if you have any problems, ask your librarian.

4.3.1   Dictionaries, encyclopaedias and books

Dictionaries and encyclopaedias are useful for extending the range of subject terms. As your research progresses, you should amend your list of key words by adding more precise words and deleting any which you find are not used. You must check that you understand the exact meaning of the words you are using, and you will probably need to *define* many of the key *terms*. Bear in mind that American spelling and terminology may differ from that used in the UK.

The following reference books are just a small selection of the many dictionaries and encyclopaedias available which you may find useful:

- Oxford English Dictionary
- Oxford Concise Dictionary of Accounting
- Oxford Concise Dictionary of Business
- Harrap's Dictionary of Business and Finance
- The M.B.A.'s Dictionary (Oran and Shafritz)
- Encyclopaedia of Management (Heyel)
- International Encyclopaedia of the Social Sciences
- Roget's Thesaurus.

It is highly unlikely that any of the *books* you already have will give adequate coverage of the specialised topic you are now investigating; even recently published books are not entirely up to date as they often take years to write and publish. Moreover, they are unlikely to go into sufficient depth. However, books are a good starting point and usually provide references to further reading. Some of these references will be other books which you can borrow from the library or obtain through interlibrary loan; others will be articles, papers and other published material. You may also find edited books which contain chapters written by different authors. These can be very useful for giving a range of views and are often highly specialised.

To find out what books are in your institution's library, you will need to use the library catalogue. This may be available in printed form (for example, on a card index), on microfiche or on a computerised database. Books are grouped together on the shelves according to the subject they cover. Each subject is given a different shelf number which is its classification number. Most public and many academic libraries in the UK use the *Dewey Decimal Classification System*. Table 4.3 shows an example of this classification system.

Table 4.3 Examples of the Dewey Decimal Classification System

Subject	Dewey classification
Management	658
Personnel management	658.3
Recruitment	658.311
Conditions of work	658.312
Motivation	658.314
Social sciences	300
Social science research	300.72

Thus, books on management usually start with 658. Books on personnel management which is a subdivision of management are listed under 658.3. This category is then further broken down into, for example, recruitment (658.311), conditions of work (658.312) and motivation (658.314). All the books in a given category are grouped together alphabetically by author and the letters following the classification number indicate the first three letters of the author's or editor's surname. For example, 658.314 WER refers to a book called *Productivity through People* by Werther, Ruch and McClure which is kept in the management section under motivation.

Books on the social sciences usually start with 300. Books on research in the social sciences are listed under 300.72. Here you will find books on research design as well as specialist texts on methodology, collection methods and methods of analysis. For example, 300.72 ROB refers to a books called *Real World Research* by Colin Robson which is kept in the social sciences section under social sciences research.

This classification system means that a book can only have one position on the library shelf. Since many books cover a number of different topics, it may be necessary to look under more than one number. For example, if you a looking for a book on decision-making you might look under:

Executive management 658.403
Psychology of decision-making 153.83
Decision-making mathematics 519.542

If you are using a computerised library catalogue, you can use the 'subject key word' facility to locate books on a specific subject. You will need to search under the different key words you identify. When you have found a relevant title and its classification number (or location), you can identify other titles on that subject by using the 'class number' search facility. If you have already identified particular books using other authors' references, then you can use the 'quick author/ title' facility to see if they are in the library. Books and articles in journals which are not stocked by your library may be obtained for you through the British Library interlibrary loan system. It can take up to three weeks for items to arrive, so this is another reason for starting your search early. You may also find that you are only allowed to request a certain number of items simultaneously.

Published bibliographies are lists of books which are currently in print or which have been published in the past. The *British National Bibliography* is a compilation of all books published each year and deposited in the British Library by copyright deposit. It is published weekly and cumulated annually It is arranged by both author and subject (according to the Dewy Classification System). The *Catalogue of the Library of Congress* is the equivalent for the USA; the *Cumulative Book*

Index and *Books in English* include both American and Canadian books. *Whitaker's Books in Print* lists books currently in print and published by commercial organisations. The listing is by author, title and by the subject which appears in the title, so you could easily miss valuable material if you rely only on this publication. The same publication is available on CD-ROM as *Bookbank*. The equivalent publication for the USA is *American Books in Print*. *Global Books in Print* includes both UK and American books.

Specialist bibliographies are similar to general bibliographies, but are specific to one subject area. They are often produced by professional bodies or institutions. If they are available in the subject area you are interested in, they can be a useful starting point for your literature search. For example, look for management bibliographies under 016.658; accounting bibliographies under 016.657.

Most libraries have basic reference books in specific subject areas. These can be useful for gaining a basic overview of the subject, clarifying concepts and familiarising yourself with the terminology. Table 4.4 shows a small selection of the many reference books in the field of management and business.

If you need to find material published by the UK government, then HMSO publications in print are listed in their own catalogue. However, not all UK government departments publish through HMSO. The others can be traced using *British Publications not published by HMSO*. Both these catalogues are available on the CD-ROM *United Kingdom Official Publications (UKOP)*.

You may need *statistical* or *technical* information to reinforce a point or refute someone's argument. Statistics are published by central and local government in the UK, and international organisations such as the OECD and the UN. To help you trace relevant statistics you should look at the *Guide to Official Statistics* and the *Sources of Unofficial UK*

Table 4.4 Examples of reference books

Type of reference book	Example	Dewey classification
Dictionaries explain terms	Dictionary of Accounting & Finance	657.03 BRO
Encyclopaedias give a general overview	Encyclopaedia of Management	658.003 HEY
Handbooks give specific information on a particular topic and can be used to gain a working knowledge of a subject	Gower Handbook of Management	658 LOC

Statistics. Technical information sources include the *British Standards Catalogue* and building regulations.

4.3.2   Articles and papers, abstracts and indexes

Books are only one of many sources of information and usually this is somewhat general in nature. You will find more specialised, specific and up-to-date information in journals. These contain academic *articles* and *papers* which will provide a preliminary review of the literature, as well as a clear explanation of what the research was intended to do, how the author went about it, together with a summary of the results and conclusions. Because journals are published several times a year, they provide a more contemporary data source than books, but because of the lengthy refereeing process adopted by many journals, they may not provide the most up-to-date view.

You may be able to start with the list of *references* given in a key article or book that you are already aware of. Although there is no reason why you should not scan relevant journals looking for articles on your specific topic, there is a quicker, easier and more systematic way of locating the information by using *abstracts* and *indexes*. Most indexes and abstracts work in a similar way and you can search either by author or, more frequently, you will use your key words. A search by key words should result in a list of references to documents which contain these key words, either in the title or in the abstract. Abstracts are extremely useful since they allow you to read a summary of the article and this is usually sufficient to enable you to decide whether the article or paper is going to be relevant to your research. If so, you should obtain a copy of the full article or paper.

Because of the complexity of many business and management topics, you may need to look at indexes and abstracts in various subject areas, not just business and management. Sometimes the process of searching the indexes and abstracts is frustrating and results in either no articles at all or too many! This problem is usually related to your choice of key words; you may find that you have not been sufficiently precise. Alternatively, your research topic may be somewhat obscure. If this is the case, you may wish to reconsider your choice, since the lack of literature could indicate that few others have found the topic of interest or value.

Most of the indexes and abstracts you use will lead you to articles and other documents which you will have found by using a combination of key words. From time to time you may find what you consider is a particularly useful article and which is extremely relevant to your own research. When this happens, you need to find out how many other researchers have subsequently referred to that article, since this will allow you to follow the development of the subject both forwards and backwards in time. *Citation indexes* allow you to do exactly this. They provide an indication of the quality and authority of particular published pieces of work by recording the number of times a particular author and work has been referred to by another author, and give references to these other works.

Table 4.5 Examples of printed abstracts and indexes

Example	Description
Anbar	Subjects include accounting and finance; information management and technology; management and technology, management services and production; marketing and distribution; personnel and training; and top management
Applied Social Science Index and Abstracts (ASSIA)	Covers economics, education, employment, health, penology, politics, psychology, race relations and social services
Applied Science and Technology Index (ASTI)	Subjects include computer technology, energy resources, engineering, industry, science and transportation
British Humanities Index	Covers arts, business, current affairs, economics, history, philosophy, politics and social issues
Business Automation, Key Issues in	Covers communications, computers and office systems in business and commerce; includes banking, financial markets and retailing
Business Periodicals Index	Subjects include business, company information, industry, management, people and trades
Employee Relations International: A Bibliographical and Abstracts Journal	Covers all aspects of employee and industrial relations
European Access, Current Awareness Guide	Covers European Union policy and activities
Personnel Management Abstracts	All subjects relating to the management of people and organisational behaviour
Social Science Citation Index (SSCI)	Citation index covering over 1000 leading social science journals and other publications
Research Index	A fortnightly guide to product as well as company and industry information published in newspapers, journals and the trade press

The information you obtain by following up the references given could have a significant impact on your own study. When you go back in time you develop your knowledge of the historical background to the original work; when you go forward in time you gain insights into other researchers' critiques of the study. This is very useful for your own literature review, but you may also find out that your own particular *research questions* have already been answered. We discuss research questions in Chapter 5.

Abstracts and indexes may be in printed or electronic form. There has been a rapid growth in the availability of information stored on computerised databases and we examine these in Section 4.4. Table 4.5 shows examples of printed forms of abstracts and indexes.

Once you have found one piece of relevant literature, whether it is a chapter in a book or an article, you will often be led to other sources if you look at the references or list of recommended readings at the end of the document. This gives you some indication of the quality of the piece of literature, and will refer you to the sources which the author has used and introduce you to new authors. If one reference is quoted often, then it could indicate that this is a standard work on the subject. This process is known as *snowballing*. However, it is important to remember that snowballing is referring you to earlier publications.

Articles should review the relevant literature, describe the author's own research, including the methodology used, discuss the results and draw conclusions. Once you have found a relevant article, follow up the references to other publications. When references start to duplicate, you are near the end of your search.

4.3.3   Research reports and conference papers

The most up-to-date information on the current state of research in any particular area is provided by *research reports* and *conference papers*. These are very valuable sources of information, but can be difficult to trace after publication. Table 4.6 shows a number of publications which should help you to trace these sources of information, many of which are available in digital form (see Section 4.4).

Table 4.6 Examples of abstracts and indexes to research reports and conference papers

Example	Dewey classification
Current Research in Britain: Social Sciences	016.3 CUR
Index to Theses	011 IND
Index to Conference Proceedings (British Library publication of its holdings listed by subject category)	011 BRI

Table 4.7 Examples of directories

Example	Dewey classification
Centres and Bureaux	062 CEN
Councils, Committees and Boards	062 COU
Directory of British Associations	062 DIR
Directory of International Sources of Business Information	016.658 BAL
Guide to Company Information in Great Britain	016.558 NOR
Trade Associations and Professional Bodies of the United Kingdom	062 MIL

If you are doing original research, you will want to ensure that your project is not duplicating another study. Conferences provide an opportunity to discuss aspects of subjects which may not yet be published. They are also good places to identify and talk to experts in your research area.

Once you have collected your list of references, you need to obtain the actual books, articles, papers, etc. You may decide some books are so useful that you wish to purchase a personal copy, but otherwise you will wish to borrow books and obtain copies of the other documents. Naturally, your first step will be to check your own institution's library. If the item you want is not available, you will need to decide how important that particular reference is and whether you should obtain it through interlibrary loan. In some cases you may wish to contact or visit other institutions such as:

▶ public libraries
▶ other academic institutions' libraries
▶ government libraries
▶ professional/association libraries
▶ commercial libraries/Companies House
▶ individual companies.

Access to other libraries and the information available will vary according to the library's status and how you approach them. In most cases it is a good idea to telephone in advance and enquire about conditions of access. Some of the information you are looking for may be available by post or telephone. Table 4.7 lists directories which you may find useful for identifying outside sources of information and provide addresses.

4.4   Computerised databases

A *computerised database* is 'a comprehensive, consistent, controlled, co-ordinated collection of structured data items' (Hussey, 1994, p. 354).

Databases available cover most areas of knowledge and can comprise either bibliographic details, full text or factual information. Bibliographical information, in the form of references to articles, books and reports, has traditionally been stored in printed indexes and abstracts. Searching these sources manually can be very time consuming and sometimes it is also inefficient. In recent years, many of the major business indexes have become available in electronic form which speeds up the search process, and enables you to carry out a more efficient search.

Computerised databases may be *on-line* or *off-line*. 'On-line means being accessible to and under the control of the processor. Off-line means not being accessible to or under the control of the processor' (Hussey, 1994, p. 328). A CD-ROM is an example of an off-line database and looks like an audio CD. CD-ROM is an acronym for Compact Disk – Read Only Memory. This means that the end user can only display or print ('read') the information and cannot add, delete or amend it in any way ('write').

In addition to bibliographical databases, there are those which have a directory function. For example, in the business area it is possible to obtain a list of companies in a given area which have an annual turnover of £1.8 million and over 250 employees. Some databases contain mailing lists which can be downloaded and used for mail merging or printing address labels.

4.4.1   On-line databases

Many on-line databases are accessible from anywhere in the world. The database is made publicly available by one or more 'hosts' who load the database onto a mainframe computer and create the search software. The host then markets and sells the information to remote users such as academic and corporate institutions. Access is via a computer terminal connected by modem to the telecommunications network. The user is connected to the remote computer which holds the database by dialling the appropriate number and using special passwords. Table 4.8 shows a small selection of the many on-line databases used in management and business.

Searching on-line databases is very expensive. For this reason you should take advantage of tutorial sessions arranged for you and read the manuals carefully before you log on. The more familiar you are with the host language and the individual database, the more cost-effective your search will be. You may find that searches are conducted by an intermediary, such as a librarian or information specialist, who is familiar with the command language used by each host, the range and scope of the databases and the principles involved in constructing an efficient and comprehensive search strategy.

Table 4.8 Examples of on-line databases

Example	Description
ABI/INFORM	Compilation of business information from over 1000 business and trade journals, but has an American bias; covers the most recent five years of the database and gives a substantial abstract of each article
Datastream	International company information in the form of accounts, share prices, etc.; includes international economic data, import–export statistics and exchange rates
Harvard Business Review	Full text, bibliographical database of the printed journal
Key British Enterprises	Directory of top British companies as measured by turnover
Kompass On-line	Directory of over 200 000 UK establishments. Comprehensive coverage by director, trade name, parent company and overseas agent
LEXIS/NEXIS	Full text retrieval system covering law, business, trade information, news and current affairs; the vast databanks are in effect computerised libraries
Management Marketing Abstracts	Bibliographic information on worldwide developments in theoretical and practical aspects of management and marketing
Public Affairs Information Service (PAIS)	Indexes articles on a range of topic areas from a selection of European newspapers and journals
Social Science Citation Index (SSCI)	Citation index covering over 1000 leading social science journals and other publications

The principles involved in searching a computerised database are fairly straightforward. Supposing you wish to find out references on the topic of the marketing of beer and cider in the UK. You have already decided that your key words are 'Marketing', 'Beer', 'Cider' and 'UK'. On-line searching allows you to link a number of words by using *logical operators* such as 'and', 'or', and 'not'. These operators enable you to specify the terms which must either occur or not occur in the item. For example, 'Marketing and Cider' specifies that both terms will appear in the abstract or article, regardless of their order. 'Cider or Beer' specifies that either or both terms must occur. 'Cider not Beer'

Table 4.9 Typical search results

Search number	Search words	Number of items
#1	Beer	712
#2	Cider	45
#3	Beer or cider	693
#4	Marketing and UK	37 872
#5	#3 and #4	283

specifies that the first term must occur and that occurrences of both terms will be excluded. Groups can be expressed using brackets. The results of a typical on-line search are shown in Table 4.9.

You might have thought of carrying out the fifth search immediately, but by doing so you risk moving towards too narrow a set of descriptions too quickly and this could result in a poor outcome. In this example, the final search resulted in 283 references to journal articles on the marketing of beer and cider. You have narrowed this down to a particular region in the UK, for example, or broadened it by substituting 'Europe' for 'UK' in your list of search words.

The next step is to download the selected records to disk, where they will be stored in ASCII (American Standard Code for Information Interchange), to send it to the printer for printing. You will probably find that saving the data to disk is much faster than waiting for it to print. In addition, you can browse through it at your leisure and delete any data which is not as useful as you first thought.

4.4.2   The Internet

Once you are familiar with on-line searching you may wish to consider searching potential sources of information available through the Internet (see Chapter 1). If you are familiar with the *Windows* or *Apple Mac* interface, you will find it easy to use the point-and-click hypertext system. Table 4.10 gives some addresses on the World Wide Web which could be useful.

Surfing the Internet can consume significant amounts of precious time and the serious researcher can find the final results disappointing. If you know the address of the relevant web site you can go directly there, otherwise you will need to use a search engine such as Google, Lycos or Yahoo.

Many people have a favourite search engine, but whichever one you use, your research strategy is the same: remain as focused on your own research question as possible. The more general or common the keyword you use, the more precisely you will need to explain or delimit it. For the most effective searches we recommend that you use Boolean operators such as:

+

The search should contain all keywords. For example, if the key-words 'labour + absenteeism + engineering' are entered, the engine will locate only documents that contain all those terms.

OR

The search result will contain one of the terms: 'stress OR anxiety' will locate web sites containing either of these terms.

NEAR

The search result will find documents where the terms are just a few words apart, for example 'labour NEAR absenteeism'.

NOT

The second term should not appear in the results. For example, 'stress NOT executives' will produce documents with only the word 'stress' in them.

FAR

This search will locate documents in which the two terms are at least 25 words apart. The search 'book FAR keeping' will find only sites containing these terms separated by 25 words and not the term 'bookkeeping'.

ADJ

This search will find terms that are directly adjacent to one another regardless of the order. Hence the search 'overtime ADJ working' will find 'overtime working' and 'working overtime'.

BEFORE

This search should contain both terms in the order given. The search 'hard BEFORE working' will not produce 'working hard'.

Table 4.10 Useful Internet addresses

ABI/INFORM Global (academic publications)
http://proquest.umi.com

Bank of England (UK economic reports)
http://www.bankofengland.co.uk

BIDS (academic publications)
http://www.bids.ac.uk

CSA (academic publications)
http:/www.csal.co.uk

DTI Publications (UK government)
http://www.dti.gov.uk/publications

Economist (magazine)
www.economist.com

Emerald (academic publications)
http://fiordiliji.emeraldinsight.com

European Union
www.europa.eu.int

FAME (financial and other data from Companies House)
http://fame.bvdep.com

Financial Times (news and annual reports service)
www.ft.com

HMSO Publications (UK government)
http://www.hmso.gov.uk

ICAEW (accounting publications)
http://www.icaew.co.uk/library

ILO (international labour publications)
http://www.ilo.org/public/english

Ingenta (academic publications)
http://www.ingentaselect.co.uk

IFS (UK taxation and economics)
http://www.ifs.org.uk

Internet Bookshop
http://www.bookshop.co.uk

ISI Web of Science (citation index)
http://wos.mimas.ac.uk

JISC (academic publications)
http://www.jisc.ac.uk

LexisNexis (academic publications)
http://web.lexis-nexis.com

Lights (publishers' catalogues)
http://www.lights.com/publisher

National Statistics Online (UK government)
http://www.statistics.gov.uk

Mintel (market analysis)
www.mintel.co.uk

NISS (news, publications and other information)
http://www.niss.ac.uk

Research Index
www.researchindex.co.uk

Small Business Portal (gateway)
http://www.smallbusinessportal.co.uk

Small Business Service (UK government)
http://www.sbs.gov.uk

UKonline (UK government)
http://www.ukonline.gov.uk

United Nations (news and publications)
http://www.un.org

WWW Virtual Library
http://www.vlib.org

4.4.3   CD-ROM databases

A CD-ROM contains permanent, digitally encoded information on a huge scale which may represent text, graphics, images or data and can be accessed very quickly. The contents of a CD-ROM cannot be altered or erased. CD-ROMs are expensive, but once the subscription has been paid, they are available for unlimited use. Thus, the cost is fixed and known in advance. On the other hand, with on-line searching the cost of a search depends on the time taken. Therefore, the cost is not known until the search has been completed. Table 4.11 shows a small selection of the many hundreds of CD-ROM databases available in the field of business and management.

Table 4.11 Examples of CD-ROM databases

Example	Description
ABI/INFORM	Covers every aspect of business and management theory and practice including accounting, computers, human resources, marketing and organisational behaviour; has an American bias
Anbar	Subjects include accounting and finance; information management and technology; management and technology, management services and production; marketing and distribution; personnel and training; and top management
Bookbank	Includes British books in print, publishers' addresses, and titles recently out of print
ECONLIT	Covers industrial relations, business finance, monetary theory and financial institutions
FAME (Financial Analysis Made Easy)	Contains the JordanWatch database of major public and private British companies with more than £1.5m turnover; up to five years of detailed financial information and some descriptive details

Table 4.11 *(continued)*	
Example	*Description*
Global Books in Print	Lists British and American books currently in print and includes publishers' addresses
Helecon	Collection of European databases; searching is conducted in English; many databases contain a key word index in English; many articles are in European languages
Institute of Management International Database (IMID)	Series of databases which include references to and information on audio-visual materials, books/IM publications, company practices, short courses, training packages, and working papers
Mintel Marketing Intelligence	Marketing database which provides current information on over 200 consumer markets, with detailed analysis of marketing data, activities, news, new products and economic, social and demographic data

4.4.4   Advantages and disadvantages of computerised searching

The advantages of computerised searching include:

- ► **Accessibility**: Many institutions would find it too expensive to purchase the printed equivalents of the wide range of abstracts and indexes which are now available as computerised databases
- ► **Cross-disciplinary searching**: Since files on many subjects are available on the same system, it is possible to transfer a search to other files and to search several specified files simultaneously to establish which are most relevant
- ► **Currency**: On-line databases in particular are often up-dated more frequently than the printed versions
- ► **Flexibility**: Although you can use key terms in your search in a similar way as you would when using a printed equivalent, you can also carry out a free-text search using any combination of terms and subjects you can think of. The result is any document which contains the word or combination of words
- ► **Speed**: Thousands of references can be searched in seconds to find the few that are relevant to your research, compared with many hours of manual searching
- ► **Versatility**: The search strategy can be altered as the search progresses to accommodate the need to broaden or narrow the search terms in order to identify the information you require.

However, some of the disadvantages include:

- **Cost**: Because charging for on-line services is usually by connect time, with additional costs for on-line or off-line printing of references found, an extensive or poorly structured search can be very expensive. Because of the high costs of on-line and CD-ROM databases, you may find that access to them is limited
- **Sources**: A database is only as useful as its sources. If the directories, journals, reports, newspapers, etc. covered by a database are limited in range or scope, then the search will also be limited
- **Structure**: The structure of the database, especially the choice of key words and the wording of the abstracts, can restrict searching.

You will probably use a combination of manual searching and electronic methods to conduct your literature search, but regardless of which method you adopt, you know you are nearing the end of your search when you begin to find many repetitions in the literature of previous works cited.

4.6 Recording references

Finding information is hard enough, but finding it again can be even harder unless you keep accurate and systematic records! It is good practice to make a note of everything you find, even if you eliminate it later because it is not relevant after all. In the long run this will save time by avoiding duplication and helping you with the selection and rejection of material. You should keep your records in the format you will need for the list of references you will need to give at the end of your project report, dissertation or thesis. This means keeping full bibliographic details.

Keeping records of any relevant and useful articles, books, quotations, etc., is essential throughout your research. Your records may be kept on index cards which are inexpensive and easy to use. Their size makes it easy to take a few blanks into the library with you so that you can jot down references as soon as you find them. In addition, index cards are easy to sort into whatever classifications you find most helpful. Alternatively, you may choose to keep your records on computer. There are some excellent software programs on the market, some of which are tailor-made for academic purposes and all have fast and efficient sorting facilities.

Whichever method of record keeping you adopt, the main reasons for maintaining a database are as follows:

- You need to be able to identify the full and accurate reference in order to find or order the material
- You can develop links amongst authors, topics, results and periods of time by resorting your database

- ▸ It prevents duplication of effort
- ▸ You will need to refer to your sources of information in your proposal and final research report
- ▸ Others reading your finished work will be able to trace the original sources of information easily.

At undergraduate and postgraduate level it is essential that you reference any work you are citing properly. A *citation* is an acknowledgement within the text of the source from which you have obtained the information. A *reference* is the detailed description of the source from which you have obtained the information. References can either be listed at the end of the document or as a footnote on the page on which they occur. Accurate citations and full references are important for three reasons:

- ▸ They help the reader to distinguish between your own ideas and findings, and those gleaned from the literature
- ▸ They help your arguments by showing the extent to which independent theoretical and empirical sources support them, although this depends on the quality and appropriateness of those sources
- ▸ They enable readers to refer to the original sources for themselves.

Failure to acknowledge the original sources of ideas or failing to use quotation marks when reproducing other people's spoken or written words is known as *plagiarism* and is treated as a serious form of academic misconduct.

All works cited are listed either alphabetically or numerically at the end of the document, usually under the heading of 'References'. If a number of different works from the same author are cited, these are given in reverse chronological order; that is, the most recent first. Some authors draw a distinction between the terms *references* and *bibliography*. Whereas references are a detailed list of the sources which have been drawn from and cited in the text of a document, a bibliography also includes items which were not cited but are relevant to the document. Other authors use the terms interchangeably. You should check with your supervisor to find out what the preferred terminology is in your institution.

There are several ways of making citations, all of which contain the same information, but display it differently. The two main systems of referencing are the *Harvard System* and the *Vancouver System*, and during the course of your studies you may come across others. The Harvard System is used principally by the social sciences, anthropology and some of the life sciences, and is the one we have used in this book. The Vancouver System is mainly used in the applied sciences such as chemistry, computer science, mathematics and physics. You should be

Table 4.12 Key data for recording references

Articles	Books
Author(s)'s surname, first name and any subsequent initials	Author(s)'s or editor(s)'s surname, first name and any subsequent initials (corporate authors may replace individual authors' names)
Year of publication (in brackets)	Year of publication (in brackets)
Title of the article (in inverted commas) with initial capitals for words except definite and indefinite articles, prepositions and conjunctions	Title of the book (in italics, underlined or bold type) with initial capitals for words except definite and indefinite articles, prepositions and conjunctions
Title of the journal (in italics, underlined or bold type)	Edition
Volume number	Place of publication
Part number (in brackets)	Publisher
Page number(s) of the article preceded by 'p.' (for a single page) or 'pp.' for multiple pages	Page numbers of author's chapter if part of an edited collection

aware that book and journal publishers may have their own house styles which result in some departures from these academic principles.

For business research we recommend the Harvard System. This is one of the easiest systems to use and is set out in British Standard 5605 : 1990. The second advantage of the Harvard System is that you can still use numbered *footnotes*, which is precluded with the Vancouver System. You will need to find out what is the preferred method in your own institution. The important thing to remember is that whichever method you choose, you must stick to it. The basic rule is that references should be correct, complete and consistent.

It is very useful to keep all your references in your chosen format so that you can easily add the appropriate ones to your *research proposal* or final report without much difficulty. The key data you need to record for showing in your list of references is shown in Table 4.12.

4.5.1   References under the Harvard System

Examples of *references* or articles and books using the Harvard System are given in Figure 4.4. There is no need to put in the words 'Volume' or 'Part'. If an article is interrupted by advertisements or other features, you should indicate this by showing all the page sequences, as shown in the example.

Figure 4.4 References for articles and books under the Harvard System

Reference for an article:
Porter, Michael E. (1990) 'Competitive advantage of nations', *Harvard Business Review*, 68 (2), pp. 73–85, 87–93.

Reference for a book:
Davidson, Alan B. (1994) *The Pursuit of Business*, London: Chapman & Hall.

Figure 4.5 Reference for a chapter in a book under the Harvard System

Thorne, Sally (1994) 'Secondary Analysis in Qualitative Research: Issues and Implications', in Morse, Janice M. (ed.) *Critical Issues in Qualitative Research Methods*, Thousand Oaks, Sage: pp. 263–79.

You may wish to refer to a chapter in a book. In such cases the editor of the book should also be acknowledged. In effect, a double reference is needed with the more specific reference coming first. An example is given in Figure 4.5.

You may come across examples of referencing in the literature which vary slightly from our examples; perhaps the date of publication has been placed at the end. The main rule is to be consistent. If you are submitting your work for publication, find out what the required house style is.

You may wish to refer to electronic information; for example, information contained in full-text or bibliographic databases, electronic conferences (interest groups), bulletin board services or electronic

Figure 4.6 General form for referencing main electronic sources

Full-text or bibliographic databases

Reference for a book:
Author (date) *Title of book*, (edition) [Type of medium]. Available: Give sufficient information to allow retrieval of book or abstract

Reference for an article:
Author (date) 'Title', *Name of journal* [Type of medium] volume number (issue number) page numbers. Available: Give sufficient information to allow retrieval of article or abstract

Electronic Conferences (Interest Groups) or Bulletin Board Services
Author of message (date) Subject of message, *Electronic Conference/Bulletin Board Services* [On-line]. Available e-mail: LISTSERV@e-mail address

Personal e-mail
Author (date) *Subject of message* [e-mail to recipient's name], [On-line]. Available e-mail: Recipient's e-mail address

mail (e-mail). Li and Crane (1995) offer a detailed guide which stresses the importance of using the generic terms offered by the information supplier to identify the path for retrieval of an item. The general approach is based on the Harvard style of referencing, but adds a type of medium statement in square brackets after the name of the publication and generally replaces the information on the place of publication and the publisher with an available statement. Examples of types of media include on-line, CD-ROM and disk. An availability statement might comprise the name of an index, a file name or an e-mail address.

Figure 4.6 shows the general form for referencing a number of electronic sources. You must take extra care with punctuation when referring to electronic information sources as a stray full stop, comma or slash could be mistaken for part of an e-mail address.

4.5.2   Citations under the Harvard System

The Harvard System shows the *citations* within the text in brackets. What is required is the surname of the author(s), the year of publication and, if you have quoted material directly, the page number(s). Figure 4.7 shows examples which demonstrate the range of possibilities. If you are clearly quoting from the same author in succeeding sentences or paragraphs, it is not necessary to be pedantic about giving the year again, as long as that particular reference cannot be confused with others in your study.

Sometimes you may wish to refer to more than one publication by the same author in the same year. In this case the date shown in the text (and in your list of references at the end of the document) will be suffixed by an 'a' for the first publication (for example, Gibbs, 1993a), a 'b' for the next, etc.

Figure 4.7 Citations under the Harvard System

In an investigation conducted in large factories, Gibbs (1993) reported that absenteeism was higher on the night shift than the day.

In an investigation conducted in large factories, it has been reported that absenteeism was higher on the night shift than the day (Gibbs, 1993).

In an investigation conducted in large factories, it has been reported that 'absenteeism on the night shift was measured and found in every instance in our sample to be significantly higher than that on the day shift' (Gibbs, 1993, p. 64).

Figure 4.8 Citing more than one authority under the Harvard System

A number of research studies have been conducted into the effect of the recession on small businesses (Smith, 1989; Anderson, 1992; Jones, 1995).

Figure 4.9 Authors with the same surname under the Harvard System

R. Hussey (1994) and J. Hussey (1996) studied the effect of the recession on small and medium-sized businesses...

Figure 4.10 Citing multiple authors under the Harvard System

First citation:

An earlier report on goodwill (Arnold, Eggington, Kirkham, Macve and Peasnell, 1992) which was commissioned by the ICAEW proposed that...

or

An earlier report on goodwill by Arnold, Eggington, Kirkham, Macve and Peasnell (1992) which was commissioned by the ICAEW proposed that...

Subsequent citation:

The ICAEW report (Arnold *et al.*, 1992) found that...

or

The report by Arnold *et al.* (1992) found that...

When citing more than one authority in the text, you should use the format shown in Figure 4.8, where the authors are placed in chronological rather than alphabetical order, the most recent last. If you need to cite two or more authors with the same surname, you should include their initials in the text, even if the dates differ, to avoid confusion. Figure 4.9 shows an example.

If there are more than three authors, all their names should appear the first time you refer to the publication. However, in subsequent citations you need only use the name of the first author follow by '*et al.*' (and others). Figure 4.10 gives examples.

4.5.3   The Vancouver System

The *Vancouver System* uses an in-text number instead of an author, date, page reference. The same superscript or bracketed number is given in the text each time the source is cited and will also appear in the list of references at the end. This is quite easily achieved by using the 'insert footnote' facility which is available on most word-processing packages. However, one of the drawbacks of this system is that it prevents you from using numbered footnotes for other purposes. We will be examining the general use of footnotes in Chapter 9. Figure 4.11 shows how the Vancouver System works in the text. The reference to Gibbs will be the first reference in your list of references, as shown in Figure 4.12. When citing more than one authority in the text, you should use the

Figure 4.11 Citations under the Vancouver System

In an investigation conducted in large factories, Gibbs[1] reported that absenteeism was higher on the night shift than on the day shift.

In an investigation conducted in large factories, it has been reported that absenteeism was higher on the night shift than on the day shift (Gibbs[1]).

In an investigation conducted in large factories, it has been reported that 'absenteeism on the night shift was measured and found in every instance in our sample to be significantly higher than that on the day shift' (Gibbs[1])..

Figure 4.12 References for articles and books under the Vancouver System

Reference for an article:
[1] Gibbs, J. M. (1993) 'Absenteeism in SMEs', *International Small Business Journal*, 13 (1), pp. 13–26.

Reference for a book:
[2] Davidson, A. B. (1994) *The Pursuit of Business*, London: Chapman & Hall.

Figure 4.13 Citing multiple authors under the Vancouver System

A number of research studies have been conducted into the effect of the recession on small businesses.[3–5]

format shown in Figure 4.13. The three sources will then become numbers 3, 4 and 5 in your list of references.

In this section we have concentrated on the most common needs of students when using citations and references. Winkler and McCuen (1994) devote two chapters to this subject and are an excellent source of further information.

4.7 The literature review

In Chapter 9 we examine in detail what is required in the *literature review* you will write for your final research report. In this section it is useful to explain what a literature review is and offer some general guidelines on how to write one. There are a number of definitions in the literature. Gill and Johnson (1991, p. 21) claim that a critical review of the literature 'should provide the reader with a statement of the state of the art and major questions and issues in the field under consideration'. A similar approach is taken by Merriam (1988, p. 6) who considers the literature review to be 'an interpretation and synthesis of published research'.

Both these definitions are concerned with the purpose of the written text, whereas there is a purpose underlying the activity which 'involves locating, reading and evaluating reports of research as well as reports of casual observation and opinion' (Borg and Gall, 1989, p. 114). We would place the emphasis on this third definition. The literature review is not merely a piece of writing but an activity which helps guide and inform the research. Unfortunately, many students do not recognise this aspect of the literature review, as evidenced by a study conducted by Bruce (1994). With a sample of 41 students who were at an early stage of their studies, she identified six ways in which they viewed their literature review:

- as a **list**, with the primary focus on listing what was read, rather than extracting and using the knowledge in the literature
- as a **search**, with the emphasis on finding the existing literature
- as a **survey**, where the researcher is interested in the knowledge in the literature, but does not relate it to his or her own activities
- as a **vehicle for learning**, where the researcher considers he or she is improving his or her own personal knowledge on the subject
- as a **research facilitator**, where the researcher improves not only his or her own knowledge, but the literature has an impact on the research project itself
- as a **report** which is a synthesis of the literature and the earlier experiences the researcher has engaged in.

If your literature review is going to be a successful part of your research study, it is the last three aspects you need to concentrate on. The literature review should improve your own knowledge of your chosen subject area, have a significant impact on your research project and demonstrate your understanding.

The literature search and review is a continuous activity and should be started as soon as possible and continued until you have finished the final draft of your project report, dissertation or thesis. You may find the questions shown in Figure 4.14 a useful checklist when reading the literature.

This analysis helps you to improve your knowledge of the literature on your chosen research topic, as well as helping you to identify a gap which will become the niche for your own research. For example, you may find that there are inconsistencies in the methods and findings of other studies, or perhaps you will be able to identify areas which have not been investigated. These weaknesses and gaps can become the justification for carrying out your own study.

If you take this approach, you will find that writing your literature review will be easier. As it will form a significant part of your *research proposal* and your final report, you need to make it as academically

Figure 4.14 Checklist for analysing the literature

By asking yourself the following questions, you will develop an analytical approach to your literature review.

1. What was the purpose of the study and how does it differ from other studies and my own research?

2. How was the research conducted and how does that differ from other studies and my own research?

3. What were the findings and how do they differ from other studies and my own research?

4. What were the limitations and weaknesses of the study?

sound as possible. Remember that it must not be a list of everything you have read; neither should it be merely descriptive. Do not be afraid to criticise other studies and identify any weaknesses you consider they have. This should enable your to argue that your own research is needed.

Whilst you are perusing the literature you are likely to read a number of other authors' literature reviews. These should offer you an additional guide to what is required. The main point to remember is that your literature review should show a competent exploration of the background to the work and a comprehensive review of recent, relevant literature. It is a written discussion of the literature and forms a significant part of your project report, dissertation or thesis. The literature review should contain a synthesis of the relevant literature as well as a critical analysis. It should also demonstrate how the literature relates to your own research and identify any deficiencies or omissions in previous research which you intend to address in your study.

Finally, we would impress on you the importance of ensuring that you have included all the major studies on your chosen research topic. You may also consider it diplomatic to refer to any relevant publications by your supervisor(s) and external examiners!

Conclusions

In this chapter we have explored a number of the practical ways in which you can generate research topics and how you can search the literature for information on your chosen subject. We have identified some of the main sources of information and compared manual and computerised methods of searching. We have also examined the importance of keeping accurate records and illustrated how you should show citations and references. Finally, we have explained what a literature search is and offered a checklist for analysing the results of your literature search.

We would emphasise the importance of starting your preliminary literature search as soon as possible. This will enable you to proceed to the next stage, which is to determine your *research design*.

5 Determining the research design

Introduction

Having decided on your research paradigm, selected a research topic and begun to investigate the relevant literature, you are now ready to determine your research design. This will enable you to write up your research proposal. The intellectual sophistication and length of your proposal will vary according to whether you are at the undergraduate or postgraduate level, but once accepted by your supervisor(s), this critical document provides you with a detailed plan for your study. The objectives of this chapter are to help you:

- ▶ to identify a research problem
- ▶ to assess the availability of information
- ▶ to develop a theoretical framework
- ▶ to write a research proposal.

5.1 Overview of research design

Research design is the 'science (and art) of planning procedures for conducting studies so as to get the most valid findings' (Vogt, 1993, p. 196). Determining your research design will give you a detailed plan which you will use to guide and focus your research. Whether you are on an undergraduate course or are a post-graduate student, you will be expected to set out your research design in a document known as a *research proposal*. This is an important step because it is on the basis of your proposal that your research study will be accepted or rejected.

Before you can begin constructing the research design for your project, you need to have determined your research *paradigm* (see Chapter 3) and chosen a *research topic* (see Chapter 4). You will remember that your choice of paradigm has important implications for your choice of *methodology*, and hence your *methods* for collecting data. It also has implications for your choice of *research problem* and *research questions* and we will be looking at these aspects later in this chapter. Figure 5.1 shows an overview of the research design process.

The first step in research design is to identify a research problem or issue. However, you must remember that this does not take place

Figure 5.1 Overview of research design

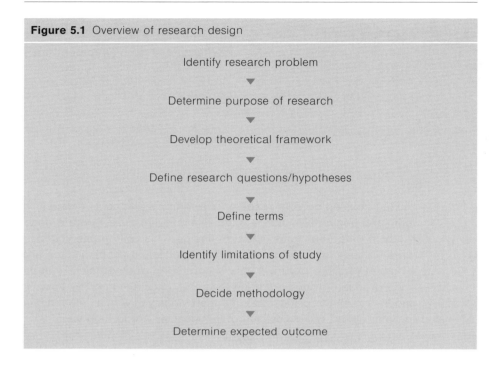

Identify research problem

▼

Determine purpose of research

▼

Develop theoretical framework

▼

Define research questions/hypotheses

▼

Define terms

▼

Identify limitations of study

▼

Decide methodology

▼

Determine expected outcome

in a vacuum, but in a particular context. Although you may have already determined your research paradigm, you might find that you have selected a research problem where you consider it is necessary to change some of your basic assumptions. Therefore, you may have to review your choice of paradigm and reflect on how appropriate it is to the problem you have identified. Another possibility is that you have picked a problem which is not acceptable to your supervisor or which for practical reasons cannot be investigated. We will discuss these issues in Section 5.2.

You will need to refine your research problem to provide a clear statement of the research. In a positivistic study, you will develop a *theoretical framework* which will lead to *hypotheses*. In a phenomenological study, you are more likely to determine the purpose of your research and construct only one or two questions which you will refine and modify, and set within a theoretical context during the course of the research itself. The final stages of your research design will be defining *terms*, establishing your *methodology* and giving an indication of the *expected outcome*.

In the following sections we consider each of these activities separately. However, it is important to remember that although we have shown them in a linked sequence, in practice, research is seldom quite so straightforward and orderly. It is highly likely that you will have to retrace your steps and review some of earlier stages as more information and more problems come to light in the later stages of constructing your research design.

We will now examine each of the stages of research design shown in Figure 5.1 in detail.

5.2 Identifying a research problem

You will remember from Chapter 1 that research must address a specific *research problem* or *issue*. The greatest failing in students' research proposals is usually the conversion of a general interest in a topic into a specific research problem which is suitable for a research project. Of course, your project must be achievable in terms of being manageable, given the resources available and all the constraints on your time. However, it must also be sufficiently challenging to meet the standards of your course or level of qualification.

Identifying a research problem is always an exploratory and reiterative phase in your research. You are attempting to establish a purpose for the research in a general area of study and the types of questions you might pose. There are a number of ways in which you can develop your general ideas and interests. Discussions with staff and fellow students are helpful. You may also find it useful to look at what other people have done; for example, other students' projects which may be available in your library, and other published research studies.

The classic way in academic research is to consider the *literature* (see Chapter 4) on your area of interest and identify any *gaps* since these will indicate original areas to research. Figure 5.2 shows a useful procedure for this. Identifying a research topic can be a lengthy business since you have to keep revising your initial ideas and referring to the literature until you arrive at a business problem or issue which you think will lead to a researchable project. Evidence that you are arriving at this stage is that you can begin to generate suitable *research questions* (see Section 5.5).

Your initial search will probably result in three or four projects within your broad area of interest. You now need to compare them so that you can select one. At this stage it is helpful to eliminate any research problem which you consider is less likely to lead to a successful outcome. Although you may select a topic which is of great interest to you and your supervisor, at the end of the day you will want to submit a research report which receives a high mark from the examiner or is accepted by the research/doctoral committee. Therefore, you need to examine your list of potential research problems critically and make certain that you select the one which is likely to give you the highest chance of success.

Figure 5.2 Procedure for identifying a research problem

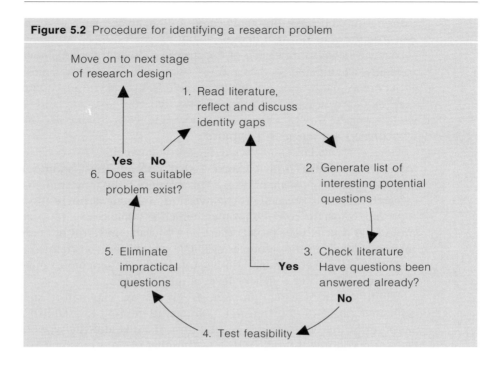

Creswell (1994, p. 3) suggests that the following questions provide a useful checklist for students planning a study:

▶ Is the project researchable, given time, resources, and availability of data?
▶ Is there a personal interest in the topic in order to sustain attention?
▶ Will the results from the study be of interest to others, especially to the research committee who will be responsible for accepting or rejecting your proposal?
▶ Does the study
  (a) fill a void
  (b) replicate
  (c) extend; or
  (d) develop new ideas in the literature?
▶ Is the research likely to be publishable in an academic journal?
▶ Will the project contribute to your career goals?

There are also some more specific issues which should indicate which of the projects is the most researchable and these are discussed below.

5.2.1   Availability of data

The *availability of data* is crucial to the successful outcome of your research. *Data* refers to known facts or things used as a basis for inference or reckoning. You will need to find out whether you will be able to collect the necessary data for your research project. Although you may be able to think of a number of very interesting problems, your final choice may be constrained because the necessary data is either not available or is very difficult to collect. Even if you are certain that the data you require is available and that you have access to it, you must make sure that you will be allowed to use it when you write up your research report and submit it.

Many students fail to appreciate the barriers to collecting data. For example, postal questionnaire response rates are often very low; 20 per cent is typical. Companies will rarely give commercially sensitive information and in many cases may not have suitable records to allow them to give the required data. Therefore, before deciding on your research project, you must be sure that you will be able to get the data and other information you will need to conduct your research.

Table 5.1 Assessing availability of data

Type of data	Source
The literature	Check in relevant libraries and databases
Official statistics	Official statistics are available covering almost every conceivable topic, if you know where to look. Refer to the official guides to published statistics
Industry data	You may need background information about a particular industry. Check in libraries for publications such as the Mintel Keynote Reports
Company data	General information about companies is available through many libraries and from the company's annual report and accounts
In-company data	This is one of the most difficult areas to assess. List exactly what information you will require and get official approval, preferably in writing. Do not try to use back door methods of getting information from your brother's girlfriend's uncle who happens to work in the accounts department!
People	How many will you need to see? Do you know them already? Have you the necessary interview skills to get what you want? Have you enough time?
Surveys	Where will you find a population of suitable respondents? How will you contact them? What response rate could you expect? Therefore, how many questionnaires will you have to send out to get a reasonable number of replies?

Table 5.1 provides a checklist which you may find useful for assessing the availability of data.

5.2.2   Knowledge gaps

You need to consider what you will need to know and do to complete your research. You should be able to gain a reasonable understanding of your subject area by conducting a systematic literature search and we discussed this in Chapter 4. You also need to think about the other types of skills you may need for your research, such as:

▶ questionnaire design and coding
▶ interpretation of completed questionnaires
▶ statistical analysis of the data
▶ use of computer software packages for analysis and presentation of the data
▶ interviewing skills
▶ analysing quantitative and qualitative data.

If you know that you have certain weaknesses, for example in statistics or interviewing skills, you need to assess realistically whether you can overcome them in the time you have available. Your project is a period of development and you should welcome any opportunity to improve your skills, but you should also make certain that you exploit any strengths you have.

5.2.3   Time and cost constraints

You must ask yourself whether you have sufficient time as well as resources. We advise that you make a rough estimate of how long you think each stage of the research will take and then discuss it with your supervisor; research always takes up much more time than you think it will! Jankowicz (1991) gives estimates of standard times for some project activities. These include one day for preparing a ten-question interview schedule and four weeks for piloting a large questionnaire. You must be realistic about the amount of time you have available and what you can achieve in that time. Moreover, if travelling is involved, for example to conduct interviews or visit other libraries, you will need to ensure that you can afford it.

5.2.4   Stating the research problem

When you have chosen your research problem, you should try to write a simple statement describing it. This will help you to remain focused whilst planning your research. Table 5.2 gives some examples of business research topics and problems other students have identified.

Table 5.2 Examples of business research problems

Research topic	Research problem or issue
Accounting regulations	Should accounting practices be regulated by the government or by the accounting profession?
Corporate governance	How can corporate governance be extended to employee communications?
Financial accounting in the NHS	How do fundholding GPs use financial accounting?
Stakeholder financial communications	What are the most effective ways of communicating financial information to stakeholders?
Environmental issues in accounting ethics	What are the criteria by which shareholders measure 'green' companies?
Environmental issues in manufacturing	How do 'green' factors influence supplier selection in manufacturing?
Equal employment opportunities for women	How do career break schemes contribute to the recruitment and retention of skilled female staff?
Public service announcements as a method of communication	How effective are public service announcements as a vehicle for communicating with students?

!

Experiential learning | **Identifying your research problem/issue**

Complete the following statement in one simple sentence.

My research project is about.. . . . .

. . . .

. . . .

If you have difficulty in describing your research in a simple statement, try discussing your ideas in small groups or with your supervisor to clarify your thoughts.

5.3   Determining the purpose of the research

5.3.1   Stating the purpose

Having chosen a suitable *research problem*, you need to decide what the *objectives* or *aims* of the research will be. The purpose of the research is normally stated in a separate section, initially in your *research proposal*, but later in your research report. It need only be a few sentences long and its aim is to convey the overall purpose of the study. *Purpose statements* vary according to whether you are adopting a positivistic or a phenomenological paradigm, as discussed in Chapter 3.

The purpose statement of a positivistic or quantitative study should identify the *variables* to be examined, the *theory* to be employed, the *methods* and refer to the *sample* being studied. You will remember that a variable is an attribute of an entity that can change and take different values which are capable of being observed and/or measured. A theory is a set of interrelated variables, definitions and propositions that presents a systematic view of phenomena which seek to explain natural phenomena (see Section 5.4). The research methods are the various means by which data can be collected and a sample consists of members of drawn from a population. A population is a body of people or any collection of items under consideration.

All terms used should be defined. It is normal to write in the passive. You will use the future tense in your proposal but the past tense when the study has been completed and you are writing up your research report. For example, instead of writing: 'I will hold interviews with ...' or 'I held interviews with ...' you would write, 'Interviews will be held with ...' or 'Interviews were held with ...'. Throughout the purpose statement you are trying to convey your assumptions on the objective nature of reality, distancing yourself from the study and emphasising your impartiality.

Creswell (1994) suggests that *scripting* can be useful when preparing a purpose statement. Scripting is the process of filling in blanks in a piece of text based on cues in the sentence. Figures 5.3 and 5.4 represent simple models for positivistic and phenomenological studies respectively, and you may find them useful as a base on which you can construct your own purpose statement. It is important to remember that the alternatives in brackets are merely prompts.

Figure 5.3 Simple model of a positivistic purpose statement

The purpose of this _____ (experimental? survey?) study _____ (is? was? will? be?) to test the theory of _____ that _____ (compares? relates?) the _____ (independent variable) to _____ (dependent variable) for _____ (subjects? sample?) at _____ (research site). The independent variable(s) _____ will be defined generally as _____ (provide general definition). The dependent variable(s) will be defined generally as _____ (provide general definitions), and the intervening variable(s), _____ (identify the intervening variables) will be statistically controlled in the study.

Source: Creswell (1994) p. 59.

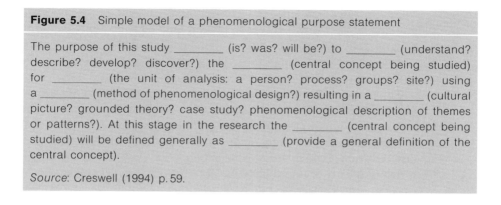

Figure 5.4 Simple model of a phenomenological purpose statement

The purpose of this study _____ (is? was? will be?) to _____ (understand? describe? develop? discover?) the _____ (central concept being studied) for _____ (the unit of analysis: a person? process? groups? site?) using a _____ (method of phenomenological design?) resulting in a _____ (cultural picture? grounded theory? case study? phenomenological description of themes or patterns?). At this stage in the research the _____ (central concept being studied) will be defined generally as _____ (provide a general definition of the central concept).

Source: Creswell (1994) p. 59.

There is more variation among the purpose statements of phenomenological studies. It is normal to emphasise the methodology employed and to imply the inductive nature of the research. The central phenomenon being explored should be described as well as the location for the study. It is normal to write in the first person rather than in the passive; for example: 'I will hold interviews with …' or 'I held interviews with …' rather than 'Interviews will be held with …'. or 'Interviews were held with …'. Throughout the purpose statement, you are trying to convey your assumption that reality is socially constructed and your involvement with the research process.

5.3.2   Choosing the unit of analysis

As you may have noticed in purpose statements shown in Figures 5.3 and 5.4, at this stage in your research you need to decide what *unit of analysis* will be appropriate for your project. You will remember from Chapter 3 that a unit of analysis is the kind of case to which the variables or phenomena under study and the research problem refer, and about which data is collected and analysed. Kervin (1992) suggests that as a rule it is best to select a unit of analysis at as low a level as possible. This should be at the level where decisions are made. Table 5.3 shows the different units of analysis, starting at the lowest and most simple level.

You should remember that you will require a number of cases of the same unit of analysis for your research project. If you are conducting a positivistic study, you must have sufficient cases to carry out the necessary statistical analyses. In addition, your unit of analysis must be appropriate to the *research problem* (see Section 5.2) you have identified.

Table 5.3 Units of analysis

Unit of analysis	Description
An individual	A person is the most common unit of analysis in business research; for example, a manager, a union member or a customer
An event	This is a particular incident; for example, a strike, a decision to relocate or a purchase
An object	In business research this is likely to be a commodity; for example, a machine, a product or a service
A body of individuals	This includes groups of people and organisations; for example, a work group, a committee or a department
A relationship	This is a connection between two or more individuals or bodies; for example, a buyer/seller relationship, a manager/employee relationship, a management/union relationship, a company/supplier relationship or a r elationship between a head office and its retail outlets. (An individual or body may be part of more than one relationship)
An aggregate	This is a collection of undifferentiated individuals or bodies with no internal structure; for example, supporters of a particular football club, parents of children at a certain school, sole traders in a particular part of a city, or companies in a specific industry

Source: Adapted from Kervin (1992) pp. 87–9.

5.4   Developing a theoretical framework

A *theory* is 'a set of interrelated constructs (variables), definitions and propositions that presents a systematic view of phenomena by specifying relationships among variables with the purpose of explaining natural phenomena' (Kerlinger, 1979, p. 64). On a more simple level, theories are 'explanations of how things function or why events occur' (Black, 1993, p. 25).

A *theoretical framework* is a collection of theories and models from the literature which underpins a positivistic research study. The theoretical framework is a fundamental part of this type of research as it explains the *research questions* or *hypotheses* (see Section 5.5). In a phenomenological study, a theoretical framework may be less important or less clear in its structure. Some researchers attempt to approach their research with no prior theories, as they believe that to do so would constrain and blinker them. However, 'even in wanting to escape theory, to be open-minded or wanting to believe that theorising was unimportant to science, we would be practising a theory' (Slife and Williams, 1995, p. 9). We will be discussing such an approach in Chapter 8.

Although much applied research has no theoretical background, if there is a theory you can develop a testable *hypothesis*. You will remember from Chapter 3 that a hypothesis is an idea or proposition which can be tested for association or causality using statistics. We will be looking more closely at how to develop hypotheses in Section 5.5.

According to Merriam (1988), theories can be classified into three types:

▶ *grand theories*, which are most often found in the natural sciences
▶ *middle-range theories*, which are placed higher than mere working hypotheses, but do not have the status of a grand theory
▶ *substantive theories*, which are developed within a certain context.

Laughlin (1995) argues that in the social sciences it is not possible to have a grand theory, only a skeletal theory. The latter would be incomplete, but 'empirical data will always be of importance to make the skeleton complete in particular contexts' (Laughlin, 1995, p. 81). This does not mean that the theory will be changed or permanently completed, but will remain as a general framework within which a study can be conducted. Glaser and Strauss (1967) emphasise the importance of substantive theories (see Chapters 3 and 8).

Given these differences of opinion, you may find it confusing trying to develop a theoretical framework. However, there are a number of theories and models in business which you can draw upon, many of which you may already be familiar with. For example:

▶ Ansoff's (1965) growth vector
▶ Chaffee's (1985) three models of strategy
▶ Jensen and Meckling's (1976) agency theory
▶ Lewin's (1951) force field analysis
▶ Parasuraman's (1991) service quality model
▶ Porter's (1985) value chain analysis
▶ Porter's (1980) five forces model
▶ Shannon and Weaver's (1949) communication model
▶ Chaos theory
▶ Game theory
▶ Efficient market hypothesis.

Refinements of these and other theories in the literature can be helpful for framing your research and giving possible explanation to what is observed.

5.5   Defining research questions or hypotheses

Whereas the purpose statement explains the general direction of the study, the *research questions* or *hypotheses* expand on this by providing detail. This is a crucial stage in your research. If you do not ask the appropriate questions, you will not be able to collect suitable data and arrive at sensible conclusions. By research questions, we do not mean the detailed questions you might use in questionnaires or interviews, but questions which identify the nature of the research problem or the issue you wish to focus on.

In a positivistic study Black (1993) recommends a specific research question, followed by a number of hypotheses. In a phenomenological study there may only be one research question, which you may need to refine during the course of the research. You will probably also need to change the title of your project to reflect your final research question(s). Creswell (1994) advises one or two *grand tour* questions, followed by no more than five to seven sub-questions. A grand tour question is a single research question posed in its most general form. We discuss the essential distinction between research questions under the two paradigms in Sections 5.5.1 and 5.5.2.

Figure 5.5 shows a simple model of how you can develop research questions. At each stage in the process you need to read, reflect

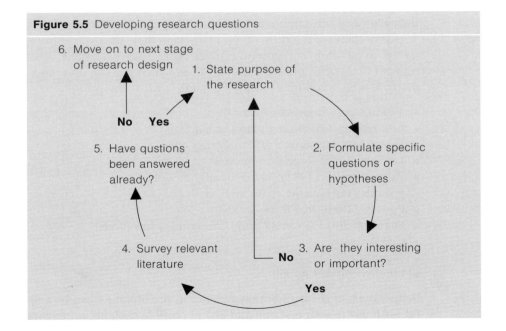

Figure 5.5 Developing research questions

and discuss what you are doing with others. The people you discuss your research with may be fellow students as well as your supervisor. We have already identified research as a process of enquiry, so the outcome of your investigation will be answers. However, you must ensure that the answers will be of interest or importance, otherwise your research will not receive much attention.

Before launching your investigations, you must conduct a survey of the relevant literature to see if anyone else has already answered your particular questions. If not, you can commence your research. However, if work has already been done in your chosen area, you may have to find ways of amending your proposed research so that it will produce new findings. If this is not possible, you will have to start the process of identifying a research topic again.

5.5.1   Research questions in positivistic studies

Kerlinger (1986) suggests that good research questions for a positivistic study should:

▶ express a relationship between variables
▶ be stated in unambiguous terms in question form
▶ imply the possibility of empirical testing.

For example, if your project was an investigation into the introduction of a career break scheme at a particular company, you might ask the following research questions:

> What impact does a career break scheme have on the recruitment of skilled female staff?
> What impact does a career break scheme have on the retention of skilled female staff?
> What is the pattern of recruitment of skilled female staff over the last ten years in the company?

Under a positivistic paradigm, it is traditional to state the research questions as *hypotheses*, particularly if you are conducting an experimental study. These will be deduced from your reading of the literature and your attempt to apply theory to the subject you are investigating. Your hypothesis will identify the *independent variable* and the *dependent variable*. A hypothesis is a statement about the relationship between them. The *null hypothesis (H_0)* states that the two variables are independent of one another and the *alternate hypothesis (H_1)* states that they are associated with one another. The null hypothesis is always stated first. For example, if you thought that older employees might work more slowly than young employees, your null hypothesis would be:

H_0 There is no relationship between an employee's age and productivity.
H_1 There is a relationship between an employee's age and productivity.

In this example, *age* is the independent variable and *productivity* is the dependent variable. The purpose of your research will be to test specific aspects of any theory you may have found in the literature which suggests that there is a relationship between age and productivity level. Using the null hypothesis ensures that you adopt a cautious and critical approach when you are conducting statistical tests on your data.

Sometimes theory suggests that there is a possible direction for the relationship. In this case, you may decide to use a *directional hypothesis*. For example:

H_0 Productivity does not decrease as an employee increases in age.
H_1 Productivity decreases as an employee increases in age.

As you will have a number of hypotheses, it is important to use a formal, rhetorical style by repeating the same key phrases in the same order. For example:

There is no relationship between an employee's age and the level of productivity.
There is no relationship between an employee's age and the level of absenteeism.
There is no relationship between an employee's age and degree of skill.

5.5.2   Research questions in phenomenological studies

The criteria for a good research question is less clear in phenomenological studies than in positivistic studies. This is due to the importance of the interaction between the researcher and the subject of the study in the former. If you are following a phenomenological paradigm, you will find that your research questions often evolve during the process of research and may need to be refined or modified as the study progresses. The best advice is to concentrate on the language of the question. Creswell (1994) suggests that you should:

▸ avoid wording that suggests a relationship between variables, such as 'effect', 'influence', 'impact', 'determine'
▸ use open-ended questions without reference to the literature or theory, unless otherwise dictated by the research design
▸ use a single focus and specify the research site.

You will find that there are different trends and fashions within different phenomenological methodologies. Reading similar research studies should help. It is usual to begin the research questions with 'what' or 'how', but to avoid words such as 'cause', 'relationship' or 'association', which might infer that a positivistic approach has been adopted.

In some phenomenological methodologies the research question may take the form of a *grand tour question* (Werner and Schoepfle, 1987). This is a single research question posed in its most general form. For example:

How do employees cope with redundancy in an area of high unemployment?

By doing this, the researcher does not block off any other potential lines of enquiry. This is particularly necessary where the methodology is considered to be of an emerging nature and one phase of the research guides the next stage, as in grounded theory (see Chapter 8). The aim is not to set a question which might restrict your enquiries, although any question will focus the study on certain phenomena or direct the study in a particular direction. Some phenomenologists pose one grand tour question and follow it with some four to eight sub-questions. These are not intended to constrain the research, but merely to delineate the focus of the study.

5.6 Defining terms

It is important to define any terms you use. You should define each term when you first use it and ensure that you are consistent in the way you use terms. You should define any term which may be new to the reader or which you are using in a novel way. If appropriate, you should use an authoritative definition, which should, of course, be referenced.

In positivistic studies it is essential to define your terms since this enhances the precision and rigour of your research. It may be necessary to show the definitions in a separate section of your *research proposal* (see Section 5.10) and later when you write your research report (see Chapter 9). It is often more difficult to define terms in a phenomenological study because the nature of the research is one of exploration and discovery. It is not until the research is in progress that the definitions emerge. However, it is still essential to explain any terms you use, if only in the form of tentative definitions in order to help explain your focus to the reader.

One approach which is useful under both paradigms is to *deconstruct* your research question or hypothesis. Parker (1994) illustrates

Figure 5.6 Deconstruction as a means of defining terms: 'Tall people have a better chance of gaining high rank in the UK'

'Tall people...'

- above average height?
- age?
- sex?
- birthplace?
- socio-economic factors?
- etc.

'...have...'

- time period?
- historical change (had)?
- etc.

'...of gaining...'

- comparison with whom?
- appropriate statistics (rationale)?
- statistical confidence?
- etc.

'...of gaining...'

- duration of career?
- positions held?
- progress?
- etc.

'...high rank...'

measured by:
- title?
- salary/perks?
- number of subordinates?
- company size?
- industry?
- commerce?

'...in the UK.'

- companies based in the UK?
- companies registered in the UK?
- other countries?

Source: Adapted from Parker (1994) p. 24

this with a hypothesis from a positivistic study, which is shown in Figure 5.6. Deconstruction is a useful means by which to analyse your research questions or hypotheses because the process enables you to define every term used in considerable detail within the context of your own research project. Not only do you gain considerable insight into your research from this process, but you will be in a better position to explain it to others.

5.7   Identifying limitations and delimitations

Whether you are conducting a large or a small research project, you will need to constrain your enquiries in a number of ways. You will have to exclude some potential areas of investigation and it will also be important that you comment on any reservations you may have. These are known as the *limitations* and *delimitations* of the study.

A limitation identifies potential weaknesses in the research. For example, when you have finished your investigation, you may consider that it is inappropriate to generalise from your research findings because of the way in which you structured your sample. A delimitation explains how the scope of your study is focused on one particular area. For example, you may confine your interviews to employees in only one company, or you may restrict your postal questionnaire to a particular geographical area.

It is usual to state your delimitations and limitations in your *research proposal* in the section dealing with methodology. There is no need to emphasise them at the proposal stage, a comment is usually sufficient. However, you should not ignore them as they serve two useful purposes. One is to identify potential difficulties which can be discussed with your supervisor to ascertain whether they need to be resolved or whether they are acceptable in the context of your research design. The other purpose is to signal at an early stage some of the issues you will need to address during the course of the research and at the writing-up stage.

5.8   Deciding the methodology

This important aspect of research design was discussed at some length in Chapter 3 because it is so closely associated with the earlier decision you had to make regarding your research paradigm. You should be fairly clear that your choice of methodology is restricted by your chosen paradigm. Some students try to evade this restriction by not admitting to a research design either explicitly or implicitly. This is a serious mistake. In your research report you will have to explain why you have selected a particular methodology and if you have a viva you will have to give an oral defence of your selection. Therefore, it is essential to recognise the paradigm you have selected for your research study and how that restricts your choice of methodology.

5.9   Determining the expected outcome

Some institutions require students to comment on the *expected outcome* of their research project. This can be very difficult when you have not even started it! However, the best strategy is to emphasise what you expect may be the outcome, but also identify any problems you think you will experience.

One way of determining the expected outcome is to refer to the purpose of the research, since ideally the outcome should complete the circle and you will achieve what you intend to achieve. For example, if your purpose is to describe the level of sales of a product in Scotland, then the expected outcome will be a description of the sale in Scotland. If the purpose of your research is to conduct an analytical investigation into why sales are higher in Scotland than in France, your expected outcome will be an identification and exploration of those factors leading to higher sales.

At all levels of research, but particularly at the Ph.D. level, it is valuable to emphasise that one outcome of the research is expected to be a contribution to knowledge. This may be written in the context of deficiencies that you have identified in the literature.

5.10 Writing the research proposal

A *research proposal* is a written account of the research topic you have chosen and why, a plan of your future research and an explanation of how you will achieve it. The main questions you are trying to answer when drafting your project proposal are:

▶ Is my proposed research interesting, important and relevant?
▶ Who has already done work in this area?
▶ What are my aims and objectives, my research questions?
▶ How do I intend to conduct the research?
▶ Where do I intend to do the research?
▶ What is my timetable for conducting the research?
▶ What do I expect the outcome of the research to be?

Some of the above questions will prove more difficult than others to answer, so the time you spend on each is also likely to vary. In the following sections we will look more closely at these questions.

Although it is best to follow a standard format, there is plenty of flexibility to allow you to put your research proposal in its best light. If your proposal is fairly long (say, over three pages) you will need to start with a brief summary. A summary is not necessary if your proposal is three pages or less. Howard and Sharp (1994) recommend preparing a topic analysis in addition to the research proposal. The topic analysis is a two- or three-page summary of the main parts of the research proposal. Their recommended content for a topic analysis is as follows:

▶ hypothesis or research objective
▶ prior research in the area
▶ value in terms of possible outcomes
▶ probable methodology or approach to the research.

Table 5.4 Indicative structure of a project proposal

Chapter/section	Percentage of proposal
Research purpose and research questions or hypotheses; explanation of why the research is important or interesting, and what your project is focusing on (the research problem); definition of key terms; limitations and delimitations	10
Theoretical framework and prior research; explanation of any assumptions and theories you are employing; literature review	30
Research paradigm and methodology; description of the sources of the data and the methods of collection and analysis	40
Expected outcome and timetable for the study	10
References	10
Total	100

On courses where students are only expected to submit a brief project proposal, the above headings, with the addition of a suggested timetable, with probably suffice. However, if your course requires a full project proposal, conducting a topic analysis is a useful exercise for collecting your thoughts together, but will need substantial development. In general terms, you will need to cover the following subjects (see Table 5.4), although you may give them different headings and arrange them in other ways. We have also added, in percentage terms, the approximate space in your project proposal that each topic will require, assuming a one-page proposal. If your proposal is longer than one page, the emphasis should be given to the theoretical framework and your own research approach. The details you put into the proposal will depend on the nature of your own particular research project. We have already discussed some items, but these are reviewed briefly below as well as the other items which you must incorporate.

5.10.1   Proposed title

The *proposed title* of your research project should be as brief as possible and yet the reader should be able to understand what the research is about from the title. If you are carrying out the research in one particular company or industry, make this clear. Wilkinson (1991) suggests that you eliminate unnecessary words such as 'An Approach to ...' and 'A Study of ...' Use a single title or a double title, such as 'An Ethnography: Understanding a Child's Perception of War'. Creswell (1994) adds that you should consider a title no longer than

12 words, eliminate most articles and prepositions, and make sure that it includes the focus or topic of the study.

5.10.2   Proposed research problem

The project objective(s) or *research problem* should be clearly stated. This statement is normally only one or two sentences long. Try to be as specific as possible. If you have a large number of research objectives it may be that your research is still not sufficiently focused. It is often useful in this section to state why the research is of interest and/or importance.

5.10.3   Proposed research questions or hypotheses

You should make certain that the *research questions* or *hypotheses* follow logically from the research problem and that you will be able to find out the answers. It is better to omit a question if you know that it will be very difficult to find the answer, rather than keep it in because it looks impressive.

5.10.4   Proposed theoretical framework

You must state clearly any theories or assumptions you are using. Some of these will be derived from your literature search (see Chapter 4).

5.10.5   Preliminary literature review

Do not write down the title of every book you have read! The preliminary *literature review* should be a critical analysis of major research studies already conducted and other key contributions. We examined how to conduct a literature search and write your review in Chapter 4. Remember, it is highly unlikely that the standard course texts you may have used will give adequate coverage of the specialised topic you are investigating. Your literature review must refer to the classical and most influential pieces of research in the topic area. You should quote from the experts, the leading commentators who write in the key academic journals.

5.10.6   Proposed research design

Your *research design* should demonstrate how you will answer the research questions. You will need to explain why you have selected your research methodology (see Chapter 3), the methods you will use to collect data (see Chapters 3 and 6) and the techniques you will use to analyse the data (see Chapters 7 and 8). You may also need to state any weaknesses in your research design and how you intend to cope with them. There should also be a statement of any resources you require, such as special computer facilities or access to particular organisations.

5.10.7 Proposed timetable

The *timetable* may be incorporated into your research design or shown separately. You should show the anticipated completion date for each activity. It is difficult to be precise on how long you should take for each activity but Gill and Johnson (1991, p. 21) quote from the example of a Ph.D. student. This allows some 20 per cent of the project time for the literature search, project design and refinements, and 25 per cent for writing the thesis. Although this may be somewhat high for an undergraduate project, do make certain that you allow sufficient time for these activities and do not get carried away by collecting too much data. Realistically, you should allow contingency time for illnesses, holidays, job interviews and other disruptions.

5.10.8 References

Your proposal must be properly referenced. The correct procedure is described in Chapter 4. You should use the term *bibliography* if you are listing books and articles which are relevant to the topic and you have read in the course of your research. You should use the term *references* if you are listing only those books and articles you have cited in your project.

5.10.9 General advice

As you get involved in the problems of selecting a suitable research topic and constructing an appropriate research design, it is easy to forget the big picture. Here are some words of general advice:

- ▶ Don't be too ambitious. It is much better to submit a modest research proposal which you can achieve than to come to grief on a project which sets out to remedy all the problems of the world
- ▶ Don't try to impress. The use of convoluted language and references to obscure articles does not help. Try to write simply and clearly so that any problems with your proposal can be identified and discussed with your supervisor
- ▶ Discuss your proposal with friends and family. Although they may not be familiar with the subject matter, they can often ask the awkward question which you have not spotted
- ▶ Be prepared to revise your proposal. It may be that you get part way through and realise that it is not possible to achieve all you set out

Figure 5.7 Project proposal checklist

1. Do you have, or can you acquire, the knowledge and skills to do the research?
2. Do you have the resources, such as computer facilities, travelling expenses?
3. If you need the cooperation of certain companies or individuals, have you obtained their consent?
4. Does your title describe your research satisfactorily?
5. Have you explained the importance and interest of your research?
6. Have you made a clear statement of the research problem and the research questions?
7. Is there a good description of your theoretical framework and research design?
8. Have you written a sound, critical analysis of previous studies and the literature?
9. Have you set out a timetable and is it realistic?
10. Are your references/bibliography complete and properly referenced?

to do. It is much better to correct this at the planning stage than to start the research and fail to complete it

▶ Remember that your proposal is a plan. You will have done a considerable amount of work preparing it; do not throw it all away. You should use your proposal to guide and manage the research. This does not mean that you cannot adapt your work as the research progresses, but the proposal is a map which should indicate your course and allow you to decide why and when to depart from it

▶ Try to allow some time between completing your research proposal and submitting it, in order to reflect on it and be critical of it.

Once you have constructed your research proposal, you can use the checklist shown in Figure 5.7 to evaluate it, before finally submitting it to your supervisor.

Finally, in case you are tempted to think that some of the items in the checklist are optional, Robson (1993) offers ten ways to get your proposal turned down. These are shown in Figure 5.8.

5.11   Examples of business research proposals

In this chapter we have described in detail what the contents of a research proposal are and what you are trying to achieve when drafting yours. However, your final proposal will reflect your own research philosophy and therefore be peculiar to your particular study. The best assessor of your proposal is your supervisor.

Figure 5.8 Ten ways to get your proposal turned down

1. Don't follow the directions or guidelines given for your kind of proposal. Omit information that is asked for. Ignore word limits

2. Ensure the title has little relationship to the stated objectives; and that neither title nor objectives link to the proposed methods or techniques

3. Produce woolly, ill-defined objectives

4. Have the statement of the central problem or research focus vague, or obscure it by other discussion

5. Leave the design and methodology implicit; let them guess

6. Have some mundane task, routine consultancy or poorly conceptualised data trawl masquerade as a research project

7. Be unrealistic in what can be achieved with the time and resources you have available

8. Be either very brief, or preferably, long-winded and repetitive in your proposal. Rely on weight rather than quality

9. Make it clear what the findings of your research are going to be, and demonstrate how your ideological stance makes this inevitable

10. Don't worry about a theoretical or conceptual framework for your research. You want to do a down-to-earth study so you can forget all that fancy stuff

Source: Robson (1993) p. 468.

Although every research proposal is unique, it is useful to look at other proposals. If you can obtain examples of successful proposals from your supervisor, these provide the best guide to what is acceptable at your own institution. The following examples are summaries of proposals submitted by potential M.Phil. and Ph.D. students. For the purpose of this book they have been abbreviated and therefore do not capture the richness of a full proposal. However, they do provide an illustration of the style and content of a typical business research proposal.

Research area | **Accounting decision making**

Evaluating investment decisions in advanced manufacturing systems: a fuzzy set theory approach

Research problem and literature overview
An important function of management accounting systems is providing managers with models that evaluate all relevant information needed for making investment decisions (Accola, 1994). Although Discounted Cash Flow Models (DCFM) have been widely accepted by both academicians and practitioners as a sound approach to investment decisions (Cheung, 1993

Accounting decision making *continued*

and Klammer *et al.*, 1991; and Wilner, 1992), many authors have criticized applying them to evaluate the investment in Advanced Manufacturing Systems (AMS) (for example: Medearis *et al.*, 1990; and Mensah and Miranti, 1989) because these models are biased in favour of short-term investments whose benefits are more easily quantified than longer-term projects. Consequently, these authors concluded that DCFM should not be applied to evaluate the investments in AMS. The most difficult task associated with applying DCFM in evaluating AMS investments lies in the existence of many variables which can hardly be measured and expressed in terms of cash flows, especially the benefits that the system will provide, such as greater manufacturing flexibility, learning effects, the effects on employee morale and decreased lead time.

Due to these criticisms some researchers (for example: Medearis *et al.*, 1990; and O'Brien and Smith, 1993) argue to ignore the financial analysis and regard the investment as a strategy that should be implemented regardless of the results of DCFM. Also, several authors suggested many approaches to evaluate the investment in AMS as a substitute of DCFM. These approaches are either numerical or non-numerical.

Thus, the main problem in the evaluation of investment decisions in AMS is how to quantify the expected benefits from these systems. In order to make these decisions in an objective manner, there is a need for a device that can properly treat qualitative variables in addition to quantitative variables. This suggests the use of Fuzzy Set Theory (FST), which reduces the need for precise numerical inputs to decision analysis, in evaluating such decisions. FST provides a method of combining qualitative and quantitative variables for decision making processes.

Research objective The main objective of this research is introducing a suggested model for evaluating investment decisions in AMS considering qualitative and quantitative variables through the use of FST.

Methodology and work plan The main aspects of the proposed research are: First, a model using the mathematical logic of FST will be constructed for evaluating the investment decisions of acquiring AMS. This will be carried on through an extensive theoretical study. So as to ensure that this model is applicable in the UK environment, a limited number of interviews with practitioners will be undertaken during the formulation of the model.Second, there will be an empirical study which can be used as a basis for evaluating the benefit and validity of the quantitative model. Input to the theoretical model will demand an in-depth understanding of particular investment decisions and the co-operation of key players in the decision making process in order to establish 'fuzzy' variables. This data can only be collected in face-to-face interviews of a semi-structured nature.

Accounting decision making *continued*

References

Accola, W. L. (1994) 'Assessing Risk and Uncertainty in New Technology Investments', *Accounting Horizons*, Vol. 8, No. 3, September, pp. 19–35.

Cheung, J. K. (1993) 'Management Flexibility in Capital Investment Decisions Literature', *Journal of Accounting Literature*, Vol. 12, pp. 29–66.

Klammer, T., Koch, B. and Wilner, N. (1991) 'Capital Budgeting Practices: A Survey of Corporate Use', *Journal of Management Accounting Research*, American Accounting Association, Vol. 3, Fall, pp. 113–130.

Medearis, H. D., Helms, M. M. and Ettkin, L. P. (1990) 'Justifying Flexible Manufacturing Systems (FMS) from a Strategic Perspective', *Manufacturing Review*, Vol. 3, No. 4, December, pp. 219–223.

Mensah, Y. M. and Miranti, P. J. (1989) 'Capital Expenditure Analysis and Automated Manufacturing Systems: A Review and Synthesis', *Journal of Accounting Literature*, Vol. 8, pp. 181–207.

O'Brien, C. and Smith, J. E. (1993) 'Design of the Decision Process for Strategic Investment in Advanced Manufacturing Systems', *International Journal of Production Economics*, Vol. 30–31, pp. 309–322.

Wilner, N., Koch, B. and Klammer, T. (1992) 'Justification of High Technology Capital Investment – An Empirical Study', *The Engineering Economist*, Vol. 37, No. 4, Summer, pp. 341–353.

Research area | **Accounting regulation**

The regulation of related party transactions

The problem

Related parties are an everyday occurrence in the business world and the transactions that take place between them are a natural process. However, in the UK, these transactions are not disclosed which gives misleading information and enables companies the chance to act fraudulently (Mason, 1979). There are a number of cases of fraud using related parties including Pergamon Press (1969), US Financial (1972) and more recently, the death of Robert Maxwell has revealed the syphoning of funds to related parties, effectively stealing people's pensions. For these reasons, it is essential that the disclosure of related party transactions should be regulated. Attempts to regulate these transactions have been made by the ASC with ED 46 (1989) but so far these have been unsuccessful.

Aim of the research

To enable any future standard concerned with the disclosure of related party transactions to be comprehensive and implementable, certain questions must be researched and answered:

Accounting regulation *continued*

(i)   Why was the earlier attempt at a standard unsuccessful?
(ii) How should 'related parties' be defined?
(iii) What information should be disclosed?
(iv) What should be the threshold of the influence of the resulting standard?
(v)   How valuable will the information be to the users of the accounts? This research will aim to answer these questions.

Methodology

The research will be conducted as a longitudinal investigation of the interest in related party transactions in the UK. This will include an extensive literature review of background papers (Brown, 1980), previous attempts at issuing a standard ED 46 (ASC, 1989) and comments made about the exposure draft (ASC, 1990 and Hinton & Anderson, 1989). A critique of ED 46 will be published as a major part of the research. The study will be conducted in the context of Agency theory (Jenson, 1976) and the 'market of excuses' thesis by Watts and Zimmerman (1979). A critical appraisal will also be made of the 'Nobes Cycle' (l991). The transfer to Ph.D. will enable the research to include international experience, including IAS 24 (IASC, 1984) and SAS no 6 (AICPA, 1975), conducted within the framework of international classification (Mueller, 1969 and Nobes, 1992).

References

ASC, 'Comments received on ED 46', 1990.
ASC, 'Exposure Draft 46 Related Party Transactions', April 1989.
AICPA, 'Statement on Auditing Standard no. 6', *Journal of Accountancy*, Vol. 140, Sept 1975, pp. 82–85.
Brown, H. R. 'Background paper on related party transactions', ICAEW, 1980.
Hinton, R. 'Relating party transactions the UK way', *Accountancy*, Vol. 103, No. 1150, June 1989, pp. 26–27.
IASC, 'International Accounting Standard 24 Related Party Disclosures', 1984.
Jenson, M. C. and Meckling, W. H. 'Theory of the firm; managerial behaviour, agency costs and ownership structure', *Journal of Financial Economics*, Vol. 3, pp. 305–360, 1976.
Mason, A. K. 'Related party transactions. A research study', CICA, 1979.
Mueller, G. '*International Accounting*', (New York: Macmillan, Part I, 1967).
Nobes, C. '*International Classification of Financial Reporting*', 2nd edn (Lava: Routledge, 1992).
Watts, R. L. and Zimmerman, J. L. 'The Demand and Supply of Accounting Theories; the Market of Excuses', *Accounting Review*, Vol. 54, April 1979,

Research area	Auditing

An analytical study of the effect of confirmatory processes on auditors' decision making and hypothesis updating

Research problem
Motivated in part by research findings in psychology, the auditing literature has recently begun to focus on auditors' use of confirmatory processes in evidence search and evaluation. Confirmatory processes mean that the auditor prefers to search for evidence confirming his initial hypotheses and also evaluates this evidence in a way that confirms his hypotheses (Church, 1990, p. 81). As the use of confirmatory processes is still a new trend in auditing, some problems are associated the use of these processes, e.g. the impact of confirming and disconfirming approaches on auditors' decisions, the role of hypotheses formulation and the use of audit evidence in hypotheses updating.

Literature review and inadequacy of current research
Most of the previous studies (for example, Bedard and Biggs, 1991; and McMillan and White, 1993) on the use of confirmatory processes in auditing focused on auditors' hypotheses formulation. These studies declared that auditors differ in their abilities to formulate correct or plausible hypotheses and these abilities are affected by various factors. Among these factors are expertise, source of hypotheses, hypotheses frame, professional skepticism, motivational factors and cognitive factors. The stated factors still need in-depth investigation, in addition to determining what other factors can trigger the use of confirmatory processes in auditing. A few studies also examined the process of hypotheses updating. Einhorn and Hogarth (1985) formulated a model called 'Contrast/Surprise Model' which investigates the effect of confirming and/or disconfirming evidence on hypotheses updating. Ashton and Ashton (1988) investigated the validity of the previous model. However, their study is insufficient for investigating the process of hypotheses updating because they concentrated only on evidence order.

Research objective
The main objective of the proposed research is determining the effect of using confirmatory processes on auditor's decision making, and investigating the process of hypotheses updating. The main research questions to be addressed are:

1 What factors trigger the use of confirmatory processes in auditing?
2 What is the process of hypotheses updating?
3 What theoretical models are relevant to the process of hypotheses updating?
4 What are the most appropriate circumstances for using confirmatory/ disconfirmatory approaches?

Auditing *continued*

Methodology and work plan

The research will be carried out through a theoretical and an empirical study. The empirical study will involve survey and experimental studies. The survey will be conducted through interviews with a number of auditors in auditing firms. It is intended to carry out 36 interview in six auditing firms; two large, two medium and two small. Interviews will be held with two highly experienced, two medium experienced and two relatively inexperienced auditors in each firm. These interviews will help in determining factors affecting auditors' use of confirmatory processes. Following the analysis of this data, 18 experimental studies will be carried out to determine the validity of the proposed model. These experimental studies will be conducted in the same auditing firms as the interviews.

References

Ashton, A. H. and Ashton, R. H. (1988) 'Sequential Belief Revision in Auditing', *Accounting Review*, Oct., pp. 623–641.

Bedard, J. C. and Biggs, S. F. (1991) 'Pattern Recognition, Hypotheses Generation and Auditor Performance in an Analytical Task', *Accounting Review*, July pp. 622–642.

Church, B. K. (1990) 'Auditors' Use of Confirmatory Processes, *Journal of Accounting Literatures*, Vol. 9, pp. 81–112.

Einhorn, H J. and Hogarth, R. M. (1985) *A Contrast/Surprise Model for Updating Beliefs*, Working Paper, University of Chicago, April.

McMillan, J. J. and White, R. A. (1993) 'Auditors' Belief Revisions and Evidence Search: The Effect of Hypothesis Frame, Confirmation Bias and Professional Skepticism'. *Accounting Review*, July, pp. 443–465.

Research area | **Buyer behaviour**

The influence of children on the family purchase of environmentally friendly grocery products in South Wales

Previous studies of environmental consumerism have addressed the implications of the individual's buyer behaviour (Peattie 1992, Charter 1992, Ottman 1989) and changes in organisational management practices (Smith 1993, Welford & Gouldson 1993, Charter 1992). The majority of studies in the area of green consumerism focus on the greening of the individual's buying behaviour, the development of green consumerism and the reactions of management in a wide sphere of industries. This research will take family buying behaviour models and build in an environmental perspective, the conceptual framework is presented briefly in Figure A.1.

Research by Charter in 1992 revealed that environmental awareness is increasing in schools throughout Europe, with the introduction of

Buyer behaviour *continued*

Figure A.1 Diagrammatic conceptual framework

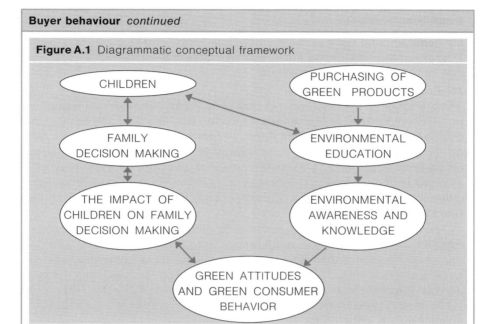

environmental topics in range of school syllabuses, together with wide recognition of the importance of environmental issues as a cross curricular subject. This has resulted in environmental awareness and concern diffusing amongst children, with the direct result of children acting as important catalysts in raising the environmental awareness of the family group by reporting back what has been learned about the environment at school.

As Buttle (1993) discovered, consumer decisions are influenced by systematic relationships of the family which have a variable and determined effect upon the actions of individuals. Most researchers in environmentally responsive buyer behaviour have employed what Buttle (1993) describes as individualistic concepts and constructs. This research intends to take the interactive phenomena of the family and the influence of children on the purchase of environmentally response grocery products.

Aims

To investigate the influence of children on the family purchase of environmentally friendly grocery products in South Wales.

The aims of this research centre on an understanding of the influence that children have on family purchase of environmentally friendly grocery products. Grocery products have been selected as the focus of this study because children have a major influence on product choice in this area, and are likely to be involved in product choice selection. The aim of this doctoral study is to determine children's attitudes to and awareness of environmental

Buyer behaviour *continued*

concerns and the family-child interaction process within the context of environmentally responsive family buying behaviour.

Methodology

The first stage of the research has been a review of the existing literature on green consumerism, environmental education and children, and family buying behaviour. The literature review concentrates on several areas – first, on the diffusion of environmentally responsive buying behaviour, secondly, on the issues surrounding the development of children's attitudes and awareness of environmental concerns; and thirdly, on the family-child interaction process within the context of family buying behaviour, as figure one illustrates.

The primary methodology consists of three stages: The exploratory research which is underway, and consists of focus group sessions with primary school children in South Wales. The aims of the exploratory study is to determine the attitudes and behaviour of children towards environmental consumerism and how they believe they influence environmentally responsive family buying behaviour. The legal and ethical aspects of research with children will be adhered to.

Stage two will be an investigation of the family group through focus group sessions in South Wales, with the objective of establishing the actual interactive decision-making process within the sample families. This will be undertaken between September 1995 and March 1996.

The third stage of the research will consist of the development of case studies in order to investigate the holistic characteristics of the real life situation. The case study sample will be developed from stage two of the research. The in-depth case study analysis will consist of semi-structured interviews and an observational study to be undertaken between March 1996 and March 1997.

Output

This doctoral research will contribute to family buyer behaviour knowledge and the understanding of environmentally responsive consumer behaviour; it will contribute to the understanding of the marketing implications of the influence of children in environmental decision making and the ways in which decision making is undertaken within the family group in the context of environmentally responsive buyer behaviour.

References

Buttle F. (1993) The Co-ordinated Management of Meaning: A Case Exemplar of a New Consumer Research Paradigm, *European Journal of Marketing*, vol. 28, nos. 8/9.

Charter, M. I. (1992) *Greener Marketing* (Sheffield: Greenleaf Publishing) Sheffield, UK.

Buyer behaviour *continued*

Ottman, J. (1989) 'Industries' Response to Green Consumerism', *Journal of Business Strategy*, vol. 13, Part 4.

Smith, D. (1993) 'Purchasing Department Contributions to Company Environmental Performance', *Purchasing Supply Management*, vol. 20, no. 1.

Welford, R. and Gouldson, A. (1993) *Environmental Management Business Strategy* (London: Pitman Publishing).

Research area | **Organisational change**

Changing the deal: The role of informal contracts in business transformation and organisational renewal

Introduction and literature review

In the last decade, the belief has grown amongst organisational theorists (Handy, 1985, 1989; Kanter, 1983, Pascale, 1990 and others) that in order to be successful in increasingly turbulent markets, organisations need to be able to assimilate – or better, instigate – dramatic shifts in their industries. Change is becoming more discontinuous (Handy, 1989) – or transformational – in nature. The management of discontinuous change demands a more 'holistic approach' (Hinings and Greenwood, 1988) and an ability to recognise – and if appropriate, act on – the limitations of the organisation's existing paradigms (Morgan, 1986, 1993). It can also require organisations to build more flexibility into their structures and contractual arrangements (Atkinson, 1984). Roles may be restructured; jobs rescoped; new skills demanded; career paths obfuscated: in short, individuals are asked to undertake a radical rethink of their role, both within the organisation and in a broader context. Formal contracts and cultures are being developed that aim to meet these challenges, but the informal side of organisational life cannot and should not be ignored.

A pilot project (in an operating company of a leading financial services group) conducted for this proposal, suggested that even when change is accepted at the 'rational' levels it may meet resistance if insufficient attention is paid to its broader implications (Jarvis, 1994). There is a growing need to understand the 'informal contract' between the employer and employee, if both parties' expectations are to be met.

A key output from the research will be a better understanding of the 'informal contract', and if and how it is evolving. At this stage, a working definition is being employed, as follows: 'the expectations – emotional and rational; conscious and unconscious – that employees bring to and take from their work and that are not covered by their job description and formal contract of employment'.

Research aim

The main aim of the M.Phil. project is to define the informal contract and establish its role in the implementation of major change programmes. Ph.D.

Organisational change *continued*

research will aim to uncover if and how the informal contract can be 'managed' to support employees through major change.

Research methodology and proposed timetable
Primary research will be qualitative, collaborative inquiry (Reason, 1988) built around 6–8 case studies, each being conducted over a period of 18–24 months. This approach has been selected for its ability to yield data at the unconscious, as well as conscious, level.

Hypotheses will be developed as the case study progresses and each case study will adopt four key research methods: interviews with senior management to provide an organisational context and an understanding of the aims and critical success factors for the change programme; depth interviews, with middle management grades and below, to provide context and a broad understanding of the individual meaning of the informal contract; individual diaries to provide a depth of information – 'felt' and rational – into the meaning of the informal contract to individuals; a series of inquiry groups to develop a shared meaning for the informal contract. Triangulation will be provided through this use of different methods and different sources, whilst an audit trail will ensure confirmability.

Ph.D. research will test hypotheses for transferability. As well as the opportunities for comparison provided by multiple case studies, it is envisaged that a series of cross organisational groups, comprising senior managers, wilt be set-up to look at how these hypotheses transfer from theory into practice.

References
Atkinson, J., *Emerging UK Work Patterns*, IMS Paper No 145 1984.
Handy, C., *The Age of Unreason* (Business Books Ltd, 1989).
Hinings, C. R. and Greenwood, R., *The Dynamics of Strategic Change* (Basil Blackwell, 1988).
Jarvis, C., *The Introduction of a Self-Assessment Appraisal System in to FSG OpCo'*, unpublished 1994.
Kanter, R. M., *The Changemasters* (Unwin Hyman, 1983).
Morgan, G., *Images of Organisation* (Sage Publications, 1986).
Morgan, G., *Imaginization* (Penguin, 1990).
Pascale, R., *Managing on the Edge* (Penguin, 1990).
Reason, P. (ed.) *Human Inquiry in Action: Developments in New Paradigm Research* (Saga Publications, 1988).

Research area | **Organisational change**

To evaluate input and effectiveness of culture change on individuals and organisations

Background
I have run and co-tutored personal, management and organisational development courses for the last ten years. Co-tutoring has given me the

Organisational change *continued*

opportunity to observe others training, receive feedback and reflect on my own practice. The dominant thought area that has emerged from this reflection is that the quality of relationship between tutor and learner, and learner and learner, is of critical importance if lasting change and development is to occur.

As a participant in a self-managed learning group at Lancaster University (MAML), I found the experience challenging and, at times frustrating. I believe this was due to the developmental relationships within the group. Whilst this subject has emerged from reflecting on my own personal experience, I believe it is relevant to tutors, learners and managers. Effective 'engaging' between individuals could be a basis for effective managerial relationships.

The project

The study will explore the nature of 'engaging' (i.e. effective developmental relationships) between tutors and learners, and learners and learners. The aim is to define and develop a working model of effective developmental relationships.

Theoretical context

Rowland (1993) has proposed a spectrum of tutoring relationships from 'didactic' to 'exploratory', with the middle ground being occupied by an 'interpretative' model. In his 'exploratory' end 'didactic' models the learning process is seen as being 'a black box, a kind of private psychological process in which the tutor cannot engage' (1993, p. 27). In the 'interpretative' models the tutor deliberately attempts to become part of the learning process. He characterises the relationship as being one in which there is a free flow of learning and the tutor becomes an important part of the students learning process. The psycho-therapeutic work of Rogers (1961) clearly defines the characteristics of what he terms a 'helping relationship'. This relationship creates a 'psychological climate' that ultimately releases human potential. Combining the work of Rowland (1993) and Rogers (1961) suggests a definition of 'engaging' as a relationship that creates a developmental psychological climate and a culture of support in which individuals develop shared meanings and collectively become an integral part of each others reflective processes.

Using Reason's (1988) post-positivist research methodology of co-operative enquiry, I will work with groups to establish how individuals successfully 'engage'. Reason provides many useful insights into establishing co-operative enquiry groups including creating the 'right' atmosphere for people to examine processes, freely challenge and support one another. He suggests this is not easy and needs to emerge from the group as it matures towards truly authentic collaboration. This is another factor within the process of 'engaging' but between researcher and researched. Thus, the theoretical context of the research methodology parodies the area under study.

Organisational change *continued*

Methodology and research process

The proposed study will use a form of co-operative enquiry, which is ontologically based on a belief in a participatory universe and attempts to undertake research with people rather than on them. Cunningham (1988) suggests a broad model of co-operative inquiry which he calls 'interactive holistic research'. This non-linear, or as he puts it is 'omni-focussed', model (p. 167) has four elements:

a Collaborative enquiry – that is with people and either of Type I – in which the group explores it's internal processes together or Type II in which the group explores a process which happens outside the group.

b Action research – research which is concerned with developing practical knowledge or praxis.

c Experimental research – research which is concerned with how and what I experience.

d Contextual locating – this represents the backdrop to the whole research study, either intellectual, socially or emotionally.

Within the M.Phil. phase, I propose to establish a collaborative enquiry group with fellow tutors and learners to explore experiences of 'engaging' (Type II according to Cunningham, 1988). The purpose of this phase is to define and develop a model of 'engaging' between tutors and learners. This will be elaborated in the Ph.D. phase by exploring the nature of developmental relationships within the group (Type I according to Cunningham, 1988) and to look further at this relationship in the context of managing. In this phase the objective is to define 'engaging' between learners and to develop a model of collaborative learning or development. The group will be assembled by invitation and consist of fellow tutors with an interest in exploring developmental relationships. Initial research with learners will be confined to participant observation to enable a working hypothesis to be established and will be undertaken with the many groups that I currently co-tutor. This will be replaced with a more formal collaborative enquiry which attempts to elicit a learners perspective on 'engaging', initially free of any hypothesis, but later to explore a hypothesis which is either given or developed.

Research with fellow tutors and with learners will take place concurrently. The synthesis of these views will take place through a critical examination of my own practice and experience, through observation and critical subjectivity. Ideas which are developed will then be available for scrutiny and development with the collaborative inquiry group. In each of the groups (i.e. learners and tutors) I will be the primary researcher.

References

Cunningham, I. (1988) *'Interactive Holistic Research: Researching Self Managed Learning'*, in Reason, P. (1988) *Human Inquiry in Action – Developments in New Paradigm Research* (London: Sage Publications).

Organisational change *continued*

Rogers, C. (1961) *On Becoming a Person* (London: Constable).
Rowland, S. (1933) *The Enquiring Tutor: Exploring the Process of
  Professional Learning* (London: Falmer Press).

Research area | **Strategic management**

Tacit knowledge and sustainable competitive advantage

Introduction and literature review

An enduring problem for strategic management is the sustainability of
competitive advantage (Porter, 1985, Barney, 1991, Black and Boal, 1994).
The proposed research is concerned with competitive advantage and the link
between a heterogeneous firm resource (in this instance tacit knowledge)
and the use of relatively homogenous information technology (IT) assets.
Much of the literature exploring the link between IT and competitive
advantage, holds that innovatory systems are quickly and widely adopted
and thus a source of enabling and not critical advantage (Banker and
Kauffman, 1988, Ciborra, 1991). Contradictory research shows that this may
not be the case as implentation of IT can produce unexpected outcomes
(Ciborra, 1991). Other research (e.g. Cash & McFarlan, 1988, Lederer and
Sethi, 1991, Kremar and Lucas, 1991) does not recognise the import of tacit
knowledge and sees deviations in performance stemming from a lack of
planning. However, recent additions to the literature question this logic,
finding that intra-firm structural differences, the source of unexpected
outcomes, can be combined with technology as complementary assets to
confer a potential source of sustainable competitive advantage (Clemons
and Row, 1995, Feeny and Ives, 1990, Heatley, Argarwal and Tanniru, 1995).

Inadequacy of current research

No empirical research has explored the role of tacit knowledge as a positive
intra-firm structural differentiator in the implementation of IT. *A priori*
observation seems to indicate that tacit knowledge is valuable, rare,
imperfectly inimitable and non-transferable (Barney, 1991). Evaluating IT
strategic successes, Ciborra (1991) identifies serendipity, trial and error, and
bricolage as elements of a process of innovation in the use of systems. None
of the literature explores the source, nor the effects of this process. Thus,
whilst the literature has speculated as to the role of tacit knowledge in
creating sustainable competitive advantage (Spender 1993), the empirical
question, 'Can tacit knowledge provide a source of sustainable competitive
advantage?' has not been addressed.

Aims and objectives of research

The research aims to fill this gap in the literature by examining the
proposition that tacit knowledge is a source of competitive advantage, and

Strategic management *continued*

asking, if it is, what the conditions are required to support it. The research also aims to answer the question how tacit knowledge can provide a source of sustainable competitive advantage. This requires an examination of pre-emption, dynamic economies of learning and continuing innovation effects from using IT and tacit knowledge as complementary assets. Thus, the research will test the proposition that combinations of tacit knowledge and IT create core competencies that lead to superior performance, and that these competencies are inimitable in the sense used by Barney (1991). Barriers to imitation can be created by combining tacit knowledge and technology.

Methodology and plan of work

At the highest level of abstraction, it is proposed to use the resource based view of the firm as a framework to understand asset combinations that can be the source of differences among firms. It is proposed that the research will operationalise measures developed by Sethi and King (1994) which were devised to assess the extent to which IT applications provide competitive advantage. In this research competitive advantage is driven by system performance, and this is the dependent variable in this study. The sample will be taken from the population of firms who use SAP business process software. The sample will be stratified for external validity according to Collis and Ghemawat's (1994) resource-based industry typology: along the dimensions of key resources and the nature of the production task. Construct validity will be established using pilot research; in depth interviews. The focus of the study will centre on deviations from expected performance of a tightly specified and robust business process oriented system which is widely used in a variety of industries. The unit of analysis is at the level of business processes. Deviations in performance between firms having the same IT system constitute differences in the dependent variable and this is a function of knowledge assets, their management and characteristics of the firm and system context. A research instrument will be designed which will be administered to collect cardinal and ordinal data on the dimensions of tacit knowledge, group dynamics, firm and system characteristics, including data collection on firm specific technology trajectories.

References

Barney, J. (1991) 'Firm Resources and Sustained Competitive Advantage', *Journal of Management*, 17(1), 99–120.

Banker, R. and Kauffman, R. (1988) 'Strategic Contributions of IT ', Proceedings of 9th Int. Conf. on IS, 141–150.

Black, J. and Boal, K. (1994) 'Strategic Resources: Traits, configuration and Paths to Sustainable Competitive Advantage', *Strat. Man. Jnl*, 15, 131–148.

Cash, J. and McFarlane, F. (1988) 'Competing Through Information Technology; (Harvard Business School Press).

Ciborra, C. U. (1991) 'The Limits of Strategic Information Systems', *International Journal of Information Resource Management*, 2(3), 11–17.

Strategic management *continued*

Clemons, E. K. and Row, M. C. (1991) 'Sustaining IT: The Role of Structural Differences', *MIS Quarterly*, Sept. 275–292.

Collis, D. and Ghemawat, P. (1994) 'Industry Analysis: Understanding Industry Structure and Dynamics', in *The Portable MBA*, ed. Fahey, L. and Randall, R. M., Wiley, pp. 171–193.

Feeny, D. and Ives, B. (1991) 'In Search of Sustainability: Reaping Long-term Advantage from Investments in IT', *Jnl Mgmt IS*, 7(1), 27–45.

Heatley, J., Agarwal, R. and Tanniru, M. (1995) 'An Evaluation of Innovative Information Technology', *Jnl Strat IS*, 4(3), 255–277.

Kremar, H. and Lucas, H. (1991) 'Success Factors for Strategic IS', *Information and Management*, 21, 137–145.

Lederer, A. and Sethi, V. (1991) 'Meeting the Challenges of Information Systems Planning', *Long Range Planning*, 25(2), 69–80.

Porter, M. E. (1980) *Competitive Advantage* (Free Press).

Spender, J. C. (1993) 'Competitive Advantage from Tacit Knowledge? Unpacking the Concept and its Strategic Implications', *Academy of Management*, pp. 37–41.

Sethi, V. and King, W. (1994), 'Development of Measures to Assess the Extent to Which IT Provides Competitive Advantage', *Management Science*, 40(12), 1601–1627.

Conclusions

In this chapter we have built on the knowledge you have gained in the first four chapters and explained how to draw up a detailed plan of your research. We have explored ways in which you can identify a potential research problem by identifying gaps in the literature. We have discussed the role of the purpose statement and the importance of defining any terms used and determining your research questions or hypotheses, any theoretical framework and your methodology. We have described how to write a research proposal and looked at an indicative structure. Finally, we have suggested a project proposal checklist to evaluate your proposal.

Once your research proposal has been accepted, you will be able to start collecting your primary data, which we discuss next.

6 Collecting original data

Introduction

By the time you have submitted your research proposal, you will have collected and collated a considerable amount of secondary data as a result of your literature search. Searching the literature is an ongoing process which you can continue while you wait to hear whether your research proposal has been accepted. As soon as you receive an affirmative answer, you will be in a position to start collecting original data for your research.

In this chapter we examine the main methods by which original data can be collected. The objectives of this chapter are to help you:

▶ to identify and classify the variables you want to collect data about
▶ to select a suitable sample
▶ to classify the sources and types of data
▶ to select your data collection method(s)
▶ to design any questions you may wish to ask
▶ to code questionnaires and data record sheets for computer analysis
▶ to choose a suitable method for recording qualitative data.

6.1 Overview of data collection

In Chapter 3 we referred to *methodology* as being concerned with the entire process of the research. As the name suggests, *data collection methods* are used in that part of the research process which is concerned with collecting data. Many research projects use more than one method. Table 6.1 lists the main methods of data collection we will be discussing in this chapter.

Qualitative (phenomenological) methods have been described as 'an array of interpretative techniques which seek to describe, decode, translate and otherwise come to terms with the meaning, not the frequency, of certain more or less naturally occurring phenomena in the social world' (Van Maanen, 1983, p. 9). However, a method is not necessarily phenomenological or positivistic by its label, but by how it is used. If you are using a method to collect data on the frequency of

Table 6.1 Main data collection methods

Method
Critical incident technique
Diaries
Focus groups
Interviews
Observation
Protocol analysis
Questionnaires

occurrence of a phenomenon or variable, you will obtain *quantitative data*. If you are collecting data on the meaning of a phenomenon, you will obtain *qualitative data*. Quantitative data is numerical data; qualitative data is nominal (named) data.

Some qualitative data collection methods are so closely intertwined with the analysis of the data that it is impossible to separate the two processes, and we examine these methods in Chapter 8. During the course of your studies you may come across authors who refer to certain methods of collecting data, such as *questionnaires* (see Section 6.5.7) and *structured interviews* (see Section 6.5.4), as *research instruments*. This term is mainly used to refer to questionnaires or interview schedules which have been used and tested in a number of different studies. In a phenomenological study, the researcher may be referred to as a research instrument to emphasise his or her close involvement under that paradigm.

Figure 6.1 shows an overview of the data collection process. However, it is important to realise that at this stage in the research, as at any other, the process is less rigid than the diagram suggests, especially in a phenomenological study.

You will remember from Chapter 5 that your overall research design includes making decisions about the methodology you will adopt. This encompasses selecting method(s) of data collection and analysis. Although we are focusing on methods of data collection in this chapter, it is important to think ahead to how you will analyse the data you have collected. We will be looking at the main methods of analysis in Chapters 7 and 8. For the time being, we will now examine each of the stages in Figure 6.1 in detail.

6.2   Variables

In your *research proposal* (see Chapter 5) you included a *purpose statement* which indicated the *unit of analysis* you have chosen for

Figure 6.1 Overview of the data collection process

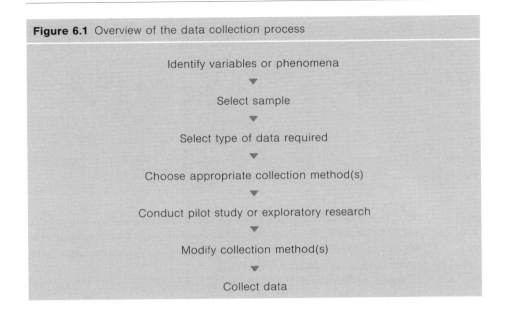

Identify variables or phenomena

▼

Select sample

▼

Select type of data required

▼

Choose appropriate collection method(s)

▼

Conduct pilot study or exploratory research

▼

Modify collection method(s)

▼

Collect data

your study. You will remember that a unit of analysis is the kind of case to which the *variables* or *phenomena* under study and the *research problem* refer, and about which *data* is gathered and analysed. The unit of analysis can range from an individual, an event or an object, to a body of individuals, a relationship or an aggregate (see Section 5.3.2).

In research we are interested in collecting data about *variables*. If you are working under a phenomenological paradigm you may prefer to use the term *phenomena* instead of variables. A *variable* is an attribute of the entity which you have chosen as your unit of analysis. The most important characteristic of a variable is that it can change; in other words, it can take more than one value, either across entities (cross-section data) or within the same entity over time (time series data). Furthermore, these different values are capable of being observed and/or measured. For example, 'age' and 'qualifications' are variables which are attributes of individuals. They can vary from one person to another and, if you are considering only one individual, over time. On the other hand 'number of employees' and 'profit margin' are attributes of organisations. These variables differ from one organisation to another and, over time, can change within the same organisation.

6.2.1   Quantitative and qualitative variables

Variables can be classified as *qualitative* or *quantitative*. A qualitative variable is a non-numerical attribute of an individual or object. Some qualitative variables, like gender or colour, simply divide people or objects into groups. Other qualitative variables, like job position or social class, which both divide and order, are known as *ordered qualitative variables*.

A quantitative variable is a numerical attribute of an individual or object. However, in order to obtain a quantitative variable, you need to find a suitable measuring tool. This is not a problem with such variables as income and age, since there are accepted measures already in use, but you may have some difficulty with other variables such as loyalty, honesty or intelligence. If there is no generally accepted measure, you may have to devise your own measuring tool or find out what other researchers have used. For example, intelligence has been measured by psychologists as an intelligence quotient (IQ) which is a score resulting from specially designed test. This measure is known as a *hypothetical construct* and you may have to devise your own if you cannot find a suitable one in the literature.

Quantitative variables are divided into *discrete quantitative variables* and *continuous quantitative variables*. A discrete quantitative variable can take only one of a range of distinct values between the start and end of a scale. For example, the number of sales assistants in a baker's shop on different days of the week might range from one to five. Between the start and end of this scale, the variable can only take the values 0, 1, 2, 3, 4 and 5. Values like 1.3 or 4.6 sales assistants are impossible.

A continuous quantitative variable can take any value between the start and end of a scale. For example, a suitable range for an adult's weight might be from 30 kg to 150 kg. Between the start and end of this scale, any value of the variable is possible. One adult might weigh 45 kg, another might weigh 45.6 kg or another weigh 45.63 kg, and so on with increasingly more accurate measurement.

In practice there is considerable blurring of these definitions. For example, it might be argued that income is a discrete variable, because any income must be one of a distinct range of values listed in pennies. But there are so many different possibilities when incomes are taken down to the last penny, that income is almost always considered to be a continuous variable. In the same way, weight is certainly a continuous variable. However, if weight is being measured with a set of scales which is only accurate to the nearest tenth of a kilogram, the results will be from the distinct range of values, 0.1, 0.2, 0.3, 0.4, etc. Table 6.2 gives examples of qualitative and quantitative variables where the *unit of analysis* is an individual.

A further distinction between quantitative and qualitative variables is that all the operations of arithmetic can be applied only to quantitative variables. For example, we can make statements such as factory A has twice as many workers as factory B; the income of person C is equal to the income of person A plus the income of person B.

Table 6.2 Qualitative and quantitative variables

Qualitative variables	Discrete quantitative variables
Name	Number of dependants
Job title	Number of subordinates
Employment status	Number of cars owned
Place of birth	Date of birth
Colour of eyes/hair	Clothes/shoe size

Ordered qualitative variables	Continuous quantitative variables
Social class	Income
Qualifications	Height
Job grade	Weight

6.2.2   Independent and dependent variables

If you are carrying out a positivist study, your *purpose statement* (see Chapter 5) would have also identified the *independent* and *dependent variables* you will be collecting data about. In such a study, the *independent variable* is the variable that can be manipulated to predict the values of the *dependent variable*. The *dependent variable* is the variable whose values are predicted by the *independent variable*. For example, you might wish to vary the intensity of lighting in a room (the independent variable) in order to observe the effect on the productivity levels of employees (the dependent variable), or place individuals in a stressful situation, perhaps by creating loud, random noises (the independent variable), in order to observe their ability to complete complex tasks (the dependent variable).

6.2.3   Extraneous and confounding variables

An *extraneous* or *exogenous variable* is any variable other than the independent variable which might have an effect on the dependent variable. For example, if your study involves an investigation of the relationship between productivity and motivation, you may find it difficult to exclude the effect on productivity of other factors such as a heat wave, a work to rule, a takeover or domestic problems. A *confounding variable* is one which obscures the effects of another; for example, the novelty for employees of being the centre of attention by the researcher or working in an unfamiliar place if the study is laboratory based.

6.3 Selecting a sample

Selecting a *sample* is a fundamental element of a positivistic study. If yours is a phenomenological study, you may have a sample of one. Nevertheless, you will find our advice on the different types of sample in this section useful. A sample is made up of some of the members of a *population*. A population may refer to a body of people or to any other collection of items under consideration for research purposes. A *sampling frame* is 'a list or other record of the population from which all the sampling units are drawn' (Vogt, 1993, p. 202). For example, in a large company you may have a list of all the employees and this will form the sampling frame from which you can take a sample.

Depending on the size of your study and the size of the population under consideration, you may find that you can use the entire population. For example, your research topic may be concerned with the performance of small companies in the paper recycling industry in the London postal area. Your *unit of analysis* (see Chapter 5) is a company. You decide that for your purposes you will define a small company as a private limited company with a turnover of less than £1 million per annum. You decide to use FAME (see Chapter 4) to identify companies which fit your criteria and your investigations show that there are 32 such companies. Obviously your research findings will relate only to paper recycling companies in London and you must be very cautious about attempting to generalise to other types of company in other parts of the country.

On the other hand, you may want to investigate the performance of small companies in all industries throughout the UK. In this case, your unit of analysis is still a company Again, you can use FAME to provide a sampling frame, but this time you find that there are many thousands of companies which fit your criteria. To save the expense and inconvenience of investigating all these companies, it is acceptable to reduce the number to a manageable size by selecting a representative sample. Figure 6.2 shows the steps involved in selecting a sample.

In a positivistic study a representative or good sample is one in which the results obtained for the sample can be taken to be true for the whole population; in other words, you will be able to generalise from the results. A good sample must be:

▶ chosen at random (every member of the population must have a chance of being chosen)
▶ large enough to satisfy the needs of the investigation being undertaken
▶ unbiased.

It is important to ensure that your sample is not *biased* and is representative of the population from which it is drawn. An example of a

Figure 6.2 Selecting a sample

Define target population

▼

Obtain or construct sampling frame

▼

Determine how to select sample members

▼

Decide how to convert sample estimates into
population estimates

biased sample is where the researcher asks for volunteers to participate in the study. This sample is likely to be biased because the volunteers may possess certain characteristics which those who did not volunteer do not possess.

The various methods which can be used to select a sample are discussed below.

6.3.1 Random sampling

For small populations, numbers might be chosen at *random*, as in a raffle where every member of the population is given a number and then the numbers are pulled out of a hat. For large populations, numbers are taken from tables of random numbers (see Appendix B) or are created by a random number generating machine such as a computer. A sample must be large enough to ensure that if some of the very high or very low (extreme) members of a population are chosen to be in the sample, they do not affect any results obtained from the sample more than they should. The larger the sample chosen, the better it will represent the population as a whole.

Bias will occur if samples are chosen deliberately by a person, as this will lead to favouritism, or chosen in a haphazard fashion. A sample from a population which has been chosen to be random and is large enough should turn out to be completely unbiased. An unbiased sample is one which will give the views of each section of a population in a balanced way and should be made up of members from each section of the population.

6.3.2 Systematic sampling

In *systematic sampling* the population is divided by the required sample size (n) and the sample chosen by taking every 'nth' subject. Figure 6.3 gives an example of systematic sampling.

Figure 6.3 Systematic sampling

Example

Population: 300
Sample size: 10

First divide the population by the required sample size:

$$\frac{300}{10} = 30$$

Start by selecting a randomly chosen number between 1 and 30, say 23. Then choose the thirtieth one after that until ten have been selected:

23, 53, 83, 113, 143, 173, 203, 233, 263, 293

6.3.3   Stratified sampling

With a relatively small sample, simple random sampling might result in some members of the population being significantly under or over-represented. *Stratified sampling* overcomes this problem as each identifiable strata of the population is taken into account. For example, if your sampling frame consists of all the employees in a particular company, you may identify the following strata: directors, managers, clerical workers and production workers, and if 25 per cent of employees were clerical workers, you would ensure that 25 per cent of your sample comprised clerical workers. Figure 6.4 gives an example of stratified sampling.

Figure 6.4 Stratified sampling

Example

Population: 850 (580 females and 270 males)
Sample size: 100

$$\frac{580}{850} \times 100 = 68 \text{ females and } \frac{270}{850} \times 100 = 32 \text{ males}$$

Example using percentages

Sample size = 1000

Age band	Percentage required	Sample size
0–20	36	360
21–40	22	220
41–60	28	280
60 +	14	140

6.3.4   Other types of sampling

Quota sampling involves giving interviewers quotas of different types of people to question. For example, 25 men under the age of 21; 30 women over 50, etc. It is widely used in marketing research.

Cluster sampling involves making a random selection from a sampling frame listing groups of units rather than individual units. Every individual belonging to the selected groups is then interviewed or examined. This can be a useful approach, particularly for face-to-face interviews, where for time or economy reasons it is necessary to reduce the physical areas covered. For example, a certain number of project teams within a company might be selected and every member of the selected teams interviewed.

Multistage sampling is used where the groups selected in a cluster sample are so large that a sub-sample must be selected from each group. For example, first select a sample of companies. From each company, select a sample of departments and from each department select a sample of managers to survey.

Snowball sampling or *networking* is associated with phenomenological studies where it is essential to include people with experience of the phenomena being studied in the sample. For example, supposing you are interested in how people cope with redundancy. Perhaps you are able to find some people who have experienced being made redundant who are willing to take part in your survey. One of the questions you would ask them would be whether they know of anyone else who has also been through the same experience they could put you in touch with. In this way you can extend your sample of participants.

Judgemental sampling is similar to snowball sampling as the participants are selected by the researcher on the strength of their experience of the phenomenon under study. However, in judgemental sampling the researcher makes the decision prior to the commencement of the survey and does not pursue other contacts which may arise during the course of the study.

Natural sampling is fairly common in business research and occurs when the researcher has little influence on the composition of the sample. For example, only particular employees are involved in the phenomenon being investigated or only certain employees are available at the time of the study. It is important to try to avoid the situation where the employer selects the sample on criteria which are not divulged to you, since it is possible that such a sample will be biased.

It can sometimes be very difficult to obtain a sample, particularly if you are dealing with sensitive issues. In addition to the sampling methods we have already identified, Lee (1993) suggests a number of other approaches which can be useful if you have difficulty in obtaining a sample by the above means, for whatever reason.

Advertising can be used, either in local or national newspapers, or you can visit locations where members of your population are likely to congregate. Lee calls this *outcropping*. For example, if you wish to find out how people cope with unemployment, you are likely to find a suitable sample of individuals with experience of this by visiting a Job Centre or employment bureaux. However, you may find that you already have access to a suitable sample. For example, Fineman (1983) used his position as a counsellor on a government-sponsored career review programme to study while-collar unemployment.

Another approach is to join a club or society which caters for the phenomenon you are investigating. For example, you might try joining a fitness club in order to meet people who use exercise as a means of controlling stress at work, or an angling club to find a sample of fishermen in order to investigate their views on licensing regulations.

Piggybacking is where you extract your sample from an existing survey or use another survey to obtain your population simultaneously. Finally, you can use *screening* to select a sample. For example, if you were interested in why people purchase a particular product, you would interview a large number of people and screen out for your sample, all those who buy the product.

Many of the above methods present problems of *sample bias*, mainly because a sampling frame cannot be unambiguously identified in advance. In other words, the sample will not be representative of the population as a whole. In a positivistic study you must recognise this limitation to your research and attempt to minimise the bias. You will need to justify your sample selection method in your research report. In a phenomenological study sample bias is not likely to be important, but you may still need to discuss the issue in your research report.

Two other problems need to be recognised. One is the ethical dilemmas concerned with some methods of sample selection; the other is your personal safety when it comes to conducting the research. We discussed both these problems in Chapter 2.

6.3.5 Sample size

There is a temptation, particularly with questionnaire surveys, to pick as large a sample as possible. Although such an approach is not necessary if you are willing to accept a degree of uncertainty in the conclusions you draw, the question of the appropriate number of subjects to include in a sample is very complex. All the various factors involved are discussed in detail by Czaja and Blair (1996). Essentially, it is a question of deciding how accurate you want your results to be and how confident you want to be in that answer. You will also need some indication of the anticipated response, possibly taken from previous studies or a pilot survey you have conducted yourself.

Clegg (1990) suggests that there are three main considerations to bear in mind:

▶ the kind of statistical analysis which is planned
▶ the expected variability within the samples and the results, based on experience (the greater the expected variation, the larger the sample)
▶ the traditions in your particular research area regarding appropriate sample size.

As well as reiterating Clegg's advice, Robson (1993, p. 139) emphasises 'the need to consider what you are going to do with the data in terms of analysis at the design stage'. You will remember from Chapter 5 that part of the process of research design is to select an appropriate methodology. This step encompasses choosing both methods by which you can collect data and also methods for its analysis. We will be discussing the former in this chapter and the methods by which you can analyse quantitative data in Chapter 7.

6.4 Data

Data refers to known facts or things used as a basis for inference or reckoning. Strictly speaking it is a plural word, the singular of which is *datum*. Some authors draw a distinction between *data* and *information*, by defining information as knowledge; data which has been organised into a useful form. This obviously depends on how the data is perceived and the use to which it will be put. For example, you may consider that the transcript of an interview you have held with a survey participant forms part of your research data which you later analyse, attempt to draw conclusions from and thus make a contribution to knowledge. On the other hand, the interviewee may consider that he or she was simply giving you information.

In both positivistic and phenomenological research we are interested in collecting data about the variables under study. In the following sections we examine the two main sources of data and the different ways in which data can be classified. These classifications have important implications when it comes to analysing quantitative data (see Chapter 7) and qualitative data (see Chapter 8).

6.4.1 Sources of data

There are two main sources of data. Original data is known as *primary data*, which is data collected at source. Examples include *survey data*, which is obtained in an uncontrolled situation by asking questions or making observations, and *experimental data*, which is obtained in a controlled situation by making experiments.

Secondary data is data which already exists, such as books, documents (for example, published statistics, annual reports and accounts of companies, and internal records kept by organisations such as personnel records) and films. We looked at the main sources of secondary data in Chapter 4 in the context of the literature search. When data is organised in a useful form it becomes information.

6.4.2   Types of data

Data can be described as *qualitative* or *quantitative*. As the names suggest, qualitative data is concerned with qualities and non-numerical characteristics, whilst quantitative data is all data that is collected in numerical form. Quantitative data can be classified as *discrete* or *continuous*. Discrete data can take only one of a range of distinct values; for example, number of employees. On the other hand, continuous data can take any value within a given range, such as time or length.

There are a number of different measurement scales for recording and describing quantitative data. The *nominal (named) scale* permits only the classification of data, which will allow you to make statements of equality or difference, but nothing else. For example, a sample of subjects can be classified according to the variable 'occupation' where you would count how many directors, managers, administrators, etc. there were in the sample. Although the *mode* (see Chapter 7) might be used, very few statistics can be properly applied to data collected in this form.

Measures on an *ordinal (ordered) scale* have the same amount of information as measures on a nominal scale, since data can be classified in terms of equality and difference. However, ordinal scales provide additional information since they permit you to order individual data and make decisions such as this score is greater than or less than another; for example, employee grades of A, B and C, or choices ranked as first, second or third. Since the *arithmetic mean* (see Chapter 7) cannot be calculated with data recorded in this form, the use of many other statistics are also excluded.

An *interval scale* has all the characteristics of both nominal and ordinal scales, but provides additional information regarding the degree of difference between individual data items within a set or group. Thus, if you have an interval scale you can place each data item precisely along the scale and determine exactly what the intervals are. Most measures of human characteristics have interval properties. For example, the interval between an IQ score of 100 and 115 is the same as the interval between 110 and 125, or the interval between an assignment mark of 50 per cent and 55 per cent is the same as the interval between 60 per cent and 65 per cent. If properly constructed, measure of attitudes may also have interval properties. However, precision in interval scales is limited; for example, it is not possible to say that an individual with an IQ of 120 is twice as intelligent as an individual with an IQ of 60. For such decisions, the scale must have *ratio* properties. Another drawback of the interval scale is that some statistics, such as the *geometric mean*, are excluded from use with data collected in this form.

Ratio scales represent the highest level of precision. A ratio scale is a mathematical number system which must have a fixed zero point to the scale as in the examples of height, weight and time. Ratio scales allow ratio as well as interval decisions to be made, thus allowing us to say that something is so many times as big, heavy, bright, etc. as another. The advantage of using the ratio scale is that any statistics can be used on data collected in this form. Some scales, such as temperature, may appear to have ratio properties, but in fact are only interval scales. For example, you cannot say that a temperature of 30°C is twice as hot as a temperature of 15°C. This is because the Centigrade scale does not represent the absolute amount of heat available, whereas temperature measured in degrees Kelvin does have ratio properties.

6.5   Data collection methods

Whether you are following a broadly *positivist* or *phenomenological paradigm* (see Chapter 3), there will always be a combination of quantitative and qualitative inputs into your data generating activities. The balance will depend on your analytical requirements and the overall purpose of your research. Quantitative and qualitative approaches to data collection present a mixture of advantages and disadvantages. Although we examine methods of data analysis separately in Chapters 7 and 8, there are some aspects which need to be considered before you choose your data collection method.

One of the main advantages of a quantitative approach to data collection is the relative ease and speed with which the research can be conducted. However, if you adopt a quantitative approach to data collection, the analytical and predictive power which can be gained from statistical analysis must be set against the issues of sample representativeness (see Section 6.2), errors in measurement and quantification, and the danger of reductionism. In a descriptive study, the use of quantitative methods can give a spurious objectivity to information which can lead to reductionist tendencies. This means that the richness of the data and its contextual implications may be lost, thus contributing to a narrower and less 'real' interpretation of phenomena.

Qualitative data collection methods can be expensive and time consuming, although it can be argued that qualitative data in business research provides a more 'real' basis for analysis and interpretation. Moreover, a qualitative approach presents problems relating to rigour and subjectivity. It is important to remember that the methods we describe in this chapter do not necessarily provide quantitative or qualitative data; it depends on how you use them.

6.5.1   Critical incident technique

Critical incident technique is widely used during in-depth interviews to generate qualitative data. Developed by Flanagan (1954), it is 'a procedure for gathering certain important facts concerning behaviour in defined situations' (Flanagan, 1954, p. 335). Although called a technique, it is not a set of rigid rules, but a flexible set of principles which should be modified and adapted according to the circumstances.

Adopting a positivistic approach, Flanagan recommends that only simple types of judgements should be required of observers, who should be qualified. All observations should be evaluated by the observer in terms of an agreed statement of the purpose of the activity. By following these principles, it is possible to gather facts 'in a rather objective fashion with only a minimum of inferences and interpretation of a more subjective nature' (Flanagan, 1954).

The procedure for establishing the general aims of an activity, the training of the interviewers and the manner in which observations should be made are all predetermined. However, what is of prime interest to researchers is the way in which Flanagan concentrates on an observable activity (the incident), where the intended purpose seems to be clear and the effect appears to be logical; hence, the incident is critical. Figure 6.5 shows an example of a form for use by an interviewer when collecting effective critical incidents.

Such a controlled approach would be an anathema to many phenomenological researchers, although their investigations might reflect this theme of exploration. A much more open approach was adopted in a study by MacKinlay (1986) which is quoted by Easterby-Smith, Thorpe and Lowe (1991, p. 84). A questionnaire was sent to householders which contained six open-ended questions. The questionnaire allowed a third of an A4 page per question for the reply, but some respondents added additional sheets. The questions were preceded by the following explanation: 'These questions are open-ended and I have kept them to a few vital areas of interest. All will require you to reflect back on decisions and reasons for decisions you have made.' The six questions shown below.

1. Please think about an occasion when you improved your home. What improvements did you make?

Figure 6.5 Example of a form for collecting effective critical incidents

'Think of the last time you saw one of your subordinates do something that was very helpful to your group in meeting your production schedule.' (Pause until he indicates that he has such an incident in mind.) 'Did his action result in increase in production of as much as one per cent for that day? – or some similar period?'

(If the answer is 'no,' say) 'I wonder if you can think of the last time that someone did something that did have this much of an effect in increasing production.' (When he indicates he has such a situation in mind, say) 'What were the general circumstances leading up to this incident?'

. . . .

. . . .

'Tell me exactly what this person did that was so helpful at that time.'

. . . .

. . . .

'Why was this so helpful in getting your group's job done?'

. . . .

. . . .

'When did this incident happen?'. . . . .

'What was this person's job?'. . . . .

'How long has he been on this job?'. . . . .

'How old is he?'. . . . .

Source: Flanagan (1954) p. 342.

2. On that occasion what made you do it?
3. Did you receive any help? If 'yes', please explain what help you received.
4. Have you wanted to improve your home in any other way but could not?
5. What improvements did you wish to make?
6. What stopped you from doing it?

This study demonstrates the simplicity and open nature of the questions which can be used with critical incident technique. It is quite likely that many researchers are employing the technique informally without realising it. The technique can be of considerable value in generating data in an interview where there is a lack of focus or the interviewees have difficulty in expressing their opinions.

Despite its advantages there are a number of problems associated with this data collection method. Respondents are being asked to remember a particular event and the reasons for their choice are not evident. There is also a danger that they may fail to remember important facts or rationalise events to impose a certain logic and coherence which did not exist at the time. Finally, there remains the problem of how to analyse the data thus collected.

6.5.2   Diaries

Diaries are a method for collecting data which can be used under either a phenomenological or a positivistic methodology. A diary is a daily record of events or thoughts and is typically used to capture and record what people do, think and feel. Participants are asked to record relevant information in diary forms or booklets over a specified period of time. The information recorded may be quantitative (for example, a form of activity sampling from which patterns may be identified statistically) or qualitative (for example, a journal or record of events kept by employees). Plummer (1983) distinguishes between:

► **Logs:** These are detailed diaries in which participants keep a record of the time they spend on their activities.
► **Diaries:** These are diaries in which participants keep descriptive records of their day-to-day lives.
► **Diary-interviews:** With this method participants are asked to keep a diary in a particular format for a short period. Detailed questions are then developed from the diaries and these form the basis of an in-depth interview.

In a business research project, the use of diaries offers a method for collecting data from the perspective of the individual. They can be a useful means of gaining sensitive information or an alternative to using direct observation. In contrast to *participant observation* (see Section 6.5.4), where the researcher is involved in the research, in a diary study, the data is collected and presented largely within the reference frame of the writer of the diary. Diary methods allow the perspectives of different writers to be compared.

Practical problems associated with diary studies include selecting participants who can express themselves well in writing, focusing the diary and providing encouragement over the record-keeping period. As with many other methods of data collection, there is also the issue of *confidentiality* (see Chapter 2). In common with participant observation, setting up a diary study may involve considerable time and

Figure 6.6 Diary methods and observation compared

Advantages of diary methods

▶ Diaries greatly increase the possible coverage of:
   numbers and types of managers
   geographical and industrial distribution
   length of time, unless only a small number are observed for a long period
▶ The classification of activities is made by the person involved and not by an observer who may be unfamiliar with all the technical aspects of the job
▶ All time can be recorded, whereas an observer may be excluded from confidential discussions

Disadvantages of diary methods

▶ There are severe limitations if the study is concerned with comparability, although these are reduced if the managers are a homogeneous group
▶ It is difficult to obtain a random sample as the researcher must rely on volunteers
▶ There is always some unreliability in recording

effort; also bias may easily occur in diary entries. For example, the participants may misreport their activities or change their behaviour so that certain activities can be reported.

Stewart (1965) used diaries as part of a study of manager's jobs and offers a useful summary of the advantages and disadvantages compared with using methods of observation. Figure 6.6 gives details.

As a sole method of data collection it would appear that diaries are more useful for generating quantitative rather than qualitative data. To do this effectively, you will need to ensure that the participants use the same format for recording information and you must be cautious over the bias and unreliability of the recording. Although diaries can be used to generate qualitative data, their best use may be as the basis for subsequent in-depth *interviews* (see Section 6.5.3).

6.5.3   Focus groups

Focus groups are normally associated with a phenomenological methodology. They are used to gather data relating to the feelings and opinions of a group of people who are involved in a common situation. Under the guidance of a group leader, selected participants are stimulated to discuss their opinions, reactions and feelings about a product, service, type of situation or concept. For example, you might wish to get a group of employees from a particular company together to discuss what they feel about the profit-sharing scheme in operation, or a group of consumers to discuss their views on a particular brand of toothpaste.

Figure 6.7 Procedure for forming a focus group

▶ Invite a group of people whom you consider have sufficient experiences in common on the topic to meet at a neutral location

▶ Introduce the group members and discuss the purpose of the study and what will happen in the focus group

▶ If possible, give visual examples of the subject matter. For example, if you want the group to discuss the merits of different brands of toothpaste, have the products on display

▶ Start the session with a broad, open question (see Section 6.6.1). This can be displayed using a flip chart or overhead projector

▶ Allow the group to discuss the topics among themselves, but intervene to ensure that all participants have an opportunity to contribute

▶ Use a prepared list of topics and intervene to ensure that all topics are covered

▶ Enlist the help of two observers and, if possible, record the proceedings on video

Listening to other group members' views encourages participants to voice their own opinions. 'The explicit use of the group interaction to produce data and insights that would be less accessible without the interaction found in a group' (Morgan, 1988, p. 12) provides the researcher with rich data.

The researcher should try to create a relaxed atmosphere and record what is said, or enlist the help of others to observe and record what is said. Figure 6.7 shows the main steps involved.

Focus groups combine both *interviewing* (see Section 6.5.4) and *observation* (see Section 6.5.5). They are often used in pilot studies to develop a *questionnaire* (see Section 6.5.7) or *interview schedule* for a quantitative study. They are mainly used in market research, but can be useful in the preliminary stages of any study.

The interaction of the participants should ensure that all the issues relating to the chosen topic(s) are covered, thus providing the boundaries of the study. The data generated from a focus group is qualitative. It will provide a guide to the matters you will need to concentrate on and the most pertinent questions to ask in any subsequent questionnaires or interviews. Because designing questions is a crucial element of many of the data collection methods in this chapter, we examine this topic separately in Section 6.6.

6.5.4   Interviews

Interviews are associated with both positivist and phenomenological methodologies. They are a method of collecting data in which selected participants are asked questions in order to find out what they do, think or feel. Interviews make it easy to compare answers and may be face-to-face, voice-to-voice or screen-to-screen; conducted with individuals or a group of individuals.

A positivistic approach suggests structured, *closed questions* (see Section 6.6.1) which have been prepared beforehand, as used in market research surveys, for example. Verbal or visual prompts may be required. A phenomenological approach suggests unstructured questions, where the questions have not been prepared beforehand. *Unstructured* or *semi-structured* interviews are likely to be very time consuming and there may be problems with recording the questions and answers, controlling the range of topics and, later, analysing the data. Many researchers find it essential to tape-record such interviews. Questions are likely to be *open-ended* and probes may be used to explore answers in more depth. Because designing questions is a crucial element of many of the data collection methods in this chapter, we examine this topic separately in Section 6.6.

Easterby-Smith, Thorpe and Lowe (1991) suggest that unstructured or semi-structured interviews are an appropriate method when:

▶ it is necessary to understand the construct that the interviewee uses as a basis for his or her opinions and beliefs about a particular matter or situation
▶ one aim of the interview is to develop an understanding of the respondent's 'world' so that the researcher might influence it, either independently or collaboratively (as might be the case with action research)
▶ the step-by-step logic of a situation is not clear
▶ the subject matter is highly confidential or commercially sensitive
▶ the interviewee may be reluctant to be truthful about this issue other than confidentially in a one-to-one situation.

One aspect of semi-structured and unstructured interviews is that the issues discussed, the questions raised and the matters explored change from one interview to the next as different aspects of the topic are revealed. This process of open discovery is the strength of such interviews, but it is important to recognise that emphasis and balance of the emerging issues may depend on the order in which you interview your participants.

There are several problems associated with conducting interviews. The whole process can be very time consuming and expensive, and in some cases a short questionnaire may be more appropriate. In common with a number of other data collection methods, there is the issue of *confidentiality* (see Chapter 2). In a positivist study, a large number of interviewees are needed and this gives rise to the problem of obtaining *access* to an appropriate sample (see Chapter 2).

You will need to ensure that all the interviews are conducted in the same way. This not only means that the same questions should be asked, but also that they should be posed in the same way. Furthermore, you must ensure that each respondent will understand the question in the same way. This is known as *stimulus equivalence* and demands considerable thought and skill in question design.

With any type of interview there is the problem of the effect the interviewer has on the process; for example, there may be an element of class, race or sex bias. This can be illustrated if we look at the possibility of sexual bias. Rosenthal (1966) argues that male and female researchers sometimes obtain significantly different data from their subjects and the following behaviour occurs:

- Female subjects tend to be treated more attentively and considerately than male subjects
- Female researchers tend to smile more often than male researchers
- Male researchers tend to place themselves closer to male subjects than do female researchers
- Male researchers tend to show higher levels of body activity than do female researchers; when the subject is male, both male and female researchers tend to show higher levels of body activity than they do when the subject is a female.
- Female subjects rate male researchers as more friendly and as having more pleasant and expressive voices than female researchers
- Both male and female researchers behave more warmly towards female subjects than they do towards male subjects, with male researchers the warmer of the two.

In addition to these problems, interviewees may have certain expectations about the interview and therefore give what they consider to be a 'correct' or 'acceptable' response. Lee (1993) suggests that to some extent these problems can be overcome by increasing the depth of the interview. It is difficult to predict or measure potential bias, but you should be alert to the fact that it can distort your data and hence your findings.

You should bear in mind that events which have taken place prior to the interview may also affect the interviewee's responses. For example, he or she may have just received promotion or a salary increase, a cut in hours or a reprimand. If time allows, you will find it useful to arrive at the interview venue 15 minutes beforehand to assimilate the atmosphere and the environment, and spend the first few minutes putting the interviewee at ease.

Generally interviews are one-to-one, but may involve other people. You may find it useful to have two interviewers conducting each interview. This can help ensure that all the points are fully explored and nuances and gestures, as well as words, are recorded.

Sometimes the interviewee is accompanied by another person. This is often to ensure that all the questions you ask can be answered. You must be alert to the fact that with two interviewees, the dynamics of the interviewing process will change. Even a single interviewee may be 'wearing two hats'. For example, the finance director of a company may also be a director of other companies or involved in other organisations; an employee may also be a trade unionist or a shareholder. When you are asking questions, you must determine which 'hat' the interviewees are wearing, and whether they are giving their own opinions or making a policy statement.

Despite their disadvantages, interviews permit the researcher to ask more complex questions and ask follow-up questions, which is not possible in a questionnaire. Thus, further information can be obtained. An interview may permit a higher degree of confidence in the replies than questionnaire responses and can take account of non-verbal communications such as the attitude and behaviour of the interviewee.

If you are conducting interviews as part of a positivistic survey, it is important that you abide by strict rules to ensure that interviewer bias is kept to the minimum. Brenner (1985) recommends the following:

- Read the questions as they are worded in the questionnaire
- Read slowly and use correct intonation and emphasis
- Ask the question in the correct order
- Ask every question that applies
- Use response cards when required
- Record exactly what the respondent says
- Do not answer for the respondent
- Show an interest in the answers given by the respondent
- Make sure that you have understood each answer adequately and that it is adequate
- Do not show approval or disapproval of any answer.

It is important to determine how you will record the responses to your questions (see Section 6.8) before you commence any interviews if you are not using a pre-designed questionnaire. One method is to use an audio recorder. After putting your interviewee at ease, you may find it useful to spend a little time establishing a rapport before starting to record. You may need to switch the recorder off if your interviewee wishes to discuss confidential or sensitive information, although he or she may be happy for you to continue to take notes. You may find that you can encourage a higher degree of frankness by ostentatiously switching off the recorder at such moments.

As well as deciding on the structure and recording of an interview, you must also be able to bring it to a satisfactory conclusion and the interviewee must be aware that it is ending. One device is to say that you have asked all the questions you wanted to and do they have any final comments that they would like to make. You should then conclude by thanking them and reassuring them that you will be treating what they have told you as confidential. It is beneficial if you can then spend a little time reflecting on the interview and, if possible, 'debrief' yourself with your supervisor or a colleague.

6.5.5   Observation

In its broadest sense, *observation* is a method for collecting data associated with either a positivistic or a phenomenological methodology. Observation can take place in a laboratory setting or in a natural setting. A *natural setting* is a 'research environment that would have existed had researchers never studied it' (Vogt, 1993, p. 150)

Observing individuals in a laboratory or natural setting may make them wonder what you are doing. They may try harder or become nervous. These are known as *demand characteristics*, because you are making demands on the individual, and this may affect the research. It may be possible to minimise the demand characteristics by not stating the exact purpose of the research. For example, instead of saying you are studying the effect of lighting on productivity levels, you could say you are investigating the effect of different environments on job satisfaction. For ethical reasons, after the experiment you should state the true purpose, although some researchers would argue that even subsequent disclosure is unethical. There is a risk that the researcher may give cues to those being observed, even if they have not been told the exact purpose of the research. This can be overcome by using a second researcher to conduct the research who does not know the purpose of the experiment.

There are two ways in which observation can be conducted: non-participant and participant observation. The purpose of *non-participant observation* is to observe and record what people do in terms of their actions and their behaviour without the researcher being involved. The observer is separate from the activities taking place and the subjects of the research may or may not be aware that they are being observed. There are a number of ways in which data can be collected without the observer writing anything down on the spot; for example, by using a video or a still camera. If the focus of the research is dialogue, audio recordings can be made. Whichever method is used, reliable records will have to be produced and in a positivistic study a grid will be used. For example, if the study involves recording activities in the workplace, the grid might show what types of activity take place, how often, the duration and the intensity.

Participant observation is a method of collecting data where the researcher is fully involved with the participants and the phenomena being researched. The aim is to provide the means of obtaining a detailed understanding of values, motives and practices of those being observed. Some of the factors which should be taken into consideration when choosing the role of the participant observer include:

- the purpose of the research
- the cost of the research
- the extent to which access can be gained
- the extent to which the researcher would be comfortable in the role
- the amount of time the researcher has available.

There are a number of problems associated with observation techniques. One problem is that you cannot control variables in a natural setting, but by observing the behaviour in two different settings you can draw comparisons. Other problems are concerned with ethics, objectivity, visibility, technology for recording what people say and/or do, boredom, and the impact the researcher has on those observed. Problems of *observer bias* may arise, such as when one observer interprets an action differently from a colleague. Another problem can be that the observer fails to observe some activities because of distractions. In addition, the grid designed for recording observations may be deficient because it is ambiguous or incomplete.

6.5.6   Protocol analysis

In business research *protocol analysis* is a data collection method used to identify the mental processes in problem solving, and is usually associated with a phenomenological methodology. The aim is to ascertain the way that people behave and think in a particular situation. The researcher gives some form of written problem to a practitioner who is experienced in that field. The participant then solves the problem, but verbally explains the way he or she is tackling it. This allows the researcher to record the process. Sometimes the participant generates further questions and these can form the basis of subsequent analysis and research.

There are a number of ways in which the verbal data can be generated. *Retrospective verbalisation* takes place when the participant is asked to describe processes after they have occurred. *Concurrent verbalisation* takes place when the participant is asked to describe and explain their thoughts as they undertake a task. There are two types of concurrent verbalisation: *directed reports* and *think-aloud protocol*. The former result when participants are asked to describe only specific behaviours, and the latter when they are asked to relay every thought that comes into their heads.

Smagorinsky (1989, p. 475) describes protocol analysis as 'an expensive and meticulous research method that has had its share of growing pains'. However, the method offers a tool for the researcher who is interested in how individuals solve business problems. Clarkson (1962) used the technique to examine the decision-making processes of a US bank trust investment officer. Day (1986) used it to establish what information is used by investment analysts when making decisions. The reasons she gave for using protocol analysis were as follows:

▶ it helps to reduce the problem of interviewer bias
▶ the possibility of omitting potentially important areas or aspects is reduced
▶ the technique is open-ended and provides considerable flexibility.

Day makes the point that a major drawback of using the retrospective verbalisation method is that it does not consider 'a real-time situation, but rather an action replay' (Day, 1986, p. 296). The alternative, concurrent verbalisation, involves the researcher maintaining a continuous presence is usually too time consuming and disruptive to be considered a feasible choice.

Protocol analysis studies tend to be small, involving fewer than a dozen participants. The process of constructing the problem which is given to the practitioners is difficult and can be regarded as part of the research process. The study must not only seek to contrive a problem which is realistic and address the fundamental issues, but also it must place some limits on its scope. Furthermore, the researcher must have sufficient knowledge to be able to understand and interpret the logic and methods the practitioners use to arrive at their solutions.

Protocol analysis has wider application than we have implied above. For example, Smagorinsky (1994) used it to study writing and Bolton (1991) used concurrent verbal protocols to pre-test questionnaires. The latter found the technique was useful for evaluating draft questionnaires and for identifying questions associated with information problems, but warns that the approach 'is time consuming and labor intensive' (Bolton, 1991, p. 565).

6.5.7   Questionnaires

Questionnaires are associated with both positivistic and phenomenological methodologies. A questionnaire is a list of carefully structured questions, chosen after considerable testing, with a view to eliciting reliable responses from a chosen sample. The aim is to find out what a selected group of participants do, think or feel.

Under a positivistic paradigm questionnaires can be used for large-scale surveys. Each question can be coded at the design stage and completed questionnaires can be computer processed for ease of analysis. A positivistic approach suggests that *closed questions* should be used, whereas a phenomenological approach suggests *open-ended questions*. The latter can only be coded after they have been completed by the respondents, after which they, too, can be computer processed, although it may be more appropriate to use one of the analytical methods we discuss in Chapter 8. Consequently, open-ended questions do not lend themselves to large-scale surveys. Because designing questions is a crucial element of many of the data collection methods in this chapter, we examine this topic separately in Section 6.6.

As with structured interviews (see Section 6.5.3), you need to be sure that each respondent will understand the question in the same way and that every respondent is asked the questions in exactly the same way as the others. This is not a problem with a postal questionnaire, but may become an issue if the questions are asked face-to-face or by telephone.

Figure 6.8 summarises the main decisions involved when using questionnaires. These decisions are fundamental to a positivistic study, but some will be less important in phenomenological research.

Questionnaires are a popular method for collecting data. A questionnaire survey is cheaper and less time-consuming than conducting interviews, and very large samples can be taken. In addition to the issue of *confidentiality* (see Chapter 2), there are a number of problems associated with the use of questionnaires which we examine next.

Question design is concerned with the type of questions, their wording, the reliability and validity of the responses. Because designing questions is a crucial element of many of the data collection methods in this chapter, we examine this topic separately in Section 6.6.

Presentation can do much to encourage and help respondents to complete a questionnaire correctly and it can also make the subsequent analysis of the data much easier. The purpose of the questionnaire must be apparent; the respondents must know the context in which the questions are being posed. This can be achieved by either attaching a covering letter or by starting off the questionnaire with an explanatory paragraph. It is necessary to give precise instructions to the respondents

Figure 6.8 Main decisions when using questionnaires

- ► Sample size
- ► Type of questions
- ► Wording of the questions and how to ensure that they are intelligible and unambiguous
- ► Design of the questionnaire, including any instructions
- ► Wording of any accompanying letter
- ► Method of distribution and return of completed questionnaires
- ► Tests for validity and reliability and when they should be applied
- ► Methods for collating and analysing the data thus collected
- ► Any action to be taken if questionnaires are not returned

regarding whether boxes have to be ticked, whether more than one box can be ticked or whether numbers or words should be circled to indicate the response. ✓

Remember to number each questionnaire. This will enable you to maintain control of the project and, if appropriate, you will be able to identify which respondents have replied and send follow-up letters to those who have not. Questions should be presented in a logical order, often moving from general to specific topics. This is known as funnelling. In more complex questionnaires it may be necessary to use filter questions. This is where only respondents who have given a certain answer are directed to another batch of particular questions. For example, 'Do you normally do the household shopping? *If YES go to Question 12; if NO, go to Question 17.*'

There is some debate regarding the best location for the classification questions which ask about the respondents age, education, etc. Some authors believe that they are best placed at the beginning, so that respondents gain confidence in answering easy questions; others prefer to place them at the end, so that the respondent starts with the more interesting questions. If your questions are of a sensitive nature, it may be best to start with the non-threatening classification questions. If you have a large number of classification questions, it could be better to put them at the end, so that the respondent is not deterred at the start.

It is essential that you *pilot* or test your questionnaire as fully as possible before distributing it. At the very least, have colleagues or friends read through it and play the role of respondents, even if they know little about the subject. It is amazing how even a non-specialist friend can spot a glaring error. However, the best advice is to try your questionnaire out on people who are similar to those in your sample. It may take several drafts, with tests at every stage, before you are satisfied that you have got it right.

Cost is often an important element when it comes to deciding on the best method to *distribute* your questionnaire and this will depend on the size and location of the sample. Each has its own strengths and weaknesses.

▶ **By post:** This is a commonly used and reasonably inexpensive method, even if you have a large sample. The questionnaire and covering letter are posted to the sample, usually with a prepaid envelope for returning the completed questionnaire. If you are conducting your survey in a particular company it may be possible to use the internal mail. Postal distribution of questionnaires is easy to administer, although the response rate can be very low. Response rates of 10 per cent or less are not uncommon and this introduces the problem of sample bias because those who respond may have a particular interest in the topic and therefore are not representative of the population. Response rates can be increased by keeping the questionnaire as short as possible (no longer than two sides of A4) and using closed questions of a simple and non-sensitive nature. It is valuable to send a follow-up questionnaire to the non-respondents and these responses can be used for checking bias.

▶ **By telephone:** This can be a valuable method to employ as it reduces the costs associated with face-to-face interviews, but still allows some aspect of personal contact. As the telephone has become more widespread so the use of this technique has grown and in the USA is the most widely used survey method. A relatively long questionnaire can be used and it can be helpful with sensitive and complex questions. Responses rates can be as high as 90 per cent, but there is the inherent problem that the results will be biased towards people who have a telephone or are willing to answer questions in this way.

▶ **Face-to-face:** The questionnaire can be presented to the respondent in the street or in the home or office, indeed in any convenient place for the interviewee. It is an expensive method and time consuming, particularly if conducted in a location which is the choice of the interviewee. However, this method offers the advantage that response rates tend to be high and comprehensive data can be collected. It is often very useful if sensitive or complex questions need to be asked. Where the interview is conducted in the interviewee's home, it is possible to use a lengthy questionnaire.

▶ **Group distribution:** This method is only appropriate where the survey is being conducted in one or a few locations; for example, a number of factories. In such instances, you may be able to agree that the sample or sub-groups are assembled in one room at the same time. You can then explain the questionnaire to them and answer any queries. This is a convenient, low cost technique for administering questionnaires and the number of usable questionnaires which are collected is high.

▶ **Individual distribution:** This is a variation of group distribution. If the sample is situated in one location, it may be possible to distribute, and collect, the questionnaires individually. As well as a place of work, this approach can be used in theatres, restaurants and even on trains and buses. It is normally necessary to supply pens or pencils for the completion of the questionnaires. You may encounter problems with sample bias if you use this method; for example, you may only capture patrons who visit a theatre on a Monday, or travel at a particular time. However, if properly designed, this method can be very precise in targeting the most appropriate sample.

The major problems associated with questionnaires, particularly those distributed by post, is what to do about *non-response bias*. There are two main types. *Questionnaire non-response* occurs if all the questionnaires are not returned; *item non-response* occurs if all the questions have not been answered. Non-response is often crucial in a questionnaire survey because your research design will be based on the fact that you are going to generalise from the sample to the population. If you have not collected responses from all the members of your sample, the data may be biased and thus not representative of the population.

Wallace and Mellor (1988) describe the following three methods for dealing with questionnaire non-response.

1. To analyse and compare responses by date of reply. One method is to send a follow-up letter to those who do not respond to the first enquiry. The questionnaires which result from the follow-up letter are then compared with those from the first request
2. A comparison of the characteristics of those who responded with those of the population, assuming you know them
3. A comparison of the characteristics of the respondents with non-respondents from the sample, assuming you have the relevant data such as age, occupation, etc.

Typical examples of item non-response include omitting to answer questions or not answering questions correctly, perhaps by ticking more than one box when only one response is required. There are a number of *ad hoc* methods for dealing with such problems, ranging from making an educated guess from the respondent's other answers to using statistical techniques. If you have a large number of non-responses to a particular question, this is usually evidence that the question was faulty and should be omitted from the analysis.

6.6   Designing questions

Many of the data collection methods we have described in this chapter rely on questions as the vehicle for extracting the primary research data. If you are conducting a positivistic study, before you can begin *designing questions* for an interview or a questionnaire you must know a substantial amount about your subject, so that you can decide what the most appropriate questions will be. This knowledge may have come from your literature search and other studies which have used questionnaires. Alternatively, you may have conducted a number of exploratory interviews.

If you are conducting a phenomenological study, you will probably want to keep an open mind. In this case, you will not design specific questions in advance, but encourage the participant to discuss various topics.

When designing questions, it is essential to bear your potential audience in mind. If your sample is composed of intelligent people who are likely to be knowledgeable and interested in the research topic, you can aim for a fairly high level of complexity. The general rules for designing questions are shown in Figure 6.9. These fundamental aspects of question design are important, because once you have asked the questions, there is often little you can do to enhance the quality of the answers or, in the case of a questionnaire, increase the response rate.

It can be helpful to the respondent if you qualify your questions in some way, perhaps by referring to a specific time period, rather than requiring the respondent to search their memory for an answer. For example, instead of asking, 'Have you ever bought Nescafé decaffeinated coffee?' you might ask, 'Have you bought Nescafé decaffeinated coffee in the last three weeks?' A question can also be qualified by referring to a particular place. For example, 'What are your views on the choice of decaffeinated coffee in your local supermarket?'

If the issue addressed in the question is complex or rigid, we might wish to add some generality to it. For example, 'Do you travel to work in your own car?' might be taken to mean every day. This can be generalised by inserting the word 'normally' or 'usually', thus: 'Do you

Figure 6.9 General rules for designing questions

1. Explain the purpose of the interview or questionnaire to all participants
2. Keep your questions as simple as possible
3. Do not use jargon or specialist language
4. Phrase each question so that only one meaning is possible
5. Avoid vague, descriptive words such as 'large' and 'small'
6. Avoid asking negative questions as these are easy to misinterpret
7. Only ask one question at a time
8. Include relevant questions only (do not be tempted to include every question you can think of)
9. Include questions which serve as cross-checks on the answers to other questions
10. Avoid questions which require the participant to perform calculations
11. Avoid leading or value-laden questions which imply what the required answer might be
12. Avoid offensive questions or insensitive questions which could cause embarrassment
13. Avoid questions which are nothing more than a memory test
14. Keep your interview schedule or questionnaire as short as possible, but include all the questions required to cover your purposes

normally travel to work in your own car?' A question can also be made more general by inserting the word 'overall' or the term 'in general'. For example, 'In general, are you satisfied with the level of service you obtain from the company?' However, in some questions precision may be important and desirable.

Coolican (1992) identifies the following pitfalls to avoid when deciding on the order in which questions should be asked:

▶ The tendency for participants to agree rather than disagree (known as response acquiescence). Mixing positive and negative questions to keeps them thinking of their answers

▶ The participant may try to interpret the aim of the question or questionnaire or set up emotional blocks to some questions. It is therefore best to ensure that both positive and negative items appear and that the less extreme statements are first

▶ Some responses may be considered as socially desirable; for example, 'How often do you shower each week?' This can lead respondents to give a certain answer because it fits in with the image they wish to present. You can try to resolve this problem by putting in some statements that only those respondents who are answering to impress would choose, but if your pilot test produces too many of these types of answers, you should discard your questionnaire or interview schedule.

In the remainder of this section we examine the different types of questions you can ask and the importance of incorporating features which will enhance your results and assist in the later analysis of the responses you receive.

6.6.1   Open and closed questions

Some of the questions you will want to ask are likely to be factual, such as those which ask for the respondent's age and occupation; others seek opinions. Questions may be described as *open-ended*, where each respondent can give a personal response or opinion in his or her own words. Other questions can be described as *closed*, where the respondent's answer is selected from a number of predetermined alternatives. Thus factual questions are likely to be closed questions, whereas questions which seek opinions are likely to be open-ended in a focus group or interview, for example, but closed in a questionnaire survey.

Open questions offer the advantage that the respondents are able to give their opinions as precisely as possible in their own words, but they can be difficult to analyse. In a questionnaire survey, open questions may deter busy respondents from replying to the questionnaire. Closed questions are very convenient for collecting factual data and are usually easy to analyse, since the range of potential answers is limited. Figure 6.10 shows an extract from a questionnaire used in a postal questionnaire survey of small businesses which gives examples of both open and closed questions.

Although the questions in Figure 6.10 have been taken from a questionnaire survey, there is no reason why they could not have be adapted for use in an interview or serve as prompts to a focus group discussion. Obviously, it is not very likely you would need to ask Question 1, you would simply make a note of whether the participant is a man or a woman. You might ask Question 2 as an open question and simply jot down the answer and collate all the responses into appropriate categories at the analysis stage. Alternatively, age might be a sensitive issue and you might retain the question's present categories so that the participant does not have to give his or her exact age. Question 3 would

Figure 6.10 Open and closed questions

Q1. Please indicate whether you are
(Closed question)

Male	(1)
or Female	(2)

Q2. What is your age?
(Closed question)

Under 21	(1)
21–30	(2)
31–40	(3)
41–50	(4)
51–60	(5)
61 or over	(6)

Q3. If the original business was established prior to incorporation as a limited company, in which year was it founded?
(Open question)

Q4. What were your reasons for starting the business?
(*Tick as many reasons as apply*)
(Closed question)

Desire to work for oneself
Redundancy
Frustration in present employment
Wish to accumulate wealth
An excellent opportunity presented itself
Other (*please state*)

remain an open question, and it is likely that you would wish to ask Question 4 as an open question in an interview and this would enable you to follow this with further questions or probes. In a focus group this question might provide the main area for discussion.

6.6.2   Multiple-choice answers

Multiple-choice answers are those where the participant is asked a closed question and selects his or her answer from a list of predetermined responses or categories. Even with factual questions, it may be difficult to provide sufficient, unambiguous categories to allow the respondent to give an unequivocal answer. An example of this is a question which seeks to ascertain respondents' occupations. Even in a fairly small organisation there may be quite a wide range of occupations; you cannot provide a full list because it would take up too much room. As a general guide approximately six predetermined responses or categories is usually sufficient.

When deciding on categories, you must take care to use terms which mean something to the participants, so that you can have confidence in their replies. For example, you may use the term 'Professional' as one of your occupation categories, meaning a person who is a member of one of the traditional professions such as accountancy or law. However, some respondents may construe this as meaning their experience in the job or the way that they conduct themselves. Thus, a sales assistant may see himself or herself as a belonging to the 'Professional' category.

In a single organisation it is usually possible to construct categories for factual questions which people will understand. If you are taking a random sample of the population it becomes much harder. In such circumstances, and wherever you are uncertain that you have covered all possibilities, you should add an 'Other' category which the respondent can use to specify the answer in their own words, or a 'Don't know' category.

Figure 6.11 shows another extract from the questionnaire used in the survey of small businesses. Both questions are closed with multiple-choice answers. Whereas Question 4 asks respondents to tick as many boxes as apply, you will see that Question 5 expects only one response. It is important to give clear instructions.

Sometimes a question is phrased so that the respondent is presented with a range of opinions and has to select the one which most closely resembles their own. Figure 6.12 shows an example of this. The drawback with this type of question is that it takes up considerable space and does not capture the respondents' opinions in their own words. As a result, you cannot be certain about how closely it matches their opinions. However, it can sometimes be useful for dealing with sensitive issues, since it identifies different responses. It can also be

---

Figure 6.11 Multiple-choice answers

Q4. What were your reasons for starting the business?
(*Tick as many reasons as apply*)

Desire to work for oneself
Redundancy
Frustration in present employment
Wish to accumulate wealth
An excellent opportunity presented itself
Other (*please state*)

Q5. How is the company managed?
(*Tick one box only*)

Solely by one director   (1)
Mainly by one director in consultation with other directors   (2)
By all directors equally   (3)
By directors with some senior managers   (4)
Other (*please state*)

---

useful as a means of cross-checking other questions by presenting the situation in a different way.

In interviews it is helpful to list any multiple-choice answers on a card. You can then present the card to the interviewee and ask him or her to select the most appropriate response to your question. This approach avoids the interviewee having to memorise a list of alternatives.

Figure 6.12 Multiple-choice answers: Opinions

Q18. Thinking about your relationship with your colleagues at work, indicate which of the following statements is closest to your own view:

We are a very happy and friendly group of workers   (1)
We get on reasonably well and better than many others   (2)
We have our ups and downs the same as any other group   (3)
We tend to be quite argumentative and less friendly
    than other groups   (4)
We do not work as a group and there is little contact   (5)
    between us

Figure 6.13 Likert scale

Q6. How important are the following characteristics to the performance of the company?

(*Please tick one box for each characteristic*)

Characteristic	Very important (5)	Quite important (4)	Undecided (3)	Of little importance (2)	Not important (1)
Access to finance					
External financial advice					
Sales/ marketing skills					
Quality of products					
Competitive pricing					
Diverse customer base					
Technical skills					
Innovation					
Loyalty of key staff					
Commitment of directors					
Good luck					
Other (*Please state*)					

6.6.3   Using rating scales

As well as answers to factual questions you will also be seeking opinions. One way to do this is to set a simple question requiring a 'Yes' or 'No' response. For example, 'Do you think your manager is good at keeping you informed about changes in work requirements?' This elicits a clear response, but does not permit any flexibility by the respondent. There is also the problem that participants may be provoked into giving an opinion where in fact they do not hold one.

It is often possible to allow participants to give more discriminating responses, and to state if they have no opinion, by providing them with some form of *rating scale*. This allows a numerical value to be given to an opinion. One of the more frequently used types of scale is the *Likert scale*. This turns the question into a statement and asks the respondent to indicate their level of agreement with the statement by ticking a box or circling a response as shown in Figure 6.13. A further advantage of this method is that a number of different statements can be provided in a list which does not take up much space, is simple for the respondent to complete and simple for the researcher to code and analyse.

Another way of obtaining numerical values from qualitative data is to pose questions where there are semantic differences. Two words or phrases are selected to represent two ends of a continuum and respondents are asked to indicate their choice on a seven-point scale. Figure 6.14 shows an example.

Another approach is to ask respondents to rank a list of items. Figure 6.15 shows an example of a question using ranking. The responses to such questions can be disappointing. Often respondents will not have gone through this type of exercise before and will be unwilling to do it just for your questionnaire. After ranking the first three they may be unable to decide what their opinions are amongst the remainder and are likely to leave them blank. If you wish to include a ranking question, keep the number of items as low as possible and definitely limit them to six.

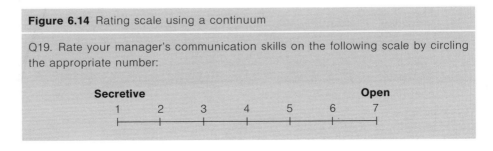

Figure 6.14 Rating scale using a continuum

Q19. Rate your manager's communication skills on the following scale by circling the appropriate number:

Secretive   Open

1   2   3   4   5   6   7

Figure 6.15 Ranking

Q20. Rank the following aspects of your job using the values 1 to 6 where

1 = the aspect you like the *most*
6 = the aspect you like the *least*

The pay
The conditions
The work itself
Relationship with superiors
Company culture

6.6.4 Classification questions

Classification questions are questions which set out to find out more about the participant; for example, his or her age and occupation. If you wish to make comparisons with other research studies, such as government statistics, etc., it is essential that your categories are complementary and that you ask all the classification questions. In most studies it is necessary to describe your sample in some way; if you are going to conduct any form of cross tabulation or statistical analysis this is essential. Remember, you must ensure that you will actually use any classification information you collect.

6.6.5 Sensitive questions

When designing questions you must be alert to the possibility that some of the issues you wish to ask about may be threatening or embarrassing to the participants. We do not recommend that you incorporate any type of *sensitive question* in a postal questionnaire because the respondent is highly likely to react by throwing it away; an interview may be a more appropriate forum for asking questions about sensitive issues.

Lee (1993) offers the following advice if you are asking questions on sensitive topics.

- ► Use words which are non-threatening and familiar to the respondents. For example, when explaining the purpose of the questionnaire, rather than saying you are conducting research into absenteeism in their workplace, say you are looking at working patterns
- ► Lead up to any sensitive question slowly
- ► You may find that participants will answer questions about past indiscretions more readily than those relating to current behaviour.

For example they may admit to stealing from their employer at some time in the past, but not be willing to disclose that they are currently doing it.

These suggestions raise ethical issues and you must determine your own position on this. If you find your interviewee is showing signs of resisting some topics, the best advice is to drop them. However, this will alert you to the likelihood that these may be interesting and important issues and you may wish to find an alternative way of collecting the data, such as *diary methods* (see Section 6.5.2) or *observation* (see Section 6.5.5).

6.6.6   Reliability and validity

You will remember from Chapter 3 that *reliability* is concerned with the findings of the research. The findings can be said to be reliable if you or anyone else repeated the research and obtained the same results. *Validity* is concerned with the extent to which the research findings accurately represent what is happening in the situation; in other words, whether the data collected is a true picture of what is being studied. For example, the use of protocol analysis in a laboratory setting might be reliable because it can be replicated, but it does not have high validity because the findings do not reflect behaviour in a natural setting.

The reliability of the responses you receive is an important issue in question design in a positivistic study. The reason why we may have doubts lies in the problem that our questions may contain errors (perhaps they are worded ambiguously), the respondent may become bored or there may be antagonism between the researcher and the participants. If you decide to use rating or attitude scales in the questions you ask, you will want to be sure that they will measure the respondents' views consistently.

There are three common ways of estimating the reliability of the responses to questions in questionnaires or interviews:

▶ **Test re-test method:** The questions are asked of the same people, but on two separate occasions. Responses for the two occasions are correlated and the *correlation coefficient* of the two sets of data computed (see Chapter 8), thus providing an index of reliability. However, this method suffers from the considerable disadvantage that it is often difficult to persuade respondents to answer questions a second time and, if they do, they may think more deeply about the questions on the second occasion and give different answers.
▶ **Split-halves method:** The questionnaires or interview record sheets are divided into two equal halves, perhaps by putting the responses to the odd numbered questions in one pile and the

responses to the even number questions in another. Alternatively, the responses to the first half of the questions are put in a separate pile from the answers to the remainder. The two piles are then correlated and the *correlation coefficient* of the two sets of data computed as above.

▶ **Internal consistency method:** Every item is correlated with every other item across the entire sample and the average inter-item correlation is taken as the index of reliability. Although this approach is a popular method of computing the reliability of the results where questions have been used as the basis of the data collection method, it requires substantial computing facilities and software which uses a special formula called *Kuder-Richardson (KR20)*.

The responses to your questions may turn out to be highly reliable, but the results will be worthless if your questions do not measure what you intended them to measure; in other words *validity* is low. Therefore, it is important that the questions you ask correspond with the explanation you give respondents regarding the purpose of your study; otherwise, they may lose interest in answering the questions as these will appear to be irrelevant.

Figure 6.16 Checklist for eliminating questions

1. Does the question measure some aspect of one of the research questions?
2. Does the question provide information needed in conjunction with some other variable?
   (If NO to both 1 and 2, drop the question;
   if YES to one or both, retain)
3. Will most respondents understand the question and in the same way?
   (If NO, revise or drop; if YES, retain)
4. Will most respondents have the information to answer it?
   (If NO, drop; if YES, retain)
5. Will most respondents be willing to answer it?
   (If NO, drop; if YES, retain)
6. Is other information needed to analyse this question?
   (If NO, retain;
   (if YES, retain only if the other information is available or can be obtained)
7. Should this question be asked of all respondents or only a subset?
   (If ALL, retain;
   If ONLY A SUBSET, retain only if the subset is identifiable beforehand
   or through questions in the interview)

Source: Adapted from Czaja and Blair (1996) p. 61.

6.6.7   Eliminating questions

Having decided on the questions you wish to ask, it is common to find that you have far too many. Use the checklist given in Figure 6.16, which is adapted from Czaja and Blair (1996), to determine which questions you should retain and which you should drop when designing questions for interviews or questionnaires.

!

Experiential learning	**Role-playing exercise**

In small groups or with your supervisor, use role play to rehearse verbal questions that you may want to ask (for example, interview questions). You can also use role play to test written questions (for example, those used in a questionnaire). If you are using observation to collect data, you may find that you can simulate the research situation to allow you to test any forms or grids you have designed. Keep this data for testing your method(s) of analysis.

6.7   Coding for computer analysis

Although *coding* is more closely related to analysis than data collection, it is important to consider at this stage how you will analyse the responses you get to the questions you ask. If you have adopted a positivistic approach, perhaps using a large questionnaire survey to collect your data, you will need the help of a computer to process and analyse the responses. This will require questions which are structured to fit in with this process.

Examples of computer software which will help you process, summarise and analyse the data you have collected include *Minitab* and *SPSS* (Statistical Package for the Social Sciences). Whatever statistical package you decide to use, you will need to take account of the format in which the program expects to find your data. In this section we will show you the most commonly used method of coding data on a questionnaire or data record sheet ready for analysis using *SPSS for Windows*.

All statistical packages expect the data to be in numerical form. Therefore, you must allocate a numerical code to each variable. Open-ended questions cannot be coded until all the replies have been received and grouped together in categories. For example, you will need to draw up a list of any answers given against 'Other' (see Section 6.8.1) and allocate codes to them.

It is usual to reserve certain code numbers for particular purposes. For example, we normally use code 9 to indicate that a question has not been answered; in other words, this is the code we use for missing values. Although at first sight it might seem logical to use code 0 for this purpose, we do not do so as this would preclude it being used in open questions where the answer takes a numerical value; for example, dates as in 1990, or figures as in £30 000. Where only one answer can be selected by the respondent, for example by ticking a box, we give a column number but no code, and would use code 1 to indicate that the respondent has ticked this box.

It is important to remember to keep a record of the codes you are using for each question and what they signify, especially those which are not incorporated in your questionnaire or data record sheet. This is essential should you decide to use a third party to input your data, and also for when you start to interpret the analysed data.

The first item to code in any questionnaire or data record sheet is the number which identifies the entire questionnaire or record sheet. This number must be printed on the document before it is distributed and/or completed. Not only will this enable you to identify the data on the form with each respondent or participant, but in a question-naire survey it will also allow you to ascertain which respondents have not replied so that they can be sent a follow-up letter.

You may have noticed that the examples of questions we used earlier in this chapter were pre-coded. Figure 6.17 shows the first page of the small business questionnaire which was pre-coded and has been returned completed by the respondent. Look carefully at the way in which the potential answers have been coded. The codes have been put in brackets as close as possible to the boxes which the respondent will use to indicate his or her response. This makes the keying in of data easier and less prone to error.

Question 4 is an example of a question where we would use code 1 to indicate a positive response (a box which has been ticked) and code 0 to indicate a negative response (not ticked). Questions 4 and 5 leave space for free text by offering an 'Other' category.

The coding of Question 6 is similar to that of Question 5, except the latter is really a collection of small, closed questions which ask the respondent to use the same scale to answer them. You may find it convenient to think of each question as Q6.1 (Access to finance), Q6.2 (External financial advice), and so on. You will see that a code 7 has been given to Q6.12 (Other). This is because all the 'Other' responses to this question have been listed, counted (see Section 6.8.1) and classified. 'Relationship with suppliers' has been allocated to a cate-gory which has been given code 7.

SPSS is available as a Windows package. The data file consists of a worksheet where data can be stored and is supported by a number of menu-driven commands. It is very similar to a spreadsheet, with num-bered rows for each respondent, record sheet or questionnaire, and columns for each variable.

You can label each variable using up to eight letters. Sometimes it is convenient to use the question number as the label; in other cases an

Figure 6.17 A pre-coded, completed questionnaire

Questionnaire number | 365 |

Q1. Please indicate whether you are

| | Male | | | (1) |
| | or Female | ✓ | (2) |

Q2. What is your age?

Under 21		(1)
21–30		(2)
31–40		(3)
41 - 50	✓	(4)
51–60		(5)
61 or over		(6)

Q3. If the original business was established prior to incorporation as a limited company, in which year was it founded?

| *1987* |

Q4. What were your reasons for starting the business?
(*Tick as many reasons as apply*)

Desire to work for oneself
Redundancy   ✓
Frustration in present employment
Wish to accumulate wealth   ✓
An excellent opportunity presented itself ✓
Other (*please state*)

Q5. How is the company managed?
(*Tick one box*)

Solely by one director		(1)
Mainly by one director in consultation with other directors	✓	(2)
By all directors equally		(3)
By directors with some senior managers		(4)
Other (*please state*)		

Q6. How important are the following characteristics to the performance of the
company?
(Please tick one box for each characteristic)

	(5) Very important	(4) Quite important	(3) Undecided	(2) Of little importance	(1) Not important
Characteristic					
Access to finance		✓			
External financial advice				✓	
Sales/ marketing skills	✓				
Quality of products	✓				
Competitive pricing		✓			
Diverse customer base		✓			
Technical skills		✓			
Innovation		✓			
Loyalty of key staff	✓				
Commitment of directors	✓				
Good luck		✓			
Other (*Please state*)	✓				

Relationship with suppliers is vital to our business

abbreviation or an acronym of the variable is more useful. Labelling
the variables helps guide you when you are entering your data and later
when you are analysing it. Table 6.3 shows how the data collected from
the respondent who completed the questionnaire shown in Figure 6.17
would appear once it has been keyed into a *SPSS* data file.

Table 6.3 Data entered into SPSS data file

	ID	Q1	Q2	Q3	Q4.1	Q4.2	Q4.3	Q4.4	Q4.5	Q4.6	Q5
1	0365	2	4	1987	1	0	0	1	1	0	2
2											
3											
etc.											

Q6.1	Q6.2	Q6.3	Q6.4	Q6.5	Q6.6	Q6.7	Q6.8	Q6.9	Q6.10	Q6.11	Q6.12
4	2	5	5	4	4	4	4	5	5	4	7

Once all the data has been entered for all the respondents, record sheets or questionnaires, you can use menu-driven commands to draw up frequency tables and cross-tabulations, and perform a wide range of statistical tests. The results can be presented in the form of both tables and graphs which you can import into your final research report.

In Section 6.6 we suggested that you should pilot your questions before commencing your data collection in earnest. We also recommend that you pilot your coding, using your test data. Amending coding errors now will save you much valuable time and energy later when errors can only be painstakingly corrected by hand on every record sheet or questionnaire.

6.8   Recording data and observations

Many of the data collection methods we have examined in this chapter, such as *focus groups* (see Section 6.5.3) *interviews* (see Section 6.5.4) and *observations* (see Section 6.5.5), generate a considerable amount of data and you will need to find methods by which to record it. This can be done in a structured way by using a prepared record sheet, or by taking notes or using an audio cassette or a video. In most cases the data thus recorded will be qualitative.

6.8.1   Recording qualitative data

The main advantage of *note taking* for recording qualitative data is that you can record your observations and responses to questions immediately. Making notes during *interviews* (see Section 6.5.4) also allows you to control the pace. However, note-taking is time consuming and you may unwittingly leave out important information, miss behavioural clues and not explore all the issues because you are busy writing. If you are using *observation* (see Section 6.5.5) to collect data, you will find that it is practically impossible to write down every event, every action and every word spoken.

Another disadvantage of note taking is that when you write your notes you are automatically screening and summarising the information. Although this can be seen as an advantage, because it means that you have already begun to analyse your data, it can lead to omissions, distortions, errors and bias, where your own perceptions act as a filter on the data you record. Therefore, we recommend that you use an *audio recording* in addition to supplement note taking. Most participants in focus groups and interviewees will agree to being recorded and you will be free to concentrate on taking notes of other aspects, such as attitude, behaviour and body language. Later, these notes can be read in conjunction with the transcripts you will make from the audio recording.

Video is not used as widely as it might be in business research as a method of recording data. Bottorff (1994, p. 258) argues that although using video is 'a complex and technically demanding process, the potential this method holds for extending our understanding of behaviour and illuminating new problems should not be underestimated'. The advantage of video is the relative completeness and complexity of the data thus captured and the permanence of the record it provides. The subsequent analysis can be conducted in any order and at different speeds.

Unfortunately this method is limited by the fact that you can only record what is within the video camera's range of vision, and cannot capture all dimensions of phenomena, such as feelings for example. Therefore, we recommend that the use of video, like audio recording, is supplemented by note taking. For many students the practicalities and cost of using video eliminates it as a method of collecting qualitative data, but if these problems can be overcome, it is an option which you should consider carefully.

6.8.2   Using tallies

If you are conducting a positivistic study and your sample is fairly small (or if you do not have access to a suitable computer software), the first task you will need to carry out once you have collected your raw data is count the *frequency* of occurrence of the value codes allocated to each variable. If you are using a statistical package, such as SPSS, the program can be instructed to do this for you.

In Section 6.7 we noted that open-ended questions cannot be pre-coded. These open-ended question are those to which you are unable to anticipate the response; for example, and those where an 'Other'

Figure 6.18 Ranking

Q4. Reasons for starting business	Frequency	Total
Desire to work for oneself	~~IIII~~ ~~IIII~~ ~~IIII~~ ~~IIII~~ ~~IIII~~ 11	27
Redundancy	~~IIII~~	5
Frustration in present employment	~~IIII~~ 1111	9
Wish to accumulate wealth	~~IIII~~ ~~IIII~~ ~~IIII~~ ~~IIII~~ ~~IIII~~ ~~IIII~~ 111	33
An excellent opportunity presented itself	~~IIII~~ ~~IIII~~ ~~IIII~~ ~~IIII~~ ~~IIII~~ 1111	29
Other:		
It's now or never/Last chance	~~IIII~~ 1	6
Mid-life crisis/Age related reasons	111	3

category is given. Even if you are using a computer to help you process the data, you will need to list and count the frequency of all the different responses you receive to these questions. The task of recording and counting frequencies accurately and methodically can be help by using *tallies*.

A tally is just a simple stroke used to represent the occurrence of values or other phenomena of a similar nature. You simply jot down one upright stroke for each occurrence until you have four; the fifth is drawn through the four upright strokes to form a bundle of five. Grouping frequencies together in fives helps when counting up the total number of frequencies. Figure 6.18 shows tallies being used to help record the frequencies in Question 4 where respondents were asked to indicate their reasons for starting the business.

Conclusions

In this chapter we have investigated the ways in which you can collect original data to supplement the secondary data you have collected, and will continue to collect, from searching the literature. We have examined how you can select a suitable sample, and identify and classify the variables you want to collect data about. We have also described the different types of data and discussed various measurement scales for recording and describing quantitative data.

We have examined the main methods of collecting and recording data in some detail and you should now be in a position to make an informed choice. It is important to remember that you can use more than one method and, depending on the way you use them, collect either qualitative or quantitative data.

Finally, in readiness for the next stage which is concerned with data analysis, we have looked at how you can code questionnaires and other data record sheets for computer analysis.

7 Analysing quantitative data

Introduction

Having collected the data for your research project, you are now in a position to start analysing it. Your choice of methods and techniques will depend on whether the data you have collected is quantitative or qualitative; you may have collected some of each. We discuss the methods for analysing qualitative data in Chapter 8. In this chapter we consider the main ways in which quantitative data can be analysed. This chapter can be used in the following ways:

- to help you select the methods and techniques of analysis which are appropriate for the data you have collected
- to revise your knowledge of basic statistical techniques
- to give guidance on how to carry out your chosen method of analysis
- to advise on how to interpret the results of statistical tests.

If your knowledge of statistics is somewhat rusty, you should find this chapter useful as it contains key formulae for some of the most widely used statistical techniques, together with step-by-step instructions and worked examples. Even if you are not analysing large amounts of quantitative data, you will find it of considerable help if you have access to a suitable computer statistics package, such as *Minitab* or *SPSS (Statistical Package for the Social Sciences)*, or a spreadsheet program, such as *Excel*. Computer programs such as these enable you to conduct a wide range of analysis, carry out statistical tests quickly and accurately and present the results in the form of tables or charts. Thus, they can be very useful, provided you know how to interpret the results!

7.1 Overview of quantitative data analysis

Statistics is a body of methods and theory that is applied to quantitative data when making decisions in the face of uncertainty. 'It enables us to recognize and evaluate the errors involved in quantifying our experience, especially when generalizing from what is known of some small group (a sample) to some wider group (the population)' (Rowntree, 1991, p. 186).

If you have adopted a *positivistic paradigm* (see Chapter 3), you will have collected mainly quantitative data on which you will normally need to conduct some form of statistical analysis. This quantitative data will take the form of numerical values which represent the total number of observations or *frequencies* for the variables under study. *Phenomenologists* may also use quantitative data, although they may not necessarily analyse it using statistics. For example, Glaser and Strauss (1967, p. 220) argue that 'if quantitative data is handled systematically by theoretical ordering of variables in elaboration tables, the analyst will indeed find rich terrain for discovering and generating theory'.

Statistics texts commonly draw a distinction between *exploratory data analysis* or *descriptive statistics*, which is used to summarise or display quantitative data, and *confirmatory data analysis* or *inferential statistics*, which involves using quantitative data collected from a sample to draw conclusions about a complete population. You will remember from Chapter 6 that a population is a body of people or any collection of items under consideration. Therefore, the population includes the totality of observations that might be made, as in a census. On the other hand, a sample comprises a subset of the population where observations will be, or have been, made.

Within confirmatory data analysis, a second distinction that is commonly made is between *non-parametric* and *parametric techniques*. The latter are important since they are more powerful. Parametric techniques compare sample statistics with population parameters, but can only be used on data which has a *normal distribution* (see Sections 7.4.3, 7.5.3 and 7.8). Non-parametric techniques are more general and can be used on *skewed data*; that is, data which is not normally distributed. They can also be used on *ordinal data* (see Chapter 6). However, because they are less discriminating, the results are correspondingly less reliable (Oakshott, 1994).

Apart from time, cost and access to suitable software, your choice of statistical technique or procedure will mainly depend on the following criteria:

▶ whether you wish to conduct **exploratory data analysis** to summarise, describe or display your data, or **confirmatory data analysis** to make inferences from your sample data
▶ whether your data has a **normal distribution** which allows you to use the more powerful parametric techniques, or is skewed and means that you will have to use a non-parametric technique
▶ the **number of variables** you wish to analyse at the same time

▶ the **measurement scale** of your data (nominal, ordinal, interval or ratio) which has implications if you decide to use an inferential technique.

!

Experiential learning	**Getting to grips with the software**

Discuss with your supervisor what instruction is available to enable you to learn or enhance your knowledge of using spreadsheets or specialist programs for analysing quantitative data(for example, Excel, Minitab or SPSS).

The analysis of a single variable is known as *univariate* data analysis; two variables, *bivariate* analysis, and more than two variables *multivariate* data analysis.

In this chapter we concentrate on examples of univariate and bivariate data analysis and focus on *exploratory data analysis* because this type of analysis can be conducted in all studies where quantitative

Table 7.1 Type of analysis by data type

	Exploratory data analysis	*Confirmatory data analysis*
Univariate data	*Presenting frequencies*	*Estimating from samples*
	Tables	Confidence intervals (P)
	Graphical forms	*Forecasting*
	Measuring location	Time series analysis
	Mean	
	Median	
	Mode	
	Measuring dispersion	
	Range and interquartile	
	range	
	Standard deviation	
	Measuring change	
	Index numbers	
Bivariate data	*Presenting frequencies*	*Measuring association*
	Cross tabulations	Pearson's coefficient (r) (P)
	Graphical forms	Spearman's rank
	Scatter diagrams	coefficient (r_S) (NP)
	Stem plots	*Measuring difference*
		Chi squared (χ^2) test (NP)
		Student t-test (P)

Note
P = Parametric technique
NP = Non-parametric technique

data has been collected. In sophisticated, positivistic studies, you will also need to conduct *confirmatory data analysis*. Although we give some introductory examples of the range of possibilities, if you wish to conduct confirmatory data analysis, you will need to refer to a statistical text, such as Clegg (1992), Coolican (1992), Bryman and Cramer (1997) or Field (2000).

We will look first at exploratory data analysis, before going on to discuss the main issues you must consider when conducting confirmatory data analysis and describing some introductory techniques. Where practical we have given formulae and instructions, as this can aid understanding of the underlying purpose of a particular technique or procedure, and hence the interpretation of the results. However, we recommend that you use either a spreadsheet or a specialist statistical package for both exploratory and confirmatory data analysis, and refer to the relevant books and articles cited in this chapter. Table 7.1 lists the techniques we will be describing in this chapter by data type and purpose.

7.2   Exploratory data analysis

We prefer the term *exploratory data analysis* to *descriptive statistics* as we consider the latter term can be misleading. It implies that this group of techniques is only concerned with describing data, whereas it is also useful for summarising and presenting the data in tables, charts, graphs and other diagrammatic forms, which enable patterns and relationships to be discerned which are not apparent in the raw data. In exploratory data analysis, techniques are applied to data as part of a preliminary analysis or even a full analysis, if great statistical rigour is not required or the data does not justify it. Graphical presentations 'do not merely present the data in a different, more compact form but the form positively *aids* subsequent hypothesis detection/confirmation' (Lovie, 1986, p. 165)

We will be looking at four main groups of techniques which can be used for:

- presenting frequencies
- measuring location (central tendency)
- measuring dispersion (spread)
- measuring change.

7.3   Presenting frequencies

Even when the raw data you have collected consists of small sets of data of less than 20 items, you will probably need to rearrange it to aid full comprehension. A useful first step in the analysis of quantitative data is to examine the *frequency distribution* for each variable. A *frequency* is a numerical value which represents the total number of observations for a variable under study. For example, you may have collected data from line managers on how many subordinates they have. A frequency distribution is an array of the frequencies arranged in size order in a table, chart, graph or other diagrammatic form.

If you have only a small amount of quantitative data, you may decide to count the frequencies yourself, but with large data sets you will need the help of a spreadsheet program, such as *Excel* or a statistical package, such as *Minitab* or *SPSS*. Even so, you may find that you have to analyse certain data before you can enter it into the program. For example, you may need to group certain raw data values into categories or classes and then count the frequencies for each. You will remember from Chapter 6 that we recommended using *tallies* to aid the counting of frequencies.

7.3.1 Frequency distribution tables

Once you have obtained a count of the frequencies you are ready to construct frequency distribution tables for your variables. A *frequency distribution table* presents the frequency data, usually in size order. The frequencies may be summarised by calculating the *average* and/or the *percentage* frequencies. An average is a convenient way of describing a data set by means of a single value. It involves calculating the arithmetic *mean*. We will be looking more closely at this in Section 7.4.1. The formula for calculating single data is:

$$\text{Mean} = \frac{\Sigma x}{n}$$

where

$x = $ each observation
$n = $ the total number of observations
$\Sigma = $ the sum of

A percentage is a statistic which summarises the data by describing the proportion or part in every 100. You can calculate a percentage relative frequency using the following formula.

$$\text{Percentage relative frequency} = \frac{f}{\Sigma f} \times 100$$

where

$f = $ the frequency
$\Sigma = $ the sum of

Example

Table 7.2 shows an example of a percentage relative frequency distribution table which has been constructed to display the responses of 12 managers to a question which asked them how many subordinates they have. We were lucky that we were able to obtain responses from all managers. If this had not been the case, we would have added a row indicating the 'no response' frequencies.

You will remember that we defined a frequency distribution as an array of frequencies arranged in size order. One important decision you need to make is whether it is more appropriate to let the frequencies or the variable dictate the order. In this table you can see that the variable (the number of subordinates) has been selected. Reading the table, you can see that 42 per cent of respondents had three subordinates, 25 per cent four subordinates and 17 per cent two subordinates. Under 10 per cent had either one or five subordinates.

Table 7.2 Frequency distribution table: number of subordinates

Number of subordinates (x)	Number of respondents (f)	% of total respondents (f%)
1	1	8
2	2	17
3	5	42
4	3	25
5	1	8
Total	**12**	**100**

In large samples, you may find it more convenient to group the observed values of the quantity variables you have collected to form non-overlapping *groups* or *classes*, which between them cover the whole range of the data. For example, if you are conducting a large survey and collect data on people's ages, you may wish to group them into classes which span five years. Normally, the number of classes should be between eight and 16. Fewer than this can obscure essential features and too many classes can emphasis minor or random features. You can then count how many of the data values fall within each class and present the results in tabular or diagrammatic form. The advantage of grouping the data in this way is that this can help you to present the overall pattern more clearly, but in the process information about the individual observed values will be lost.

However, there are several problems associated with grouping data. First of all, you need to decide whether the data is *discrete* or *continuous*. You will remember from Chapter 6 that a discrete quantitative variable can only take one of a range of distinct values between the start and end of a scale. For example, if your discrete data refers to the number of employees, you could use a class interval of 5, for example: 1 to 5; 6 to 10; 11 to 15, etc.

If your data is continuous, for example the number of hours worked per week, you will need to form classes so that you can allocate each item of data within the range to the appropriate group without ambiguity. A value recorded as being on the boundary between two classes is placed in the upper one. For example, if the range was between 10 and 49 hours per week, you might use equal class intervals of 10, as shown in Table 7.3. A value of 20 would be placed in the $20 < 30$ band.

Example
Table 7.3 shows an example of a frequency distribution table which presents interval data. As you can see, the intervals have been used to order the frequencies.

Table 7.3 Frequency distribution table: hours worked per week

Hours per week *Class boundaries*	*Class mid-value* (x)	Number of responses *Class frequency* (f)	% of total respondents $(f\%)$	Cumulative % of total respondents $(cum\ f\%)$
$10 < 20$	15	1	8	8
$20 < 30$	25	2	17	25
$30 < 40$	35	5	42	67
$40 < 50$	45	4	33	100
	Total	**12**	**100**	

The use of class boundaries allows us to use the whole range without leaving any gaps The reason for doing this will become apparent when we look at histograms in Section 7.3.3.

7.3.2   Cross tabulations

In the above examples we have only analysed *univariate* data. However, if you wish to analyse *bivariate* data you may wish to construct a table which is known as a *cross tabulation*. Although cross tabulations can be constructed with any type of quantitative data, they are particularly useful for analysing nominal (named) data.

Example

Table 7.4 shows an example of a cross tabulation which presents the number of managers in a particular company by functional department and by sex.

There is no reason why you should not order the data in this table alphabetically by department, but as the main message the table is communicating concerns the distribution of male and female managers, the table is ordered by frequency. In this example, both male and female categories follow the same order. However, if your data does not conveniently coincide in this way, simply order the category which contains the larger frequencies and let the other follow. As with other frequency distribution tables, further analysis can be provided by adding percentage figures.

Table 7.4 Cross tabulation: number of managers by department and sex

Department	Number of male managers	Number of female managers	Total number of managers
Production	16	22	38
Sales	11	16	27
Accounting	9	8	17
Human resources	5	9	14
Marketing	1	3	4

7.3.3   Charts and graphs

Charts and *graphs* are suitable for both presenting and summarising frequency data and, like tables, can be constructed to convey information precisely. In fact, research suggests that while some people prefer information presented in tabular form, others prefer it in graphical form. Charts and graphs which conform to one or more conventions can help you display your data and communicate your ideas, but they should always be accompanied by a paragraph or two of explanation. Table 7.5 shows the advantages and disadvantages of using graphical forms to represent data.

If you have entered your frequency data onto a spreadsheet or into a specialist statistical program, you will find it easy to produce a variety of different charts and graphs. Table 7.6 shows how your choice of chart is constrained by the type of data you have collected.

You will remember from Chapter 6 that *nominal* data is data which has been classified into named categories; for example, occupation or colour of eyes. *Ordinal* data is nominal data which has been ordered in some way; for example, respondents' choices which have been ranked

Table 7.5 Graphical representation of data

Advantages	Disadvantages
Good for communicating general points	Poor for communicating specific details
Attractive to look at	Design may detract from message
Appeals to a more general audience	Can be time consuming to prepare
Relationships can be seen more clearly	Can be misinterpreted
Easier to compare sets of data	Open to abuse

Table 7.6 Type of chart by type of data

Type of data	Bar chart	Pie chart	Histogram	Frequency polygon
Nominal	✓	✓		
Ordinal	✓			
Interval			✓	✓

as first, second or third. *Interval* data is data which is measured on a scale which determines exactly what the intervals are; for example, with students' assignment marks you can say that the interval between 50 per cent and 55 per cent is the same as the interval between 60 per cent and 65 per cent. *Ratio* data represents the highest level of precision since the data is measured on a scale which has a fixed zero point and permits both ratio and interval decisions to be made; for example, height, weight or time data. Therefore you can say that a speed of 60 mph is twice as fast as a speed of 30 mph, and you can say that the interval between 50 mph and 60 mph is the same as the interval between 30 mph and 40 mph.

In a simple *bar chart* the data is represented by a series of separate bars which can be drawn vertically or horizontally. The ordering of the bars is not important. The frequency is indicated by the height or length of the bar and there must be a fixed zero point to the scale (Morris, 1993).

Example
Figure 7.1 shows a horizontal bar chart which displays the frequency data relating to the number of subordinates from Table 7.2.

In a *component/segmented bar chart* the bars are divided into segments. Some commentators do not recommend their use, as the segments lack a common axis or base line for visual reference, which

Figure 7.1 Horizontal bar chart: number of subordinates

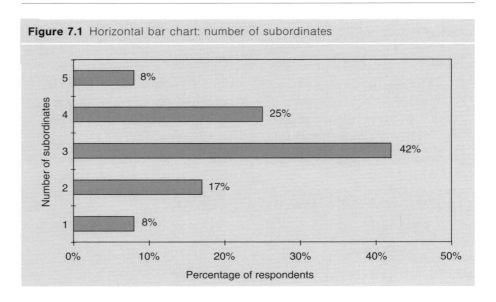

makes it difficult for the reader to extract information. The alternative is a *multiple bar chart* in which the segments adjoin one another and each starts at the base line. This allows the reader to compare several component parts, but the comparison of the total is lost.

Figure 7.2 Pie chart: number of subordinates by percentage of respondents

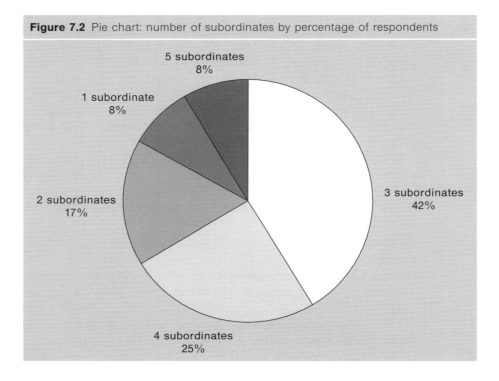

A *pie chart* is a circular diagram divided into segments so that the area of each is proportional to the segment represented. Its construction involves the calculation of the angles at the centre of the diagram.

Example
Figure 7.2 shows the frequency data from Table 7.2 again, but this time a pie chart has been used. Since pie charts should be used to present proportional data only, you will see that the chart uses the percentage relative frequencies.

The axes on a *line graph* represent *continuous* scales. The independent variable is shown on the horizontal axis and the dependent variable on the vertical axis.

Example
Figure 7.3 shows an example of a line graph. Since it not appropriate to use a line graph for discrete data, we will the continuous data from Table 7.3 which relates to the number of weekly hours worked.

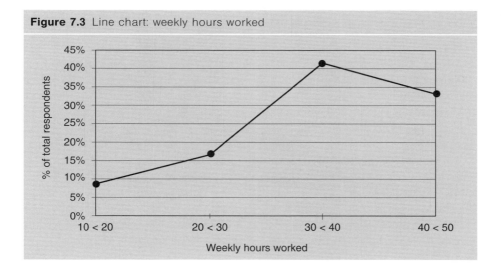

Figure 7.3 Line chart: weekly hours worked

One advantage of line graphs over other forms is that a number of graphs can be superimposed on the same axes. This enables comparisons to be made very clearly.

Frequency distributions can usefully be displayed as a *histogram*. A histogram is a refinement of a *bar chart* where adjoining bars touch, indicating *continuous interval* or *ratio* data. The width of each bar is the class interval or width of the group and may be unequal; the height is the frequency of the class. Thus, frequency is represented by area. The *frequency density* is plotted instead of the frequencies and is calculated by dividing the frequency by the class width.

If the your data has been grouped together in *equal* class intervals, the widths of the bars will be constant and the height of each bar will represent the frequencies (because area equals width multiplied by height). If your data has been grouped together in *unequal* class intervals, you can calculate the height of the rectangle by dividing the frequency of the class interval by the width of the class interval. You may need to choose an upper limit for an open-ended class. If the frequency is less than the adjoining one, the same class width is probably appropriate; otherwise, err on the small side, for example, two-thirds of the expected absolute upper limit.

Example

Figure 7.4 shows an example of a histogram which uses the continuous data from Table 7.3 again (as used in the line chart in Figure 7.3).

Figure 7.4 Histogram: weekly hours worked

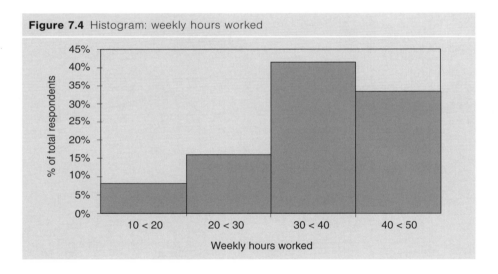

You may wish to consider using a *frequency polygon* for representing *discrete* data. A frequency polygon can be obtained by joining the mid-points of the tops of the rectangles of a frequency distribution histogram. The resulting polygon has the same area as the histogram. For discrete data with equal class intervals, it is acceptable to use class boundaries such as 10 to 19; 20 to 29, 30 to 39, 40 to 49, 50 to 59, etc.

An *ogive* or *cumulative frequency polygon* is a graphical form of a cumulative frequency table. The cumulative frequency is plotted against the upper class boundary of each class, so that you can estimate the number of observations which lie between given limits of the variable.

7.3.4   Diagrams

Scatter diagrams are used to illustrate the relationship between two variables. One variable is plotted against the other on a graph which thus displays a pattern of points. Therefore, this type of graph is useful for *bivariate* analysis. The pattern of points indicates the strength and direction of the *correlation* between the two variables. Correlation is concerned with measuring the strength of association between two variables (see Section 7.9). The more the points tend to cluster around a straight line, the stronger and the higher the correlation.

Example
If the line around which the points tend to cluster runs from lower left to upper right, the relation is positive (direct) as in Figure 7.5. Positive correlation occurs when an increase in the value of one variable is associated with an increase in the value of the other. For example, increased orders may be associated with increased calls by the sales staff.

Figure 7.5 Scatter diagram showing strong positive linear correlation

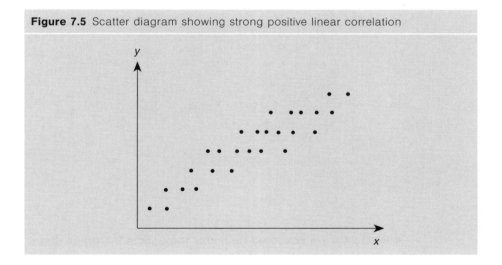

If the line around which the points tend to cluster runs from upper left to lower right, the relation is negative (inverse) as in Figure 7.6. Negative correlation occurs when an increase in the value of one variable is associated with a decrease in the value of the other. For example, higher interest rates may be associated with lower house sales.

Figure 7.6 Scatter diagram showing perfect negative linear correlation

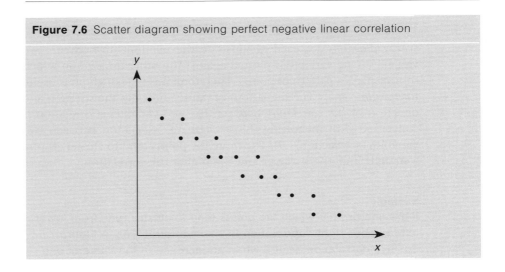

Figure 7.7 Scatter diagram indicating no correlation

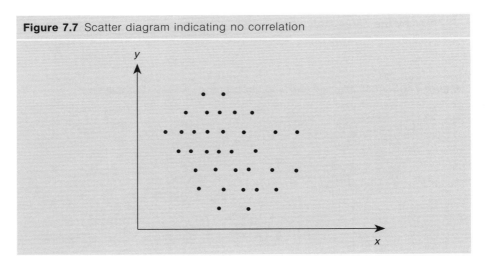

If the points are scattered randomly throughout the graph, there is no correlation relationship between the two variables as in Figure 7.7. Alternatively, the pattern may show non-linear correlation as in Figure 7.8.

A *dot diagram* can be constructed to present small sets of *univariate* frequency data and is also very useful for identifying patterns in the data. A dot diagram consists of a line covering the range of the values of the measurements. The individual values are plotted as dots over the line.

Figure 7.8 Scatter diagram showing non-linear correlation

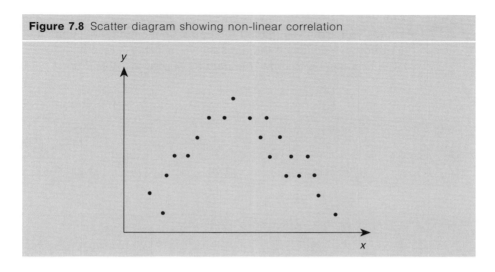

Figure 7.9 Dot diagram: number of subordinates

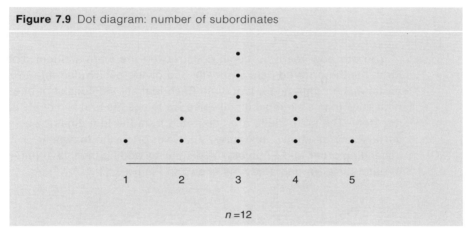

Example

Figure 7.9 displays the frequency data given in Table 7.2 which referred to the number of subordinates. The total number of respondents is shown as n.

Stem-and-leaf plots give a picture of the data using the actual values to create the display. The diagram gives the same information as the raw data, but presents it in a more compact and useable form, highlighting any gaps and *outliers*. An outlier is an outlying value; in other words, an extreme value or item of data which does not seem to conform to the general pattern. Outliers are important because they can distort the interpretation of data.

Example

Perhaps you are investigating the petrol consumption of company cars and have collected the data shown in Table 7.7.

The first step is to order the data as shown in Table 7.8.

Table 7.7 Petrol consumption data (mpg)

40.6	34.6	38.8	39.7	38.3	39.2	38.3	36.4	35.3	37.7
38.5	37.0	36.0	29.8	32.6	35.3	34.7	30.2	35.9	

Table 7.8 Ordering the data: petrol consumption (mpg)

29.8	30.2	32.6	34.6	34.7	35.3	35.3	35.9	36.0	36.4
37.0	37.7	38.3	38.3	38.5	38.8	39.2	39.7	40.6	

You are now ready to begin constructing the stem-and-leaf plot. First, list the ordered data vertically and divide each value into two parts: a stem digit and a leaf digit. Each leaf should consist of one digit only. In this example it makes sense to use the first two digits as the stem. The stem digits are separated from the leaf digits by a vertical line as shown in Figure 7.10. Next, order the leaves in ascending order and complete the display by adding the total number of data items (*n*) and a key, as shown in Figure 7.11.

Figure 7.10 Separating the stem from the leaves: petrol consumption (mpg)

Stem	Leaves			
29	8			
30	2			
31				
32	6			
33				
34	6	7		
35	3	3	9	
36	4	0		
37	7	0		
38	8	3	3	5
39	7	2		
40	6			

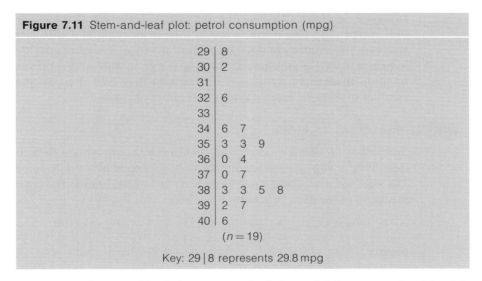

Figure 7.11 Stem-and-leaf plot: petrol consumption (mpg)

```
                29 │ 8
                30 │ 2
                31 │
                32 │ 6
                33 │
                34 │ 6  7
                35 │ 3  3  9
                36 │ 0  4
                37 │ 0  7
                38 │ 3  3  5  8
                39 │ 2  7
                40 │ 6
                    (n = 19)
          Key: 29│8 represents 29.8 mpg
```

Stem-and-leaf plots are particularly useful for comparing *bivariate* data analysis.

Example
Perhaps you have collected both summer and winter data. The two batches of data share a common stem and can be shown as a back-to-back stem-and-leaf plot, as in Figure 7.12.

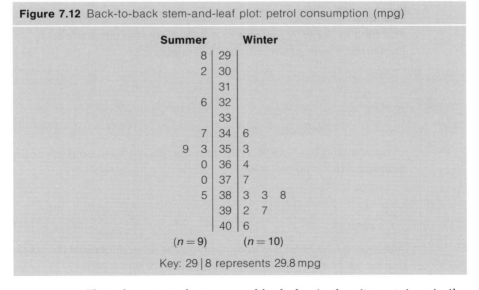

Figure 7.12 Back-to-back stem-and-leaf plot: petrol consumption (mpg)

```
           Summer        Winter
               8 │ 29 │
               2 │ 30 │
                 │ 31 │
               6 │ 32 │
                 │ 33 │
               7 │ 34 │ 6
           9   3 │ 35 │ 3
               0 │ 36 │ 4
               0 │ 37 │ 7
               5 │ 38 │ 3  3  8
                 │ 39 │ 2  7
                 │ 40 │ 6
           (n = 9)        (n = 10)
        Key: 29│8 represents 29.8 mpg
```

The advantage of a stem-and-leaf plot is that it contains similar information to a histogram if it were drawn horizontally. However, none of the data is lost since the stem-and-leaf plot presents the complete set of raw data, but in a more useful form. The disadvantage of this type of display is that it can be time consuming to construct as well as cumbersome when the number of observations, and hence the leaves, is large. In addition, if the data range is wide and expressed to more than three significant figures, you may find the potential number of stems is greater than the number of leaves.

7.4   Measuring location

A *measure of location* or *central tendency* is a convenient way of describing a large frequency distribution by means of a single value. The data to be analysed must be at least of interval status. The main measures of location in common use are:

▶ the *mean* ($\bar{x}$)   ▶ the *median* (M)   ▶ the *mode* (m)

7.4.1   Mean

The *mean* ($\bar{x}$) is the arithmetical average of a frequency distribution. The formula for calculating single data is:

$$\bar{x} = \frac{\Sigma x}{n}$$

where

$x =$ each observation
$n =$ the total number of observations
$\Sigma =$ the sum of

Example
The data in Table 7.9 relates to a sales representative's weekly commission over seven consecutive weeks.

Table 7.9 Commission data

Week 1	Week 2	Week 3	Week 4	Week 5	Week 6	Week 7
£42	£36	£39	£38	£40	£34	£32

Substituting the figures in the formula, you can work out his or her average weekly commission.

$$\frac{£261}{7}$$

$$= £37.29$$

Although this is helpful in summarising the data, in none of the weeks did the sales representative actually receive this figure.

The formula for calculating the mean of grouped data is:

$$\bar{x} = \frac{\Sigma x}{\Sigma f}$$

where

f = the frequency
x = each observation
Σ = the sum of

Example
The data in Table 7.10 relates to employees' pay in a particular department of an organisation and is grouped together in classes or bands.

Table 7.10 Employees' pay data

Weekly pay	Number of workers (f)
£90–£99.99	6
£100–£109.99	9
£110–£119.99	8
£120–£129.99	5
£130–£139.99	7

To determine the average weekly pay, you need to take the class mid-points of the pay bands and multiply by the frequency (numbers of workers) as shown in Table 7.11.

Table 7.11 Calculating the mean (grouped data): Employees' pay

Weekly pay	Mid-point (x)	Number of workers (f)	(fx)
£90–£99.99	£95	6	570
£100–£109.99	£105	9	945
£110–£119.99	£115	8	920
£120–£129.99	£125	5	625
£130–£139.99	£135	7	945
Total		35	4005

Substituting the figures in the formula, the mean pay is:

$$\frac{£4,505}{35}$$

$$= £114.43$$

The advantages of the mean as a measure of location are:

▶ the mean can be calculated exactly
▶ it makes use of all the data
▶ it can be used in further statistical work.

The disadvantages of the mean are:

▶ the mean is greatly affected by outliers
▶ it can give an impossible figure when the data is discrete; for example, the statistic that the average family has 1.8 children.

7.4.2   Median

The *median* (M) is the mid-value in a frequency distribution which has been arranged in size order. It can be used with all types of data, except those of nominal status. The formula is:

$$M = \frac{n+1}{2}$$

where

n = number of observations

By adding 1 to the number of observations and dividing by 2, you arrive at the mid-point of a data set that has been arranged in order of size.

Example
To illustrate the median we will use the sales representative's commission data from Section 7.4.1 (Table 7.12). All you need to do is to arrange the data in size order and ascertain which data item falls in the middle of the series. The value of this data item, the mid value, is the median. Table 7.13 illustrates this. In this series, the median is the fourth item, £38.

Table 7.12 Commission data

Week 1	Week 2	Week 3	Week 4	Week 5	Week 6	Week 7
£42	£36	£39	£38	£40	£34	£32

Table 7.13 Finding the median (uneven number of items): sales commission

£32	£34	£36	**£38**	£39	£40	£42

As you can see, this is fairly straightforward with an *uneven* number of data items, but you may have an *even* number of data items. Perhaps you have collected details of the sales representative's commission for an eighth week and this was £44. Table 7.14 illustrates this. Now the mid-value lies between the fourth and the fifth data items, £38 and £39. Therefore the median is £38.50.

Table 7.14 Finding the median (even number of items): sales commission

£32	£34	£36	**£38**	**£39**	£40	£42	£44

The advantages of the median as a measure of location are:

▶ the median is not affected by outliers
▶ it can be determined even if some of the values in the distribution are unknown
▶ it is unaffected by open-ended classes and irregular class widths it can represent an actual value in the data.

The disadvantages of the median are:

▶ the value of the median can only be roughly estimated for a grouped distribution
▶ it cannot be used in further statistical calculations
▶ when the distribution is irregular, the median may not be characteristic of the distribution.

7.4.3   Mode

The *mode* (*m*) is the most frequently occurring value in a frequency distribution.

Example
Perhaps you are investigating the purchase of protective helmets for a security firm. The company has nine guards and has decided to buy one size and rely on the straps to adjust the helmet to fit the guards. The data in Table 7.15 relates to the size of the guards' heads. The most frequently occurring size is 7 inches. Thus, if you decided to use the mode, three guards would have a perfect fit, two guards would find them a bit large, and four would find them too tight.

Table 7.15 Size of guards' heads

6″	$6\frac{1}{2}$″	7″	7″	7″	$7\frac{1}{2}$″	8	$8\frac{1}{2}$″	9″

If you used the median (7 in.), in this example the result would be the same. However, if you used the mean (7.38 in.), and bought the nearest size ($7\frac{1}{2}$ in.), it is worth noting that the helmet would fit only one of the guards properly.

The advantages of the mode as a measure of location are:

► the mode is unaffected by outliers
► it is easy to obtain by histogram or calculation
► only values near the modal class are required

The disadvantages of the mode are:

► the mode is an unstable figure and can change dramatically as other observations are added
► it cannot be found exactly when the distribution is grouped
► the distribution may be *multimodal* (contain more than one mode)
► it cannot be used in further statistical work.

The mean, the median and the mode are descriptive statistics which provide you with a view of where the approximate 'middle' of a set of data lies; that is, they are measures of *central tendency*. However, they all use different definitions of central tendency, so you can get very different answers from the same set of values.

When a frequency distribution curve is *symmetrical*, the median, mean and mode all share the same value. This is known as *normal distribution* and is illustrated in Figure 7.13.

When the frequency curve is *skewed*, the mean, the median and the mode have different values. With *positively* skewed data, the tail is on the right (positive side) and most of the data is at the lower end of the range. Figure 7.14 shows an example.

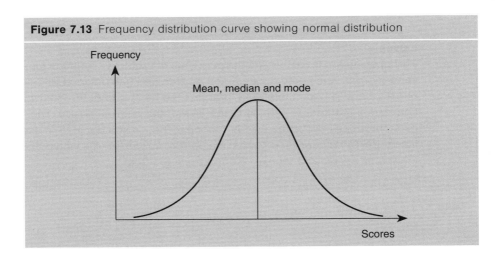

Figure 7.13 Frequency distribution curve showing normal distribution

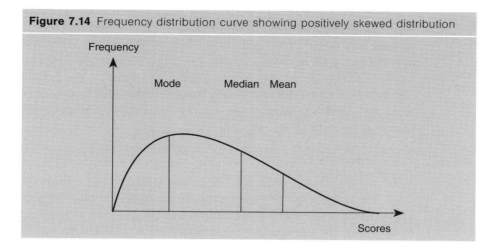

Figure 7.14 Frequency distribution curve showing positively skewed distribution

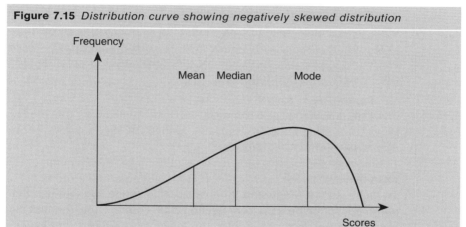

Figure 7.15 *Distribution curve showing negatively skewed distribution*

With *negatively* skewed data, the tail is on the left (negative side) and most of the data is at the upper end of the range. Figure 7.15 shows an example.

When a frequency curve is unimodal (in other words, has only one mode) and is moderately skewed, the following equation gives an approximate relationship between the median, mean and mode:

$$\text{Mean} - \text{Mode} = 3(\text{Mean} - \text{Median})$$

7.5 Measuring dispersion

A simple measure of location on its own does not give us any idea of the shape of the data distribution. A measure which helps describe the spread of values in a data distribution is called a *measure of dispersion* or *spread*. If the measures of location and dispersion are used together, you can obtain a concise and useful description of the distribution of your data set.

If the data set is quite large (more than 30), it is sometimes useful to divide the ordered data into quarters. Just as the point for the division into halves is called the *median*, the points for divisions into quarters is called *quartiles*. Quartiles are usually calculated from frequency distributions rather than raw data.

7.5.1   Range and interquartile range

Two simple measures of dispersion are the *range* and the *interquartile range*. The range is the difference between the upper extreme (highest) value (E_U) and the lower extreme (lowest) value (E_L) in a frequency distribution. The interquartile range measures the spread of the middle 50 per cent of observations and is the difference between the upper quartile (Q_3) and the lower quartile (Q_1). The interquartile range is often preferred to the range when making a comparison between two distributions, because the range is more easily affected by outliers (extreme values). The formulae for the range and interquartile range can be summarised as follows:

$$Range = E_U - E_L$$
$$Interquartile\ range = Q_3 - Q_1$$
$$Semi\text{-}interquartile\ range = \frac{Q_3 - Q_1}{2}$$

Example

To illustrate the range and the interquartile range, we will use the petrol consumption data from Section 7.4.5 (Table 7.16). The first step is to order the data and identify the lower extreme (E_L), the lower quartile (Q_1), the median (M), the upper quartile (Q_3) and the upper extreme (E_U). You will remember from Section 7.5 that the median is the mid-value and n = the total number of observations. The calculations you need to make are as follows.

$$Quartiles = \frac{n+1}{4}$$
$$= \frac{19+1}{4}$$
$$= 5th\ number\ (Q_1 = 34.7;\ Q_3 = 38.5)$$

Table 7.16 Petrol consumption data (mpg)

40.6	34.6	38.8	39.7	38.3	39.2	38.3	36.4	35.3	37.7
38.5	37.0	36.0	29.8	32.6	35.3	34.7	30.2	35.9	

$$\text{Median} = \frac{n+1}{2}$$

$$= \frac{19+1}{2}$$

$$= \text{10th number (36.4)}$$

Table 7.17 shows the ordered data, together with the above five measures of dispersion.

Table 7.17 Ordered data, together with the above five measures of dispersion

E_L				Q_1					M
29.8	30.2	32.6	34.6	**34.7**	35.3	35.3	35.9	36.0	**36.4**

				Q_3				E_U	
37.0	37.7	38.3	38.3	**38.5**	38.8	39.2	39.7	**40.6**	

Next, substitute the figures for the formulae.

$$\text{Range} = E_U - E_L$$

$$= 40.6 - 29.8$$

$$= 10.8\,\text{mpg}$$

$$\text{Interquartile range} = Q_3 - Q_1$$

$$= 38.5 - 34.7$$

$$= 3.8\,\text{mpg}$$

$$\text{Semi-interquartile range} = \frac{Q_3 - Q_1}{2}$$

$$= \frac{38.5 - 34.7}{2}$$

$$= 1.9\,\text{mpg}$$

The lower quartile (Q_1) contains the petrol consumption figures for the bottom 25 per cent of cars in the sample, and the upper quartile (Q_3), the figures for the top 25 per cent. This means that you can make such statements as 50 per cent of company cars under investigation have a petrol consumption of between 34.7 mpg and 38.5 mpg.

7.5.2 Box plots

A *box plot* is a very useful diagram that presents four important measures of dispersion and one of location and illustrates the shape of a frequency distribution: the upper and lower extremes, the median and the upper and lower quartiles. The 'box' represents the middle 50 per cent of the data and each 'whisker' 25 per cent

Example
Figure 7.16 shows an example of a box plot which presents the petrol consumption data from Section 7.5.1.

Figure 7.16 Box plot: petrol consumption (mpg)

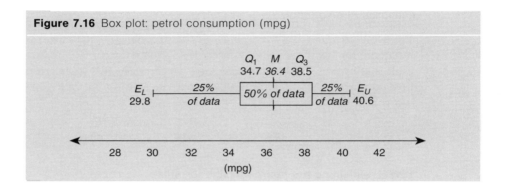

You can see that a box plot allows you to get an idea of the spread and shape of the data. 'If the box is small compared with the whiskers this indicates that the distribution is bunched in the middle with long tails. A box shifted to one side or the other indicates skewness, as does the position of the median within the box' (Oakshott, 1994, p. 48). This example shows that the data is *negatively skewed*; in other words, the values are bunched to the right-hand side of the central tendency and tail out on the left. If it were *positively skewed*, the data would be bunched to the left-hand side of the central tendency and tail out on the right.

Unfortunately, the drawback of using the range as a measure of dispersion is that it only takes into account two items, and the inter-quartile range only takes account of half the values. What we really want is a measure of spread which uses all the values and we discuss this next.

7.5.3   Standard deviation

One solution to the limitations of the *range* and the *interquartile range* (see Section 7.5.1) is to use the *standard deviation*. This is calculated by adding together all the differences (deviations) between each observation and the mean, and making some adjustments. We have to make adjustments because the difference between each observation below the mean and the mean would result in a negative figure and the difference between each observation above the mean and the mean would result in a positive figure; when added together, the answer would always be zero. What we need to do is to get rid of all the plus and minus signs. Mathematically, the way to do this is to square the differences (deviations), since the squares of positive and negative quantities are both positive.

The *variance* is the term used to describe the mean of the deviations squared. The variance uses every item, but always gives an answer in squared units. Therefore, if you are measuring length, the variance is in squared lengths (areas); if you are measuring times in hours, the variance is in squared hours. To avoid the problem of squared units, the square root of the variance is used to de-square the units. The final result is known as the *standard deviation*. To carry out this calculation, the data must be at least of interval status. The formula for individual data is as follows.

$$S = \sqrt{\frac{\Sigma(x - \bar{x})^2}{n}}$$

where

x = an observation
$\bar{x}$ = the mean
n = the total number of observations
$\sqrt{}$ = the square root
Σ = the sum of

The formula for grouped data is:

$$S = \sqrt{\frac{\Sigma x^2 f}{\Sigma f} - \frac{(\Sigma x f)^2}{\Sigma f}}$$

where

x = the mid-point of each data class
f = the frequency of each class
$\sqrt{}$ = the square root
Σ = the sum of

Example

To illustrate the standard deviation, let us suppose that you are investigating wastage of materials in a manufacturing company and have collected the data shown in Table 7.18 over a six-week period.

Table 7.18 Material wastage data

Week 1	Week 2	Week 3	Week 4	Week 5	Week 6
12 kg	10 kg	8 kg	4 kg	18 kg	8 kg

Before you can calculate the standard deviation, you need to calculate the mean ($\bar{x}$) (see Section 7.4.1) as shown below.

$$\bar{x} = \frac{\Sigma x}{n}$$

$$= \frac{60 \text{ kg}}{6}$$

$$= 10 \text{ kg}$$

Now you are ready to calculate the other figures you will need for the formula by constructing a table (7.19) as follows.

Table 7.19 Calculating $(x - \bar{x})^2$

x	$(x - \bar{x})$	$(x - \bar{x})^2$
12	2	4
10	0	0
8	−2	4
4	−6	36
18	8	64
8	−2	4
	Total	**112**

The final step is to substitute the figures you have calculated in the formula.

$$S = \sqrt{\frac{\Sigma(x - \bar{x})^2}{n}}$$

$$= \sqrt{\frac{112}{6}}$$

$$= 4.32 \text{ kg}$$

The standard deviation is the most important measure of spread because it uses every value and is in the same units as the original data. The bigger the spread, the bigger the standard deviation. The mean and the standard deviation go together since they both use all the items. The mean gives the centre of the distribution of data and the standard deviation gives a measure of the spread of the distribution.

The most important reason for using the standard deviation as a measure of spread is that it is related to a very common theoretical frequency distribution called the *normal distribution*. One important feature of the standard deviation is that if you have a normal distribution, 68.26 per cent of all your observations will fall within one standard deviation (1 S) of the mean. In other words, 34.13 per cent of

Figure 7.17 Proportions of the normal distribution curve cut off by one standard deviation below and one standard deviation above the mean

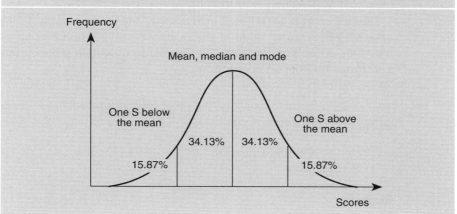

the total set of scores will fall one standard deviation below the mean and 34.13 per cent will fall one standard deviation above the mean, as shown in Figure 7.17.

If you take two standard deviations above and below the mean, 95.4 per cent of your observations will be covered. We will be looking more closely at the implications of this in Section 7.8.

7.6   Measuring change

An *index number* is a statistical measure which shows the *percentage change* in a variable, such as costs or prices, from some fixed point in the past. The *base period* of an index is the period against which all other periods are compared.

7.6.1   Simple index numbers

A *simple index* shows each item in a series relative to some chosen base period value. For example, you may have collected data about a variable whose value changes over time, such as property prices, the cost of a certain component, the average pay of employees in a particular industry, or consumers' annual expenditure on durable goods. For a clearer indication of the pattern of movement of the value of such a variable over time, it is customary to choose an appropriate point in time as a base; for example, a particular year for a variable that is observed annually; a week for a variable that is observed weekly. The base time-point should be a time when values of the variable are relatively stable. Then the values of the variable at other points in time are expressed as percentages of its value at the base time-point.

The percentages are referred to as *relatives* and are the simplest form of *index number*. The value of the relative (or index number) at the base time-point is always 100. The formula for calculating the current year index number (I) is as follows.

$$I = \frac{P_C}{P_B} \times 100$$

where

$P_C =$ Current price
$P_B =$ Base price

Example
To illustrate how to construct simple index we will examine house prices in the 1970s (Table 7.20).

Table 7.20 House price data

Year	Average house price
1971	£5,632
1972	£7,374
1973	£9,942
1974	£11,073
1975	£12,144
1976	£13,006

You have decided that 1971, which is the first year for which you have data, will be your base year, in other words, $1971 = 100$. Next, you need to make the necessary calculations using the formula, as shown in Table 7.21.

Index figures are very useful for reducing sets of data to a form which allows them to be compared directly.

Example
The data shown in Table 7.22 relates to a production department in a particular company.

By constructing a simple index for each variable, you can make direct comparisons as shown in Table 7.23.

As well as using a table to present the index figures, they can be plotted as a multiple line graph as shown in Figure 7.18. The graph

Table 7.21   Index of house prices, 1971–6

Year	Average house price	$\dfrac{P_C}{P_B} \times 100$	Index number (1971 = 100)
1971	£5,632	$\dfrac{5\ ,\ 632}{5\ ,\ 632} \times 100$	100.0
1972	£7,374	$\dfrac{7\ ,\ 374}{5\ ,\ 632} \times 100$	130.9
1973	£9,942	$\dfrac{9\ ,\ 942}{5\ ,\ 632} \times 100$	176.5
1974	£11,073	$\dfrac{11\ ,\ 073}{5\ ,\ 632} \times 100$	196.6
1975	£12,144	$\dfrac{12\ ,\ 144}{5\ ,\ 632} \times 100$	215.6
1976	£13,006	$\dfrac{13\ ,\ 006}{5\ ,\ 632} \times 100$	230.9

Table 7.22 Production department data

Year	Production units (mn)	Number of employees	Units per manshift
1980	184	602	1.40
1981	180	571	1.45
1982	188	551	1.56
1983	188	524	1.65
1984	185	498	1.72
1985	179	466	1.80

Table 7.23 Indices of production department data (1980 = 100)

Year	Production units (mn)	Number of employees	Units per manshift
1980	100	100	100
1981	98	95	104
1982	102	92	112
1983	102	87	116
1984	101	83	123
1985	97	78	128

Figure 7.18 Multiple line graph: indices of production department data (1980 = 100)

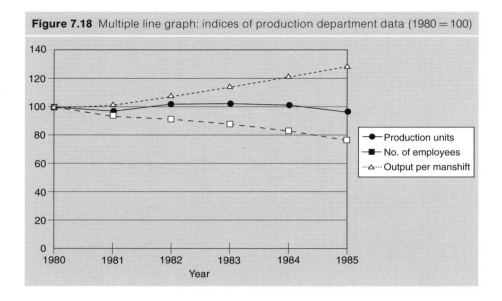

shows that there has been an increase in production per manshift. However, production has remained stable, despite a rapid reduction in the number of employees.

7.6.2   Deflating data

Deflating a data series using an index is a method of removing the effect of inflation from the data which otherwise obscures the underlying trend. To deflate a figure, divide the figure by the index number for that year and multiply by 100. The result will then be expressed in terms of the value of money in the base year.

Example
Perhaps you have collected the profit figures shown in Table 7.24 for a certain company for the five years 1982 to 1987.

Table 7.24 Profit data (£mn)

1982	1983	1984	1985	1986
12	13.5	15.1	17	19

The figures look impressive, but you want to find out how much of the increase was due to inflation. You will need to look up the published values for the Retail Price Index (RPI) for these five years, and these are reproduced below (Table 7.25).

Table 7.25 Retail Price Index (1974 = 100)

1982	1983	1984	1985	1986
320.4	335.1	351.8	373.2	385.9

You can use the RPI to deflate the profit data so that the profit figures for each year will be based on the same values they would have had in 1974, because that was the base year for the index. The deflated profit figures can be calculated using the following formula:

$$\frac{\text{Base year RPI}}{\text{Current year RPI}} \times \text{Profit}$$

Applying the formula we can calculate the deflated profit figures as shown in Table 7.26.

Table 7.26 Deflating a series: profit data

Year	RPI	$\dfrac{\text{Base year RPI}}{\text{Current year RPI}} \times \text{Profit}$	Deflated profit (£mn)
1982	320.4	$\dfrac{100}{320.4} \times 12.0$	3.7
1983	335.1	$\dfrac{100}{335.1} \times 13.5$	4.0
1984	351.8	$\dfrac{100}{351.8} \times 15.1$	4.2
1985	373.2	$\dfrac{100}{373.8} \times 17.0$	4.5
1986	385.9	$\dfrac{100}{385.9} \times 19.0$	4.9

These results can be plotted on a line graph, as shown in Figure 7.19, which highlights the distorting effects of inflation very clearly. Far from showing the dramatic increase which appears in the original data, the deflated profits show only a modest increase over the period, which puts a different complexion on the general financial health of the company and demonstrates the impact of inflation since 1974.

7.6.3   Weighted index numbers

A *weighted (composite or aggregate) index number* is constructed by calculating a weighted average of some set of values, where the weights show the relative importance of each item in the data set. For

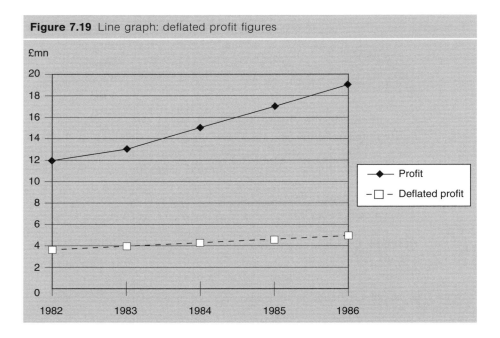

Figure 7.19 Line graph: deflated profit figures

example, the Retail Price Index (RPI), or the Consumer Price Index as it is known in the USA and some other countries, is an index of the price of goods and services in retail shops. The prices are weighted to reflect the spending habits of 'average' households and expressed in percentage terms relative to a base year, which is taken as 100. For example, if 1987 is taken as the base year (in other words, 1987 = 100), then in 1946 the RPI stood at 7.4 and in 1990 at 126.1.

The Financial Times Stock Exchange 100 Share Index (FT-SE 100) 'is a weighted arithmetic index representing the price of 100 securities with a base of 1,000 on 3 January 1984' (Hussey, 1995, p. 157). Unlike other index numbers, it is indexed with a base of 1,000 rather than 100 at the base time-point.

When calculating weighted index numbers, you should remember that the weights are held constant at their values for the base time-point. Since the weights (for example, quantities purchased) may change dramatically over a long period of time, it is only realistic to use weighted index numbers with fixed weights over relatively short periods of time. An index can be calculated which is the average of a series of price relatives. For it to be realistic, it should take into account the amount of each commodity used. The method of weighting allows this to be done.

A *Laspeyres index* is a base period weighted index, where the weights used relate to some chosen base period. It can be calculated using the following formula:

$$\frac{\Sigma PcQb}{\Sigma PbQb} \times 100$$

where

Pc = Current price
Pb = Base price
Qb = Base quantity

The advantages of a Laspeyres index are:

▶ The index is easy to calculate for series of years as it uses the same set of weights each time
▶ It allows a comparison of any one year with any other as all use the same weights
▶ It requires little data in terms of weights.

The disadvantages of a Laspeyres index are:

▶ The weights used will gradually become out of date and will no longer represent the contemporary situation
▶ It tends to overestimate price increase because it uses out-of-date weights.

A *Paasche index* is a current period weighted average where the weights used rebase to the current period. It can be calculated using the following formula:

$$\frac{\Sigma PcQc}{\Sigma PbQc} \times 100$$

where

Pc = Current price
Pb = Base price
Qc = Current quantity

The advantage of a Paasche index is:

▶ The index always uses the current weights and thus reflects today's situation.

The disadvantages of a Paasche index are:

▶ The index involves more calculation for a series of years as the weights used a constantly changing
▶ It can only be compared against the base year as the weights for each year change
It tends to underestimate price increases
▶ It requires new weights each period which can be both costly and time consuming to collect.

7.7   Confirmatory data analysis

In this section we will be looking at four main groups of *inferential statistics* which are used when conducting *confirmatory data analysis*:

▶ estimating from samples
▶ measuring association
▶ measuring difference
▶ forecasting.

It is important to remember that we are only looking at a small selection of the more common techniques and procedures available. If you are interested in conducting confirmatory data analysis and are not a statistician, you may find it helpful to seek the advice of someone with a good knowledge of the range of techniques available and 'to get that advice at the design stage of the project, not after you have collected the data' (Robson, 1993, p. 307). You will also need to consult a specialist text and obtain access to suitable computer software.

When conducting *confirmatory data analysis*, it is important that you bear in mind the nature of your data and what you are trying to find out. These two factors will help you determine the most appropriate technique to use. You will remember from Section 7.1 that a *non-parametric technique* can be used on skewed data, whereas a *parametric technique* can only be used on data which is normally distributed. Table 7.27 shows the inferential statistics we will be examining in this second half of the chapter analysed by type of data.

Table 7.27 Confirmatory data analysis by type of data

Technique or procedure	Type of data
Estimating from samples	
Confidence intervals (P)	Univariate; must be normally distributed
Forecasting	
Time series analysis	Univariate; must be available for several past periods of time
Measuring association	
Pearson's coefficient (r) (P)	Bivariate; only suitable for interval or ratio data
Spearman's rank coefficient (r_S) (P)	Bivariate; must be at least of ordinal status
Measuring difference	
Chi squared (χ^2) test (NP)	Bivariate; nominal data
Student *t-test* (P)	Bivariate; must be at least of interval status

Note
P = Parametric technique
NP = Non-parametric technique

In carrying out your analysis, you will have to identify the independent variable and the dependent variable. For example, you may want to find out whether, if employees are paid more (independent variable), their productivity levels increase (dependent variable). Indeed, you may have predicted that there will be an effect in a specific direction. In this example, you may have predicted that more pay will lead to higher productivity. This example of a prediction is known as a *one-tailed hypothesis*. You will remember that a hypothesis is an idea or proposition which can be tested for association or causality by deducing logical consequences, which can be tested against *empirical evidence* (data which is based on observation or experience).

A *two-tailed hypothesis* is where you suspect that the independent variable has an effect on the dependent variable, but you cannot predict the direction. Your hypothesis that the independent variable will have an effect on the dependent variable is known as the *alternate*, (*experimental* or *research*) *hypothesis* (H_1). However, when you conduct your analysis, you will assume that there is no effect by establishing a *null hypothesis* (H_0).

As well as determining the nature of your data, you must also take into account the type of your samples. They must either be *related samples* or *independent (unrelated) samples*. Related samples can occur in two different ways. For example, in a 'before-and-after' research design two scores are obtained from each of the subjects and analysed. alternatively, subjects may be paired off on the basis of relevant variables and then the scores obtained in one group are compared with the scores in the other. This type of research often involves identical twins. Independent samples occur when all available subjects are divided into two groups which are assumed to be comparable on all the relevant variables and different treatments are given to the two groups.

Having identified the nature of your data and samples, you need to determine your reasons for using the test. This will depend on your hypothesis. Either your hypothesis will predict a *difference* (for example, long-service employees work harder than new employees) or a *correlation* (for example, increased advertising expenditure leads to increased sales). Of course, you will be anxious to know whether any difference you find is one which matters or not; in other words, whether the difference is statistically significant and not merely due to random variables (chance). Thus, *significance* refers to how certain you are that your manipulation of the independent variable really has altered the dependent variable. You can express the significance of your results as a numerical *probability* value. There are traditional probability levels used in statistics and if there is more than a 5 per cent (1 in 20) probability that the results are due to chance, we would not accept them. If your results are significant at the 5 per cent level, you can state that the probability (p) is 0.05. If there is only a 1 per cent

Figure 7.20 Examples of the principal decisions to be made when analysing data

1. Determine the type of data. If your data is normally distributed, use a parametric technique; if your data is skewed, use a non-parametric technique
2. Decide whether you have related or independent samples
3. Decide whether you wish to measure difference or association as this will determine which specific technique to use
4. Decide whether you have a one-tailed or a two-tailed hypothesis
5. Establish the level of significance you will accept

chance that the results are due to chance, we are even more are confident in accepting the alternate hypothesis.

As you can see, there are a number of decisions you need to make. Depending on the nature of your particular research, the decisions you have to make and the order in which you make them will vary. In Figure 7.20 we summarise the above paragraphs and suggest a logical sequence.

When you have completed your analysis, you will state that you have accepted or rejected the null hypothesis at a set level of significance; usually, 5 per cent or, less often, 1 per cent. It could be that through faulty research design you accept the null hypothesis, even though the effect does exist. In this case, you will have made what is know as a *type two error*. Alternatively, you may claim that an effect exists when it has occurred merely by chance. In this situation, you will have made a *type one error*. If you set your level of significance too high (that is, $p \geq 1$ per cent), you are more likely to make a type two error.

7.8   Estimating from samples

If you are conducting confirmatory data analysis, your reason for obtaining a sample from a population will be to obtain estimates of various *population parameters*. A population parameter is a characteristic of a population, such as the mean or the standard deviation, and is usually symbolised by Greek letters. Traditionally, sample statistics are represented by Roman letters. Table 7.28 shows the symbols we will be using in this chapter to denote population (theoretical) parameters and sample statistics.

Sampling theory is the study of relationships existing between a *population* and *samples* drawn from it. For conclusions of sampling theory to be valid, the chosen samples must be representative of the population. This may be achieved through *random sampling* (see

Table 7.28 Symbols for denoting population parameters and sample statistics

Parameter	Population	Sample
Mean	μ (mu)	$\bar{x}$
Standard deviation	σ (sigma)	S
Percentage	π (pi)	P

Chapter 6) or by using the *random number tables* given in Appendix B. Much sampling theory is based on the assumption that random samples have been taken.

Sampling theory states that the sampling distribution of means is a *normal distribution* (see Section 7.1), with mean equal to the population mean (μ) and standard error $\sigma/\sqrt{n}$.

The quantity $\sigma/\sqrt{n}$ is called the standard error of the means ($\sigma\bar{x}$) to differentiate it from the standard deviation of a population (σ). Even if the parent population is not normally distributed, the distribution of sample means is sufficiently close to normal to be treated as such, provided it is larger than 25. If you subtract the mean and divide by the standard deviation, you can standardise $\bar{x}$ and obtain a variable which has a standard normal distribution. This enables you to use standard normal tables to answer questions about sample means.

The theoretical frequency distribution known as the *normal distribution* (see Section 7.4.3) is an important concept in inferential statistics. Frequency distributions are not normally known for populations, since often only a sample is taken and not a census. The normal distribution is used to represent the population frequency distribution of variables, especially those which can be physically measured. The frequency curve of such a population, known as a *normal curve*, is bell shaped and symmetrical with tails extending indefinitely either side of the centre. Three measures of central tendency coincide at the centre of a normal curve: the mean, the median and the mode. A distribution which is not symmetrical and has its peak offset to one side is known as *skewed*. In such a distribution the mean, median and mode will not coincide. The properties of the normal distribution are shown in Figure 7.21.

Figure 7.21 Properties of the normal distribution

1. The curve is symmetrical about the mean (μ)
2. The total area under the curve is unity (1)
3. The probability that a particular value of the variable under study lies between two points, equals the area under the curve between those two points

If you know the value of the mean and the standard deviation of a data set with a normal distribution, the following is always true:

▶ The mean ± 2/3 standard deviation will give you the middle 50% of the data
▶ The mean ± 1 standard deviation will give you the middle 68.3% of the data
▶ The mean ± 2 standard deviations will give you the middle 95.4% of the data
▶ The mean ± 3 standard deviations will give you the middle 99.7% of the data.

7.8.1   Confidence intervals

The principle of sampling theory underpins a parametric technique for estimating *confidence intervals*. A confidence interval is a range of values of a sample statistic that is likely to contain an unknown *population parameter* at a given level of probability. The wider the confidence interval, the higher the confidence level. The normal distribution is used to calculate the limits if the population is normal and the standard deviation of the population is known. If normality cannot be assumed, a large sample size will ensure that the sampling distribution of the means is approximately normal (Oakshott, 1994).

Confidence intervals allow you to give an estimate of the reliability of your estimate by specifying some limits within which the true population value is expected to lie. The estimate is expressed as a range of figures together with a statement of the *level of confidence* (*probability*) that the interval contains the true population parameter. The formulae are as follows:

$$\mu = \bar{x} \pm 2.58 \, \frac{\sigma}{\sqrt{n}} \text{ at a 99\% confidence interval}$$

or

$$\mu = \bar{x} \pm 1.96 \, \frac{\sigma}{\sqrt{n}} \text{ at a 95\% confidence interval}$$

or

$$\mu = \bar{x} \pm 1.64 \, \frac{\sigma}{\sqrt{n}} \text{ at a 90\% confidence interval}$$

where

μ = the population mean
$\bar{x}$ = sample mean
σ = standard deviation (of the population)
n = sample size
$\sqrt{}$ = square root

Example

Perhaps you are investigating management stress and have collected data relating to the heart rates of 25 managers who have been diagnosed as suffering from stress and are taking part in an exercise programme. You find out that the mean heart rate is 85 beats per minute. Assuming that the overall standard deviation of heart rate increase is 15 beats per minute, you now wish to establish a 95 per cent confidence interval for the overall mean heart rate increase of all stressed managers who undergo this exercise programme.

$$\mu = 85 \pm 1.96 \left(\frac{15}{\sqrt{25}} \right)$$

$$= 85 \pm 1.96(3)$$

$$= 85 \pm 5.88$$

$$= 79.12, 90.88 \text{ beats per minute}$$

7.8.2   Confidence intervals of a percentage

Percentages are a useful descriptive statistic which are commonly calculated when analysing quantitative research data. For example, the proportion of managers with a certain number of subordinates in a sample or the percentage of workers in a certain pay band. You can estimate an unknown *population percentage*, providing you have a sample size of at least 30. The formulae are as follows:

$$\pi = P \pm 2.58 \sqrt{P \frac{(100 - P)}{n}} \text{ at a 99\% confidence interval}$$

or

$$\pi = P \pm 1.96 \sqrt{P \frac{(100 - P)}{n}} \text{ at a 95\% confidence interval}$$

or

$$\pi = P \pm 1.64 \sqrt{P \frac{(100 - P)}{n}} \text{ at a 90\% confidence interval}$$

where

$\pi =$ population percentage
$P =$ sample percentage
$n =$ sample size
$\sqrt{} =$ square root

Example

Perhaps you have collected data from a random sample of 500 families in Bristol and find that 160 own CD players. Now you want to calculate a 95 per cent confidence interval for the proportion of families in the city owning CD players. First, you need to work out the sample percentage (*P*) as follows

$$P = \frac{160}{500} \times 100$$

$$= 32\%$$

Therefore, the 95 per cent confidence internal for the unknown population percentage (π) is as follows:

$$\pi = P \pm 1.96 \sqrt{P\frac{(100 - P)}{n}}$$

$$= 32 \pm 1.96(2.09)$$

$$= 32 \pm 4.10$$

$$= 36.1\%, 27.9\%$$

This means that the true percentage lies somewhere between 36.1 per cent and 27.9 per cent.

7.9   Measuring association

Distributions in which the data consists of pairs of measurements, such as a sales representative's commission and the number of sales made or the age and weight of babies, are known as *bivariate data*. If you have collected such data you may wish to investigate a possible association between the two variables concerned (*correlation*). If you find that an association exists, you may then wish to express it in mathematical terms (*regression*).

7.9.1   Pearson's product moment correlation coefficient

Pearson's product moment correlation coefficient (*r*) is a parametric technique which gives a measure of the strength of association between two variables. 'Pearson's correlation is so frequently used that it is often assumed that the word 'correlation' by itself refers to it; other kinds of correlation, such as Spearman's have to be specified by name' (Vogt, 1993, p. 169). The data must be *interval* or *ratio* status (see Chapter 6) and normally distributed. The data must be *bivariate* and the two sets must have similar variances. The relations between the two quantity variables must be linear. This is more conveniently calculated by computer. The formula is as follows:

$$r = \frac{\Sigma xy - \dfrac{\Sigma x \Sigma y}{n}}{\sqrt{\left[\Sigma x^2 - \dfrac{(\Sigma x)^2}{n}\right]\left[\Sigma y^2 - \dfrac{(\Sigma y)^2}{n}\right]}}$$

where

y = the dependent variable
x = the independent variable
n = the number of data pairs
$\sqrt{\ }$ = square root
Σ = the sum of

Example

The data shown in Table 7.29 relates to the number of calls made by a sales representative during an eight-week period and the corresponding number of orders taken. First, you need to perform some initial calculations as shown in Table 7.30.

In this example, the number of data pairs is eight ($n = 8$). Now you are ready to substitute the figures in the formula as follows.

$$r = \frac{\Sigma xy - \dfrac{\Sigma x \Sigma y}{n}}{\sqrt{\left[\Sigma x^2 - \dfrac{(\Sigma x)^2}{n}\right]\left[\Sigma y^2 - \dfrac{(\Sigma y)^2}{n}\right]}}$$

$$= \frac{668 - \dfrac{(32)(144)}{8}}{\sqrt{\left[170 - \dfrac{(32)(32)}{8}\right]\left[2{,}816 - \dfrac{(144)(144)}{8}\right]}}$$

$$= \frac{668 - 576}{\sqrt{[170 - 128][2{,}816 - 2{,}592]}}$$

$$= \frac{92}{\sqrt{(42)(224)}}$$

$$= \frac{92}{96.9948}$$

$$= 0.95 \text{ to two significant figures}$$

Table 7.29 Sales data

Week	Number of orders	Number of calls
1	1	10
2	2	14
3	2	12
4	4	20
5	3	18
6	6	20
7	8	26
8	6	24

Table 7.30 Calculating xy, x^2 and y^2: sales orders and calls data

Week	Number of order (x)	Number of calls (y)	(xy)	(x^2)	(y^2)
1	1	10	10	1	100
2	2	14	28	4	196
3	2	12	24	4	144
4	4	20	80	16	400
5	3	18	54	9	324
6	6	20	120	36	400
7	8	26	208	64	676
8	6	24	144	36	576
Total	**32**	**144**	**668**	**170**	**2,816**

Next, you need to look up the critical value of r in the correlation coefficient table (see Appendix C). The following should help you interpret your results:

$r = 1$ represents a perfect positive linear association
$r = 0$ represents no linear association
$r = -1$ represents a perfect negative linear association

Therefore, values in between can be graded roughly as:

$r = 0.90$ to 0.99 (very high positive correlation)
$r = 0.70$ to 0.89 (high positive correlation)
$r = 0.40$ to 0.69 (medium positive correlation)
$r = 0$ to 0.39 (low positive correlation)
$r = 0$ to -0.39 (low negative correlation)

$r = -0.40$ to -0.69 (medium negative correlation)
$r = -0.70$ to -0.89 (high negative correlation)
$r = -0.90$ to -0.99 (very high negative correlation)

In this example the result is significant at the 5 per cent level. In other words, there is positive correlation between the number of calls made by the sales representative and the number of orders.

Correlation coefficients should be interpreted with care, since a correlation between two variables does not prove the existence of a causal link between them; two causally unrelated variables can be correlated because they both relate to a third variable. For example, sales of ice-cream and sales of suntan lotion may be correlated because they both related to higher temperatures.

7.9.2   Spearman's rank correlation coefficient

Spearman's rank correlation coefficient (r_S) is a non-parametric technique used to obtain a measure of linear association between two variables where it is not possible or it is difficult to measure accurately, but where ranking is possible. It can also be used to obtain a quick approximate value of the product moment coefficient when you have a large number of values which make it tedious to calculate Pearson's r (see Section 7.9.1).

In order to calculate Spearman's rank correlation coefficient, the data must be *bivariate* and at least of *ordinal* status (see Chapter 6). Again, this is more conveniently calculated by computer. However, the formula is as follows:

$$r_S = 1 - \frac{6\Sigma d^2}{n(n^2 - 1)}$$

where

$d =$ difference between the two ranked variables
$n =$ number of data pairs
$\Sigma =$ the sum of

Before you proceed, the two data sets must be ranked. The purpose of ranking is to give the variables in each data set a number according to its relative size, with either the largest or the smallest variable being ranked as 1. If you have equal rankings for the same variable, calculate the mean rank. For example, four variables coming fourth equal would each be given the rank of 5.5 ($4 + 5 + 6 + 7$, divided by 4), so the next rank would be 8. Next, obtain the difference between the rankings for each data set, square the differences, total the squared differences and substitute them in the formula.

Example

The data shown in Table 7.31 relates to production levels and material wastage in a factory during a seven-month period. First, you need to rank the data and perform some initial calculations as shown in Table 7.32.

Table 7.31 Production and material wastage data

Month	Production (units)	Material wastage (kg)
January	13,900	290
February	12,700	210
March	10,800	180
April	12,200	270
May	11,800	230
June	11,300	140
July	14,700	245

Table 7.32 Calculating d^2 : production and material wastage data

Month	Production Rank	Wastage Rank	(d)	(d^2)
January	2	1	1	1
February	3	5	2	4
March	7	6	1	1
April	4	2	2	4
May	5	4	1	1
June	6	7	1	1
July	1	3	2	4
x			**Total**	**16**

In this example, the number of data pairs is seven ($n = 7$). Now you are ready to substitute the figures in the formula as follows.

$$r_S = 1 - \frac{6\Sigma d^2}{n(n^2 - 1)}$$

$$= 1 - \frac{6(16)}{7(49 - 1)}$$

$$= 1 - \frac{96}{336}$$

$$= 0.714$$

Next you need to look up the critical value of r_S in the correlation coefficient table (see Appendix C). The following should help you interpret your results:

▸ When $r_S = 1$ there is perfect positive linear association
▸ When $r_S = 0$ there is no linear association
▸ When $r_S = -1$ there is perfect negative linear association

In this example the result is significant at the 5 per cent level. In other words, there is a correlation between production levels and material wastage. However, you must remember that this result does not mean you have established direct causality.

7.10   Measuring differences

7.10.1   Chi squared test

Pearson's product moment coefficient (see Section 7.9.1) measures the strength of association between two quantity variables; Spearman's rank coefficient (see Section 7.9.2) does the same for two ordinal variables, but sometimes the data is in *nominal* form, such as categories (see Chapter 6). A *Chi squared* (χ^2) test is a non-parametric technique which is used to assess the statistical significance of a finding, by testing for *contingency* (uncertainty of occurrence) or *goodness of fit*.

You will need to have collected frequency data from two situations. There will almost always be a difference between the two sets of data. The test involves setting up two hypotheses. The *null hypothesis* (H_0) states that the two variables are independent of one another and the *alternate hypothesis* (H_1) states that they are associated with one another. The null hypothesis is always stated first. The χ^2 test allows you to find out whether there are any statistically significant differences between the actual (observed) frequencies and hypothesised (expected) frequencies. In other words, whether the differences are due to some underlying, universal difference or merely to chance. The procedure is as follows.

1. Set up the two hypotheses
2. Draw up a contingency table of the observed frequencies (O) and total the rows and columns
3. Draw up a contingency table of the expected frequencies (E) if H_0 were true. The *E*s need not be whole numbers. If an *E* value is less than 5, combine the *O* and the *E* values of this cell with an adjacent cell, thereby reducing the size of the table. The expected frequencies can be calculated as follows:

$$\frac{\text{Row total} \times \text{Column total}}{\text{Grand total}}$$

4. The χ^2 test summarises the differences between the O and E values. This is more conveniently calculated by computer. However, the formula is:

$$\chi^2 = \Sigma \frac{(O-E)^2}{E}$$

where

$O =$ observed frequencies
$E =$ expected frequencies
and all the cells in the table are summed

If the Os and Es agree well this test statistic has a low value; a high value shows a poor agreement. If the H_0 is true, this test statistic will have approximately an χ^2 distribution.

5. To find the 5 per cent critical values beyond which you will want to reject H_0 in favour of H_1, you need χ^2 tables. The formula is:

$$v = (r-1)(c-1)$$

where

$v =$ degrees of freedom
$r =$ number of rows in the table (excluding totals)
$c =$ number of columns in the table (excluding totals)

This observed value of χ^2 represents the number of cells you are free to fill, given the marginal totals.

6. Look up v in the contingency table given in Appendix D at the 5 per cent critical value. This gives you evidence that an observed value higher than the figure you read off from the table is unlikely at the 5 per cent significance level and therefore grounds to reject the null hypothesis.

Example
Perhaps you have collected the data shown in Table 7.33 which relates to 180 employees' use of the company canteen and absenteeism over a four-week period.

Table 7.33 Use of canteen and absenteeism data (number of employees)

	Use canteen	Don't use canteen
Number absent	20	30
Number working	80	50

The first step is to state your two hypotheses.

H_0 = The use of the company canteen and absenteeism are independent of one another

H_1 = The use of the company canteen and absenteeism are associated with one another

Now you need to draw up your frequency table of observed frequencies (Table 7.34).

Table 7.34 Calculating the observed frequencies (O)

	Use canteen	Don't use canteen	Total
Number absent	20	30	50
Number working	80	50	130
Total	100	80	180

Next you need to calculate how many absences you would expect if there were no differences between the two data sets (Table 7.35).

Table 7.35 Calculating the expected frequencies (E)

	Use canteen	Don't use canteen	Total
Number absent	28	22	50
Number working	72	58	130
Total	100	80	180

Now you are ready to calculate χ^2 using the formula (Table 7.36).

Table 7.36 Calculating χ^2

Cell	O	E	$O - E$	$\dfrac{(O-E)^2}{E}$
1	20	28	-8	$\dfrac{64}{28} = 2.286$
2	30	22	$+8$	$\dfrac{64}{22} = 2.909$
3	80	72	$+8$	$\dfrac{64}{72} = 0.888$
4	50	58	-8	$\dfrac{64}{58} = 1.103$
			Total	7.186

Using the table given in Appendix D, the 5 per cent critical value at 1 degree of freedom is 3.841. Our observed value of χ^2 is 7.186 and this is greater than the 5 per cent critical value (and also greater than the 1 per cent critical value). It is therefore highly unlikely to have occurred by chance and we have strong evidence to reject the null hypothesis. Therefore, there is strong evidence that non-use of the canteen and absenteeism among employees are positively associated.

7.10.2   Student *t*-test

The *student t-test* is a parametric technique which can be used for either *independent* or *related samples*. Statistical investigations involving controlled experiments often compare the parameters of two populations, commonly the means. Separate samples are selected from each population. One sample may be referred to as the *control group*; the other, the *experimental group*. When making inferences about the means of the populations, the actual observations may have come from *independent* (unrelated) samples or *matched-pairs* (related) samples.

If you want to use a *t*-test for independent samples, your data should meet the following criteria:

▶ the data must be at least of interval status
▶ the data in each data set must be normally distributed
▶ the two data sets must have similar variances.

If you want to use a *t*-test for matched-pairs samples the same criteria apply, but each data pair must also be related.

Before you can apply the appropriate *t*-test, you must decide whether you are dealing with independent or matched-pairs samples. In a research design where independent samples are used, you might take groups to participate in difference phases of an experiment. For example, perhaps you are interested in the fuel consumption of vehicles where some drivers have been on a safe driving course and others have not. The first group is the experimental group and the second group is the control group. One problem with this is that as the two groups of drivers are independent, difference between them could be due to other variables. For example, some drivers may be more experienced or more cautious than others.

One way round this problem is to adopt a matched-pairs design. In this case, you would match a driver in the experimental group with a driver in the control group with similar characteristics which might affect their driving performance, such as age, driving experience, accident rate, etc.

The basic procedures for drawing inferences using large and small independent samples, and matched-pairs samples involve constructing confidence intervals, but the formulae are too complex to include here. If you decide to undertake this form of analysis, we advise that you refer to a statistics textbook and obtain access to suitable computer software.

Whether you are using the *t*-test for related or unrelated samples, the underlying principles are the same, although there are differences in the calculations. Essentially, you will adopt the null hypothesis which states that there is no difference between the experimental group and the control group. In our example any differences would be due to chance and not to the fact that the experimental group had received training.

The *t*-test result indicates the extent to which the two samples need to differ in order for you to reject the null hypothesis. You will need to refer to the table of critical values in Appendix E to establish the significance level and identify the acceptance and rejection regions. Your result must exceed the values stated in the table for significance at the various probability levels. These depend on whether you have a one-tailed or a two-tailed hypothesis. If the critical value given in the table exceeds the value at the selected probability level (usually 5 per cent or less), you can reject the null hypothesis. In other words, you have found out that there is a difference between the two samples which is not due to chance.

7.11 Forecasting

You can use *time series analysis* to transform the data you have collected into *forecasts* of future events, providing the data is available for several past periods of time. The series of values of a variable over a period of time is called a *time series*, hence a statistical procedure which uses such values is known as time series analysis.

There are two main models: the *additive model* and the *multiplicative model*. The formulae are as follows.

The additive model:

$$Y = T + S + C + I$$

The multiplicative model:

$$Y = T \times S \times C \times I$$

where

$Y =$ the observed variable
$T =$ trend
$S =$ seasonal variation
$C =$ cyclical component
$I =$ irregular component

Although the additive model is simpler to analyse, the multiplicative (or classical) model is generally considered to be more realistic. The adequacy of the multiplicative model may be tested by analysing the irregular component. If this component is not random, the suitability of the chosen model must be questioned. Any component may be absent from a particular time series. For example, annual data cannot include the seasonal variation component.

7.11.1   Predicting trends

The main use of time series analysis is to predict *trends*. The time periods may be even or uneven. The trend is calculated using *moving averages*. This gives an artificially constructed time series in which each value is replaced by the arithmetic mean of itself and values at a number of preceding and succeeding points. The number of points in a moving average is referred to as the period of that moving average. A moving average has a smoothing effect on a time series, no matter what period is chosen, since the averaging process heightens troughs and lowers peaks.

Example
Perhaps you have collected quarterly data which relates to number of ice-creams sold by a particular company over a five-year period. It is possible to make these calculations without the help of a computer, but if suitable software is available it will save you considerable time.

The first step is to calculate the four-quarter moving total by adding in fours. Next you need to calculate the eight-quarter moving total by adding in two; finally, you divide by eight to obtain the trend. Table 7.37 gives details.

7.11.2   Eliminating seasonal variations

Having calculated the trend, you are now in a position to eliminate any seasonal variations in your time series ($Y \div S$).

Example
To illustrate how you can eliminate the seasonal variations we will use the ice-cream data from Table 7.37. First, you need to calculate the de-trended series by dividing your data by the trend ($Y \div T$) as shown in Table 7.38.

The next step is to calculate the seasonal variations (S) which you do by averaging the detrended series ($Y \div T$) as shown in Table 7.39. The averages should add up to 4 for quarterly data, 12 for monthly data, etc.

Table 7.37 Calculating the trend: ice-cream sales 1991–5 (mn)

Date		Data (Y)	Four-quarter moving total	Eight-quarter moving total	Trend (T)
1991	Quarter 1	106			
	Quarter 2	192			
			726		
	Quarter 3	278		1,463	183
			737		
	Quarter 4	150		1,481	185
			744		
1992	Quarter 1	117		1,488	186
			744		
	Quarter 2	199		1,492	187
			748		
	Quarter 3	278		1,518	190
			770		
	Quarter 4	154		1,541	193
			771		
1993	Quarter 1	139		1,575	197
			804		
	Quarter 2	200		1,631	204
			827		
	Quarter 3	311		1,652	207
			825		
	Quarter 4	177		1,670	209
			845		
1994	Quarter 1	137		1,692	212
			847		
	Quarter 2	220		1,694	212
			847		
	Quarter 3	313		1,701	213
			854		
	Quarter 4	177		1,672	209
			818		
1995	Quarter 1	144		1,591	199
			773		
	Quarter 2	184		1,551	194
			778		
	Quarter 3	268		1,412	177
			634		
	Quarter 4	182			

Table 7.38 Calculating the de-trended series: ice-cream sales 1991–5 (mn)

Date		Data (Y)	Trend (T)	De-trended series (Y ÷ T)
1991	Quarter 1	106		
	Quarter 2	192		
	Quarter 3	278	183	1.52
	uarter 4	150	185	0.81
1992	Quarter 1	117	186	0.63
	Quarter 2	199	187	1.06
	Quarter 3	278	190	1.46
	Quarter 4	154	193	0.80
1993	Quarter 1	139	197	0.71
	Quarter 2	200	204	0.98
	Quarter 3	311	207	1.50
	Quarter 4	177	209	0.85
1994	Quarter 1	137	212	0.65
	Quarter 2	220	212	1.04
	Quarter 3	313	213	1.47
	Quarter 4	177	209	0.85
1995	Quarter 1	144	199	0.72
	Quarter 2	184	194	0.95
	Quarter 3	268	177	1.51
	Quarter 4	182		

Table 7.39 Calculating the seasonal variation: ice-cream sales 1991–5 (mn)

Year	De-trended series			
	Quarter 1	Quarter 2	Quarter 3	Quarter 4
1991	–	–	1.52	0.81
1992	0.63	1.06	1.46	0.80
1993	0.71	0.98	1.50	0.85
1994	0.65	1.04	1.47	0.85
1995	0.72	0.95	–	–
Total	**2.70**	**4.03**	**5.95**	**3.39**
Average	**0.68**	**1.01**	**1.49**	**0.83**
Seasonal index	**68**	**101**	**149**	**83**

Note
Discrepancies due to rounding may occur if you use a spreadsheet program to aid these calculations.

Table 7.40 Calculating the de-seasonal variation: ice-cream sales 1991–5 (mn)

Date		Data (Y)	Trend (T)	De-trended series (Y ÷ T)	Seasonal variation (S)	De-seasonalise data (Y ÷ S)
1991	Quarter 1	106			0.68	156
	Quarter 2	192			1.01	190
	Quarter 3	278	183	1.52	1.49	187
	Quarter 4	150	185	0.81	0.83	181
1992	Quarter 1	117	186	0.63	0.68	172
	Quarter 2	199	187	1.06	1.01	197
	Quarter 3	278	190	1.46	1.49	187
	Quarter 4	154	193	0.80	0.83	186
1993	Quarter 1	139	197	0.71	0.68	204
	Quarter 2	200	204	0.98	1.01	198
	Quarter 3	311	207	1.50	1.49	209
	Quarter 4	177	209	0.85	0.83	213
1994	Quarter 1	137	212	0.65	0.68	201
	Quarter 2	220	212	1.04	1.01	218
	Quarter 3	313	213	1.47	1.49	210
	Quarter 4	177	209	0.85	0.83	213
1995	Quarter 1	144	199	0.72	0.68	212
	Quarter 2	184	194	0.95	1.01	182
	Quarter 3	268	177	1.51	1.49	180
	Quarter 4	182			0.83	219

The averages you have calculated are the seasonal variations. Now you are in a position to calculate the de-seasonalised data ($Y \div S$) as shown in Table 7.40.

Now you can plot the trend for ice-cream sales over the period on a graph and use the seasonal indices to forecast the data for 1996.

7.11.3 Cyclical and irregular variation

In order to evaluate the cyclical variation (C) you need to obtain the de-trended, de-seasonalised series:

$$\frac{Y}{T \times S} = C \times I$$

Next, smooth out the irregular component (I) by means of a moving average performed on the $Y/(T \times S)$ series.

Since the aim is to smooth and not to remove the cycle, a three-point moving average could be used.

The irregular component (I) is obtained from $Y/(T \times S \times C)$.

This should be random in nature, otherwise the adequacy of the proposed model must be questioned. Therefore, evaluation of the irregular component yields a measure of method suitability. For multiplicative models, the irregular component should be random about unity (± 1). If the irregular component is evaluated and shown to be random, it can be removed from the series, producing an error-free series:

$$\frac{Y}{I} = T \times S \times C$$

In order to be reasonably certain that components exist in a time series, there should be sufficient data to establish the reality of these components or complementary information to suggest their presence. In a short span of data, random phenomena can appear to be systematic and, conversely, systematic effects can be masked by random variation.

Conclusions

In this chapter we have provided an introduction to exploratory and confirmatory data analysis. We have focused on exploratory data analysis because all students carrying out business research who have collected quantitative data will need to use this group of statistical techniques. We have discussed some of the issues you will need to bear in mind if you wish to use inferential statistics and given some examples from the wide range available. If you are conducting a sophisticated positivistic study, you will need to refer to some of the statistical texts given at the end of this chapter.

We recommend that you use either a spreadsheet or specialist statistical software for both exploratory and confirmatory data analysis; both normally incorporate a graphics package. Although it is possible to calculate simple statistics, such as percentages, averages and the standard deviation using a calculator, when time and accuracy are at a premium you will find it invaluable to obtain access to appropriate computer facilities.

You can use the checklist given in Figure 7.22 to ensure the successful completion of your quantitative data analysis.

In Chapter 8 we discuss the methods by which you can analyse any qualitative data you may have collected. When you have finished your

Figure 7.22 Checklist for conducting quantitative data analysis

1. Are you confident that your research design was sound?
2. Have you been systematic and rigorous in the collection of your data?
3. Is your identification of variables adequate?
4. Are your measurements of the variables reliable?
5. Have you used appropriate statistical techniques in the analysis of your data?
6. Is the analysis suitable for the type of scale (nominal, ordinal, interval or ratio)?
7. Does the statistical analysis adequately test your hypotheses?

data analysis, you will need to summarise and present it in the results section of your dissertation or thesis. We offer guidance on this and other aspects of writing up your research in Chapter 9.

8 Analysing qualitative data

Introduction

Your choice of data analysis method depends on whether the data you have collected is quantitative or qualitative; you may have collected some of each. We discussed the techniques and procedures for analysing quantitative data in Chapter 7. In this chapter we consider the main methods by which qualitative data can be analysed.

Our overall aim is to help you select the method(s) of analysis which are appropriate to the paradigm you have adopted and the data you have collected. In this chapter we:

▶ identify the main problems associated with analysing qualitative data
▶ describe formal and informal methods of quantifying qualitative data
▶ offer guidance on a general analytical procedure for non-quantifying methods of analysis;
▶ examine specific non-quantifying methods and techniques for analysing qualitative data
▶ offer advice on how a qualitative analysis might be evaluated.

Wherever possible we refer to specific research studies which explain the use of qualitative methods of analysis in practice. It will be up to you to determine which is the most suitable for your project.

8.1 Overview of qualitative data analysis

Analysing qualitative data presents both positivists and phenomenologists with a number of problems. 'Despite the proliferation of qualitative methodology texts detailing techniques for conducting a qualitative project, the actual process of data analysis remains poorly described' (Morse, 1994, p. 23). Moreover, since the data collection method can also be the basis on which it is analysed, it is often difficult to distinguish between methods of collection and methods of analysis.

The main challenge to *qualitative data analysis* is that there is 'no clear and accepted set of conventions for analysis corresponding to those observed with quantitative data' (Robson, 1993, p. 370). In some published studies we are aware that the researcher must have had hundreds, if not thousands, of pages of qualitative data, but it is difficult to appreciate how this data has been summarised and structured to arrive at conclusions. 'Brief conversations, snippets from unstructured interviews, or examples of a particular activity are used to provide evidence for a particular contention. There are grounds for disquiet in that the representativeness or generality of these fragments is rarely addressed' (Bryman, 1988, p. 77).

Although 'reports of successes and problems with attempts to collect and analyse qualitative data in practice are not often published' (Jinkerson, Cummings, Neisendorf & Schwandt, 1992, p. 273), there are a number of different approaches which we will be examining in this chapter. One approach is to *quantify* the data, either *formally* or

Figure 8.1 Overview of the main challenges to qualitative data analysis

1. **Reducing the data:** Data reduction is 'a form of analysis that sharpens, sorts, focuses, discards and reorganises data in such a way that 'final' conclusions can be drawn and verified (Miles and Huberman, 1994, p. 11). In a phenomenological study you will have collected a mass of field notes, documents, transcripts of interviews, etc., which must be condensed and made manageable. One solution is to find a systematic way of summarising the data and this usually involves some form of coding.

2. **Structuring the data:** Often the data is collected in a chronological structure, which may not be the most suitable form for its analysis. If you have commenced your study with a theoretical framework, this will provide a structure and may give an *a priori* (pre-existing) specification of categories into which data can be fitted. If there is no pre-existing structure, a suitable one may emerge during the data collection phase.

Anticipatory data reduction can occur where the researcher has constructed some particular theoretical framework or highly structured research instrument which will result in certain data being ignored. You will remember from Chapter 5 that a theoretical framework is a collection of theories and models from the literature which underpins a positivistic research study (research instrument is an alternative term for certain data collection methods).

Anticipatory data reduction is not usually recommended in a phenomenological study as it restricts deep understanding and the collection of rich data.

3. **Detextualising the data:** Most qualitative data is collected in the form of extended text. This may not be the most suitable form for analysis or presentation to various audiences. Therefore, it may be more appropriate to convert the text into diagrams and illustrations for analysis and presentation.

Table 8.1 Main methods of analysing qualitative data

Quantifying methods	*Non-quantifying methods*
Informal methods	General analytical procedure
Formal methods	Cognitive mapping
Content analysis	Data displays
Repertory grid	Grounded theory
	Quasi-judicial methods

informally; in other words, turn the qualitative data into numerical data. This is an approach which some phenomenologists find abhorrent, but which takes place to a greater extent than many care to admit.

If this is not possible, or you consider it would be undesirable to quantify the data, you must find a *non-quantifying* method of analysing your qualitative data. Figure 8.1 gives an overview of the main challenges faced by those seeking a non-quantifying method of analysis. Usually, if you can resolve one of these problems, you will find that you are simultaneously resolving the other two. Table 8.1 shows the main methods used to analyse qualitative data which have been divided into two categories: quantifying methods and non-quantifying methods. Your choice of method depends on your research *paradigm* (see Chapter 3). If you have adopted a *positivistic paradigm*, you are likely to use one of the formal, quantifying methods; if you have adopted a *phenomenological paradigm*, you may be willing to adopt an informal, quantifying method, but are more likely to want to use a non-quantifying method.

8.2   Quantifying methods of qualitative data analysis

The increasing use of *mixed methodologies* in a research study (see Chapter 3) and the greater flexibility in *data collection methods* (see Chapter 6) means that you may have collected both qualitative and quantitative data. Even if you have adopted a positivistic approach, you may have collected qualitative data in order to provide richness and give insight to the numerical data. In such circumstances, you may have no philosophical objections to attempting to quantify qualitative data. However, some phenomenologists regard such an attempt as an anathema. If this is how you feel about quantifying qualitative data, our remarks in this section are not addressed to you.

8.2.1   Informal methods

Researchers often quantify data *informally* in the process of reducing it or examining 'such things as repetitive or patterned behaviours'

(Lindlof, 1995, p. 216). One procedure is dependent on the frequency of something occurring. If a phenomenon occurs very frequently, the researcher may omit some references to it to avoid repetition. Of course, this relies on counting frequencies to determine which data should be omitted. Frequency is also used to determine whether an action or event normally happens or whether it is a rare occurrence.

Another approach is to use some form of scaling to determine which data should be included. The scaling may be as simple as deciding that certain data will be labelled 'Important' and other data, which can be omitted, as 'Not important'. Unfortunately, the basis for constructing and applying the scale is rarely explained.

If you decide to use these informal methods for quantifying data in your research, it is important to decide why you are using them and where it is appropriate to apply them. In using these informal methods make certain that you do not lose the richness and meaning of the qualitative data and explain what you are doing. Also ensure that your informal methods do not lead to a lack of precision in circumstances where it is justifiable and, perhaps, even necessary to use numbers.

8.2.2   Content analysis

Content analysis represents a formal approach to qualitative data analysis. It is mainly associated with a positivistic approach, although it is advocated by Easterby-Smith, Thorpe and Lowe (1991) as a means of analysing qualitative data. Mostyn (1985, p. 117) refers to it as 'the diagnostic tool of qualitative researchers, which they use when faced with a mass of open-ended material to make sense of'.

Content analysis is a way of systematically converting text to numerical variables for quantitative data analysis. Mostyn (1985) claims that the technique is known to have been used as early as 1740 to analyse communications. Normally a document is examined, although other forms of communication, such as audio cassette or video may be analysed. The analysed material is classified into various coding units which are normally preconstructed by the researcher.

Silverman (1993) explains how he drew up a simple table to analyse text. However, his process was not a simple count of arbitrary items, but was based on analysis and theoretical understanding of the substance of the text. The first stage in the analysis is *sampling*. If a large volume of written, oral or visual research data exists, a decision must be made on the rationale for extracting a sample. Where the material is less substantial, it may be possible to analyse all of it. The next stage is to determine *coding units*, such as a particular word, character, item or theme which is found in the material. Table 8.2 gives some examples of units which could be used for coding.

Table 8.2 Examples of coding units

Coding unit	Example
Word/phrases	Examine minutes of company/union meetings for the word 'dispute' Examine circulars to shareholders for the words 'increased dividends'
Theme	Examine minutes of company/union meetings for occasions where discussions lead to agreements Examine circulars to shareholders for examples where increases in productivity are linked to increased profits
Item	Examine newspapers for whole articles dealing with redundancies Examine company annual reports for entire pieces on environmental issues
Time	Measure the time allocated in broadcast news bulletins to industrial issues

A *coding frame* is then constructed which lists the coding units vertically, thus permitting the analysis of each communication to be added on the horizontal axis. The analysis can be conducted purely on frequency; alternatively, it may incorporate the placing of the items or words (in documents) or the duration (for audio or filmed communications).

Content analysis is often used for analysing newspapers and advertisements. Czepiec (1994) used the technique to analyse 454 advertisements appearing in the *People's Daily* between 1980 and 1989 to determine which factors Chinese businessmen consider most important when promoting their industrial products. She analysed the text of the advertisements for mention of 21 advertising traits which had been generated from previous studies concerned with buying behaviour. Her results are shown in Table 8.3.

A study by Todd, McKeen and Gallupe (1995) demonstrates the volume of data that content analysis can generate, the sophistication of analysis and the range of data displays that can be used. The researchers examined changes in the knowledge and skill requirements of information systems (IS) positions by analysing the content of advertisements for IS professionals placed in four major newspapers between 1970 and 1990. For each different type of IS job, the data was summarised over three main skills levels, then detailed over seven sub-categories. The data was also summarised to show the proportion of advertisements which referred to a main skill category at least once; and the average number of phrases per skill category was expressed as a percentage of the total number of phrases.

Table 8.3 Content analysis: traits found in Chinese advertising, 1980–1989

Trait	Proportion of advertisements (%)
Claims about product	40.5
Quality	37.0
Uniform/Made to standards	29.1
Dependability	26.4
Economy in operation	17.4
Received award	15.6
Years of experience	14.3
Guarantee	13.9
Maintenance available	13.0
Made in China	11.2
New or improved	10.1
Foreign connection	9.7
Made to customer specifications	9.0
General reference to price	8.8
Durability	8.8
Safety	8.4
Government endorsement	7.9
Price specified	5.7
Sold internationally	5.5
Labour-saving in operation	4.8
Ease of installation	4.2
Time-saving in operation	4.0

Source: Czepiec (1993) p. 261.

Content analysis offers a number of advantages as a method of analysing qualitative data. If you are dealing with public documents, there are no problems with access and it is a relatively inexpensive method. Once you have constructed your sample, it is a permanent record which can be revisited and re-examined; the pressures of time associated with interviews and observations are not an issue. You can choose to conduct your analysis when you wish. It is also a non-obtrusive measure which requires neither observation, interviews or questionnaires, so that the subjects of your study are normally unaware and unaffected by your interest. Finally, the systems and procedures for carrying out content analysis are very clear, so a researcher who is concerned with the *reliability* and *validity* (see Chapters 3 and 6) of their study will find the method highly acceptable.

Unfortunately, there are also a number of criticisms and problems associated with content analysis. It has been argued that 'its theoretical basis is unclear and its conclusions can often be trite' (Silverman, 1993, p. 59). Moreover, if you decide to use content analysis, you will be going through a process of data reduction at an early stage of the research. To record only the words or phrases you consider are of particular interest, may mean that you discard large amounts of data which could help you understand the phenomenon you are studying more thoroughly and at a deeper level.

Even with public documents there can be omissions, so that your sample may be incomplete. There is also the problem that the documents may have been written for purposes other than those for which you are using them, or they may be worded for a public audience. Even though you can conduct the analysis when it best suits you, it is time consuming and you may find it tedious. But despite these reservations, content analysis can be useful to the researcher who has collected qualitative data and wishes to convert it into quantitative data.

8.2.3   Repertory grid technique

Based on personal construct theory (Kelly, 1955), *repertory grid technique* is another example of a formal method of quantifying qualitative data. The technique 'allows the interviewer to get a mental map of how the interviewee views the world, and to write this map with the minimum of observer bias' (Stewart and Stewart, 1981, p. 5). It provides a mathematical representation of the perceptions and constructs an individual uses to understand and manage their own world. Although some might argue that 'at one level the repertory grid is nothing more than a labelled set of numbers' (Taylor, 1990 p. 105), a skilled and sensitive researcher can attribute deeper meaning to those numbers. Therefore, when used appropriately, the technique 'is a framework for the patterning of subjective experiences that has the advantage of being available for statistical analysis' (Taylor, 1990, p. 117).

Repertory grid technique is particularly useful if the researcher finds it difficult to formulate appropriate questions in the interview situation and the interviewee is unable to structure his or her opinions and experiences with sufficient clarity. The main features of the grid are as follows:

▸ **Elements** or the **objects of the perceptions:** In many studies these are the people in our world we consider to be important, but elements can also be such matters as the skills needed to do a particular job or, in marketing research, a range of products a company is seeking to promote

▶ **Constructs:** These are the qualities which an individual uses to describe and differentiate between the elements. Kelly suggests that these personal constructs are bi-polar. This means that they can be set on a continuum; for example, 'Good' to 'Bad'; 'Easy to get along with' to 'Difficult to get along with'; 'High manual dexterity required' to 'Low manual dexterity required'

▶ **Linking mechanisms:** These are methods for indicating the strength of relationships and positions between elements and constructs.

The various stages in repertory grid technique are shown in Figure 8.2.

Table 8.4 shows a completed grid. This example has been taken from Dunn and Ginsberg (1986). The grid represents a hypothetical employee's constructs of a set of elements based on organisational systems. You will see from Table 8.4 that at a very simple level you can detect emerging patterns. However, it is also possible to take a statistical approach. Dunn and Ginsberg used the data to calculate three indices of cognitive content, thus allowing them to measure differences in the structure and content of reference frames.

Figure 8.2 Stages in repertory grid technique

1. Determine the focus of the grid. It must be as specific as possible; for example, the qualities required of a personnel manager, the features of comptitive products.
2. Agree with the interviewee the elements which are relevant to the chosen focus. A good range is required; usually between 6 and 12 elements. Larger ranges are possible, although may be hard to manage.
3. Write each of the elements on a separate card and select three (known as triads) at random. Ask the interviewee to decide which pair are similar and what distinguishes them from the remaining one. Then ask the interviewee to provide a word or phrase which describes the pair and another word or phrase to describe the third element.
4. These words or phrases become the constructs and the process of discussing triads of elements with the interviewee continues until a construct has been generated for each element.
5. Next, the relationship between the elements and constructs must be measured. One method is for the researcher to use a rating scale for the constructs (for example, a scale of between 1 and 7) and ask the interviewee to indicate where he or she would place each of the elements on the scale. Alternatively, the researcher may prefer to ask the interviewee to rank the constructs (for example, placing them in order from 'Very good' to 'Very poor').
6. A matrix is then constructed for each interviewee from the resulting information, using the elements as the column headings and the constructs as the rows. Finally, the number which has arisen from the rating or ranking is entered into the appropriate cell.

Table 8.4 A repertory grid

	Elements					
Constructs	Inventory management system	Strategic planning system	Office automation	Decision support system	Quality working circle	Collateral organisation
Technical quality	6	5	4	2	1	3
Cost	2	1	4	6	5	3
Challenge to status quo	6	1	2	4	5	3
Actionability	1	6	2	4	5	3
Evaluability	6	1	2	5	4	3

Source: Adapted from Dunn and Ginsberg (1986) p. 964.

Although it is possible to examine a relatively small matrix for patterns and differences between constructs and elements, a larger matrix would require the use of a computer to generate the grid and analyse the data. Whether the analysis is performed manually or electronically, the results can be discussed with the interviewee. It must be remembered that the analysis shows how the individual is currently giving meaning to events and experiences in their environment. This could change over time.

An example of business research using repertory grid technique is provided by a study in the workplace by Brook (1986). Using the technique in addition to interviews and questionnaires, she sought to measure the effectiveness of a management training programme. The grid she used consisted of typical interpersonal situations encountered by managers in their daily work, together with two elements referring to performance before and after training, plus two elements referring to examples of their best and worse performance. The situations she used to elicit elements in the managers' repertory grid are shown in Figure 8.3. Brook reports that the repertory grid provided 'rich and varied data on individual subjects which could then be validated against other information obtained from before-and-after interviews and questionnaires.' (Brook, 1986, p. 495).

Repertory grid technique offers a number of advantages and, if you wish to obtain data for statistical analysis, it may be an appropriate technique for your study. It also enables interviewees to verbalise constructs and demonstrate relationships which might otherwise remain hidden. Moreover, the data is generated from the individual's

Figure 8.3 Example of situations used to elicit elements for repertory grid

1. A time when I delegated an important task to a co-worker
2. The time when I actively opposed the ideas of my controlling officer (or someone in authority)
3. A time when I had to deal with a problem brought to me by a member of my staff
4. A time when I had to make an important decision concerning my research or other work
5. A time when I had a professional association with some outside organisation
6. The occasion when I made or proposed changes in the running and conduct of section meetings or other procedures of a similar nature
7. An occasion when I felt most satisfied with my work performance
8. An occasion when I felt least satisfied with my work performance
9. My professional self now
10. My professional self a year ago

Source: Brook (1986) p. 495.

own framework and not from one that is imposed by the researcher. This provides deeper insights.

However, there are also a number of problems. It is very time consuming and participants are not always as able to compare and contrast the triads of elements or to describe constructs in the prescribed manner. There is also the difficulty of how to aggregate individual grid matrices to obtain data averaged over a number of interviewees.

Comprehensive instructions on the full use of a repertory grid in a business setting are given by Stewart and Stewart (1981).

8.3 Non-quantifying methods of qualitative data analysis

If you have adopted a *phenomenological* approach, you may prefer not to use quantifying methods to analyse your qualitative data, or you may find that it is not practical to do so. In either case you will need to find other ways of resolving the three main problems of how to reduce, structure and detextualise the data (see Section 8.1).

A number of authors have attempted to identify what they regard as the main elements of an analysis of qualitative data. Lindlof (1995) refers to four interrelated domains which he describes as follows:

> ▶ **A process** where the analysis of data takes place continuously throughout the study. Some tentative analysis takes place at the preliminary stage of making field notes or transcribing audio or video tapes. These initial thoughts are compared with new data as it arises and are modified and improved

▶ **Reduction in data** takes place at the physical level and at the conceptual level. The physical reduction in data involves sorting, categorising, prioritising and interrelating data. To do this, either some form of coding takes place or the data is displayed in the form of matrices and flow charts. Both these methods are described later in this chapter. Conceptual reduction involves devising a conceptual structure which can be communicated to others

▶ **Explaining** is what Lindlof describes as understanding the coherence of meaning and action in the case(s) under study. This is a process whereby the researcher makes sense of the way that the participants in the research make sense of their own actions, goals and motives

▶ **Theory** is the context in which the analysis of qualitative data offers explanations.

A similar model has been proposed by Morse (1994), who argues that all the different approaches to analysing qualitative data are based on the four processes described below.

▶ **Comprehending** is the acquisition of a full understanding of the setting, culture and study topic before the research commences. There is considerable debate in phenomenological research on how much prior knowledge the researcher should have. There are those who believe that the researcher should not approach the study with pre-knowledge and the mind should be uncluttered by previous theories and concepts which might block out new perspectives and discoveries. Morse argues that the researcher does need to be familiar with the literature at the commencement of the study, but should remain distanced from it so that new discoveries can be made without being contaminated by preconceptions

▶ **Synthesising** is the drawing together of different themes and concepts from the research and forming them into new, integrated patterns. It is where the individual data are reduced and sifted to give a general explanation of what is occurring

▶ **Theorising** is defined as the 'constant development and manipulation of malleable theoretical schemes until the best theoretical scheme is developed' (Morse, 1994, p. 32). It is theory which gives qualitative data structure and application and involves confronting the data with alternative explanations. Morse describes four methods to achieve this. The first is to identify the beliefs and values in the data and attempt to make links with theory. The second method is to use lateral thinking by examining and comparing the concepts and data from other settings. The third method is the construction of theory from the data by induction. Finally, causal links or patterns can be hypothesised and these can be 'tested' with selected informants who may refute or verify them

▶ **Recontextualising** is the process of generalisation so that the theory emerging from the study can be applied to other settings and populations. In the process the researcher will return to existing theories to place the results in a context and establish any developments they have introduced or new linkages and models.

Although these processes occur almost sequentially, the emphasis and timing of them will vary according to the particular qualitative approach used; grounded theory or ethnography, for example.

The suggestions made by Lindlof (1995) and Morse (1994) provide some useful general guidance for researchers who are faced with the task of analysing qualitative data. Implicit in their advice is the fact that you must be very familiar with your data. This requires procedures and systems so that the data can be managed effectively. In the following sections we discuss a number of methods you can adopt.

8.3.1   General analytical procedure

In this section we consider a *general analytical procedure* (Miles and Huberman, 1994) for dealing with qualitative data. This can be used with any *methodology* (see Chapter 3) and emphasises the methodical rigour and systematic processes which are required. All qualitative data collection methods generate a considerable volume of material and the procedure shown in Figure 8.4 offers a method by which it can be managed and controlled.

The extent to which your analysis is structured will depend on the extent to which you structured the collection of your data. A highly structured application of the above procedure is described in an evaluation conducted in an international business setting by Jinkerson, Cummings, Neisendorf and Schwandt (1992). The study was complex. It was concerned with the analysis of training needs in the tax practice of a firm of consultants and involved a number of researchers using personal interviews, telephone interviews and a postal questionnaire survey in 14 European countries.

Two specific research instruments were used: a master questionnaire, which provided the conceptual framework for data collection, and a data checklist to track the collection of data from respondents. The questionnaire identified themes, key points and questions and each received a unique code, as did each country, office and participant. The data checklist was completed by the project researchers upon the completion of an interview or receipt of data from respondents and showed the data collected. This permitted any missing data to be identified and subsequently collected. The researchers maintained six sets of files for the study and these are described in Table 8.5. The process of research was conducted through the use of workpapers which were contained in the first three files.

Figure 8.4 General analytical procedure for qualitative data

1. Convert any rough field notes you have made into some form of written record which you and your supervisors will still be able to understand in later months. When writing your field notes you may wish to add your own thoughts and reflections. This will be the start of your tentative analysis. You should distinguish your interpretations and speculation from your factual field notes.
2. Ensure that any material you have collected from interviews, observations or original documents is properly referenced. The reference should indicate who was involved, the date and time, the context, the circumstances leading to the data collection and the possible implications for the research. You may find it useful to record your references on a *pro-forma* summary sheet, which you can then keep in an indexed system for ease of retrieval.
3. Start coding the data as early as possible. This will involve allocating a specific code to each variable, concept or theme that you with to identify. The code may be allocated to a specific word or to a phrase and the use of exemplars is helpful in applying the code and explaining its significance in your thesis. The code will allow you to store the data, retrieve it and reorganise it in a variety of ways. You will find it easier if you start with as many codes as you feel necessary and later collapse them into a smaller number.
4. When data is coded, you can start grouping the codes into smaller categories according to patterns or themes which emerge. This is not a mechanical task, but will require some considerable effort and thought. If you are not using a strong theoretical framwork, do not attempt to impose categories, but allow them to emerge from the data. Compare new data as it is collected with your existing codes and categories, and modify them as required.
5. At various stages write summaries of your findings at that point. The discipline of putting your thoughts on paper will help with your analysis and highlight any deficiencies to be remedied.
6. Use your summaries to construct generalisations with which you can confront existing theories or use to construct a new theory.
7. Continue the process until you are satisfied that the generalisations arising from your data are sufficiently robust to stand the analysis of existing theories or the construction of a new theory.

> ► Workpaper 1 contained the raw data from interview notes
> ► Workpaper 2 summarised the raw data in Workbook 1 for each of the main points for each of the offices in the study
> ► Workpaper 3 reconstructed the data in Workbook 2 to create a picture across all key points within a single theme for all offices in each country
> ► Workpaper 4 was a country summary where the researchers wrote an overall assessment of the tax practice and training situation in that country
> ► Workpaper 5 contained the findings of the research and the recommendations.

Table 8.5 Files documenting the study

File type	Description of contents
Raw data	Interview notes; documents describing existing training strategies etc.; completed questionnaires; Workpaper 1
Data summaries	Summaries of raw data; Workpaper 2
Data reconstruction	Relationship within and across countries on key themes; notes about insights, hunches, developing interpretations; drafts of reports including findings and conclusions; Workpapers 3, 4 and 5
Methodology	Descriptions of methodology and its limitations; descriptions of instrument development processes and procedures for administration; correspondence with management about the study
Plans, proposal and budget	Work programme and timeliness, proposal, budget for personnel level, payroll and non-payroll
Instruments and tools	Data collection and analysis tools

Source: Jinkerson *et al.* (1992) p. 278.

This may appear to be a very elaborate system, but it must be remembered that this was a particularly large and complex project. In addition to illustrating the use of systems and procedures to manage and analyse qualitative data, this example demonstrates the amount of planning and management required for a research project.

In this section we have focused on methods of analysing qualitative data through coding, summarising, categorising and identifying patterns or themes. Some qualitative researchers prefer a more intuitive approach to data analysis and 'assume that through continued readings of the source material and through vigilance over one's presuppositions, one can capture the essence of an account' (Miles and Huberman, 1994, p. 8). Although we have suggested ways in which you can analyse the qualitative data you have collected, the value of the analysis will depend on the quality of your interpretation.

8.3.2   Cognitive mapping

Cognitive mapping is a method of analysis which can be used to structure, analyse and make sense of written or verbal accounts of problems. It is based on Kelly's (1955) theory of personal constructs which suggests that 'we make sense of the world in order to predict how, all things being equal, the world will be in the future, and to decide how we might act or intervene in order to achieve what we prefer within that world – a predict-and-control view of problem solving' (Ackermann, Eden and Cropper, 1990, p. 1).

This technique attempts to extend personal construct theory beyond the use of the repertory grid and can provide a powerful interviewing device when used as a note-taking method during an interview. It can also be used to record transcripts of interviews or other documentary data in a way that promotes analysis, questioning and understanding of the data.

The main stages in cognitive mapping are as follows:

1. An account of the problem is broken into phrases of about ten words which retain the language of the person providing the account. These are treated as distinct concepts which are then reconnected to represent the account in a graphical format. This reveals the pattern of reasoning about a problem in a way that linear text cannot.
2. Pairs of phrases can be united in a single concept where one provides a meaningful contrast to the other. These phrases are Kelly's constructs where meaning is retained through contrast.
3. The distinct phrases are linked to form a hierarchy of means and ends; essentially explanations leading to consequences. This involves deciding on the status of one concept relative to another. There are a number of categories or levels defined in a notional hierarchy that help the user make these decisions. Meaning is retained through the context.

The technique has frequently been used in projects concerned with the development of strategy and can be useful in action research studies. Ackermann, Eden and Cropper (1990) offer some useful advice for cognitive mapping which is shown in Figure 8.5.

Recently, cognitive mapping software has been developed by the name of *Cope*. Cropper, Eden and Ackermann (1990) describe how this can be used to build models, and analyse and retain the meaning of field data. '*Cope* can also be used to assist in the development of theoretical accounts of phenomena' (Cropper, Eden and Ackermann, 1990, p. 347), thus making it a useful tool for researchers using a grounded theory methodology.

Cope contains a database which holds the data in a form amenable to analysis and presentation; the presentation of research findings satisfies the recommendations of Miles and Huberman (1994). There is no pre-set framework, other than the nodes and linkages convention; the researcher can impose any structuring convention that seems appropriate. The program can handle complex data and, on one

---

Figure 8.5 Guidelines for cognitive mapping

► Attempt to construct your map on one sheet of A4 so that links can be made
► Start mapping about two-thirds of the way up the paper in the middle and try to keep concepts in small rectangles of text rather than as continuous lines
► Separate the sentences into phrases
► Build up a hierarchy
► Watch out for goals as the discussion unfolds and for potential 'strategic issues'
► Hold on to opposite poles for additional clarification
► Add meaning to concepts by placing them in the imperative form; include actors and actions if possible
► Retain ownership by not abbreviating words and phrases used by the problem owner
► Identify the option and outcome within each pair of concepts
► Ensure that a generic concept is superordinate to specific items that contribute to it
► Code the first pole as that which the problem owner sees as the primary idea
► Tidying up can provide a more complete understanding of the problem

Source: Adapted from Ackermann, Eden and Cropper (1990).

---

level, its advantage is the support it gives the researcher in managing qualitative data.

Cropper, Eden and Ackermann (1990) also claim that using the software has methodological benefits as it reduces the need for early data reduction, structures the data and compels the researcher to be explicit about the assumptions he or she is using to structure and analyse the data. Figure 8.6 shows an example of a cognitive map using *Cope*, which has been taken from Cropper, Eden and Ackermann (1990).

| Experiential learning | **Getting to grips with the software** |

Discuss with your supervisor what instruction is available to enable you to learn or enhance your knowledge of using specialist programs for analysing qualitative data (for example, NUD.IST).

8.3.3 Data displays

Miles and Huberman (1994) provide a comprehensive guide to the analysis of qualitative data using *data displays* such as networks, matrices, charts and graphs. Indeed, their approach not only spans the analysis of qualitative data, but the entire *research design* from the beginning to the writing the final report. In this section we

Figure 8.6 Example of a cognitive map using Cope software

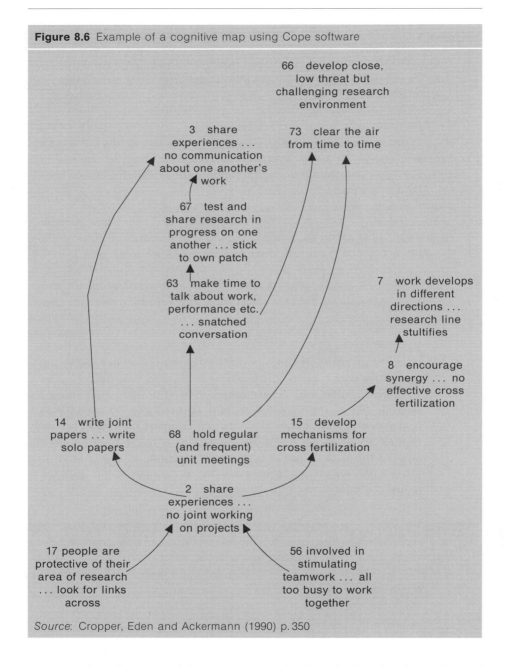

Source: Cropper, Eden and Ackermann (1990) p. 350

describe some of their suggestions for data displays for the analysis of qualitative data.

A display is 'a visual format that presents information system-atically, so the user can draw valid conclusions and take needed action' (Miles and Huberman, 1994, p. 91). There are no limits to the types of displays which can be generated, but they fall into two major categories: *networks*, with a series of nodes with links between them; and *matrices* with defined rows and columns. The data entries are blocks of text, phrases, abbreviations, symbolic figures, labelled lines, arrows, etc.

Networks are a collection of points connected by lines which illustrate relationships. These are familiar to most people, one example being an organisation chart. Matrices are sets of rows and columns and are familiar to many computer users as worksheets or spreadsheets. The rows and columns will have appropriate headings and Miles and Huberman give very detailed instructions for constructing displays for different purposes.

A matrix can take a number of formats. It may be time ordered to display a chronological sequence of events. In this case, the headings of each column are labelled with the relevant dates, which can be days, months or years, and the rows labelled with the actions, events or locations being studied. This type of display is useful for aiding understanding of the flow, location and possible causality of events. Alternatively, the matrix may be partially ordered and little more than a checklist, or very complex and illustrate variables, periods of time and conditions, as well as the researcher's own thoughts and evaluations. Whether a matrix is simple or complex, you will have to spend considerable time designing it and summarising your raw data.

Miles and Huberman have developed variations within these two main display categories to deal with a number of situations which can confront the researcher. For a study in its early stages they recommend some form of *partially ordered display*. However, if time is a crucial aspect of a study, they recommend a *time-ordered display*. If you are considering the reactions and relationships of people you may wish to prepare a role-ordered matrix where you are examining a clearly defined set of key variables. In this case, a conceptually oriented display would be appropriate. Figure 8.7 is taken from Miles and Huberman (1994) who offer general advice for constructing data displays.

An *events flow network* is useful for displaying a complex sequence of events, in terms of both chronological order and relationships. It will also lay the foundation for a causal analysis: 'what events led to what further events and what mechanisms underlay those associations' (ibid., p. 113). Figure 8.8 shows an example of an events flow network where the researcher had interviewed university students who had interrupted their studies. The student's experiences are presented in the boxes in the left-hand column, and the researcher's summary of the major forces moving the student to the next experience are shown on the right. The '+' signs indicate the strength of the various forces; the '−' signs, the strength of the student's dissatisfaction with the succeeding experiences.

Figure 8.7 General advice for constructing data displays

▶ Consider what appropriate displays can be used to bring together qualitative data so that conclusions can be drawn

▶ Be inventive in using displays; there are no limits on the types of diagrams and illustrations which can be used

▶ Constructing displays is an iterative process where you construct an initial display and draw some tentative conclusions which will be modified, or even overturned, as new data becomes available and new displays are constructed

▶ Be systematic in your approach to constructing displays and analysing data, but be aware that by becoming more formal in your approach there are the dangers of becoming narrow, obsessive or blind to new meaning which might emerge from the data

▶ Use mixed models in your analysis and draw from different methodologies and approaches in your analysis

▶ Remain self-aware of the entire research process and use supportive friends to act as critical voices on matters and issues you are taking for granted

▶ Communicate what you learn with colleagues who are interested in qualitative studies. In particular share your analytical experiences

Source: Miles and Huberman (1994) p. 310.

Figure 8.8 Events flow network: a student's learning and work experience

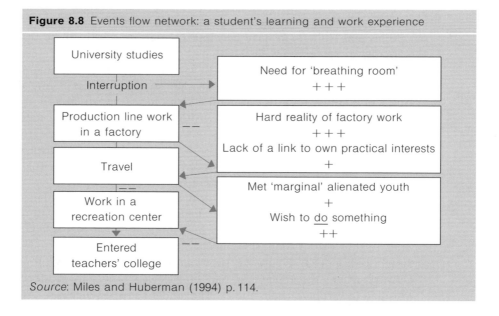

Source: Miles and Huberman (1994) p. 114.

An *effects matrix* is useful for selecting and displaying data which represents the changed state of individuals, relationships, groups or organisations. Figure 8.9 shows an effects matrix which displays data on one or more outcomes where the researcher was examining

Figure 8.9 Effects matrix: organisation changes after implementation of the ECRI Program

EFFECT TYPES	Early use 1st and 2nd yrs.		Later use 3rd yr.	
	PRIMARY CHANGES	SPIN-OFFS	PRIMARY CHANGES	SPIN-OFFS
Structural	Scheduling: ECRI all morning, rescheduling music, phys. ed. Helping teacher named: has dual status (teach/admin)	Cutting back on math, optional activities Two separate regimens in school Ambiguity of status and role	Integrated scheduling, cross-age grouping in grades 2–6	Less individual latitude: classroom problems become organizational problems
Procedural	No letter grades, no norms	Parents uneasy 2 regimens in class Teachers insecure Loosens age-grading system	ECRI evaluation sheets, tightening supervision	Teachers more visible, inspectable
	Institutionalizing assistance via helping teacher implanted	In-house assistance mechanism	More uniformity in work in all classes	Problems, solution more common, public
Relations/ Climate	Users are minority, band together	Cliques, friction between users, non-users	Tighter academic press	Reduction in "fun activities", projects (e.g. Xmas)
			Perception by teachers of collective venture	More lateral help More 'public' distress

Source: Miles and Huberman (1994) p. 138.

organisational change in a school. The researcher has divided the outcome of change at the school into structural changes, procedural or operating changes and more general relational or social climate changes, where the conceptual sequence is from 'hard' to 'soft' change. In addition, these aspects are displayed separately for the early use period (the first and second years) and the later use period (the third year). The researcher also distinguishes between primary changes, which followed directly from the requirements of change, and 'spin-offs', some of which had not been fully anticipated. Thus, the matrix displays effects, time of use and primary as well as spin-off outcomes.

Both the event flow network and the effects matrix are examples of simpler forms of diagrams and it is possible to construct far more complex displays. It is important to remember that constructing the display is only one aspect of the analytical process. The first step in constructing any type of display is to become very familiar with your data; then construct your display and, finally, write up your conclusions.

8.3.4   Grounded theory

We discussed *grounded theory* as a methodology in Chapter 3. In this section we examine how it is used as a method of analysing qualitative data. Like many other methodologies, grounded theory has its critics, but it is widely employed and can be very helpful in analysing qualitative data where there is no preconceived theoretical framework. There are a number of different approaches and developments within grounded theory, but we are basing our explanation on the work by Strauss and Corbin (1990), without implying any criticisms of other approaches. It should also be noted that even their approach has been subsequently developed in different directions.

The initial stage of grounded theory is *coding*. The codes are labels which enable the qualitative data to be separated, compiled and organised. At a basic level (*open coding*) they are simple and topical; at more complex levels (*axial coding* and *selective coding*) the codes are more general and conceptually abstract to aid theory development. The higher up the hierarchical framework of codes, from concepts through to the core category, the more abstract the label. It is important to emphasise that grounded theory requires the discovery and creation of codes from interpretation of the data. This contrasts with a *positivistic* approach, where coding requires logically deduced, pre-determined codes into which the data is placed.

Although there are separate levels or stages of coding, in practice the processes are often carried out simultaneously, with no distinction between which process is being completed. This is especially true of open coding and axial coding; these two processes are often performed simultaneously.

Open coding is the process of identifying, analysing and categorising the raw data. This involves a number of processes. First, the researcher breaks down and labels the individual elements of information, making the data more easily recognisable and less complicated to manage. These codes are then organised into a pattern of concepts and categories, together with their properties. This is accomplished by classifying the different elements into distinct ideas (the concepts) and grouping similar concepts into categories and sub-categories. The properties are those characteristics and attributes by which the concepts and categories can be recognised. The properties of each category of concepts must be defined along a continuum.

The labels by which the concepts and categories of concepts are known are entirely subjective and are chosen by the researcher. However, the label should reflect their nature and content. As the concepts are grouped into more abstract categories, so too should the labels become more conceptual. The labels can come from a variety of sources; for example, technical literature, interviewees and informants – *in vivo* codes (Glaser, 1978, p. 70; Strauss, 1987, p. 33) or from the researcher's own imagination and vocabulary. However, the labels should be explained. Labels with technical content or unfamiliar jargon can cause problems of interpretation to readers outside the field. Other problems can arise when common terms are used as codes; sometimes readers can be biased by a prior knowledge or understanding of a term which conflicts with or does not reflect what is intended by the researcher. Therefore, it is important that the researcher's interpretation of the code labels is given.

Axial coding is a more extended and evolved form of open coding and enables the researcher to build on the research. It is the process of connecting categories and sub-categories together on a more conceptual level than was adopted at the open coding stage. Whereas the earlier stage of coding involved the breaking down and separation of individual elements, axial coding is the restructuring and rebuilding of the data into various patterns with the intention of revealing links and relationships. The process includes the development of the properties of concepts and categories of concepts, and linking them at the dimensional level.

At this stage, the researcher will construct mini-theories about the relationships that might exist within the data and which need to be verified. Although the overall theoretical framework will not be discovered during axial coding, the mini-theories can be incorporated into and form part of the overall paradigm model that is being developed alongside the research. Figure 8.10 shows the main stages of axial coding.

Selective coding is the process of selecting the core category, systematically relating it to other categories, validating these relationships and filling in categories that need further refinement. This process enables themes to be generated which can then be 'grounded' by referring back to the original data.

Although conceived in the medical field, the use of grounded theory methodology is becoming increasingly popular in business research. Unfortunately, there are still very few full explanations of

Figure 8.10 Main stages of axial coding

1. **Identifying the phenomenon:** The phenomenon should be defined in terms of the conditions that give rise to its existence, and what causes its presence. It should be characterised in terms of the context in which it is situated. The action and interactional strategies which are used to manage the phenomenon should be developed and linked to the phenomenon, as well as the consequences of those strategies. This will form a pattern showing the relationships between specific categories, as follows:

Causal conditions

▼

Phenomenon

▼

Context

▼

Intervening conditions

▼

Action/Interaction strategies

▼

Consequences

2. **Linking and developing by means of the paradigm:** This is achieved through rigorous questioning and reflection, and by continually making comparisons. By identifying and defining the phenomenon, the researcher has already asked questions about the possible relationship between certain categories and sub-categories and has linked them together in the sequence shown above. These statements which relate to categories and sub-categories must be verified against data. This is part of the inductive/deductive process of grounded theory. Where further data supports the statements of relationships, the researcher can turn the statements into hypotheses.

3. **Further development of categories and sub-categories in terms of properties and dimensions:** This develops the ideas already generated within the identification of the phenomenon. It builds on the relationships discovered and purposefully tracks down other relationships, some of which will fall outside the paradigm model. The categories should be linked at the dimensional level. Within this further development is the recognition of the complexity of the real world. Although relationships are being discovered, not all the data will apply to the theory at all the times. These anomalies must not only be accepted, but must be incorporated into the research.

how qualitative data can be analysed. However, Figure 8.11, which is taken from Pidgeon, Turner and Blockley (1991), shows an example transcript together with coded concepts.

Although we have emphasised the coding procedures to demonstrate the analysis of qualitative data, this is only part of grounded theory methodology. Strauss and Corbin (1994, p. 277) complain that

---

Figure 8.11 Example transcript and coded concepts

(A)   Paragraphs for an interview relating to Hazardous Waste case-study

Interview S, 27 April

Paragraph 8
I don't think there is any doubt that on this job I readily accepted the advice of the civil engineering consultant, L, and didn't have the experience to question that advice adequately. I was not aware of the appropriate site investigation procedure, and was more than willing to be seduced by the idea that we could cut corners to save time and money.

Paragraph 9
But L's motives were entirely honorable in this respect. He had done a bit of prior work on a site nearby. And his whole approach was based upon the expectation that there would be fairly massive gravel beds lying over the clay valley bottom, and the fundamental question in that area was to establish what depth of piling was required for the factory foundation. He was assuming all along that piling was the problem. And he was not (and he knew he was not) experienced in looking for trouble for roads. His experience said that we merely needed a flight auger test to establish the pile depths.

Source: Architect S, a member of the design team involved in the incident, describing the decision of the civil engineering consultant, L, restricting the scope of the initial site investigation to the question of the need to piled foundations for warehouse units.

(B)   Significant concepts identified within paragraphs

Paragraph 8
Accepting professional advice
Criticizing other's work
Cutting corners
Experience

Paragraph 9
Knowledge of local conditions
Selective problem representation obscures wider view
Experience

Source: Pidgeon, Turner and Blockley (1991) p. 160.

---

researchers 'often seem to concentrate on coding as this methodology's chief and almost exclusive feature, but do not do theoretical coding ... some researchers deliberately do not aim at developing theories'. If you intend to use the coding procedures only from grounded theory, you must justify your reasons in your research report for isolating this activity from the overall methodology. You should also explain why you have adopted this methodology and why other analytical procedures are not appropriate.

8.3.5   Quasi-judicial method

Bromley (1986) suggests a *quasi-judicial* method for analysing qualitative data. The name is derived from the fact that the procedures are drawn from the legal profession and involve applying rational argument to interpret *empirical evidence*. You will remember from Chapter 5 that empirical evidence is data which is based on observation or experience. Thus, the quasi-judicial approach is concerned with the nature, source and quality of the evidence and the argument it supports.

Bromley emphasises that with this approach data analysis is not left until the end, but is a continuous process during which the researcher should bear in mind the following questions:

▶ What is at issue?
▶ What other relevant evidence might there be?
▶ How else might one make sense of the data?
▶ How were the data obtained?

Bromley (1986) identifies six rules which must be applied when adopting a quasi-judicial method of analysis. Table 8.6, which has

Table 8.6 Rules for the quasi-judicial method and their legal equivalent

Bromley's six rules	Legal equivalent
1. Investigator reports results truthfully	Testimony under oath
2. Aims and objectives of the investigation are stated explicitly	Formal charges are laid
3. Assessment of the achievement of aims and objectives	Presentation of evidence in court
4. Investigator is properly trained	Legal qualifications required to play formal role in court
5. The person is placed in his or her ecological (physical, cultural, social, symbolic) context	Extenuating/mitigating circumstances are considered
6. The account is written in good plain English	Case law/understandable to jury/as viewed by a reasonable person

Source: Brown and Canter (1985) p. 227.

been taken from Brown and Canter (1985), shows Bromley's rules and their legal equivalent. Brown and Canter illustrate how these rules can be used to analyse interviews in a number of studies they have conducted. In their view, 'the researcher's task is to construct a multi-perspective account of the particular event he or she is investigating, drawn from the explanations given by the primary participants' (Brown and Canter, 1985, p. 243). Robson (1993) has adapted Bromley's rules and procedures to provide a framework for the analysis of a qualitative case study data. These are shown in Figure 8.12.

If you examine these procedures, you will see that they are under-pinned by the main elements of an analysis identified by Lindlof (1995) and Morse (1994) at the beginning of Section 8.3. The empha-sis is on the importance of examining and re-examining the data (the evidence) and seeking explanations which fit the data. For a sub-stantial study you may find that the detailed procedures are difficult to apply, but the principles will be of help in assisting you to reflect on your data at various stages within the research. We have also found that the procedures, using the four questions set down by Bromley, are very helpful if you reach a sticking point in your analysis or are confronted by data which does not seem to fit.

Figure 8.12 Procedural steps in the quasi-judicial method

1. State the initial problem and issues as clearly as possible
2. Collect background information to provide a context in terms of which the problems and issues are to be understood
3. Put forward *prima facie* explanations of the problems and issues
4. Use these explanations to guide the search for additional evidence. If they do not fit the available evidence, work out alternative explanations
5. Continue the search for sufficient evidence to eliminate as many of the suggested explanations as possible, in the hope that one will account for all of the available evidence and be contradicted by none of it. Evidence may be direct or indirect, but must be admissible, relevant and obtained from competent and credible sources
6. Closely examine the sources of evidence, as well as the evidence itself. All items should be checked for consistency and accuracy. This is analogous to legal cross-examination in the case of personal testimony
7. Enquire critically into the internal coherence, logic and external validity of the network of argument claiming to settle the issues and solve the problems
8. Select the most likely interpretation compatible with the evidence
9. Formulating the acceptable explanation usually carries an implication for action which has to be worked out
10. Prepare an account in the form of a report. It should contribute to 'case law' by virtue of the general principles employed in explaining the specific case

8.4 Evaluating the analysis

Once you have selected a method of analysis and applied it, following the most appropriate procedures and techniques described in this chapter, you will want to know how to *evaluate* your analysis. A number of authors have suggested various criteria which can be used to evaluate a phenomenological study in its entirety and these can be used to assess the quality of your analysis.

Lincoln and Guba (1985) suggest that four criteria should be used:

▶ Credibility
▶ Transferability
▶ Dependability
▶ Confirmability.

Credibility demonstrates that the research was conducted in such a manner that the subject of the enquiry was correctly identified and described. Credibility can be improved by the researcher involving him or herself in the study for a prolonged period of time, by persistent observation of the subject under study to obtain depth of understanding, by triangulation by using different sources and collection methods of data, and by peer debriefing by colleagues on a continuous basis. *Transferability* is concerned about whether the findings can be applied to another situation which is sufficiently similar to permit the generalisation. *Dependability* should show that the research processes are systematic, rigorous and well documented. *Confirmability* should be used as a criterion where the study has described the research process fully and it is possible to assess whether the findings flow from the data.

Leininger (1994) has developed six criteria:

▶ Credibility
▶ Confirmability
▶ Transferability
▶ Saturation
▶ Meaning-in-context
▶ Recurrent patterning.

Although there are some differences between her definitions of the first three terms and those of Lincoln and Guba, the general thrust is similar. *Saturation* is concerned with the researcher being fully immersed and understanding the project. This is very similar to the recommendations used by Lincoln and Guba to enhance credibility. *Meaning-in-context* 'refers to data that have become understandable within holistic contexts or with special referent meanings to the informants or people studied in different or similar environmental contexts' (Leininger, 1994, p. 106). *Recurrent patterning* refers to the repetition of experiences, expressions and events that reflect identifiable patterns of sequenced behaviour, expressions or actions over time.

The above recommendations stress how important it is that you are highly familiar with the qualitative data you have collected during its analysis. You will need to be systematic and rigorous in your approach, which means that you must be explicit in the methodology you are using, your data collection methods and the techniques and procedure you use to analyse your data. One procedure adopted by a number of researchers is to obtain *respondent validity* for the analysis of qualitative data. This involves discussing your findings from the analysis with those who have participated in your study to obtain their reactions and opinions. The aim is to give the researcher greater confidence in the validity of his or her conclusions.

Conclusions

In this chapter we have examine a number of different methods of analysing qualitative data. If you are conducting your research under a phenomenological paradigm, the majority of the data you will have collected is likely to be qualitative in nature. Even if you have taken a *positivistic* approach, some of the data you have collected may be qualitative. The main challenges when attempting to analyse qualitative data is how to reduce the data, give it structure and use it in a form other than extended text, both in the analysis itself and later when presenting the findings. Unfortunately, few studies describe the methods adopted to analyse qualitative data sufficiently explicitly to provide a comprehensive guide.

There are a number of methods and techniques which can be used to quantify the data. If that is not possible, or is philosophically unacceptable, you must devise some form of coding to represent the data so that it can be stored, retrieved and rearranged. The synthesis and reorganisation of data should lead to the development of themes and patterns which can be confronted by existing theories or used to construct new theories. Many researchers find that the use of displays is extremely valuable for part, if not all, of their data analysis. Others decide a particular technique is more appropriate. Whichever approach you adopt, it is essential that you establish systems and procedures to allow you to manage and organise the raw data you have collected.

You need to remember that your purpose, when analysing the data, is to find answers to your research questions. Therefore, you need to keep your research questions at the front of your mind while you are conducting the analysis. Secondly, no matter how good the systems and procedures you adopt are, the quality of your analysis will depend on the quality of the data you have collected and your interpretations.

Once you have completed your data analysis you are ready to start writing your research report, which we discuss in Chapter 9.

9 Writing up the research

Introduction

By the time you get to the final writing-up stage in your research, you should have collected and generated a significant amount of data and material. During the course of conducting your research, you should have been writing draft sections of your report, discussing them with your supervisor(s) and making amendments. Therefore, you should now be ready to start writing the first complete draft of your final report. For those of you who are not in this position, we include some advice on how, even at this late stage, you might retrieve the position. In this chapter we offer guidance on:

► planning the report, including report design, structure and format
► setting a timetable
► the content of individual sections of the report
► presenting qualitative and quantitative data
► eleventh-hour strategies
► standards
► the viva
► getting published.

9.1 Planning the research report

Writing up often presents the greatest challenge to research students, but it is made somewhat easier if you have been writing notes and rough drafts throughout the period of your research. If you are a Ph.D. student and have put off writing until your final year, you are likely to encounter major difficulties or even failure (Torrance, Thomas and Robinson, 1992). In our experience, this applies to all researchers who put off writing until the last minute and that is why throughout this book we have urged you to commit your thoughts to paper (or disk) at the onset.

There are a number of strategies you can adopt when it comes to writing up your final research report. In a survey of 110 social science research students at British universities, Torrance, Thomas and Robinson (1992) found that 104 reported using the specified planning and writing strategies when producing their last substantial piece of academic *text*. These are shown in Table 9.1.

We can use advice from the general literature to expand these strategies into activities you can pursue. Most authors emphasise the importance in getting your thoughts committed to paper in one way or another. Phillips and Pugh (1994) advocate using a brainstorming approach and putting down all the main points that come to mind. Some people may prefer to do this in the sequential order of their dissertation or thesis structure. They will first concentrate on the main points from the literature, then consider the methodology they adopted before writing the main points from their research. Others may prefer to generate all the main points in a random order. They claim that this frees the mind and often a point from the literature or methodology will generate points concerned with the research results and analysis.

Creswell (1994) suggests that visual maps can be helpful (see Chapter 4). He recommends that once you have constructed a mind map in the most appropriate structure, you can then proceed to construct the points into grammatical paragraphs made up of well-balanced

Table 9.1 Planning and writing strategies adopted by students

Strategy	Students reporting (%)
Brainstorming or writing down a checklist of ideas which might be included in the final document but which does not specify the order in which they might be presented	80
Taking verbatim notes from the relevant literature	78
Putting notes into some kind of order	63
Constructing a 'mind map' which gives a spatial representation of the links between particular ideas	54
Constructing a plan that details not only the content of the finished piece, but also the order in which it will be presented	84
Writing out full drafts in continuous prose but not necessarily in polished English	94
Revising full drafts	94

Source: Torrance, Thomas and Robinson (1992) p. 159.

sentences We prefer to do this a chapter at a time, organising the points into each of the sections in the chapter, and then concentrate on writing the paragraphs.

However, it is important to remember that you do not have to write your thesis in any particular order. Many researchers start by writing up the literature review (see Chapter 4), as in many cases it forms part of the research proposal (see Chapter 5). If you have been diligent, you will have given conference papers or written articles on various parts of your research and you may choose to use these as a basis from which to commence writing various parts of your final research report. In many respects, it does not matter what strategy you adopt; the important thing is not to delay writing.

Some students put off writing up because they are still updating their literature or collecting more data because there has been a change. You must be strong willed and decide to impose a definite cut-off point on your research. Your dissertation or thesis will be an account of your research up to the chosen date and you need not worry about events after that time. Your supervisor(s) and examiners appreciate that you are not writing a newspaper which must contain the latest news!

9.1.1   Report design

In this section we consider the overall *report design*. When planning your research report, it is useful to bear in mind the concept of synergy: your dissertation or thesis should be greater than the sum of its parts. To achieve this, you must remember that the chapters which comprise your report do not exist in isolation from one another; they are interrelated and need to be integrated to form a cohesive whole. In Figure 9.1 we offer a logical and structured approach to report design.

9.1.2   Format

Even at the first draft stage, it is valuable to put the material in the format required by your institution. This will save you considerable time later on when you are trying to refine and improve the content of the document. You will need to ascertain from your university or college what the requirements are with regard to style, length and structure of your research report. You will be expected to submit your work typed or word processed with double (or, possibly, one-and-a-half) line spacing, printed only on one side of the page. There are also likely to be requirements to meet regarding page numbering, font size and margin widths.

For example, a left-hand margin of at least 1.25 inches leaves room for the document to be bound; a right-hand margin of 1 inch allows

Figure 9.1 Guide to report design

Structure and content

► The information should be presented in a logical sequence. Each section should have a logical progression and support a central message. Each item should lead to the next.
► A standard hierarchy of headings and sub-headings should be adopted to structure the report.
► The chapters, main sections and sub-sections should be numbered sequentially. Thus Section 3.5.5 refers to the fifth sub-section in section 5 of chapter 3. Three is normally considered to be the maximum number of subdivisions. Therefore it is usual to divide the report into chapters which contain a number of main sections and, in turn, these are divided into sub-sections. As a general rule, paragraphs should not be numbered.
► Titles and headings used for tables, graphs and other illustrations should also be standardised and numbered sequentially. The first digit should refer to the chapter number and the second digit to the table/chart number. Thus, Table 3.5 refers to the fifth table in Chapter 3.
► The pages should be numbered sequentially.

Style and layout

► Throughout the document there should be consistency of style in terms of page size, layout, headings, fonts, colour, justification, etc.
► A reasonable sized font, say 10 or 12 pitch, should be used to ensure legibility. The design and layout should be attractive; colour and/or white space should be used to complement the layout.
► If available, colour should be used to attract the reader's attention to key information.
► Different colours may be useful for highlighting key variables throughout a report.
► Avoid the combination of red and green for adjacent data, which is a problem for colour-blind and colour-deficient people.
► Do not distract the reader by using more than four or five colours (except for illustrations and photographs).
► Use dark colours for text and figures, since light colours are less legible.

Presentational forms

► Tables, graphs and other illustrations should relate to the text so that the information is supported by the different representations.
► To maintain the interest of the reader, a variety of presentations should be used, as dictated by the type of data (for example, interval or continuous) and the purpose (for example, for comparison).

Table 9.2 Approximate length of research reports

Type of research report	Typical length
Undergraduate dissertation	15,000–20,000 words
Taught Master's dissertation	20,000 words
M.Phil. thesis	40,000 words
Ph.D. thesis	80,000 words

examiners to write their comments in the margin. For higher degrees, the requirements are likely to be precise. You must ensure that your document complies with your institution's regulations.

You will be restricted in the maximum length of your research report, and this is likely to be measured by the number of words it contains. In Table 9.2 we give a general indication of the word length for different types of research reports. The appendices are not usually included in the word count. If you are having difficulty in keeping within the maximum word count, you could consider whether it might be appropriate to place some of your material in an appendix. At the same time, you should bear in mind that examiners are aware of students ploys in this respect and a thesis accompanied by a voluminous set of appendices is likely to be viewed with some dismay.

9.1.3 Structure

Before we consider the writing of the individual chapters that will make up your research report, it is useful to consider some general points. First, the overall structure of your final research report, dissertation or thesis should be logical and clear, and you should apply this principle to each chapter, section, paragraph and sentence. Although individual research reports differ according to the problem being investigated and the methodology employed, there are some common features. Table 9.3 shows a typical structure of a research report, together with an indication of the size of each chapter.

It is important to note that this structure is only a guide; you will need to modify it to reflect your own research project after discussions with your supervisor. In practice the size of each chapter will vary according to the nature of the research problem, the methodology adopted and the use of tables, charts and diagrams. For example, in an undergraduate dissertation there is often less scope for primary research and therefore the literature review will form a more substantial part of the report. In a Ph.D., particularly where a phenomenological approach without an *a priori* theoretical framework has been adopted, the methodology chapter will be a crucial and significant part of the thesis.

Table 9.3 Typical structure of a research report

Chapter/section	Description	Percentage of report
Introduction	A precise explanation of what research is about and why it is important and interesting, the research questions or hypotheses should also be stated	10
Literature review	A critical analysis of what other researchers have said on the subject and where your project fits in	20
Methodology	An explanation of why you collected certain data, what data you collected, from where you collected it, when you collected it, how you collected it and how you analysed it	15
Results	A presentation of your research results	22
Analysis and discussion	An analysis of your results showing the contribution to knowledge and pointing out any weaknesses/limitations	20
Conclusions	A description of the main lessons to be learnt from your study and what future research should be conducted	12
References	A detailed, alphabetical or numerical list of the sources from which information has been obtained and which have been cited in the text	1
Appendices	Detailed data referred to but not shown elsewhere	
Total		**100**

It is useful if the chapter titles you use reflect the contents, but do not be over-imaginative; the examiner will have certain expectations about the content and the order in which it will appear. Therefore, it is best not too depart too far from a traditional structure, unless you have good reasons. There are no hard and fast rules about how individual chapters should be structured, but in Figure 9.2 we show an example of how to structure (and number) chapters. The example takes the first two chapters of a study which examined the UK company practice of giving printed reports on the financial performance to employees. The structure may be too complex for your needs, but it demonstrates the general principles. For example, for an

Figure 9.2 Example of how to structure and number chapters

FINANCIAL REPORTS TO EMPLOYEES

Chapter 1. Introduction

1.1   Background to the study
1.2   Overview of financial reporting
1.3   Aims of the study
1.4   Definition of terms
1.5   Structure of the thesis

Chapter 2. Literature review

2.1   The background to financial reporting to employees
    2.1.1   The legal framework
    2.1.2   The theoretical framework
2.2   The case for financial reporting to employees
    2.2.1   Accountability
    2.2.2   Information demands
    2.2.3   Company self-interest
2.3   The development of current practices
    2.3.1   The extent of the practice
    2.3.2   The content of financial reports
    2.3.3   The presentation of financial reports
    2.3.4   The distribution of financial reports
2.4   Prior research studies
    2.4.1   Surveys of company practice
    2.4.2   Surveys of employee opinions
    2.4.3   Case studies
    2.4.4   Experimental studies

undergraduate dissertation you may find that you only need chapters and sections within each chapter, and have no need to use sub-sections, such as 2.2.1, 2.2.2, etc. For a M.Phil. or Ph.D. thesis, such subsections will be necessary, but you should consider carefully before you dividing your subsections any further, as this may lead to a fragmented appearance.

The more logical you can make your structure, the easier it will be for you to write the report and for the examiner to read it. The ordering of the sections in the chapters is very much a matter of choice, influenced by the nature of the research and the arguments you are trying to make. Howard and Sharp (1983) suggest a number of different ways that the sections can be ordered.

> ▶ **chronologically**, where you describe events in the order in which they occurred, is clearly most appropriate when you are trying to give an historical perspective or describe developments

▶ **categorically**, where you group the issues into various categories or groups, a good example of which is a geographical classification, although in business research you may choose to group matters by activity (for example, production, administration sales, etc.)

▶ **sequentially**, where you describe the events in the sequence in which they occur, is useful when explaining or analysing the events in a process, and is very similar to chronological ordering, but is not so closely time related

▶ by **perceived importance**, where you present the information starting with the least important and moving to the most important or vice versa. The direction in which you move will depend on the nature of the argument you are making.

Experiential learning	**Structuring your project**

Draw up a draft structure for your own research, based on Table 9.3 and Figure 9.2.

9.1.4   Writing style

The means by which you will communicate the majority of information in your research report is the *narrative* or *text*. Therefore, it is important that the meaning of the text you write is clear, even if the content is technically or conceptually difficult to understand. Some students adopt a long-winded and complicated *style of writing* in the belief that this will make the document look more 'academic'. Try to resist this temptation! We recommend that you keep your sentences relatively short and expressing your thoughts as coherently as you can. You should be trying to give the examiners the impression that they are sharing privileged information; in other words, your dissertation or thesis should allow them to understand and have access to your research project in its entirety, which is a unique piece of work.

You should aim to present your report in a way that invites the reader to start reading and is easy to follow through. This is important, because you want to attract and keep the examiner's attention. By using certain techniques, such as dividing the text up into digestible chunks, interspersing it with graphical and other illustrations, using headings, sub-headings, different fonts and typefaces, providing wide margins and a clear layout, 'a reader can be virtually "forced" to read' (Martin, 1989, p. 49). Chall (1958) identifies three key, interrelated elements of the *readability* of text which we advise that you take into account:

▶ interest (the ability to hold the reader's attention)
▶ legibility (the impact of factors such as typography and layout on the reader)
▶ ease of understanding (reading comprehension).

We recommend that you use up-to-date reference books such as an authoritative dictionary, thesaurus and grammar guide. Although quick and easy, take care when using computerised spelling and grammar checkers, as they do not take account of the sense in which the words are used, or whether they represent an interesting or dull form of expression. Nor do they consider cultural differences between English-speaking nations which give rise to differences in spelling and usage. In Figure 9.3 we offer some general guidance on the presentation of text.

Although spelling, grammar and punctuation play an important role, writing is more than a matter of correct usage; it involves a careful choice of words to create a lucid, flowing style, which both attracts and maintains the interest of the reader. Therefore, it is important not to become pedantic over rules. This should allow a personal style of writing to develop. If you already have a good writing style, the above principles will be relatively easy to apply. Unfortunately, most of us are not so blessed, but we can, at least, aim to be competent!

One way to improve your style is to look at how the academic authors you admire express themselves. In addition you should get others to comment on your work. Your supervisor can do this, but is more likely to be concerned with the way that you conducted the research and the results. Therefore, you may find it more useful if you can agree to exchange your written work with fellow students for comment. This kind of mutual support can be very encouraging and may also help you keep ahead of the various deadlines you set yourself.

Figure 9.3 Guide to the presentation of text

Structure and style

▶ Text should be written as lucidly and clearly as possible.
▶ The level of formality and style of writing should be appropriate for the intended audience.
▶ Sentences should be kept short; preferably no longer than 20 words.
▶ A new paragraph should be started for each new idea.

Grammar and semantics

▶ The grammar, punctuation and spelling (especially of names) should be checked. Computerised spelling and grammar checkers should be used judiciously.
▶ Precise words, rather than general or abstract words, should be used.
▶ The meaning of words and phrases should be checked for correct usage.
▶ Jargon should be avoided and a glossary provided for any technical terms.
▶ The document should be carefully proof-read for typographical mistakes, repetition, clichés, errors and omissions.

9.1.5   Setting a timetable

Whilst determining the structure of your thesis, it is also useful to draw up a timetable showing the critical dates when different sections will be completed. You will have a deadline for submission of your dissertation or thesis, and it is easy to think of this as coinciding with when you have finished writing up. However, finishing writing is not the final stage; you will also need time for editing, proof-reading and binding of the finished report.

It is difficult to estimate exactly how long the writing up and final tasks should take, as there are so many variables involved. In Table 9.4 we give a breakdown of the main tasks for a full-time Ph.D. student.

The schedule shown in Table 9.4 assumes that some preliminary work has been done; for example, most of the references are known and listed, some of the diagrams are drawn up and are ready to be incorporated, and the analysis of the results has been completed. Even allowing for this, you will see that five weeks (over 20 per cent) of the time is concerned with getting the results in order once it has been word processed. We would also recommend that you build in a contingency factor to allow for illness and domestic interruptions (both yours and your supervisor's), computer breakdowns and searching for lost documents.

Editing is a process which involves re-reading and identifying errors and omissions in the content and structure of your work, and consequently amending it. There are no short cuts, but if your supervisor, colleagues and family will read and comment on your early drafts, it will make your job easier. Before you start editing try to have a break of a week or two, so that you can return to it with a fresh eye and,

Table 9.4 Typical time taken to write a Ph.D. thesis

Chapter or task	Number of weeks
Introduction	2
Literature review	4
Methodology	2
Results	4
Analysis and discussion	4
Conclusions	2
Tables, figures, references, appendices, etc.	1
Consultation with supervisor and/or others and revisions	2
Editing, proof reading and binding	3
Total	**24**

possibly, a more open perspective. When you have finished editing your research report, you are ready to begin reading it for errors in spelling, grammar, chapter and section numbering, table and figure numbering, pages numbering, etc.

9.2 Content of the report

Having looked at the overall design, we are now ready to examine the *content* of the report in detail. In designing the structure of your thesis, you will have decided the content of each chapter and divided them into numbered sections. Each chapter should have an introductory section and a concluding section. They may not always be given that heading, but they must be present. This allows you to make connections between chapters. Some students get confused with this advice because it may mean that they have to think harder about their chapter and section titles. For example, if you want to call the first section in each chapter 'Introduction', then you cannot call Chapter 1 'Introduction' as well because it would repetitive. A simple way round this is to call Chapter 1 'Background to the Study' or 'An Overview of . . .' and insert the name of the research topic .

9.2.1 Preliminary pages

The *preliminary pages* or *prelims* are the introductory pages which precede the first chapter. The page numbers for these pages are normally small Roman numerals (i, ii, iii, etc.). This allows the pages of the chapters to be numbered in Arabic numerals (1, 2, 3, etc.). The preliminary pages usually comprise the following order:

- ▶ a title page
- ▶ any copyright notice
- ▶ a list of contents with page numbers
- ▶ a list of figures and tables
- ▶ any acknowledgements
- ▶ declaration (if the research is being submitted for a degree or other academic qualification)
- ▶ an abstract.

We suggest that you adopt the above order for your preliminary pages, unless your university or college follows an alternative convention.

Your research project will have been registered with a particul*ar* *title*, but you may wish to revise this to ensure that it reflects *the* research you have conducted. Keep your title as short as possib*le,* eliminate unnecessary words. Do not include such phrase*s as 'An* Approach to . . .', 'A Study of . . .', 'An Investigation into . . .' *which* have a good reason for doing so. Either a single or a double title (where a colon is used to separate two themes) is suitable. You will find a number of examples of double titles in the references we give in this book. The most important aspect of the title is that it should clearly indicate the topic or focus of the research.

The *acknowledgements* consist of one or two sentences thanking those who have helped you with your research; for example, companies who have given you access to data and individuals who have helped you, such as your supervisor, colleagues and family.

If you are required to include an *abstract*, remember that it is not an introduction. It is a very short, summary of the entire document of about 100 words. The purpose of an abstract is:

▶ to introduce the topic
▶ to describe how you did the research
▶ to discuss the results of what was done
▶ to explain the implications of the results.

Having described the preliminary pages, we are now ready to look at the main part of the research report.

9.2.2   Introduction

The first two parts of your thesis or dissertation which your examiner will read are the *introduction* and the *conclusions*, so these two chapters are very important. We advise that you do not write your introductory chapter until you have finished writing your conclusions, because these two chapters are so closely related. A common mistake that students make is to start discussing the research findings, or even the conclusions, in the introduction. To avoid this, you may find it a useful ploy to pretend that you have not yet conducted the study.

The introductory chapter will probably have four or five sections. In the early sections you must demonstrate the importance and relevance of your research. It is best to start with a broad view of the general research area and then narrow it down to explain where your research fits in. There is no need to go into great detail, as subsequent chapters of your thesis will explain and describe what you did and what you found out.

Once you have established the place of your own research, you will ⁓⁓⁓⁓ ⁓ion explaining the aims of the research and your research ⁓⁓⁓⁓⁓theses (see Chapter 5). You may have refined your ⁓⁓⁓⁓⁓⁓⁓s during the course of the research, so do not copy ⁓⁓⁓⁓⁓⁓m your proposal. The final part of your introduction ⁓⁓⁓⁓⁓to the subsequent chapters of your research report. This ⁓⁓⁓⁓ some three or four paragraphs describing the content of each chapter.

Figure 9.4 Guide to starting the introduction

1. Use an appropriate quotation. This has the advantage of taking the reader directly into the topic. The subsequent sentences can either support or refute the quotation. However, you must make certain that the quotation is applicable to your topic and does lead on to the development of an argument.
2. Pose a question which draws the reader into your discussion. This has the advantage that you can word the question to best fit the arguments you wish to present.
3. Use an illustration. If carefully chosen, this can capture your reader's interest immediately.

Source: Winkler and McCuen (1994).

The first few sentences of the introduction are crucial, as these will attract the reader's attention and set the tone for the entire document. Winkler and McCuen (1994) offer three strategies for beginning a research paper which we believe can be used as a guide to the opening of the introduction in any research report. Figure 9.4 gives details.

9.2.3   Literature review

The purpose of the *literature review* is to provide proof of scholarship; in other words, to show that you know the literature and you have the intellectual capacity to read it and criticise it constructively. Although you will have conducted your literature search, you have to put this in some sort of order before you can conduct any analysis and synthesis of the literature. Drawing on the network theory of models by Hesse (1980) and Ryan, Scapens and Theobald (1992), we recommend the following procedure:

1. Select a small number of high-quality journals for the most recent year and select articles on your topic.
2. Identify the most important articles cited by the author.
3. Put the most important articles in a time chart using the author's name, and distinguishing between the most significant which are at the core of the literature and those which are significant but not as important. Place the most important articles in square boxes.
4. Determine the motivation for each article, its literary antecedents and the methodological rationale which binds them together.
5. Go back in time and repeat the process at five-yearly intervals.

When you have completed this process, you will have constructed a network diagram which will differentiate between primary and secondary articles, and show the links between them. This will provide a structure for the literature review and a basis on which to conduct your analysis and synthesis. In Figure 9.5 we offer guidance on writing the literature review.

Figure 9.5 Guide to writing the literature review

▶ Select relevant material only.
▶ Group the material into categories and comment on the most important features.
▶ Compare the results of different studies, picking out those which have the most bearing on your research.
▶ Set the context for your own study.
▶ Be critical. You are not recording or describing other people's work, you are providing a critique by pointing out the strengths and weaknesses of other research and evaluating other studies, theories, etc., with reference to your own study.

By now you should know the names of the leading authors in your field and the main journals which cover your research topic. You must cite these references often. If you have had your own work published as a conference paper, professional journal or referred journal, you should cite it. This will demonstrate to your supervisor(s) and examiners that your work is considered acceptable at a certain level.

On the subject of *citations*, we have a few tips to offer. If you are referring to an author whose work you think is important or whose argument you consider supports yours, you should start the sentence with his or her name. For example, 'Smith (1994) has demonstrated an important link between . . .' On the other hand, if you are referring to an author you do not consider is very important, or whose arguments you do not wish to promote, cite the name within the sentence. For example, 'Although it is claimed (Smith, 1994) that there is a link between . . .' Remember that it is your research and you are setting out to be the authority in this specialised area, so do not give too much prominence to others, and do not be afraid to criticise their work, even if they are world famous. However, you must make certain that you justify any criticisms you make.

If you are concerned that your literature review is too long, you may need to go through it summarising where you have become too verbose; you may even need to delete some of the less important items. If you have to do so, we advise that you start by deleting references to newspapers or popular journals and then move on to the professional journals. Do not delete references to articles in refereed journals unless you are confident that the article is not relevant to your research after all. If you still have problems, you may be able to find a good article which summarises or reviews many other articles, and you can refer to that as a main source.

If you know the name of your external examiner in advance, and he or she has published in your research area, you may consider it prudent to quote from his or her work!

9.2.4   Methodology

The *methodology* chapter is a critical part of the report in both a positivistic and a phenomenological study, but will vary according to which paradigm you have adopted. From a general point of view, both approaches require a section which 'explains how the problem was investigated and why particular methods and techniques were used.' (Bell, 1993, p. 155). Both will start with an introductory paragraph which briefly describes the main features of the methodology and the organisation of the chapter. In a positivistic study, this will be followed by a statement of the procedures adopted, description of the sampling methods, formulation of hypotheses and the statistical techniques of analysis employed. In a phenomenological study the structure is more flexible and will be closely related to the methodology employed.

In a *positivistic study* the methodology section 'describes the exact steps that will be undertaken to address your hypotheses and/or research questions' (Rudestam and Newton, 1992, p. 60). If you are using well-known procedures and tests, there is no need to describe them in detail; you need only refer to them. If you have modified or refined any standard tests and procedures, you will need to describe them in detail. You will also need to describe any little known techniques or those you have devised yourself in detail. In a positivistic study, the methodology chapter can usually be divided into five main sections as shown in Figure 9.6.

Figure 9.6 Positivistic studies: guide to writing the methodology

The chapter should be divided into the following main sections:

1. A general description of the study, an explanation of the structure and main contents of the chapters. This introductory section is a good place to discuss the limitations and delimitations of your study (see Chapter 5), if you have not done so in the first chapter.
2. A description of the source and number of subjects in the study. This will require a description of the population and your sampling procedure (see Chapter 6).
3. An explanation of the appropriateness of the research instruments or measures you have used and their reliability and validity (see Chapter 6) as discussed in the literature. If you have designed your own research instruments, you will need to justify this and discuss the issues of reliability and validity in some depth.
4. A description of the data collection method(s) (see Chapter 6) you have adopted: how, where and when you collected the data. It is sometimes helpful to incorporate a chronological flow chart in this section.
5. A description of the methods of data analysis (see Chapter 7) you have used, why they were appropriate given the nature of your hypotheses, the number of independent and dependent variables and the level of measurement of each of the variables.

In a *phenomenological study* the methodology section should stress the nature and rationale for the chosen methodology, before leading on to discuss the method(s) of data collection and analysis. You may consider that the philosophy and assumptions underpinning the methodology, and its appropriateness to the research problem, are so important that you devote a separate chapter to it. The following chapter will then discuss how you employed it in your research. In Figure 9.7 we offer guidance on writing the methodology chapter(s) in a phenomenological study.

Throughout the methodology chapter(s) you must weave into your text the assumptions of the phenomenological paradigm. Merriam (1988) identifies the following six assumptions which can provide a platform for your writing.

1. You are concerned primarily with process, rather than outcomes or products.
2. You are interested not in frequency, but in meaning; that is, how people make sense of their experiences and the world around them.
3. You are the primary research instrument. It is by and through you that data is collected, analysed and interpreted.

Figure 9.7 Phenomenological studies: guide to writing the methodology

The chapter should be divided into the following main sections:

1. Explain how your paradigm (see Chapter 3) is appropriate to the research topic.
2. If you have a theoretical framework (see Chapter 5), explain how it relates to the research problem and guides the research.
3. Explain the place of the methodology (see Chapter 3) within your paradigm, its nature and development, making reference to any similar studies which have adopted it. As there are variations within a phenomenological approach, it is useful to quote a number of definitions of the methodology you are using, explain the main features, your own position and justify your choice.
4. Describe the data collection method(s) (see Chapter 6) you have used, their strengths and weaknesses, and justify your choice by referring to the alternatives you considered but thought were unsuitable. You should state where the data was collected, from whom and why. Data collection will normally have taken place over a period of time, so it is helpful to include a timetable showing when specific activities took place and any critical events which occurred.
5. Describe the data analysis method(s) you have used at a very general level (see Chapter 8). This is sometimes difficult, but you should emphasise the main features and leave the discussion of the details until the 'Results' chapter.
6. In some studies you will also need to include a discussion on validity and reliability (see Chapter 6). There are differences of opinion on this and you should seek guidance from your supervisor. If there is uncertainty, we consider it prudent to discuss issues of verification, generalisability and the limitations of the study.

4. Your research is placed in a natural, rather than an artificial, setting. It is conducted in the field by you visiting the places where the activity takes place so that you can observe and record it.
5. The research is descriptive and seeks to capture process, meaning and understanding.
6. The process of research is mainly inductive because you are attempting to construct abstractions, concepts, hypotheses and theories from abstractions.

9.2.5   Results

The *results* chapter in a positivistic study is often far easier than in a phenomenological one. In a *positivistic study* you only have to give the results; in other words, you need only state the facts. The analysis and interpretation will appear in the next chapter of your research report. Normally, you would begin with a description of your sample, such as age, occupation, etc. If your *unit of analysis* is not a person you would describe the characteristics of the units in your study.

In this chapter you will address the research questions or hypotheses in the sequence which seems most appropriate. Most of the data will be given in the form of tables and graphs. In Section 9.4 we provide some guidance on the presentation of quantitative data, but a more exhaustive treatment on the construction of tables to present quantitative results is given by Rudestam and Newton (1992).

In a *phenomenological study* it is often impossible to disentangle the results and the analysis. Whether you need one or two chapters to do this will depend on the amount of data you have collected and the depth of your analysis. If two chapters are required, you must try to find a rational division so that each of the chapters are complete in themselves, yet linked. As with quantitative data, the aim in a phenomenological study is to make sense of the data you have collected. In phenomenological studies the use of *diagrams* and other illustrations can be very effective (see Chapter 8). However, you need to be careful not to let them overshadow the text. Any diagrams or illustrations are for support and clarification; the main thrust of your discussion should be carried by the *text*.

9.2.6   Analysis and discussion

At an early stage in the *analysis and discussion* chapter you should restate the purpose of the research and the research questions from your first chapter, since these should underpin and direct your analysis and discussions. You should demonstrate how your results contribute to existing knowledge and draw out any implications for future

Figure 9.8 Guide to writing the analysis and discussion chapter

The chapter should be divided into the following main sections:

1. An overview of the significant findings of the study
2. A consideration of the findings in light of existing research studies
3. Implications of the study for current theory (except in purely applied studies)
4. A careful examination of findings that fail to support or only partially support your hypotheses
5. Limitations of the study that may affect the validity or generalisation of the results
6. Recommendations for further research
7. Implications of the study for professional practice or applied settings (optional)

Source: Rudestam and Newton (1992) p. 121.

research. In this chapter you need to show that you can be self-critical. This is the chapter where you discuss any weaknesses or faults in your research design. Do not be reluctant to be self critical, but take the opportunity to demonstrate that you have learnt from the experience. You may also wish to indicate how future studies might be conducted which would remedy these deficiencies. Rudestam and Newton (1992) suggest that the analysis and discussion chapter can be divided into seven main sections as shown in Figure 9.8.

If you are going to have a *viva* (see Section 9.7), which is a verbal defence of your dissertation or thesis, it is often this chapter which receives the greatest attention. Therefore, be careful not to make any sweeping statements or exaggerated claims. If you have found out something which is interesting and worthwhile, and we hope you have, discuss it fully and with enthusiasm. However, remember to acknowledge the contribution made by previous and future studies.

9.2.7 Summary and conclusions

Whilst your introductory chapter should start broadly and then became focused, your final chapter, the *summary and conclusions*, should be the opposite. You should commence by summarising the main parts of your research, then widen your discussion to explain how it is important for any further research in the same area; and finally, why it is of general interest and importance, without being too ambitious in your claims.

After reading the introductory chapter, many examiners turn immediately to the conclusions. You need to ensure that these first and last chapters complement each other, even though they are separated by thousands of words in the intervening chapters. Make sure that the same key words and phrases that were used in the

Figure 9.9 Guide to writing the summary and conclusions chapter

- ▶ Restate the purpose of the research.
- ▶ Summarise the main points from the results and show how they address your research questions.
- ▶ Give guidance on the implications of your research, such as who might be affected by your findings and how that will affect behaviour, attitudes and policies, etc.
- ▶ Do not offer new opinions.
- ▶ Identify the weaknesses in your research an the limitations of your study.
- ▶ Suggest what future research might be conducted and how your study helps. In the same way that you spent quite a bit of time choosing the opening of the introductory chapter, you should spend a long time on the last sentence. Aim for a convincing ending.

introduction are used in the conclusions chapter. Look at the aims of your research in the introductory chapter and ensure that your conclusions either show that they have been achieved or explain why they have not. In Figure 9.9. we offer guidance on writing the summary and conclusions chapter.

9.2.8   Appendices

The *appendix* or *appendices* will contain information which was either too detailed or not sufficiently relevant to be included in the main document, such as copies of statistical data drawn from other sources, background information on the industry or company, specifications of products or processes or regulations applying to employment or production. Do not make the appendices a dustbin for all those bits and pieces you could not fit into the main part of the document!

Each item should be placed in a separate, numbered appendix which is as clearly labelled and structured as the chapters in your main document. You must make sure that you make reference to any material you have put in an appendix, otherwise it is not likely to be read or taken into account. Each appendix should be numbered in the order in which you refer to them in the main part of the report.

9.3   Presenting qualitative data

Presenting qualitative data you have collected can pose a number of difficulties. The process involves taking your field notes and other documentation and making an initial draft before writing a working, interpretative document which 'contains the writer's initial attempts to make sense of what has been learned' (Denzin, 1994, p. 501). Note that this is only a working document which you will wish to reflect on and discuss with your supervisor(s) and colleagues. You may make a number of drafts before you arrive at the final document which 'embodies the writer's self-understandings, which are now inscribed in the experiences of those studied' (Denzin, 1994, p. 502).

If your data is mainly qualitative, it is essential that you intersperse your *text* with quotations. This will give your text authenticity and vibrancy, and will enable the reader to share the world you are analysing. However, you must be careful that any illustrations or quotations you give are relevant and part of the fabric of the study. 'Provided they are supported by other forms of data and tie in clearly with other aspects of the analysis, using individual episodes can provide a powerful means of getting a hold on the problems of presenting complex qualitative data' (Allan, 1991, p. 187).

You may also need to use *footnotes*, which may be at the bottom of the page or at the end of each chapter. The purpose of the footnote is to quote the authority upon which the statement in the text is made to add further information or to refer to some other passages in the text. Table 9.5 shows some of the more common abbreviations used in footnotes.

Table 9.5 Common abbreviations used in footnotes

Term	Meaning
a priori	'from the cause to the effect'
cf.	compare
et seq.	'and the following'
ff	'on subsequent pages'
	Used instead of listing pages following the first quoted in the reference
ibid.	'the same place'
	Used instead of repeating the whole of the previous reference if it is exactly the same
idem	'the same'
	Used instead of repeating the author's name if it is the same as that of the immediately preceding reference
op. cit.	'the work/place cited'
	Used instead of repeating the name of a work if it is the same as the preceding reference

The displays you used for analysing the data, as described in Chapter 8, can be used to great effect when presenting your qualitative data, although your main discussions will be in the *text*. You may find that diagrams and even photographs can help. In an article reporting an ethnographic study conducted in a retail gift store, McGrath (1989) used data from participant observation, in-depth interviews and photography to provide description and interpretative insights into the consumer gift selection and retailer socialisation process.

9.4 Presenting quantitative data

The general rule for expressing numbers in the *text* is to use words to express numbers one to nine, and numerals to express numbers 10 onwards. For example, 'Only five of the respondents answered this question', as opposed to 'There were 32 respondents in total', There are many exceptions to this rule. For example when numbers below 10 are grouped together for comparison with numbers 10 and above in the same paragraph, they should all appear as numerals. For example, 'Only 5 of the 32 respondents answered this question'. Other exceptions are described in a useful chapter by Rudestam and Newton (1992).

In the sections which follow, we have drawn together a number principles to form guidelines for different forms of presentation. However, you may find that it is not feasible to apply every suggestion we offer. Deciding whether a rule or principle is optional requires some experience and there is considerable merit in experimenting to find the best form of presentation for your data. This may lead you to new discoveries and the development of further principles.

9.4.1 Tables

The data in a *table* is tabulated or classified by arranging it in a framework of columns and rows. Research shows that some people prefer data presented in tabular form, although 'even quite sophisticated people need time to get the main points from a table (often much more time than they would need with a bar chart or pictorial chart)' (Macdonald-Ross, 1977, p. 379). However, tables offer the advantage of being compact and exact, and 'usually outperform graphics in reporting on small data sets of 20 numbers or less' (Tufte, 1983, p. 56).

Iselin (1972) suggests that the way in which a table is constructed can aid the reader's comprehension. Construction signalling allows items which are grouped together to be identified, as well as differentiating names of items from names of groups. Iselin uses three different methods of construction signalling:

- lower and upper case letters
- the indentation of items under a group heading
- spacing between groups of items.

Although Iselin's experiments were confined to students and some of his findings require further research, he shows that effective construction signalling has a significant effect on the speed and accuracy of the extraction of information.

Drawing from the literature and our own experience, in Figure 9.10 we offer guidance on the construction of tables in your research report.

To illustrate these principles we will take a table from a research report (Hussey, 1995) which analysed and compared quantitative data collected from two regional offices of a firm of accountants. We have

Figure 9.10 Guide to constructing tables

General advice
- Use a tabular presentation for an educated audience.
- Use columns rather than rows to compare figures. If comparison is the main purpose of the presentation, consider using a comparative bar chart.
- Restrict the size to 20 numbers or less. This can be done by dividing a large table into small tables. Consider a graph for large data sets.
  Minimise the number of words used, but spell words out rather than using abbreviations or codes.

Structure and layout
- Place the table number and title at the top to allow the reader to identify and understand the purpose of the presentation before proceeding to the body of the table.
- Use different fonts and styles to distinguish the table title, headings and sub-headings.
- In pairs or sequences of tables, use identical labels for common headings and labels.
- Indent items under a group variable label.
- Set columns compactly so that the eye does not have to travel too far between labels and each column of figures.
- Add grid lines to facilitate the reading of columns and rows.

The quantitative data
- Round numbers to two significant digits, unless precision of data is important.
- Where possible, order columns/rows by size of numbers. Place any miscellaneous variable last, regardless of size.
- Provide column/row averages or totals where apropriate.
- Draw attention to key figures with colour, shading or bold typeface.

Table 9.6 Southton and Northton: fee income by service

Service	Southton		Northton	
	Fee income £	Percentage of total fee income	Fee income £	Percentage of total fee income
Accounts	97,023	30.77	92,814	32.64
Audit	184,606	58.56	74,321	26.13
Management accounts	270	0.09	10,526	3.70
Special	4,022	1.28	42,206	14.84
Tax	25,402	8.06	51,695	18.18
VAT	3,875	1.23	2,969	1.04
Unidentified	36	0.01	9,857	3.47
Total	315,234	100.00	284,388	100.00

given them fictitious names to preserve the confidentiality of the data. In Table 9.6 we reproduce the original table which gave a breakdown of fee income in alphabetical order by service. In addition to the absolute figures, percentages were calculated.

The use of a table is appropriate, given the sophisticated audience, and many of the principles for the presentation of tables we have described are already present. However, the literature suggests that communication of the data can be further improved simply by decreasing the amount of data, or presenting it graphically. One way to reduce the amount of data is to divide the table into a number of smaller tables. We have done this and Tables 9.7 and 9.8 show the results.

Although not reproduced here, the most striking aspect of the tables is that they were colour coded: red for Southton and blue for Northton. The same coding was adopted throughout the analysis so that the reader could tell at a glance which office the data referred to. Further improvements were achieved by rounding the percentages to whole numbers, but full details of the fee income are shown to avoid the loss of precise information. Totals were already present and these remove the need for mental arithmetic. The rows have been ranked by size, rather than alphabetical ordering by service. This allows attention to be drawn to the relative importance of the different services. Both the rows and the columns are compactly set and percentage signs have been used to minimise the number of words.

Attention has been drawn to key figures through the use of shading and the totals are in bold. Grid lines have been used to facilitate the reading of rows and columns. The tables are contained within a border, which distinguishes the body of the table (headings, labels and

Table 9.7 Southton: fee income by service

Service	Fee income £	% of total fee income
Audit	184,606	**59**
Accounts	97,023	31
Tax	25,402	8
Special	4,022	1
VAT	3,875	1
Management accounts	270	<1
Unidentified	36	<1
Total	**315,234**	**100**

Note: Care should be taken when drawing conclusions from this table because of unidentified fee income of £36.

Table 9.8 Northton: fee income by service

Service	Fee income £	% of total fee income
Accounts	92,814	33
Audit	74,321	26
Tax	51,695	18
Special	42,206	15
Management accounts	10,526	4
VAT	2,969	1
Unidentified	9,857	3
Total	**284,388**	**100**

Note: Care should be taken when drawing conclusions from this table because of unidentified fee income of £9,857.

data) from the title and any subsequent material. Unidentified income has been placed last, regardless of its size. Because the tables have headings and labels in common, care has been taken to ensure that these are identical. It is important to remember that however clearly presented your tables are, it is still necessary to offer some interpretation and, if possible, further analysis of the data. This should be given immediately after the table.

However, a major drawback of any tabular presentation is that it does not offer the 'at a glance' comparison of a graph. Therefore, we will look at graphical presentations next.

9.5.2   Charts and graphs

When using a graphical presentation for quantitative data, it is important to remember that you must endeavour at all times to present the information 'in a manner that is clear and concise, simple and effective, uncluttered and understandable' (Martin, 1989, p. 46). Research shows that some people prefer data presented in graphics, such as *charts* and *graphs*. Playfair, the eighteenth- century political economist, developed nearly all the basic graphical designs when looking for ways in which to communicate substantial amounts of quantitative data. He preferred graphics to tables because they show the shape of the data in a comparative perspective (Playfair, 1786). 'Often the most effective way to describe, explore, and summarise a set of numbers – even a very large set – is to look at pictures of those numbers' (Tufte, 1983, p. 9).

Graphics, especially when colour is used, can attract and hold the reader's attention and help identify trends in the data. Therefore, quantitative information displayed in a graph 'has the *potential* to be both read and understood. But effective communication does not follow automatically from graph use; the graph must comply with certain principles of graph design and construction' (Beattie and Jones, 1992, p. 30).

Although most commentators promote the graphical presentation of comparative data, there appears to be some conflict over acceptable levels of complexity. Ehrenberg (1975; 1976) advises that a graph should communicate a simple story, since many readers concentrate on the visual patterns, rather than reading the actual data. Tufte (1983) and Martin (1989) suggest that both colour and monochrome presentations require careful handling to avoid detracting from the message or misleading the reader. In Figure 9.11 we offer general guidance on constructing charts and graphs in your research report.

There is general agreement that a graph must represent the facts accurately; it must be clear and easily understood and must hold the reader's attention. To achieve these aims, the best type of graph to use in particular circumstances must be identified and general standards are necessary to avoid misleading the reader. Davis (1987) suggests that the type of graph (see Chapter 7) depends on the nature of the information to be conveyed; if it is important to give specific amounts, then a table remains the most appropriate form of presentation.

Hussey and Everitt (1991) suggest the following:

- a **bar chart** is valuable for making comparisons, for example when there are two amounts, one larger than the other
- a **pie chart** can be used if the information is expressed as a part or percentage of a total

Figure 9.11 General guide to constructing charts and graphs

General advice

▶ Do not mix different types of data (for example, percentage and absolute figures) on the same chart, but draw up separate charts.

▶ Items should only be compared on the same chart if they have the same basic data structure and a clear relationship.

▶ Label the axes.

▶ Label data elements directly and include the unit of measurement. If there is insufficient room to label the elements directly, provide a key.

▶ Minimise the number of words used, but if possible, spell words out, rather than using abbreviations or codes. The majority of ink used to produce the graph should present the quantitative data. Delete anything which does not present fresh information, since this represents a barrier to communication.

Structure and layout

▶ Place the chart number and title at the top to allow the reader to identify and understand the purpose of the presentation before proceeding to the body of the graph.

▶ Use different fonts and styles to distinguish the chart title, axes and data element labels.

▶ Select an unobtrusive background.

The quantitative data

▶ Select colours for the data elements with high contrast from adjacent items.

▶ Avoid the commonest colour blind deficient combination of red and green on adjacent elements.

▶ a **line graph** is best used where changes over a period of time are presented, although bar charts are often easier to read than line graphs.

We offer specific guidance on the best way to present these three commonly used graphical forms next.

9.4.3   Bar charts

Macdonald-Ross (1977) suggests that the elements of bars should be labelled directly; horizontal bars give room for labels and figures near the elements. However, for time sequences, he recommends vertical bar charts.

Thibadoux, Cooper and Greenberg (1986) advise that bars should be of uniform width and evenly spaced; they are easier to read and interpret if space of half the width of the bar is left as the distance between the bars. The scale should begin with zero and normally should remain unbroken. The number of intervals should assist with measuring distances and generally should be in round numbers, marked off with lines or ticks. They recommend that in general graphics which use horizontal and vertical scale lines should be proportioned so that the horizontal scale is greater than the height. This view is shared by Tufte (1983) who proposes that if the nature of the data suggests the shape of the graphic, follow that suggestion; otherwise move towards a horizontal graphical presentation about 50 per cent wider than tall.

With regard to shading, Thibadoux, Cooper and Greenberg (1986) suggest that black is appropriate if the bars are not extremely wide, when diagonal line shading or cross hatching may be used. However, horizontal and vertical shadings should not be used in segmented bars because they may affect the perceived width and shape of the bar. Care must also be taken with cross-hatching not to create optical illusions. In Figure 9.12 we offer some specific advice on constructing bar charts which should be applied in addition to the guidance offered in Figure 9.11.

We will draw on the same research report we used in the previous section to provide an example of these principles in practice. We have already mentioned that a major drawback of a tabular presentation is that it does not offer the 'at a glance' comparison of a graph. The chart shown in Figure 9.13, which is taken from the original report, attempted to address this problem.

The literature supports the choice of a bar chart for making comparisons, but perhaps percentage figures rather than the absolute figures are more useful, since they offer a more equitable comparison, given the difference in size of total fee income between the two offices. Many of the principles for the presentation of graphs, and bar charts in particular, are already present. The scale is on the left, and the bars are of uniform width and evenly spaced. To avoid misleading the reader, the single scale commences at zero and the range is not extended much beyond the highest or lowest points plotted on the graph.

However, the literature suggests that communication of the data could be further improved by adopting a horizontal form which allows figures to be added close to the bars and encourages the eye to compare different pieces of data. We have done this and Figure 9.14 shows the results.

It is interesting to note that although VAT at both offices is shown as representing 1 per cent of total fee income, the bar for Southton is fractionally longer than that for Northton. This is not an error, but is due to rounding. In fact, VAT represents 1.23 per cent of total fee income at Southton and 1.04 per cent at Northton. Therefore, the difference in the lengths of the bars is justified. It is suggested that anomalies due to rounding are inevitable, but attention should be drawn to them and explanation given.

Figure 9.12 Additional principles for constructing bar charts

General advice

▶ Use a bar chart for comparing data.

▶ In a bar chart the bars represent different categories of data. The frequency should be shown by the length (horizontal bar chart) or height (vertical bar chart) of each bar. In a histogram, the frequency is indicated by the area of the bar.

▶ Use a vertical bar chart for time sequences with the scale on the left. The time elements should move from left to right on the horizontal axis.

▶ Use a multiple bar chart, rather than a segmented bar chart, since the former provides a common base for the segments.

▶ Use a histogram for continuous, ratio or interval data where the class widths are unequal.

The bars

▶ In a bar chart, the bars should be of uniform width and evenly spaced.

▶ The bar end should be straight.

▶ Horizontal bars give room for labels and figures near the elements. Values should only be given if the result is legible and does not look cluttered.

▶ When using three-dimensional bars, clearly label the reading dimension.

▶ In multiple bar charts, do not use more than four elements.

▶ In histograms, the ordering of the bars should be sequential.

▶ If you are using pictograms, take care that the dimensions (length, area or volume) correctly reflect the changing value of the variable.

▶ Avoid pictograms with undefined reading points, such as piles of coins.

▶ Black is appropriate if the bars are not extremely wide; alternatively use shades of grey.

▶ Horizontal, vertical and diagonal lines should be avoided, as they can create optical illusions.

The scale

▶ Commence the scale at zero.

▶ If a break in the scale is unavoidable, it must be clearly indicated.

▶ Proportion the horizontal scale so that it is about 50% greater than the vertical scale.

The new graph conforms to the principle that the horizontal scale should be about 50 per cent greater than the vertical scale. In addition, it now concurs with Tufte's (1983) views on friendly graphs; the majority of the data ink is devoted to the data and although not reproduced here, the red and clue colouring is suitable for colour-deficient readers. Furthermore, the chart complies with the general requirement for consistency of layout, font, etc.; the style will match that of subsequent charts.

Figure 9.13 Southton and Northton: fee income by service compared
(original chart)

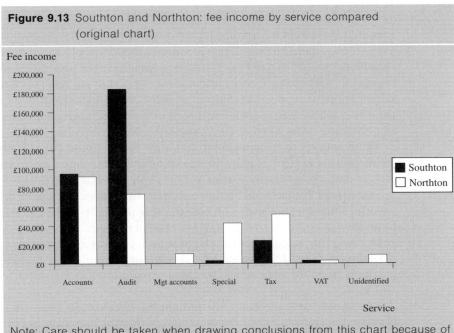

Note: Care should be taken when drawing conclusions from this chart because of
unidentified fee income of £36 at Southton and £9,857 at Northton.

Figure 9.14 Southton and Northton: percentage fee income by service
compared (new chart)

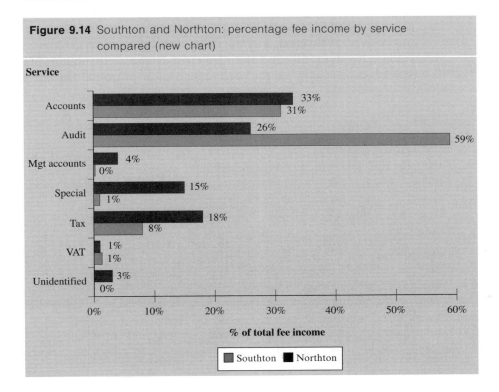

9.4.4   Pie charts

Invented by Florence Nightingale, *pie charts* are useful for presenting proportional data. Morris (1993) recommends that labels and figures should be placed nearby to facilitate comparison of the different segments. Thibadoux, Cooper and Greenberg (1986) suggest that the largest segment is placed at the central point of the upper right half of the circle, followed in a clockwise direction by the remaining segments in decreasing order, with any miscellaneous segment placed last.

There appears to be agreement that a pie chart should contain no more than six categories and should not be used to compare different sets of data. Research by Flannery (1971) shows that if quantity is related to area, readers tend to underestimate differences. In Figure 9.15 we offer some specific advice on constructing pie charts which should be applied in addition to the guidance offered in Figure 9.11.

Drawing our example from the consultancy report again, a pair of pie charts were used to provide a breakdown of percentage fee income by client trade for each office. These are reproduced in Figures 9.16 and 9.17.

The choice of a pie chart for presenting information when it is expressed as a percentage of a total is supported by the literature, but the general advice is that pie charts should not be used to compare differ-ent sets of data. Therefore, the communication of this data can be im-proved by replacing the pie charts with a single, comparative bar chart. This has the added advantage of removing potential 'noise' (Shannon and Weaver, 1949) created by the elaborate shading and hatching.

We have done this and the new chart (Figure 9.18) follows the prescribed principles for the presentation of a horizontal bar chart.

Figure 9.15 Additional principles for constructing pie charts

General advice
▶ Use a pie chart to present proportional data only.
▶ Use the angle at the centre to divide the circle into segments; the area of each segment should be proportional to the segment represented.
▶ Do not use pie charts to compare different sets of data; instead, consider a bar chart.

The segments
▶ Use no more than six segments.
▶ Place the largest segment at the central point of the upper right half of the circle, followed in a clockwise direction by the remaining segments in decreasing order.
▶ Place any miscellaneous variable last, regardless of size.
▶ Each segment should be labelled and its value given as a percentage of the whole.

Figure 9.16 Southton: percentage fee income by client trade (original chart)

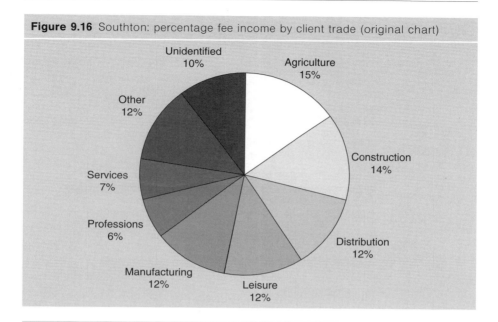

Figure 9.17 Northton: percentage fee income by client trade (original chart)

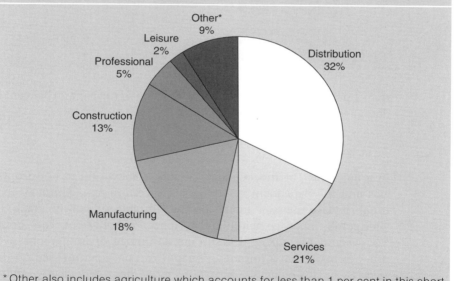

*Other also includes agriculture which accounts for less than 1 per cent in this chart.

Moreover, it now vividly illustrates the differences in the distribution of clients within each industry sector between the two offices. The chart shows that at Southton agriculture accounts for 0 per cent of total fee income, but a very small bar can be discerned. This is not as misleading is it might appear. In fact, agriculture accounts for less

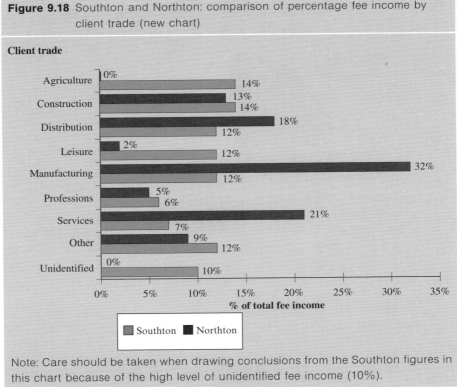

Figure 9.18 Southton and Northton: comparison of percentage fee income by client trade (new chart)

Client trade

Note: Care should be taken when drawing conclusions from the Southton figures in this chart because of the high level of unidentified fee income (10%).

than 1 per cent at Southton and the labelling of the bar as 0 per cent is due to rounding.

9.4.5   Line graphs

In a *line graph* the independent variable is shown on the horizontal axis and the dependent variable on the vertical axis. Although it is usual to place the scale figures on the left-hand side of the graph, in wide graphs it may be helpful if they appear on both sides (Thibadoux, Cooper and Greenberg, 1986). One advantage of line graphs over other forms is that a number of graphs can be superimposed on the same axes. This enables comparisons to be made very clearly. Thibadoux, Cooper and Greenberg recommend that if the curves are close together or cross, colour coding may be used to differentiate them or different patterns, such as solid, dash, dotted or dot-dash lines. However, Bergwerk (1970) found that experts on the communication of financial data preferred one or two-element charts. In Figure 9.19 we offer some specific advice on constructing line charts which should be applied in addition to the guidance offered in Figure 9.11.

Figure 9.19 Additional principles for constructing line charts

▶ The component categories should be represented by a series of points joined by a line.

▶ The axes must represent continuous scales with the independent variable shown on the horizontal axis and the dependent variable on the vertical axis.

▶ Place the scale figures for the vertical axis on the left. In a wide graph show the scale on both sides.

▶ Use no more than two elements.

As with tabular presentations, it is important to remember that however clearly presented your graphs and charts are, it is still necessary to offer some interpretation and, if possible, further analysis of the data. This should be given immediately after the graphical presentation.

9.5 Eleventh-hour strategies

Even if you have allowed plenty of time to write your final draft, you may find that you face unexpected problems because there are defects in your research. However, it may not be too late to rectify such flaws and we suggest you refer to the trouble-shooting guide in Chapter 10 for help.

If you have not been writing up during the course of your research, but have left it all until the end, you will be feeling very panicky. You have a deadline and only blank sheets of paper. Even with the best will in the world, students sometimes find themselves in this position. If this applies to you, we can offer the following advice:

1. Decide on an initial structure and do not take too long over it; no more than half a day, even for a Ph.D. Use the sample structures given in this chapter and put in as many of the sub-sections as you can. Work out the approximate word count you are aiming for with each chapter.

2. We assume that you are using a word processing package, so the next step is to open a file for each of the chapters, set up the required margins, font size, spacing, etc., and type in your section headings.

3. Now aim for volume. Do not worry unduly about grammar, punctuation or references. You must get as many words down as possible in each of the chapters. Leave the introductory chapter and concentrate on those sections you know well. You should find that the act of writing one part will spark off other aspects which

you want to include. This will entail switching from chapter to chapter and in this first rush through you may put things in the wrong places, but it doesn't matter.

4. When you have written approximately two-thirds of your target word count, stop and print each chapter. This will use up a lot of paper, but you are in a crisis situation and cost must come second to speed now. Put your print-out in a ring binder file, using dividers to separate each chapter.

5. Read all the chapters, marking any changes on the hard copy in a bright colour as you go, adding text wherever possible as well as references and quotations from other authors. Now make these corrections and additions to the computer files and open a new file for the references/bibliography. You should find that you are now within 10 to 15 per cent of your target number of words.

6. Print two copies and co-opt a friend or member of the family to read through one and mark down any comments. We imagine that your supervisor has washed his or her hands of you and has told you just to hand in the final copy.

7. Meanwhile, collect all your articles and other source materials together and skim through them looking for quotations, illustrations or other items you can fit into your thesis. As you have just read it, it should be easy to spot items. Write each item on a separate piece of paper and insert them into your ring binder containing your copy of your latest print-out.

8. When you receive your friend's comments, carefully work through your own and his or her amendments and make the changes on the computer, a chapter at a time, in order. Use the computer spell/grammar checker and check that the page layout meets requirements. As you finish each chapter print it off and read it. If you are lucky, you may just be able to persuade your supervisor into giving some guidance.

9. Make final changes, print off the required number of copies and arrange binding.

10. Now you can buy a drink for all those who have helped you, but make sure that you are never tempted to procrastinate again!

9.6   Standards

When writing up it is useful to consider the *standards* your supervisors will be looking for. Table 9.9 gives a summary of the general marking criteria of a research report.

The extent to which your research report must achieve these attributes depends on the level of your degree. Table 9.10, which is taken from Howard and Sharp (1994), gives details.

Table 9.9 General marking criteria of a research report

Element	Criteria
Objectives	Clarity Relevance Achieved

Research design	Appropriate
	Rationale
	Assessment:
	    Reliable (replicable)
	    Valid (accurate)

Literature review	Relevant Sources
Data collection and analysis	Primary/secondary Relevant to objectives Quality of analysis
Conclusions and recommendations	Persuasiveness/supported by evidence Practicality/cost/imaginative
Presentation	Style/use of language Clarity Tables/diagrams/summaries Length
Internal consistency	Continuity Objectives/conclusions
Integration of academic knowledge	Originality/initiative 'A learning process'

9.7   The viva

A *viva* is an individual oral examination, always held for post-graduate students and often for undergraduates as well. It is always a nerve-racking experience, but you can lessen the agony and improve your performance by practising making presentations. First, you should attempt to find out who the examiners will be and the format your viva will take. At the undergraduate level, your examiners are likely to be lecturers at your own institution, so you will already know them. At the postgraduate level, particularly for M.Phil. and Ph.D. students, your examiners will be external and you may only know them by reputation. In either case, it is useful if you can find out what their views are on research and your topic in particular. Your supervisors

Table 9.10 Criteria to be satisfied by reports on student research

Level	Description	Criteria
First degrees and some Master's degrees which require the completion of a project	Dissertation	1. A well structured and convincing account of a study, the resolution of a problem, or the outcome of an experiment
Master's degree by study and dissertation	Dissertation	1. An ordered, critical and reasoned exposition of knowledge gained through the student's efforts 2. Evidence of awareness of the literature
Master's degree by research	Thesis	1. Evidence of an original investigation or the testing of ideas 2. Competence in independent work or experimentation 3. An understanding of appropriate techniques 4. Ability to make critical use of published work and source materials 5. Appreciation of the relationship of the special theme to the wider field of knowledge 6. Worthy, in part, of publication
Doctoral degree	Thesis	1. to 6. as for Master's degree by research 7. Originality as shown by the topic researched or the methodology employed 8. Distinct contribution to knowledge

Source: Howard and Sharp (1994) p. 177.

may be able to tell you or you may be able to glean it from their writing. This can help you avoid pitfalls or getting into heated discussions on topics where you know their opinions are very different from your own.

As far as the format is concerned, the atmosphere tends to be fairly informal at the undergraduate level. At the postgraduate level the atmosphere may be politely cordial, but do not forget that you are there to defend your thesis and you need to argue a coherent case. You and the examiners will have copies of your document to refer to during the viva. The early part of the viva is often taken up with the examiners asking questions and the student responding. These may be clarification questions or questions centred on some weakness the examiner considers is present. In either case, he or she is testing your knowledge. As the viva progresses, it is likely to become a discussion, with the student taking the lead in explaining the research. At both undergraduate and postgraduate levels, the examiners will not be trying to trip you up, but they will want to explore any weaknesses in your dissertation or thesis. They will expect you to know your subject.

You need to be very familiar with your research report. It may have been several weeks or months since you submitted it, and it is imperative that you do know and understand the document. Phillips and Pugh (1994) give detailed instructions on how to revise your research report by summarising every page into a few words which capture the main idea. You can then list the ideas with the page numbers and use the summaries for revision before the viva and take them in with you to the viva so that you can refer the examiners to particular pages.

Ask your supervisors if they can arrange a mock viva. If not, persuade colleagues, family and friends to help you. At the M.Phil. and Ph.D. level it is imperative that you have practised presenting your research and this is why attending conferences, seminars and workshops is so valuable. These activities should have alerted you to potential weaknesses and the sort of questions which might arise in your viva.

Be careful not to argue with the examiners, but where you have strong opinions and you can support them, do not hesitate to voice them strongly. Play to your strengths and not your weaknesses. Some of the questions put to you may appear to be on the edge of the scope of your study, so attempt to place them in a context where you are certain of the facts. You need to accept that there may be defects in your study and explain to the examiners how they arose and how you would set about remedying them.

If you do not understand a question ask for clarification. This is far better than giving an inept response. Do not rush into giving replies. Many of the questions will be complex and you should take time to reflect on the question and your answer. Your responses should be balanced, with a review of the advantages and disadvantages, and conclude with your own opinions.

The major advantage you have is that you conducted the research, not the external examiners. Therefore, you will certainly know more about the details than they do. Try to keep the discussions in this area and explain any interesting factors or aspects. Even an amusing anecdote of an event whilst you were conducting the research would not go amiss, provided it is not too long.

The outcome of a viva will depending on the nature of the qualification. For an undergraduate degree or a taught Masters, the research project and the viva is only one element of your studies. Although the result of your research may be important for determining the final class of the award you receive, it is not likely in itself to determine whether you pass or fail the entire award.

With a M.Phil. and a Ph.D., the thesis and the viva are the examination and the following outcomes are possible:

▶ The award is made immediately after the viva and you have nothing else to do except receive the congratulations of friends and family
▶ The award is made, subject to minor amendments to be made within a specified period. These are usually modest changes and should cause you no problems. You will not be subjected to another viva and your internal examiner will be responsible for making certain that the final, bound thesis incorporates the amendments
▶ The award is not made and you are asked to make substantial revisions. You have not failed and have the opportunity to re-submit and be re-examined. In this case the changes will be major and will take you a number of months to complete. However, you will have the benefit of having received guidance from the examiners on what is expected, and as long as you can meet these requirements you will receive the award
▶ An outright fail with no possibility of being able to resubmit. This is a disaster
▶ With a Ph.D. it is possible that the examiners may decide that although the work is of merit, it does not achieve the standard required for a doctorate. They may, therefore, recommend that a M.Phil. is awarded instead.

9.8   Writing papers and articles

At the undergraduate and taught Master's level you are likely to find that your time is fully taken up with your studies and doing your research. At M.Phil. and Ph.D. level, at the very least, you should have written and presented a number of *papers* at conferences and possibly had one or two *articles* published. Once you have successfully completed your research, all students should consider giving conference papers and writing articles. This will improve your academic reputation, enhance your career and may even be financially rewarding.

The main factor to remember is that you will not be able to take your research report or thesis as it stands and publish it. Your research report has been written for a particular audience and conference papers and articles have different audiences. Therefore, you need to find out the requirements of these new audiences before you can be published.

9.8.1   Conferences

Conferences can be divided into commercial and academic conferences. Commercial conferences are well advertised and the business people attending often pay several hundred pounds for a day's conference. Usually there are a number of speakers who are regarded as experts in their chosen fields. If you are fortunate enough to be regarded as an expert, you can expect a fee of over £100 for a 45-minute presentation, but you must be articulate and know your subject. The audience will not be interested in your research design, literature review or methodology, but in your research results and what it means to them and their companies.

Academic conferences are less lavish affairs and can range from small regional conferences, with only a dozen participants, to large international conferences with an audience of thousands. Despite differences of size and location, both audiences will be interested in and critical of your research. The call for papers usually goes out several months before the conference and you are usually expected to submit a paper for consideration of approximately 5000 words, together with an abstract. If the conference organisers consider it is worthy, they will allocate a certain length of time for you to present it. With some conferences this can be as short as 20 minutes; with others you may be allocated an hour. You should devise a presentation based on your paper, bearing in mind the time available and allowing time at the end for questions.

If you are looking for an academic career, you must present papers at academic conferences. You may find that this also leads to a publication, as some organisers publish a collection of selected papers presented at the conference. You will find out details of academic conferences from your supervisor(s), departmental notice boards and journals. The costs are usually fairly low, often involving little more than accommodation, meals, travel and hire of rooms. Once you have attended one or two conferences, you will find a network of other researchers.

9.8.2   Articles

There are three main types of publication which may be interested in receiving an *article* about your research; each with its own style and word length. Table 9.11 gives details.

Table 9.11 Academic and commercial articles

Publication	Approximate length
Popular publications, such as newspapers and magazines	800–1,500 words
Professional journals	1,200–2,000 words
Refereed journals	2,500–5,000 words

Popular publications include the local and national press, as well as weekly magazines and some of the lighter monthly magazines. With these types of publication, it is likely that the editor will want your article to be highly topical. Therefore, a study of the hardships suffered by textile workers in the nineteenth century is unlikely to be accepted, but if you can use your research to illuminate and explain current events you may find an outlet for it. However, if your research is not topical but focuses on local industry or events, you may find that your local press is interested.

Before you submit an article read past copies of the publication so that you are familiar with the style and the topics they cover. At the local level you may not receive any payment, but at the national level you will normally receive payment based on the length of the article, but do not expect much more than £100.

The associations and societies of professional people, such as accountants, lawyers, engineers etc., produce their own *professional journals*, usually on a monthly basis. These concentrate not so much on topical issues, but on items which are relevant to their members. Thus, quite a range of stories may be relevant, although they may only be of historic importance. You might find that your research can be adapted to fit this type of audience. It is often best to send the editor a synopsis of the article before you write it, to see if the journal is interested. They may want you to put a certain slant on your story. You can expect payment, but again this is likely to be modest.

Refereed journals are known as such because it is usual to submit two or three copies of your article, together with the abstract to the journal. If the editor thinks the topic is suitable for the journal in principle, the copies of your article will be sent to other academics, who will act as referees. This means that your name will not be revealed to them and they may not even know the name of the other referee. Thus, the referees decide whether the article is worthy of publication as it is, needs amendments or will be rejected. If your article is published in a refereed journal, you receive no payment and may even have to pay a fee when you submit your article. However, because publication in a refereed journal is hard to achieve, it is the most prestigious form of publication. It is essential to strive for this type of publication if you wish to have an academic career.

Before submitting your article it is essential that you read the guide to authors which is normally given in each journal. It is also important to go through copies of the last five years or so of the journal looking for articles in the same general area and making certain that you quote them. The number of rejections by journals is high and for an inexperienced author there is considerable merit in writing the article jointly with someone with greater experience. If you are a Ph.D. student, your supervisor(s) will expect to co-author articles with you, even if in your opinion they have done little more than basic editing.

Conclusions

In this chapter we have looked at the planning and the practical side of writing, from designing the report to developing a suitable writing style and presenting the data. Writing up your research can be a highly rewarding process once you get started. The secret to completing on time is to write notes and draft sections of your dissertation or thesis from the outset, rather than leave it until the last minute. If, for one reason or another, you have not managed to start writing early enough, you will face major problems which can only be overcome by making a massive effort at the eleventh hour.

By the time you read this chapter, you should be familiar with all the research terms we have used. If you are experiencing any problems with particular aspects of writing up your research report, you should follow up the cross-references we have given to earlier chapters. We also recommend that you read Chapter 10 which contains a trouble-shooting guide.

10 Trouble shooting

Introduction

Even if you have studied every word of the nine chapters in this book before you start your research, you will still encounter difficulties of one type or another. As we explained in Chapter 1, business research is not a simple linear process and it is inevitable that you will experience some problems and have to make decisions on the best way of overcoming them.

In this chapter we examine typical problems associated with the main stages of the research process. The solutions to these problems are presented in dia-grammatic form and refer you to different sections and chapters in this book where you will be able to obtain the appropriate guidance. The topics we cover are:

- getting started
- managing the research
- identifying a research topic
- the research proposal
- deciding the methodology
- searching and reviewing the literature
- collecting data
- analysing data
- writing the research report
- achieving the required standards.

Regardless of how much support and guidance you receive from your supervisor(s), colleagues, family and friends, you are bound to make some mistakes, and this is true for researchers at all levels. However, you should aim to minimise the number of errors you make and explain where things have not worked out as you expected, and how the study might be improved. In some cases there is no right or wrong answer to problems, but you will still need to justify the decisions you make and show that you recognise the alternative approaches you might have adopted.

10.1 Getting started

> **Problem** You are unable to start because you are totally confused over what research is all about and what you are expected to do.

Before you can start your research, you will find it useful to gain an understanding of what business research entails by implementing the following plan of action:

1. Read about the various

   ► definitions of research (Section 1.1)
   ► types of research (Section 1.3).

2. Next, you can begin to

   ► identify a research topic (Section 1.4.1)
   ► define a research problem (Section 1.4.2)
   ► design the project (Section 1.4.3 & Chapter 5)
   ► collect the data (Section 1.4.4 & Chapter 6)
   ► analyse the data (Section 1.4.5, Chapters 7 & 8).

3. Then you should be able to start writing your research report, dissertation or thesis (Section 1.4.6 & Chapter 9).

10.2   Managing the research

> **Problem**   You are worried about how to complete the
> project in the allotted time.

To manage your research efficiently and in the time available, you will
need to implement the following plan of action:

1. Find out when you will have to submit your dissertation/thesis.

2. Then you should

   ▸ set yourself a timetable (Section 2.6.1)
   ▸ agree it with your supervisor (Section 2.2.1).

3. To ensure that your time is spent efficiently, you must

   ▸ organise your materials (Section 2.6.2)
   ▸ maintain adequate records (Section 2.6.4).

10.3 Identifying a research topic

> **Problem**   You are unable to find a suitable research topic or need to find an alternative research topic.

If you are unable to identify a research topic or need to change your first choice because it is unsuitable, you should implement the following plan of action:

1. Discuss the problem straight away with your supervisor (Section 2.3.1) and colleagues (Section 2.3.2).

2. You should also try such techniques as

   ▶ brainstorming
   ▶ analogy
   ▶ mind mapping
   ▶ morphological analysis
   ▶ relevance trees (Section 4.1).

3. Once you have identified a potential topic you should conduct a literature search (Section 4.3) to identify any gaps in the literature that you can investigate.

10.4 Making a preliminary plan of action

> **Problem**   You know the research topic you want to investigate but you do not know how to plan the first stages of the research.

The research proposal is going to be your detailed research plan, but you have to carry out some preliminary investigations before you can start to write the proposal. Your preliminary plan of action should be as follows:

1. Carry out a literature search (Section 4.3).

2. This should help you identify a research problem (Section 5.2.4), which will enable you to frame a research question (Sections 5.5.1 & 5.5.2).

3. You will then be able to make a decision on the appropriate method(s) for collecting the data (Section 6.5).

10.5 Applying a theoretical framework

> **Problem** You cannot write a research proposal because you have difficulty in applying an appropriate theoretical framework.

If your research requires a theoretical framework your plan of action should be to:

1. Ensure that you have clearly specified the purpose of the research (Section 5.3.1) and that you have conducted a literature search (Section 4.3).

2. You should then be able to develop a theoretical framework (Section 5.4).

3. This should allow you to

   ▸ define the unit of analysis (Section 5.3.2)
   ▸ construct one or more hypotheses (Section 3.2.3).

10.6   The research proposal

> **Problem**   You are uncertain about how to write a research proposal that will be acceptable to your supervisor(s).

If you are worried about how to draw up a research proposal, you should implement the following plan of action:

1. Look at a typical proposal structure (Section 5.11) and read about the key elements:

   ▶ the purpose statement (Section 5.3)
   ▶ any theoretical framework (Section 5.10.4 & Chapter 4)
   ▶ your chosen methodology (Section 5.10.6 & Chapter 3).

2. A major part of your proposal will consist of a literature review (Sections 4.6 & 9.2.3).

3. You must mention how you will solve any problems of access (Section 2.4).

10.7   Deciding the methodology

Problem   You are unable to decide which
methodology to use.

Deciding which methodology to use is made easier when you realise
that your choice is limited by a number of factors. Your action plan
should be as follows.

1. Start by considering the constraints placed by your

   ▸ research problem (Section 5.2)
   ▸ and the paradigm (Section 3.1).

2. Identify which methodologies are usually associated with your
   research paradigm

   ▸ methodologies associated with a positivistic paradigm
     (Section 3.4)
   ▸ methodologies associated with a phenomenological paradigm
     (Section 3.4).

3. You may decide to mix methodologies (Section 3.6).

10.8   Searching and reviewing the literature

> **Problem**   You are unable to find articles or books on
> the research topic and/or unable to write the literature
> review.

The secret of a successful literature search and review is to plan the
activity as follows:

1. Before you begin your search, you need to

   ▶ define your terms (Section 4.2)
   ▶ determine the scope of your research (Section 4.3).

2. Then you should start searching in a logical order (Section 4.3).

3. You must be certain to record references (Section 4.5), as this will
   prevent problems when writing the literature review (Sections 4.6
   & 9.2.3).

10.9   Collecting data

> **Problem**   You are unable to decide how to collect the research data.

Deciding which data collection method to use is made easier when you realise that your choice is limited by a number of factors as follows:

1. Start by considering

   ▶ the nature of your research problem (Section 5.2)
   ▶ your research paradigm (Section 3.1)
   ▶ your chosen methodology (Sections 3.4 & 3.5)
   ▶ any access you have been able to negotiate (Section 2.4).

2. This should enable you to select appropriate methods for collecting the data (Section 6.1).

3. You may also need to bear in mind your methods of data analysis (Chapters 7 & 8).

10.10 Organising the data in a phenomenological study

> **Problem** You are collecting data, but you do not know when to start analysing it.

In a phenomenological study, it is useful to commence analysing data as you collect it. Your plan of action should be as follows:

1. As you collect the data, you need to be clear about

   ▶ your choice of methodology (Section 3.5)
   ▶ issues of reliability and validity (Section 6.6.6).

2. You need to ensure your recording of the data is comprehensive and detailed if you are collecting data via

   ▶ interviews (Section 6.5.4)
   ▶ observation (Section 6.5.5).

3. As you collect the data reflect on your research by using techniques such as

   ▶ general analytical procedures (Section 8.3.1)
   ▶ data displays (Section 8.3.3).

10.11 Analysing data

> **Problem**   You are unable to decide how to analyse the data you have collected.

Deciding which method of data analysis to use is made easier when you realise that your choice is limited by a number of factors as follows:

1. First, you need to consider whether

   ▶ you are adopting a positivistic or phenomenological paradigm (Section 3.1)
   ▶ your data is qualitative or quantitative (Section 3.2.1). If the latter, you may need to determine the status of the data (Section 6.4.2).

2. It may be sufficient to conduct explanatory data analysis (Sections 7.2–7.6). In more sophisticated studies you will need to use confirmatory data analysis (Sections 7.7–7.11).

3. If you have collected qualitative data, you can use either

   ▶ quantifying techniques (Section 8.2)
   ▶ non-quantifying techniques (Sections 8.3).

10.12 Structuring the research report

> **Problem** You cannot decide the appropriate structure for your report.

You should re-read your initial research proposal and the structure described in Chapter 9. Your plan of action should be as follows:

1. Draw up a proposed structure (Section 9.1.3).

2. Allocate an approximate number of words to each main section (Table 9.3).

3. You should now be able to determine the subsections (Figure 9.2) and the presentation of any quantitative data (Section 9.4).

10.13 Writing the research report

> **Problem**   You are unable to start writing up the reserch

If you have followed the guidance in this book, at a very early stage you will have decided on the main structure of your project report and made initial drafts of some of the contents. You should now adopt the following plan of action:

1. You will need to

  ▶ draw up a plan (Section 9.1)
  ▶ give some thought to the overall design of the report (Section 9.1.1).

2. You will then be in a position to

  ▶ write drafts of the individual contents (Section 9.2),
  ▶ bear in mind the best way to present qualitative data (Section 9.3) and quantitative data (Section 9.4).

3. If you have run out of time, use our eleventh-hour strategies (Section 9.5).

10.14 Dealing with writer's block

> **Problem** You are part way through writing up your research, but suffering from writer's block.

Apart from the obvious advice to take a short break, some or all of the following will help:

1. Stop trying to write that particular section and

   ▶ start writing a totally different section of the report
   ▶ spend time checking the spelling and improving the grammar of what you have already written
   ▶ try presenting quantitative data in different ways (e.g. tables as diagrams) and write about the results.

2. Write a very harsh critique of a section you have already written.

3. Identify what is holding you up by

   ▶ recording your thoughts onto tape and transcribing them
   ▶ discussing any particular problems with your supervisor or a sympathetic friend.

10.15   Achieving the standards

> **Problem**   You are unable to decide what standard of work is required.

Apart from the obvious recommendation that you should always do your best, you will find the following advice helpful:

1. The most important source of guidance on standards is your supervisor (Section 2.2.1) but there are general characteristics of a good research project that you should aim to achieve (Section 1.5).

2. There will also be specific criteria related to your course requirements (Section 2.1).

3. There are some general guidelines on the marking criteria (Section 9.6) and the expectations for different levels of award (Section 9.6).

Random number tables

```
03 47 43 73 86   36 96 47 36 61   46 98 63 71 62   33 26 16 80 45   60 11 14 10 95
97 74 24 67 62   42 81 14 57 20   42 53 32 37 32   27 07 36 07 51   24 51 79 89 73
16 76 62 27 66   56 50 26 71 07   32 90 79 78 53   13 55 38 58 59   88 97 54 14 10
12 56 85 99 26   96 96 68 27 31   05 03 72 93 15   57 12 10 14 21   88 26 49 81 76
55 59 56 35 64   38 54 82 46 22   31 62 43 09 90   06 18 44 32 53   23 83 01 30 30

16 22 77 94 39   49 54 43 54 82   17 37 93 23 78   87 35 20 96 43   84 26 34 91 64
84 42 17 53 31   57 24 55 06 88   77 04 74 47 67   21 76 33 50 25   83 92 12 06 76
63 01 63 78 59   16 95 55 67 19   98 10 50 71 75   12 86 73 58 07   44 39 52 38 79
33 21 12 34 29   78 64 56 07 82   52 42 07 44 38   15 51 00 13 42   99 66 02 79 54
57 60 86 32 44   09 47 27 96 54   49 17 46 09 62   90 52 84 77 27   08 02 73 43 28

18 18 07 92 46   44 17 16 58 09   79 83 86 16 62   06 76 50 03 10   55 23 64 05 05
26 62 38 97 75   84 16 07 44 99   83 11 46 32 24   20 14 85 88 45   10 93 72 88 71
23 42 40 64 74   82 97 77 77 81   07 45 32 14 08   32 98 94 07 72   93 85 79 10 75
52 36 28 19 95   50 92 26 11 97   00 56 76 31 38   80 22 02 53 53   86 60 42 04 53
37 85 94 35 12   83 39 50 08 30   42 34 07 96 88   54 42 06 87 98   35 85 29 48 38

70 29 17 12 13   40 33 20 38 26   13 89 51 03 74   17 76 37 13 04   07 74 21 19 30
56 62 18 37 35   96 83 50 87 75   97 12 25 93 47   70 33 24 03 54   97 77 46 44 80
99 49 57 22 77   88 42 95 45 72   16 64 36 16 00   04 43 18 66 79   94 77 24 21 90
16 08 15 04 72   33 27 14 34 90   45 59 34 68 49   12 72 07 34 45   99 27 72 95 14
31 16 93 32 43   50 27 89 87 19   20 15 37 00 49   52 85 66 60 44   38 68 88 11 80

68 34 30 13 70   55 74 30 77 40   44 22 78 84 26   04 33 46 09 52   68 07 97 06 57
74 57 25 65 76   59 29 97 68 60   71 91 38 67 54   13 58 18 24 76   15 54 55 95 52
27 42 37 86 53   48 55 90 65 72   96 57 69 36 10   96 46 92 42 45   97 60 49 04 91
00 39 68 29 61   66 37 32 20 30   77 84 57 03 29   10 45 65 04 26   11 04 96 67 24
29 94 98 94 24   68 49 69 10 82   53 75 91 93 30   34 25 20 57 27   40 48 73 51 92

16 90 82 66 59   83 62 64 11 12   67 19 00 71 74   60 47 21 29 68   02 02 37 03 31
11 27 94 75 06   06 09 19 74 66   02 94 37 34 02   76 70 90 30 86   38 45 94 30 38
35 24 10 16 20   33 32 51 26 38   79 78 45 04 91   16 92 53 56 16   02 75 50 95 98
38 23 16 86 38   42 38 97 01 50   87 75 66 81 41   40 01 74 91 62   48 51 84 08 32
31 96 25 91 47   96 44 33 49 13   34 86 82 53 91   00 52 43 48 85   27 55 26 89 62

66 67 40 67 14   64 05 71 95 86   11 05 65 09 68   76 83 20 37 90   57 16 00 11 66
14 90 84 45 11   75 73 88 05 90   52 27 41 14 86   22 98 12 22 08   07 52 74 95 80
68 05 51 18 00   33 96 02 75 19   07 60 62 93 55   59 33 82 43 90   49 37 38 44 59
20 46 78 73 90   97 51 40 14 02   04 02 33 31 08   39 54 16 49 36   47 95 93 13 30
64 19 58 97 79   15 06 15 93 20   01 90 10 75 06   40 78 78 89 62   02 67 74 17 33

05 26 93 70 60   22 35 85 15 13   92 03 51 59 77   59 56 78 06 83   52 91 05 70 74
07 97 10 88 23   09 98 42 99 64   61 71 62 99 15   06 51 29 16 93   58 05 77 09 51
68 71 86 85 85   54 87 66 47 54   73 32 08 11 12   44 95 92 63 16   29 56 24 29 48
26 99 61 65 53   58 37 78 80 70   42 10 50 67 42   32 17 55 85 74   94 44 67 16 94
14 65 52 68 75   87 59 36 22 41   26 78 63 06 55   13 08 27 01 50   15 29 39 39 43
```

Abridged from R. A. Fisher and F. Yate (1953), *Statistical Tables for Biological, Agricultural and Medical Research*, Edinburgh: Oliver and Boyd by permission of the authors and publishers (Longman Group UK Ltd).

Appendix B
Critical values of Pearson's *r*

df (N − 2)	Level of significance for a one-tailed test			
	0.05	0.025	0.005	0.0005
	Level of insignificance for two-tailed test			
	0.10	0.05	0.01	0.001
2	0.9000	0.9500	0.9900	0.9999
3	0.805	0.878	0.9587	0.9911
4	0.729	0.811	0.9172	0.9741
5	0.669	0.754	0.875	0.9509
6	0.621	0.707	0.834	0.9241
7	0.582	0.666	0.798	0.898
8	0.549	0.632	0.765	0.872
9	0.521	0.602	0.735	0.847
10	0 497	0.576	0.708	0.823
11	0.476	0.553	0.684	0.801
12	0.475	0.532	0.661	0.780
13	0.441	0.514	0.641	0.760
14	0.426	0.497	0.623	0.742
15	0.412	0.482	0.606	0.725
16	0.400	0.468	0.590	0.708
17	0.389	0.456	0.575	0.693
18	0.378	0.444	0.561	0.679
19	0.369	0.433	0.549	0.665
20	0.360	0.423	0.537	0.652
25	0.323	0.381	0.487	0.597
30	0.296	0.349	0.449	0.554
35	0.275	0.325	0.418	0.519
40	0.257	0.304	0.393	0.490
45	0.243	0.288	0.372	0.465
50	0.231	0.273	0.354	0.443
60	0.211	0.250	0.325	0.408
70	0.195	0.232	0.302	0.380
80	0.183	0.217	0.283	0.357
90	0.173	0.205	0.267	0.338
100	0.164	0.195	0.254	0.321

Calculated *r* must EQUAL or EXCEED the table (critical) value for significance at the level shown.
Source: F. C. Powell (1976), *Cambridge Mathematical and Statistical Tables*, Cambridge: Cambridge University Press.

Critical values of Spearman's r_s

	Level of significance for a two-tailed test			
	0.10	0.05	0.02	0.01
	Level of insignificance for a one-tailed test			
	0.05	0.025	0.01	0.005
$n = 4$	1.000			
5	0.900	1.000	1.000	
6	0.829	0.886	0.943	1.000
7	0.714	0.786	0.893	0.929
8	0.643	0.738	0.833	0.881
9	0.600	0.700	0.783	0.833
10	0.564	0.648	0.745	0.794
11	0.536	0.618	0.709	0.755
12	0.503	0.587	0.671	0.727
13	0.484	0.560	0.648	0.703
14	0.464	0.538	0.622	0.675
15	0.443	0.521	0.604	0.654
16	0.429	0.503	0.582	0.635
17	0.414	0.485	0.566	0.615
18	0.401	0.472	0.550	0.600
19	0.391	0.460	0.535	0.584
20	0.380	0.447	0.520	0.570
21	0.370	0.435	0.508	0.556
22	0.361	0.425	0.496	0.544
23	0.353	0.415	0.486	0.532
24	0.344	0.406	0.476	0.521
25	0.337	0.398	0.466	0.511
26	0.331	0.390	0.457	0.501
27	0.324	0.382	0.448	0.491
28	0.317	0.375	0.440	0.483
29	0.312	0.368	0.433	0.475
30	0.306	0.362	0.425	0.467

For $n > 30$, the significance of r_s can be tested by using the formula

$$t - r_s = \sqrt{\frac{n - 2}{1 - r_s^2}} \qquad df = n - 2$$

and checking the value of t in table 8.

Calculated r must EQUAL or EXCEED the table (critical) value for significance at the level shown.

Source: J. H. Zar, 'Significance Testing of the Spearman Rank Correlation Coefficient', *Journal of the American Statistical Association*, 67, pp. 578–80.

Appendix D
Critical values of χ^2

	Level of significance for a one-tailed test					
	0.10	0.05	0.025	0.01	0.005	0.0005
	Level of insignificance for two-tailed test					
df	0.20	0.10	0.05	0.02	0.02	0.001
1	1.64	2.71	3.84	5.41	6.64	10.83
2	3.22	4.60	5.99	7.82	9.21	13.28
3	4.64	6.25	7.82	9.84	11.34	16.27
4	5.99	7.78	9.49	11.67	13.28	18.46
5	7.29	9.24	11.07	13.39	15.09	20.52
6	8.56	10.64	12.59	15.03	16.81	22.46
7	9.80	12.02	14.07	16.62	18.48	24.32
8	11.03	13.36	15.51	18.17	20.09	26.12
9	12.24	14.68	16.92	19.68	21.67	27.88
10	13.44	15.99	18.31	21.16	23.21	29.59
11	14.63	17.28	19.68	22.62	24.72	31.26
12	15.81	18.55	21.03	24.05	26.22	32.91
13	16.98	19.81	22.36	25.47	27.69	34.53
14	18.15	21.06	23.68	26.87	29.14	36.12
15	19.31	22.31	25.00	28.26	30.58	37.70
16	20.46	23.54	26.30	29.63	32.00	39.29
17	21.62	24.77	27.59	31.00	33.41	40.75
18	22.76	25.99	28.87	32.35	34.80	42.31
19	23.90	27.20	30.14	33.69	36.19	43.82
20	25.04	28.41	31.41	35.02	37.57	45.32
21	26.17	29.62	32.67	36.34	38.93	46.80
22	27.30	30.81	33.92	37.66	40.29	48.27
23	28.43	32.01	35.17	38.97	41.64	49.73
24	29.55	33.20	36.42	40.27	42.98	51.18
25	30.68	34.38	37.65	41.57	44.31	52.62
26	31.80	35.56	38.88	42.86	45.64	54.05
27	32.91	36.74	40.11	44.14	46.96	55.48
28	34.03	37.92	41.34	45.42	48.28	56.89
29	35.14	39.09	42.69	49.69	49.59	58.30
30	36.25	40.26	43.77	47.96	50.89	59.70
32	38.47	42.59	46.19	50.49	53.49	62.49
34	40.68	44.90	48.60	53.00	56.06	65.25
36	42.88	47.21	51.00	55.49	58.62	67.99
38	45.08	49.51	53.38	57.97	61.16	70.70
40	47.27	51.81	55.76	60.44	63.69	73.40
44	51.64	56.37	60.48	65.34	68.71	78.75
48	55.99	60.91	65.17	70.20	73.68	84.04
52	60.33	65.42	69.83	75.02	78.62	89.27
56	64.66	69.92	74.47	79.82	83.51	94.46
60	68.97	74.40	79.08	84.58	88.38	99.61

Calculated value of χ^2 must EQUAL or EXCEED the table (critical) value for significance at the level shown.

Source: Abridged from Fisher and Yates (1963), *Statistical Tables for Biological, Agricultural and Medical Research*, Edinburgh: Oliver and Boyd Ltd (Longman Group Ltd).

Appendix E
Critical values of *t*

Degrees of freedom	Level of significance for a one-tailed test			
	0.05	0.025	0.01	0.0005
	Level of insignificance for two-tailed test			
	0.10	0.05	0.02	0.01
1	6.314	12.706	31.821	63.657
2	2.920	4.303	6.965	9.925
3	2.353	3.182	4.541	5.841
4	2.132	2.776	3.747	4.604
5	2.015	2.571	3.365	4.032
6	1.943	2.447	3.143	3.707
7	1.895	2.365	2.998	3.499
8	1.860	2.306	2.896	3.355
9	1.833	2.262	2.821	3.250
10	1.812	2.228	2.764	3.169
11	1.796	2.201	2.718	3.106
12	1.782	2.179	2.681	3.055
13	1.771	2.160	2.650	3.012
14	1.761	3.145	2.624	2.977
15	1.753	2.131	2.602	2.947
16	1.746	2.120	2.583	2.921
17	1.740	2.110	2.567	2.898
18	1.734	2.101	2.552	2.878
19	1.729	2.093	2.539	2.861
20	1.725	2.086	2.528	2.845
21	1.721	2.080	2.518	2.831
22	1.717	2.074	2.508	2.819
23	1.714	2.069	2.500	2.807
24	1.711	2.064	2.492	2.797
25	1.708	2.060	2.485	2.787
26	1.706	2.056	2.479	2.779
27	1.703	2.052	2.473	2.771
28	1.701	2.048	2.467	2.763
29	1.699	2.045	2.462	2.756
30	1.697	2.042	2.457	2.750
40	1.684	2.021	2.423	2.704
60	1.671	2.000	2.390	2.660
120	1.658	1.950	2.358	2.617
∞	1.645	1.960	2.326	2.576

Calculated *t* must EQUAL or EXCEED the table (critical) value for significance at the level shown.
Source: Abridged from Fisher and Yates (1963), *Statistical Tables for Biological, Agricultural and Medical Research*, Edinburgh: Oliver and Boyd Ltd (Longman Group Ltd).

Glossary

Term	Definition
Abstract	A summary of a report, article or paper
Action research	A *methodology* which is used in *applied research* to find an effective way of bringing about a conscious change in a partly controlled environment
Analogy	Designing a study in one subject by importing ideas and procedures from another area where there are similarities
Analysis	The ability to break down information into its various parts
Analytical/explanatory research	Studies which aim to understand phenomena by discovering and measuring causal relations among them
Anonymity	Protection for the participants in the research by not identifying them with any of the opinions they express
Anthropology	The study of people, especially of societies and customs
Anticipatory data reduction	Ignoring certain *data* which does not fit into a particular *theoretical framework* or highly structured *research instrument*
Application skills	The ability to apply knowledge, experience and skill to a new situation presented in a novel manner
Applied research	A study which aims to apply its findings to solving a specific, existing problem
ASCII	American Standard Code for Information Interchange
Axiological assumption	People's assumptions about the role of values
Bachelor of Arts (B.A.)	A taught, *undergraduate degree* course in the arts/humanities which may include a *dissertation*
Bachelor of Science (B.Sc.)	A taught, *undergraduate degree* course in the sciences which may include a *dissertation*

Term	Definition
Bar chart	A graphical presentation of a *frequency distribution* in which the *data* is represented by a series of separate vertical or horizontal bars
Basic/fundamental/ pure research	A study which aims to make a contribution to general knowledge and theoretical understanding, rather than solve a specific problem
Bibliography	A detailed list of *references* as well as items which are not cited in the text but are relevant to the document
Bivariate data analysis	Analysis of two *variables*
Box plot	A diagram which presents four *measures of dispersion* and one *measure of location*: the upper and lower extremes, the *median*, and the upper and lower quartiles
Brainstorming	A technique which can be used for generating *research topics* by listing spontaneous ideas with one or more interested people
Case study	A *methodology* which focuses on understanding the dynamics present within single setting; often used in the *exploratory* stages of research
CD-ROM	An acronym for Compact Disk – Read Only Memory; an *off-line* database
Chi squared (χ^2) test	A *non-parametric technique* for assessing the statistical significance of a finding by setting up two *hypotheses* to test for contingency (uncertainty of occurrence) or goodness of fit
Citation	An acknowledgement within the text of a document of the source from which you have obtained information
Closed question	A question where respondents select the answer from a number of predetermined alternatives
Coding frame	A list of *coding units* against which the analysed material is classified
Coding unit	A particular word, character, item, theme or concept identified in the *data* and allocated a specific code
Cognitive mapping	A *method* of analysis used to structure, analyse and make sense of written or verbal accounts of problems
Component bar chart	A graphical presentation of a *frequency distribution* in which the *data* is represented by a series of separate vertical or horizontal bars divided into segments

Term	Definition
Comprehension	The ability to translate data from one form to another; to interpret or deduce the significance of data; to solve simple problems relying on these abilities
Confidence intervals	A *parametric technique* for estimating a range of values of a *sample statistic* that is likely to contain an unknown *population parameter* at a given level of probability; the wider the confidence interval, the higher the confidence level
Confidentiality	Protection for the participants in the research by not disclosing sensitive information and ensuring that any data used is not traceable to the organisations or individuals participating
Confirmatory data analysis	The use of *inferential statistics* to draw conclusions about a *population* from *quantitative data* collected from a sample
Confounding variable	A *variable* that obscures the effects of another
Constructs	Qualities used to describe and differentiate between elements or the objects of perceptions
Consultancy research report	The report resulting from a commercial research project
Content analysis	A *method* of collecting data where text is systematically converted to numerical variables for quantitative data analysis
Continuous quantitative variable	A numerical attribute of an individual or object which can take any value between the start and end of a measurement scale
Continuous data	Data that can take any value within a given range, such as time or length
Correlation	*Measure of the strength* of association between two *variables*; may be linear or non-linear, positive or negative
Critical incident technique	A *method* of collecting *data* which focuses on gathering important facts concerning behaviour in defined situations
Critical path analysis	A simplified model of a project which can be used to plan when tasks should be carried out
Cross tabulation	A tabular presentation of a *frequency distribution* which presents *bivariate data*

Term	Definition
Cross-sectional study	A *methodology* designed to obtain information on variables in different contexts, but at the same time
Data	Known facts or things used as a basis for inference or reckoning
Data display	A *method* for analysing *data* into a visual format which presents the information systematically so that the user can draw valid conclusions
Data integrity	Those characteristics of research which affect error and bias in the research results
Data reduction	A form of *data* analysis which sharpens, sorts, focuses, discards and reorganises *data*
Data triangulation	Where *data* is collected at different times or from different sources in the study of a phenomenon
Database	A comprehensive, consistent, controlled, co-ordinated collection of structured data items held in a computer
Deductive research	A study in which a conceptual and theoretical structure is developed which is then tested by empirical observation; thus particular instances are deducted from general inferences
Delimitation	The scope of the research
Dependent variable	The *variable* whose values are predicted by the *independent variable*
Descriptive research	A study which aims to describe phenomena as they exist; it identifies and obtains information on the characteristics of a particular problem or issue
Descriptive statistics	A group of statistical techniques used to summarise, describe or display *quantitative data* used in *exploratory data analysis*
Diaries	A *method* of collecting *data* where selected participants are asked to record relevant information in diary forms or booklets over a specified period of time
Discrete data	*Data* which can take only one of a range of distinct values, such as number of employees
Discrete quantitative variable	A numerical attribute of an individual or object which can take only one of a range of distinct values between the start and end of a measurement scale
Dissertation	The report resulting from an *undergraduate* or taught *Master's* research project

Term	Definition
Doctor of Philosophy (Ph.D.)	A *postgraduate degree* by research in either the arts or the sciences at a higher level than a *M.Phil.* which includes a thesis
Doctoral degree	A *postgraduate degree* at a higher level than a *Master's degree* (usually a Ph.D., D.B.A. or D.Phil.)
Dot diagram	A diagram which presents *univariate data* where the frequencies are plotted as dots; used for identifying patterns in the *data*
Empirical evidence	*Data* based on observation or experience
Epistemological assumption	People's assumptions about the relationship of the researcher to that researched and its effect on the validity of knowledge
Epistemology	The study of knowledge and what we accept as valid knowledge
Ethnography	A *methodology* derived from *anthropology* whereby the researcher uses socially acquired and shared knowledge to understand the observed patterns of human activity
Evaluation	The ability to make qualitative or quantitative judgements; to set out a reasoned argument through a series of steps, usually of gradually increasing difficulty; to criticise constructively
Experimental data	*Data* that is obtained in a controlled situation by making experiments
Experimental study	A *methodology* that is used to investigate the relationship between two variables. The *independent variable* is deliberately manipulated in order to observe the effect on the *dependent variable*
Experimentalist paradigm	An alternative term for a *positivistic paradigm*
Exploratory data analysis	The use of *descriptive statistics* to summarise, describe or display *quantitative data*
Exploratory research	A study which aims to find patterns, ideas or *hypotheses*; the focus is on gaining familiarity with the subject area and gaining insights for more rigorous investigation at a later stage
Extraneous variable	Any *variable* other than the *independent variable* which might have an effect on the *dependent variable*
Feminist perspective	A challenge to the traditional research paradigm from the point of view of the politics and ideology of the women's movement

Term	Definition
Field experiment	An *experimental study* conducted in a natural location where the situation is not artificial as in a *laboratory experiment*
Focus groups	A *method* of collecting *data* whereby selected participants discuss their reactions and feelings about a product, service, type of situation or concept under the guidance of a group leader
Frequency	A numerical value that represents the number of observations for a *variable* under study (the number of times a particular *data* item occurs)
Frequency distribution	An array of *frequencies* arranged in size order in a table, chart, graph or other diagrammatic form
Frequency distribution table	A tabular presentation of a *frequency distribution*, which may be summarised to show the *mean* and/or *percentage* relative frequencies
Frequency polygon	A refinement of a *histogram* used for *discrete data* and obtained by joining the mid-points of the tops of the bars. The resulting polygon has the same area as the histogram
Generalisability	The extent to which you can come to conclusions about one thing (often a *population*) based on information about another (often a *sample*)
Generalisation	The application of research results to cases or situations beyond those examined
Grand tour question	A single *research question* posed in its most general form
Grounded theory	A *methodology* in which a systematic set of procedures are used to develop an inductively derived theory about a phenomenon
Harvard System	A system of referencing favoured by the social sciences, anthropology and some of the life sciences which shows citations as author, date and page number in brackets within the text and lists full *references* at the end of the document
Hermeneutics	A *methodology* which focuses on the historical and social context surrounding an action when interpreting a text and assumes a relationship exists between the direct conscious description of experience and the underlying dynamics or structures
Histogram	A refinement of a *bar chart* where adjoining bars touch, indicating *continuous interval* or *ratio data*. The

Term	Definition
	width of each bar is the class interval and may be unequal; the height is the frequency of the class. Thus, *frequency* is represented by area
Hypothesis	An idea or proposition which can be tested for association or causality by deducing logical consequences which can be tested against *empirical evidence*
Hypothetical construct	A tool which provides a scale for measuring a *quantitative variable*
Independent variable	The *variable* that can be manipulated to predict the values of the *dependent variable*
Index	A publication which contains a systematic list of references to academic publications
Index number	A statistical measure which shows the *percentage* change in a *variable*
Inductive research	A study in which theory is developed from the observation of empirical reality; thus general inferences are induced from particular instances
Inferential statistics	A group of statistical techniques and procedures used in *confirmatory data analysis* to draw conclusions about a *population* from *quantitative data* collected from a *sample*
Interpretative paradigm	An alternative term for a *phenomenological paradigm*
Interquartile range	A *measure of dispersion*: the difference between the upper and lower quartiles (the middle 50 per cent of values) in a *frequency distribution*
Interval scale	A measure that permits *data* to be placed precisely along the scale and determines exactly what the intervals are
Interviews	A *method* of collecting *data* in which selected participants are asked questions to find out what they do, think or feel
Investigator triangulation	Where different researchers independently collect *data* on the same phenomenon and compare the results
Laboratory experiment	An *experimental study* conducted in an artificial setting, removed from the natural *location*
Limitation	Any potential weakness in the research
Line graph	A graphical presentation of a *frequency distribution* in which the data is represented by a series of points joined by a line; only suitable for *continuous data*

Term	Definition
Literature	All sources of published *data*
Literature review	A written summary of the finding of a *literature search* which demonstrates that the *literature* has been located, read and evaluated
Literature search	The process of exploring the existing *literature* to ascertain what has been written or otherwise published on a particular subject
Location	The setting in which the research is conducted
Longitudinal study	A *methodology* which involves the study of a *variable* or group of subjects over a long period of time
Master of Art (M.A.)	A taught, *postgraduate degree* course in the arts/humanities which includes a *dissertation*
Master of Business Administration (M.B.A.)	A taught, *postgraduate* business degree course which includes a *dissertation*
Master of Philosophy (M.Phil.)	A *postgraduate degree* by research in either the arts or the sciences which includes a *thesis*
Master of Science (M.Sc.)	A taught, *postgraduate degree* course in the sciences which includes a *dissertation*
Matrix	A *data display* which consists of defined rows and columns
Mean	A *measure of location*: the arithmetic average of a *frequency distribution*. Not suitable for *discrete* data
Measure of central tendency	Alternative term for a *measure of location*
Measure of dispersion	A convenient way of describing the spread of values in a *frequency distribution*
Measure of location	A convenient way of describing a *frequency distribution* by means of a single value. The data must be at least of *interval* status
Measure of spread	Alternative term for a *measure of dispersion*
Measures of association	*Statistics* which measure *correlation* in *bivariate data*
Median	A *measure of location*: the mid-value in a *frequency distribution* which has been arranged in size order. Not suitable for *nominal* data
Method	The various means by which data can be collected and/or analysed
Methodological assumption	People's assumptions about the process of research

Term	Definition
Methodological rigour	The application of systematic and methodical methods in conducting the research; the clarity, appropriateness and intellectual soundness of the overall methodology
Methodological triangulation	Where quantitative and qualitative *methods* of data collection are used in the study of a phenomenon
Methodology	The approach to the entire process of a research study
Mind map	An individual's idea of the key aspects of a subject illustrated in an informal diagram which shows connections and relationships
Mode	A *measure of location*: the most frequently occurring value in a *frequency distribution*. Distributions may contain more than one mode.
Morphological analysis	A technique for generating *research topics* whereby the subject is analysed into its key attributes and a 'mix and match' approach adopted
Morphology	The study of form
Multivariate data analysis	Analysis of more than two *variables*
Natural setting	A research environment that would have existed had researchers never studied it
Network	A *data display* which consists of a collection of nodes or points connected by lines illustrating relationships
Nominal scale	A measure that permits *data* to be classified into named categories
Non-parametric techniques	*Inferential statistics* which can be used on *skewed data*
Non-participant observation	A *method* used to observe and record people's actions and behaviour in which the observer is separated from the activities taking place
Normal distribution	A theoretical *frequency distribution* which is bell-shaped and symmetrical with tails extending indefinitely either side of the centre
Objectivist paradigm	An alternative term for a *positivistic paradigm*
Observation	A *method* for collecting *data* used in the laboratory or in the field to observe and record people's actions and behaviour
Off-line	Not being accessible to or under the control of the computer processor

Term	Definition
Ogive	A cumulative *frequency polygon*; the cumulative frequency is plotted against the upper class boundary of each class so that the number of observations which lie between given limits of a *variable* can° be estimated
On-line	Being accessible to and under the control of the computer processor
Ontological assumption	People's assumptions about the nature of reality
Open question	A question to which respondents can answer in their own words
Ordinal scale	A measure that permits *nominal data* to be ordered or ranked
Paradigm	The progress of scientific practice based on people's philosophies and assumptions about the world and the nature of knowledge
Parametric techniques	Powerful *inferential statistics* which compare *sample statistics* with *population parameters*, but can only be used on *data* which has a *normal distribution*
Participant observation	A *method* used to observe and record people's actions and behaviour in which the observer is involved in the activities taking place
Participative enquiry	A *methodology* which involves the participants in the research as fully as possible in the study which is conducted in their own group or organisation
Pearson's product moment coefficient	A *parametric technique* which gives a *measure of association* between two variables; only suitable for *bivariate*, *interval* or *ratio data*
Percentage	A *descriptive statistic* which summarises the *data* by describing the proportion or part in every 100
Phenomenological paradigm	A *paradigm* that assumes that social reality is in our minds; a reaction to the *positivistic paradigm*. Therefore, the act of investigating reality has an effect on that reality and considerable regard is paid to the subjective state of the individual
Pie chart	A graphical presentation of *proportional data* which consists of a circular diagram divided into segments so that the area of each is proportional to the segment represented

Term	Definition
Population	A body of people or any collection of items under consideration
Population parameter	A characteristic of a *population*, such as the mean or the standard deviation, usually symbolised by Greek letters
Positivist paradigm	A *paradigm* based on the natural sciences which assumes that social reality is independent of us and exists regardless of whether we are aware of it. Therefore, the act of investigating reality has no effect on that reality and little regard is paid to the subjective state of the individual. It is usual to associate a positivistic paradigm with measurement
Postgraduate degree	Research, with or without a taught element, leading to a *Master's* or *Doctor's* degree
Predictive research	A study which aims to generalise from the analysis of phenomena and make predictions based on hypothesised general relationships
Primary data	Original *data* which is collected at source, such as survey data or experimental data
Problem statement	A short statement (usually one sentence) describing the *research problem*
Proportional data	*Data* which takes the form of a *percentage*
Protocol analysis	A *method* for collecting *data* used to identify a practitioner's mental processes in solving a problem in a particular situation, including the logic and methods used
Published bibliography	A list of books which are currently in print or which have been published in the past
Purpose statement	A statement (usually two or three sentences long) that describes the overall purpose of the research study
Qualitative data	Nominal *data*
Qualitative paradigm	An alternative term for a *phenomenological paradigm*
Qualitative research	A subjective approach which includes examining and reflecting on perceptions in order to gain an understanding of social and human activities
Qualitative variable	A non-numerical attribute of an individual or object
Quantifying method	A *method* of analysing *qualitative data* by transforming it into *quantitative data*
Quantitative data	Numerical *data*

Term	Definition
Quantitative paradigm	An alternative term for a *positivistic paradigm*
Quantitative research	An objective approach which includes collecting and analysing numerical data and applying statistical tests
Quantitative variable	A numerical attribute of an individual or object
Quasi-judicial method	A method of analysing *qualitative data* which involves applying rational argument to interpret *empirical evidence*
Questionnaires	A *method* for collecting *data* in which a selected group of participants are asked to complete a written set of structured questions to find out what they do, think or feel
Random sampling	A sampling technique where every member of the *population* stands a chance of being chosen for the *sample*
Range	A *measure of dispersion*: the difference between the upper and lower extremes (the highest and lowest values) in a *frequency distribution*
Ranking	A device for obtaining numerical values from *qualitative data* where respondents are asked to indicate their views by ordering a list of items
Rating scale	A device, such as the Likert scale, for obtaining numerical values from *qualitative data* where respondents are asked to indicate their views by circling the number on a scale which most closely matches their opinion
Ratio scale	A mathematical number system that has a fixed zero point and permits ratio as well as interval decisions to be made
Recontextualising data	A process of generalisation so that the *theory* emerging from a study can be applied to other settings and *populations*
References	A detailed, alphabetical (*Harvard System*) or numerical (*Vancouver System*) list of the sources from which information has been obtained and which have been cited in the text of a document
Relevance tree	A diagram which can be used as a device for generating *research topics* and develops clusters of related ideas from a fairly broad starting concept
Reliability	Being able to obtain the same results if the research were to be repeated by any researcher

Term	Definition
Repertory grid	A *method* used to provide mathematical representation of the perceptions and *constructs* an individual uses to understand and manage their world
Replication	Repeating a research study to test the *reliability* of the results
Research	A systematic and methodical process of enquiry and investigation which increases knowledge
Research design	The detailed plan for conducting a research study
Research instrument	Alternative term for certain *methods of data collection*, which usually refers to questionnaires which have been used and tested in a number of studies and can be adopted by any researcher
Research problem	The specific problem or issue which will be addressed by the research
Research proposal	The document which sets out the *research design* for a study
Research questions	The specific questions that the research will be designed to investigate and attempt to answer
Research topic	The general area of research interest
Results currency	The *generalisability* of the research results
Rhetorical assumption	People's assumptions about the language of research
Sample	A subset of a *population*
Sampling theory	The study of relationships existing between a *population* and *samples* drawn from it
Scatter diagram	A diagram for presenting *bivariate data* where one *variable* is plotted against the other on a graph, thus displaying a pattern of points which indicates the strength and direction of the *correlation* between the two variables
Scientific paradigm	An alternative term for a *positivistic paradigm*
Secondary data	*Data* that already exists such as books, documents and films
Segmented bar chart	Alternative name for a *component bar chart*
Significance	Level of confidence that the results of a statistical analysis are not due to chance; usually expressed as the probability that the results of the statistical analysis are due to chance (often 5 per cent or less)
Skewed data	*Data* which does not have a *normal distribution* but has its peak offset to one side

Term	Definition
Snowballing	The practice of using the list of *references* at the end of a piece of *literature* as a guide to other works on the subject
Spearman's rank coefficient	A *non-parametric* technique which gives a *measure of association* between two ranked variables; *data* must be *bivariate* and at least of ordinal status
Specialist bibliography	A list of books that is specific to one subject area
Standard deviation	A *measure of dispersion*, related to the *normal distribution*, which uses every value and is in the same units as the original data; the bigger the spread, the bigger the standard deviation
Statistics	A body of methods and theory that is applied to *quantitative data* when making decisions in the face of uncertainty
Stem-and-leaf plot	A diagram for presenting *univariate* or *bivariate data* where the *frequencies* themselves are used to create the display; used for identifying patterns in the data and highlighting gaps and outliers
Stratified sampling	A sampling technique where the *sample* is chosen by taking the required number of subjects from each identifiable strata of the *population*
Structuring data	Reorganising *data* into suitable categories or sequences
Student *t*-test	A *parametric technique* which compares *population parameters* using two independent or related (matched pair) *samples* drawn from two *populations*; *data* must be at least of interval status
Subjectivist paradigm	An alternative term for a *phenomenological paradigm*
Supervisor	The academic member of staff who oversees and guides the research
Survey	A *methodology* whereby a *sample* of subjects is drawn from a *population* and studied to make inferences about the population
Survey data	*Data* which is obtained in an uncontrolled situation by asking questions or making observations
Synthesis/creativity	The ability to build up information from other information
Systematic sampling	A sampling technique where the *population* is divided by the required sample size (*n*) and the *sample* chosen by taking every '*n*th' subject

Term	Definition
Tally	A simple stroke used to represent occurrence of values, or other phenomena, of a similar nature
Theoretical framework	A collection of *theories* and models from the *literature* which underpins a positivistic research study
Theory	A set of interrelated *variables*, definitions and propositions that presents a systematic view of phenomena by specifying relationships among variables with the purpose of explaining natural phenomena
Thesis	The report resulting from a *M.Phil.* or *Ph.D.* research project
Time series analysis	A statistical technique for forecasting future events; *data* must be available for several past periods of time
Traditional paradigm	An alternative term for a *positivistic paradigm*
Triangulation	The use of different research techniques in the same study
Triangulation of theories	Where a *theory* is taken from one discipline and used to explain a phenomenon in another discipline
Undergraduate degree	A taught course in either the arts or the sciences leading to a *Bachelor's degree*
Unit of analysis	The kind of case to which the *variables* or phenomena under study and the *research problem* refer, and about which data is collected and analysed
Univariate data analysis	Analysis of a single *variable*
Validity	The extent to which the research findings accurately represent what is really happening in the situation
Vancouver System	A system of referencing favoured by the natural sciences which shows *citations* as an in-text number each time the source is cited and lists the numbered, full *references* at the end of the document
Variable	An attribute of an entity that can change and take different values which are capable of being observed and/or measured
Viva	A defence of a thesis by oral examination
Weighted index number	An *index number* constructed by calculating a weighted average of some set of values, where the weights show the relative importance of each item in the data set

References

Ackermann, F., Eden, C. and Cropper, S. (1990) 'Cognitive Mapping: A User Guide', Working Paper No. 12, Glasgow, Strathclyde University, Department of Management Science.

Adams, G. and Schvaneveldt, J. (1991) *Understanding Research Methods*, 2nd edition, New York: Longman.

Allan, G. (1991) 'Qualitative Research' in Allan, G. and Skinner, C., *Handbook for Research Students in the Social Sciences*, London: The Falmer Press, pp. 177–89.

Allen, R. E. (1990) (ed.) *The Concise Oxford Dictionary of Current English*, Oxford: Clarendon Press.

Ansoff, H. I. (1965) *Corporate Strategy*, New York: McGraw-Hill.

Barber, T. X. (1976) *Pitfalls in Human Research*, Oxford: Pergamon.

Beattie, V. and Jones, M. (1992) 'Graphic Accounts', *Certified Accountant*, November, pp. 30–5.

Bell, J. (1993) *Doing Your Research Project*, Buckingham: Open University Press.

Bergwerk, R. J. (1970) 'Effective Communication of Financial Data', *Journal of Accountancy*, February, pp. 47–54.

Black, T. R. (1993) *Evaluating Social Science Research*, London: Sage.

Bloom, B. (1956) *Taxonomy of Educational Objectives: The Cognitive Domain*, London: Longman.

Blumer, H. (1980) 'Social Behaviourism and Symbolic Interactionism', *American Sociological Review*, 45, pp. 405–19.

Bogdan, R. and Taylor, S. (1975) *Introduction to Qualitative Research Methods*, New York: Wiley.

Bolton, R. N. (1991) 'An Exploratory Investigation of Questionnaire Pretesting with Verbal Protocol Analysis', *Advances in Consumer Research*, 18, pp. 558–65.

Bonoma, T. V. (1985) 'Case Research in Marketing: Opportunities, Problems, and a Process', *Journal of Marketing Research*, XXII, May, pp. 199–208.

Borg, W. R. and Gall, M. D. (1989) *Educational Research: An Introduction*, 5th edition, New York: Longman.

Bottorff, J. L. (1994) 'Using Videotaped Recordings in Qualitative Research', in Morse, J. M. (ed.) *Critical Issues in Qualitative Research Methods*, Thousand Oaks: Sage, pp. 224–61.

Boyle, J. S. (1994) 'Styles of Ethnography' in Morse, Janice M. (ed.) *Critical Issues on Qualitative Methods*, Thousand Oaks: Sage, pp. 159–85.

Brenner, M. (1985) 'Survey Interviewing' in Brenner, M., Brown, J. and Canter, D. (eds.) *The Research Interview, Uses and Approaches*, London: Academic Press, pp. 9–36.

Bromley, D. B. (1986) *The Case Study Methodology in Psychology and Related Disciplines*, Chichester: Wiley.

Brook, J. A. (1986) 'Research Applications of the Repertory Grid Technique', *International Review of Applied Psychology*, 35, pp. 489–500.

Brown, J. and Canter, D. (1985) 'The Uses of Explanation in the Research Interview', in Brenner, M., Brown, J. and Canter, D. (eds) *The Research Interview, Uses and Approaches*, London, Academic Press, pp. 217–45.

Bruce, C. S. (1994) 'Research Students' Early Experiences of the Dissertation Literature Review', *Studies in Higher Education*, 9 (2), pp. 217–29.

Bryman, A. (1988) *Quantity and Quality in Social Research*, London: Unwin Hyman.

Bryman, A. and Cramer, D. (1997) *Quantitative Data Analysis with SPSS for Windows*, London: Routledge.

Burgoyne, J. and Stuart, R. (1976) 'The Nature, Use and Acquisition of Managerial Skills and Other Attributes', *Personnel Review*, 15 (4), pp. 19–29.

Chaffee, E. E. (1985) 'Three Models of Strategy', *Academy of Management Review*, 10 (1), pp. 89–98.

Chall, J. S. (1958) *Readability – An Appraisal of Research and Application*, Ohio: Ohio State University Press.

Clarkson, G. P. E. (1962) *Portfolio Selection: A Simulation of Trust Investment*, Englewood Cliffs: Prentice Hall.

Clegg, F. G. (1992) *Simple Statistics*, Cambridge: Cambridge University Press.

Coolican, H. (1992) *Research Methods and Statistics in Psychology*, London: Hodder & Stoughton.

Cooper, H. M. (1988) 'The Structure of Knowledge Synthesis', *Knowledge in Society*, 1, pp. 104–26.

Couch, C. J. (1987) *Researching Social Processes in the Laboratory*, Connecticut: JAI Press.

Creswell, J. W. (1994) *Research Design: Qualitative and Quantitative Approaches*, Thousand Oaks: Sage.

Cropper, S., Eden, C. and Ackermann, F. (1990) 'Keeping Sense of Accounts Using Computer-Based Cognitive Maps', *Social Science Computer Review*, 8, 3, Fall, pp. 345–66.

Czaja, R. and Blair, J. (1996) *Designing Surveys: A Guide to Decisions and Procedures*, Thousand Oaks: Pine Forge Press.

Czepiec, H. (1993) 'Promoting Industrial Goods in China: Identifying the Key Appeals', *International Journal of Advertising*, 13, pp. 257–64.

Davis, L. R. (1987) 'Reporting Financial Information Graphically', *Journal of Accountancy*, December, pp. 108–15.

Day, J. (1986) 'The Use of Annual Reports by UK Investment Analysts', *Accounting & Business Research*, Autumn, pp. 295–307.

De Venney-Tiernan, M., Goldband, A., Rackham, L. and Reilly, N. (1994) 'Creating Collaborative Relationships in a Co-operative Inquiry Group' in Reason, P. (ed.) *Participation in Human Inquiry*, London: Sage, pp. 120–37.

Denzin, N. K. (1970) *The Research Act: A Theoretical Introduction to Sociological Methods*, Chicago: Aldine.

Denzin, N. K. (1994) 'The Arts and Politics of Interpretation', in Denzin, N. K. and Lincoln, Y. S. (eds) *Handbook of Qualitative Research*, Thousand Oaks: Sage, pp. 500–15.

Denzin, N. K. and Lincoln, Y. S. (eds) (1994) *Handbook of Qualitative Research*, Thousand Oaks: Sage.

DeVault, M. L. (1990) 'Talking and Listening from Women's Standpoint: Feminist Strategies for Interviewing and Analysis', *Social Problems*, 31 (1), February, pp. 96–116.

Dilthey, W. (1976) *Selected Writings*, (ed. and trans. H. P. Rickman) Cambridge: Cambridge University Press.

Dobbins, G. H., Lane, I. M. and Steiner, D. D. (1988) 'A Note on the Role of Laboratory Methodologies in Applied Behavioural Research: Don't Throw Out the Baby with the Bath Water', *Journal of Organisational Behaviour*, 9, pp. 281–6.

Dunn, W. and Ginsberg, A. (1986) 'A Sociocognitive Network Approach to Organisational Analysis', *Human Relations*, 40, 11, pp. 955–76.

Easterby-Smith, M., Thorpe, R. and Lowe, A. (1991) *Management Research: An Introduction*, London: Sage.

Ehrenberg, A. S. C. (1975) *Data Reduction*, New York: Wiley.

Ehrenberg, A. S. C. (1976) 'Annual Reports Don't Have to be Obscure', *Journal of Accountancy*, August, pp. 88–91.

Eisenhardt, K. M. (1989) 'Building Theories from Case Study Research' *Academy of Management Review*, 14 (4), pp. 532–50.

Field, A. (2000) *Discovering Statistics Using SPSS for Windows*, London: Sage.

Fineman, S. (1983) *White Collar Unemployment: Impact and Stress*, Chichester: Wiley.

Flanagan, J. C. (1954) 'The Critical Incident Technique', *Psychological Bulletin*, 51 (4), July, pp. 327–58.

Flannery, J. J. (1971) 'The Relative Effectiveness of Some Common Graduated Point Symbols in the Presentation of Quantitative Data', *Canadian Cartographer*, pp. 96–109.

Gill, J. and Johnson, P. (1991) *Research Methods for Managers,* London: Paul Chapman.

Glaser, B. (1978) *Theoretical Sensitivity,* Mill Valley: Sociology Press.

Glaser, B. and Strauss, A. (1967) *The Discovery of Grounded Theory,* Chicago: Aldine.

Gregg, R. (1994) 'Explorations of Pregnancy and Choice in a High-Tech Age', in Riessman, C. K. (ed.) *Qualitative Studies in Social Work Research,* Thousand Oaks: Sage, pp. 49–66.

Gummesson, E. (1991) *Qualitative Methods in Management Research,* Newbury Park: Sage.

Haywood, J. (1989) *Assessment in Higher Education,* 2nd edition, Chichester: Wiley.

Hesse, M. (1980) *Revolutions and Reconstructions in the Philosophy of Science,* Brighton: Harvester Press.

Howard, K. and Sharp, J. A. (1994) *The Management of a Student Research Project,* Aldershot: Gower.

Hussey, J. (1994) 'Business Systems' in Hussey, Jill (ed.) *Understanding Business and Finance,* 2nd edition, London: D.P. Publications, pp. 324–61.

Hussey, J. (1995) *The Methodology of the Presentation of Quantitative Data,* Bristol: University of the West of England, Bristol.

Hussey, R. (1995) (ed.) *Oxford Dictionary of Accounting,* Oxford: Oxford University Press.

Hussey, R. and Everitt, H. (1991) *Summary and Simplified Financial Reporting,* London: Butterworths.

Hyde, C. (1994) 'Reflections on a Journey: A Research Story', in Riessman, C. K. (ed.) *Qualitative Studies in Social Work Research,* Thousand Oaks: Sage, pp. 169–89.

Iselin, E. R. (1972) 'Accounting and Communication Theory', *The Singapore Accountant,* 7, pp. 31–7.

Jankowicz, A. D. (1991) *Business Research Projects for Students,* London: Chapman & Hall.

Jense, M. C. and Meckling, W. H. (1976) 'Theory of the Firm: Managerial Behavior, Agency Costs and the Ownership Structure', *Journal of Financial Economics,* 3, pp. 305–60.

Jick, T. D. (1979) 'Mixing Qualitative and Quantitative Methods: Triangulation in Action', *Administrative Science Quarterly,* December, 24, pp. 602–11.

Jinkerson, D. L., Cummings, O. W., Neisendorf, B. J. and Schwandt, T. A. (1992) 'A Case Study of Methodological Issues in Cross-Cultural Evaluation', *Evaluation and Program Planning,* 15, pp. 273–85.

Johnston, S. (1995) 'Building a Sense of Community in a Research Master's Course', *Studies in Higher Education,* 20 (3), pp. 279–303.

Kelly, G. A. (1955) *The Psychology of Personal Constructs: A Theory of Personality,* New York: Norton.

Kerlinger, F. N. (1979) *Behavioural Research: A Conceptual Approach*, New York: Holt, Rinehart & Winston.

Kervin, John B. (1992) *Methods for Business Research*, New York: HarperCollins.

Kuhn, T. S. (1962) *The Structure of Scientific Revolutions*, Chicago: University of Chicago Press.

Laughlin, R. (1995) 'Methodological Themes – Empirical Research in Accounting: Alternative Approaches and a Case for "Middle-Range" Thinking', *Accounting, Auditing and Accountability Journal*, 8 (1), pp. 63–87.

Lee, R. M. (1993) *Doing Research on Sensitive Topics*, London: Sage.

Leininger, M. (1994) 'Evaluation Criteria and Critique of Qualitative Research Studies' in Morse, J. M. (ed.) *Critical Issues in Qualitative Research Methods*, Thousand Oaks: Sage, pp. 95–115.

Lewin, K. (1946) 'Action Research and Minority Problems', *Journal of Social Issues,* 2, pp. 34–6.

Lewin, K. (1951) *Field Theory in Social Sciences*, London: Harper & Row.

Li, X. and Crane, N. B. (1995) *Electronic Style: A Guide to Citing Electronic Information*, London: Mecklermedia.

Lincoln, Y. S. and Guba, E. G. (1985) *Naturalistic Enquiry*, Newbury Park: Sage.

Lindlof, T. R. (1995) *Qualitative Communication Research Methods*, Thousand Oaks: Sage.

Lovie, P. (1986) 'Identifying Outliers' in Lovie, A. D. (ed.) *New Developments in Statistics for Psychology and the Social Sciences* 1, London: Methuen.

Macdonald-Ross, M. (1977), 'How Numbers are Shown – A Review of Research on the Presentation of Quantitative Data in Texts', *AV Communication Review*, 25 (4), Winter, pp. 359–409.

MacKinlay, T. (1986) *The Development of a Personal Strategy of Management*, M.Sc. thesis, Manchester Polytechnic, Department of Management.

Martin, D. M. (1989) *How to Prepare the Annual Report*, Cambridge: Director Books, Simon & Schuster.

McGrath, M. A. (1989*)* 'An Ethnography of a Gift Store: Trappings, Wrappings, and Rapture', *Journal of Retailing*, 65 (4), Winter, pp. 421–49.

Merriam, S. B. (1988) *Case Study Research in Education: A Qualitative Approach,* San Francisco: Jossey-Bass.

Miles, M. B. and Huberman, A. M. (1994) *Qualitative Data Analysis*, Thousand Oaks: Sage.

Morgan, D. L. (1988) *Focus Groups as Qualitative Research*, Newbury Park: Sage.

Morgan, G. (1979) 'Response to Mintzberg', *Administrative Science Quarterly*, 24 (1), pp. 137–9.

Morgan, G. and Smircich, L. (1980) 'The Case of Qualitative Research', *Academy of Management Review*, 5, pp. 491–500.

Morris, C. (1993) *Quantitative Approaches in Business Studies*, London: Pitman.

Morse, J. M. (1994) 'Emerging from the Data: The Cognitive Processes of Analysis in Qualitative Inquiry' in Morse, J. M. (ed.) *Critical Issues in Qualitative Research Methods*, Thousand Oaks: Sage, pp. 23–43.

Mostyn, B. (1985) 'The Content Analysis of Qualitative Research Data: A Dynamic Approach', in Brenner, M., Brown, J. and Canter, D. (eds) *The Research Interview, Uses and Approaches*, London: Academic Press, pp. 115–46.

Normann, R. (1970) *A Personal Quest for Methodology*, Stockholm: Scandinavian Institutes for Administrative Research.

Oakshott, L. (1994) *Essential Elements of Business Statistics*, London: D.P. Publications.

Otley, D. and Berry, A. (1994) 'Case Study Research in Management Accounting and Control', *Management Accounting Research*, 5, pp. 45–65.

Parasuraman, A., Berry, L. L. and Zeithaml, V. A. (1991) 'Understanding Customer Expectations of Service', *Sloan Management Review*, 39, Spring, pp. 10–18.

Parker, D. (1994) *Tackling Coursework*, London: D.P. Publications.

Patton, M. (1990) *Qualitative Evaluation and Research Methods*, Newbury Park: Sage.

Phillips, E. M. (1984) 'Learning to do Research', *Graduate Management Research*, Autumn, pp. 6–18.

Phillips, E. M. and Pugh, D. S. (1994) *How to Get a Ph.D.*, Buckingham: Open University Press.

Pidgeon, N. F., Turner, B. A. and Blockley, D. I. (1991) 'The Use of Grounded Theory for Conceptual Analysis in Knowledge Elicitation', *International Journal of Man-Machine Studies*, 35, pp. 151–73.

Playfair, W. (1786) *The Commercial and Political Atlas*, London.

Plummer, K. (1983) *Documents of Life: An Introduction to the Problems and Literature of a Humanistic Method*, London: Allen & Unwin.

Porter, M. E. (1980) *Competitive Strategy*, New York: The Free Press.

Raimond, P. (1993) *Management Projects: Design, Research and Presentation*, London: Chapman & Hall.

Reason, P. (1994a) (ed.) *Participation in Human Inquiry*, London: Sage.

Reason, P. (1994b) 'Three Approaches to Participative Inquiry', in Denzin, N. K. and Lincoln, Y. S. (eds) *Handbook of Qualitative Research*, Thousand Oaks: Sage, pp. 324–39.

Ricoeur, P. (1977) 'The Model of the Text: Meaningful Action Considered as a Text' in Dallmayr, F. R. and McCarthy, T. A. (eds) *Understanding and Social Enquiry*, Notre Dame: University of Notre Dame Press, pp. 316–34.

Ricoeur, P. (1981) *Hermeneutics and the Human Sciences* (trans. J. B. Thompson), Cambridge: Cambridge University Press.

Robson, C. (1993) *Real World Research: A Resource for Social Scientists and Practitioner Researchers*, Oxford: Blackwell.

Rosenthal, R. (1966) *Experimenter Effects in Behavioural Research*, New York: Appleton-Century-Crofts.

Rowntree, D. (1991) *Statistics Without Tears: A Primer for Non-mathematicians*, Harmondsworth: Penguin.

Rudestam, K. E. and Newton, R. R. (1992) *Surviving Your Dissertation*, Newbury Park: Sage.

Ryan, B., Scapens, R. W. and Theobald, M. (1992) *Research Methods and Methodology in Finance and Accounting*, London: Academic Press.

Scapens, R. W. (1990) 'Researching Management Accounting Practice: The Role of Case Study Methods', *British Accounting Review*, 22, pp. 259–81.

Shannon, C. and Weaver, W. (1949) *The Mathematical Theory of Communication*, Illinois: University of Illinois Press.

Silverman, D. (1993) *Interpreting Qualitative Data: Methods for Analysing Talk, Text and Interaction*, London: Sage.

Silverman, D. (1994) *Interpreting Qualitative Data*, London: Sage.

Slife, Brent D. and Williams, Richard N. (1995) *What's Behind the Research: Discovering Hidden Assumptions in the Behavioural Sciences*, Thousand Oaks: Sage.

Smagorinsky, P. (1989) 'The Reliability and Validity of Protocol Analysis', *Written Communication*, 6 (4), October, pp. 463–79.

Smagorinsky, P. (1994) *Speaking about Writing: Reflections on Research Methodology*, Thousand Oaks: Sage.

Smith, J. K. (1983) 'Quantitative v. Qualitative Research: An Attempt to Classify the Issue', *Educational Research*, March, pp. 6–13.

Stebbins, R. A. (1992) 'Concatenated Exploration: Notes on a Neglected Type of Longitudinal Research', *Quality and Quantity*, 26, pp. 435–42.

Stern, P. N. (1994) 'Eroding Grounded Theory' in Morse, J. M. (ed.) *Qualitative Research Methods*, Thousand Oaks: Sage, pp. 212–23.

Stewart, R. (1965) 'The Use of Diaries to Study Managers' Jobs', *Journal of Management Studies*, 2, pp. 228–35.

Stewart, V. and Stewart, A. (1981) *Business Applications of Repertory Grid*, Maidenhead: McGraw-Hill.

Strauss, A. (1987) *Qualitative Analysis for Social Scientists*, New York: Cambridge University Press.

Strauss, A. and Corbin, J. (1990) *Basics of Qualitative Research: Grounded Theory Procedures and Techniques*, Newbury Park: Sage.

Strauss, A. and Corbin, J. (1994) 'Grounded Theory Methodology: An Overview', in Denzin, N. K. and Lincoln, Y. S. (eds) (1994) *Handbook of Qualitative Research*, Thousand Oaks: Sage.

Taylor, D. S. (1990) 'Making the Most of your Matrices: Hermeneutics, Statistics and the Repertory Grid', *International Journal of Personal Construct Psychology*, 3, pp. 105–19.

Thibadoux, G., Cooper, W. D. and Greenberg, I. S. (1986) 'Flowcharts and Graphics: Part II', *CPA Journal*, March, pp. 17–23.

Todd, P. A., McKeen, J. D. and Gallupe, R. B. (1995) 'The Evolution of IS Job Skills: A Content Analysis of IS Job Advertisements from 1970 to 1990', *MIS Quarterly*, March, pp. 1–24.

Torrance, M., Thomas, G. V. and Robinson, E. J. (1992) 'The Writing Experiences of Social Science Research Students', *Studies in Higher Education*, 17 (2), pp. 155–67.

Traylen, H. (1994) 'Confronting Hidden Agendas: Co-operative Inquiry with Health Visitors' in Reason, P. (ed.) *Participation in Human Inquiry*, London: Sage, pp. 59–81.

Treleaven, L. (1994) 'Making a Space: A Collaborative Inquiry with Women as Staff Development', in Reason, P. (ed.) *Participation in Human Inquiry*, London: Sage, pp. 138–62.

Tufte, E. R. (1983) *The Visual Display of Quantitative Information*, Cheshire: Graphic Press.

Turner, B. A. (1981) 'Some Practical Aspects of Qualitative Data Analysis: One Way of Organizing the Cognitive Processes Associated with the Generation of Grounded Theory', *Quality and Quantity*, 15 (3), pp. 225–47.

Van Maanen, J. (1983) *Qualitative Methodology*, London: Sage.

Vogt, W. P. (1993) *Dictionary of Statistics and Methodology*, Newbury Park: Sage.

Wallace, R. S. O. and Mellor, C. J. (1988) 'Non-Response Bias in Mail Accounting Surveys: A Pedagogical Note', *British Accounting Review*, 20, pp. 131–9.

Werner, O. and Schoepfle, G. (1987) *Systematic Fieldwork: Foundations of Ethnography and Interviewing*, Newbury Park: Sage.

Wilkinson, A. M. (1991) *The Scientist's Handbook for Writing Papers and Dissertations*, Englewood Cliffs: Prentice Hall.

Winkler, A. C. and McCuen, J. R. (1994) *Writing the Research Paper: A Handbook*, Orlando: Harcourt Brace.

Yin, R. K. (1994) *Case Study Research: Design and Methods*, Beverly Hills: Sage.

Index of names

Index of subjects

THE LEARNING CENTRE
HAMMERSMITH AND WEST
LONDON COLLEGE
GLIDDON ROAD
LONDON W14 9BL